DC COMICS: GENERATIONS

DC COMICS

GENER

writers
DAN JURGENS
ROBERT VENDITTI
ANDY SCHMIDT

JOHN ROMITA JR.
DOUG BRAITHWAITE
RAGS MORALES
MIKE PERKINS
MARCO SANTUCCI
NORM RAPMUND
COLLEEN DORAN
BRYAN HITCH

line artists
(in order of appearance)
IVAN REIS
JOE PRADO
SCOTT HANNA
FERNANDO PASARIN
OCLAIR ALBERT
AARON LOPRESTI
MATT RYAN
EMANUELA LUPACCHINO
WADE VON GRAWBADGER
BERNARD CHANG
YANICK PAQUETTE
KEVIN NOWLAN
DAN JURGENS
KLAUS JANSON
PAUL PELLETIER
SANDRA HOPE

colorist
HI-FI

letterer
TOM NAPOLITANO

collection cover artists
IVAN REIS
JOE PRADO
HI-FI

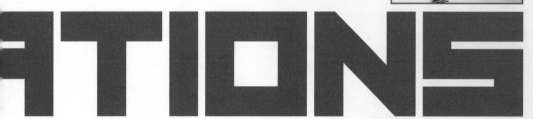

ANDREA SHEA
Editor – Original Series & Collected Edition

BRIAN CUNNINGHAM
Editor – Original Series

STEVE COOK
Design Director – Books

MEGEN BELLERSEN
Publication Design

SUZANNAH ROWNTREE
Publication Production

MARIE JAVINS
Editor-in-Chief, DC Comics

DANIEL CHERRY III
Senior VP – General Manager

JIM LEE
Publisher & Chief Creative Officer

JOEN CHOE
VP – Global Brand & Creative Services

DON FALLETTI
VP – Manufacturing Operations & Workflow Management

LAWRENCE GANEM
VP – Talent Services

ALISON GILL
Senior VP – Manufacturing & Operations

NICK J. NAPOLITANO
VP – Manufacturing Administration & Design

NANCY SPEARS
VP – Revenue

DC COMICS: GENERATIONS

DC Comics, 2900 West Alameda Ave., Burbank, CA 91505
Printed by Transcontinental Interglobe, Beauceville, QC, Canada. 4/30/21. First Printing.
ISBN: 978-1-77951-009-9

Library of Congress Cataloging-in-Publication Data is available.

PEFC Certified

This product is
from sustainably
managed forests and
controlled sources

PEFC/01-31-106   www.pefc.org

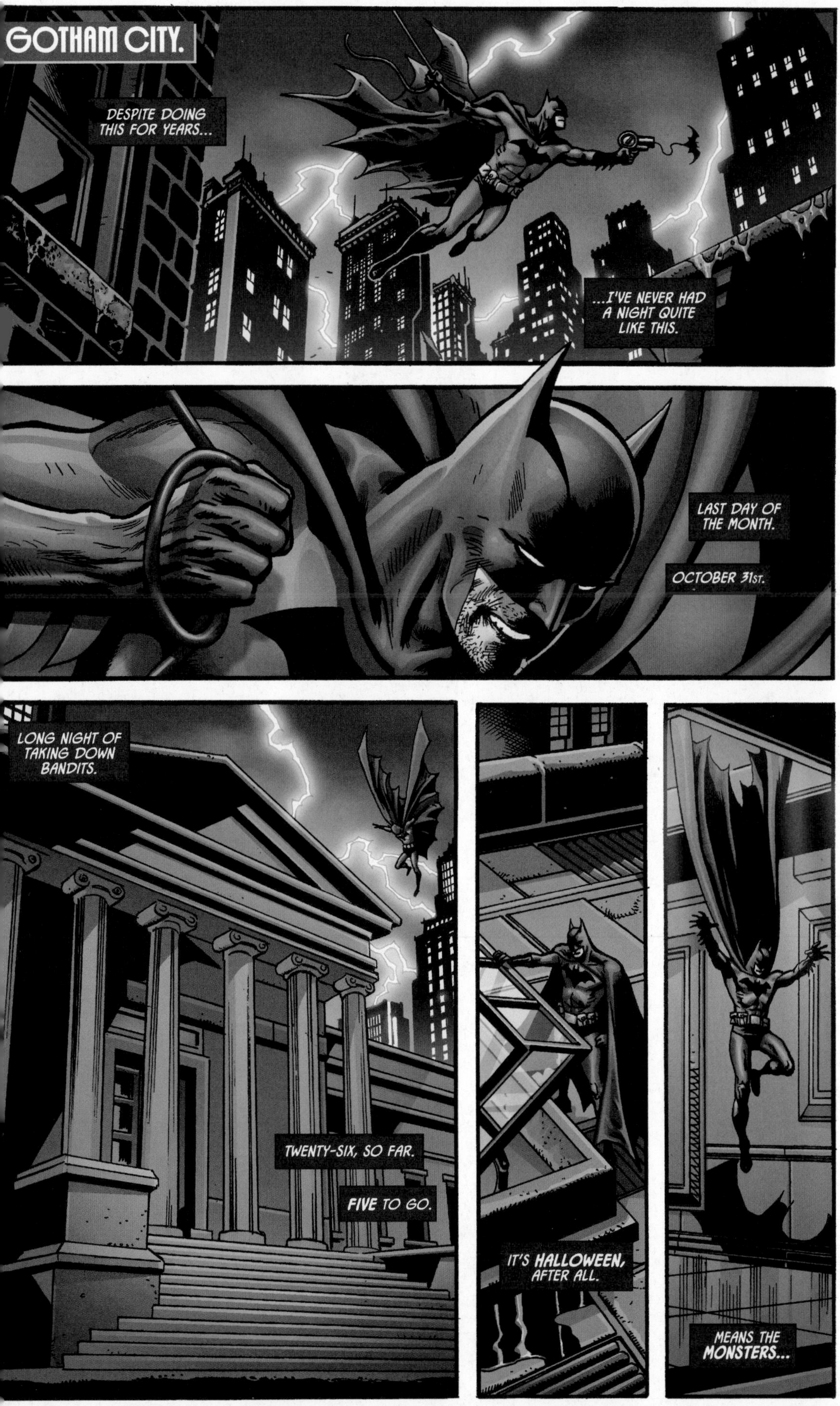
GOTHAM CITY.
DESPITE DOING THIS FOR YEARS...
...I'VE NEVER HAD A NIGHT QUITE LIKE THIS.
LAST DAY OF THE MONTH.
OCTOBER 31ST.
LONG NIGHT OF TAKING DOWN BANDITS.
TWENTY-SIX, SO FAR.
FIVE TO GO.
IT'S HALLOWEEN, AFTER ALL.
MEANS THE MONSTERS...

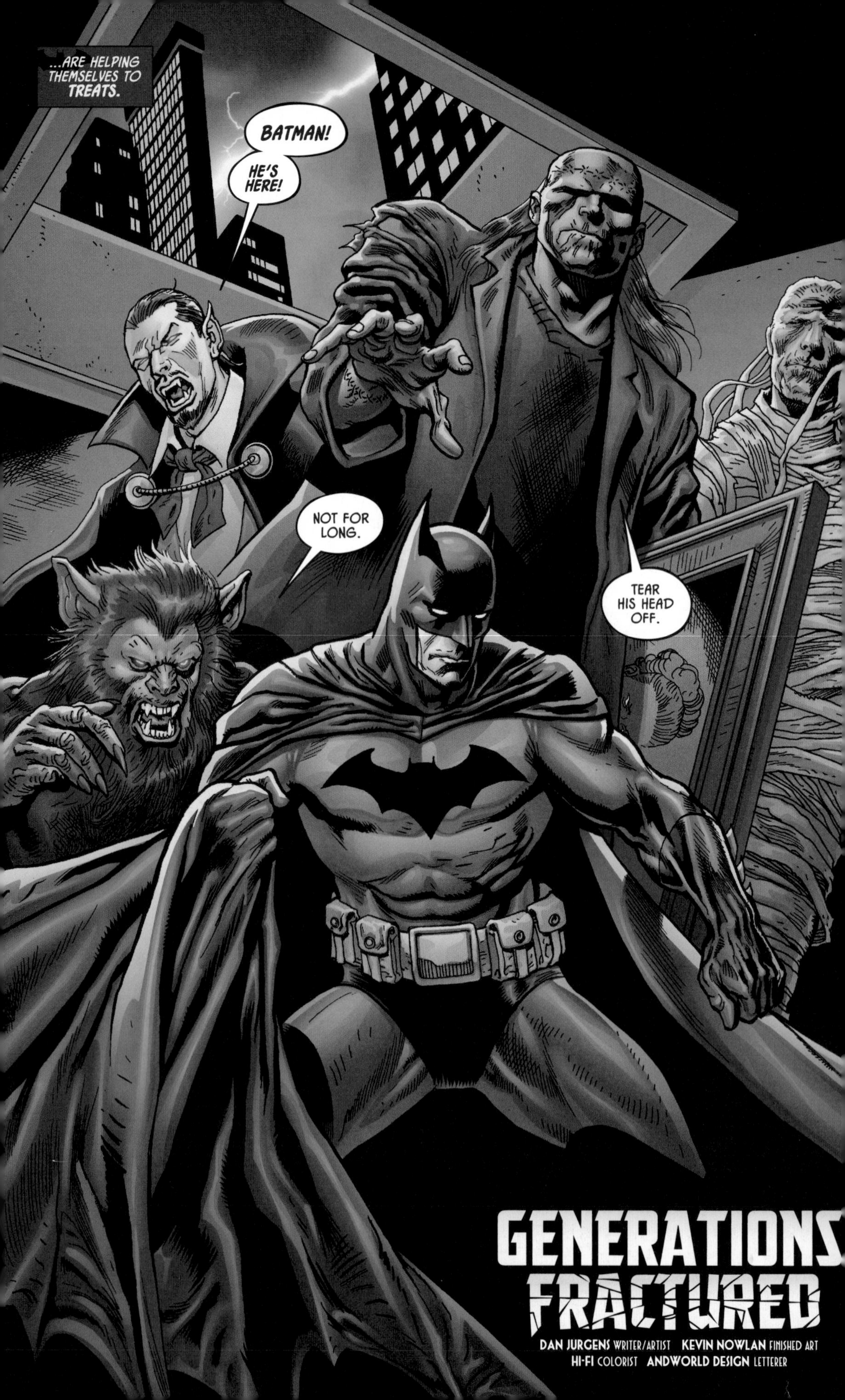
...ARE HELPING THEMSELVES TO TREATS.
BATMAN!
HE'S HERE!
NOT FOR LONG.
TEAR HIS HEAD OFF.
GENERATIONS FRACTURED
DAN JURGENS WRITER/ARTIST KEVIN NOWLAN FINISHED ART
HI-FI COLORIST ANDWORLD DESIGN LETTERER

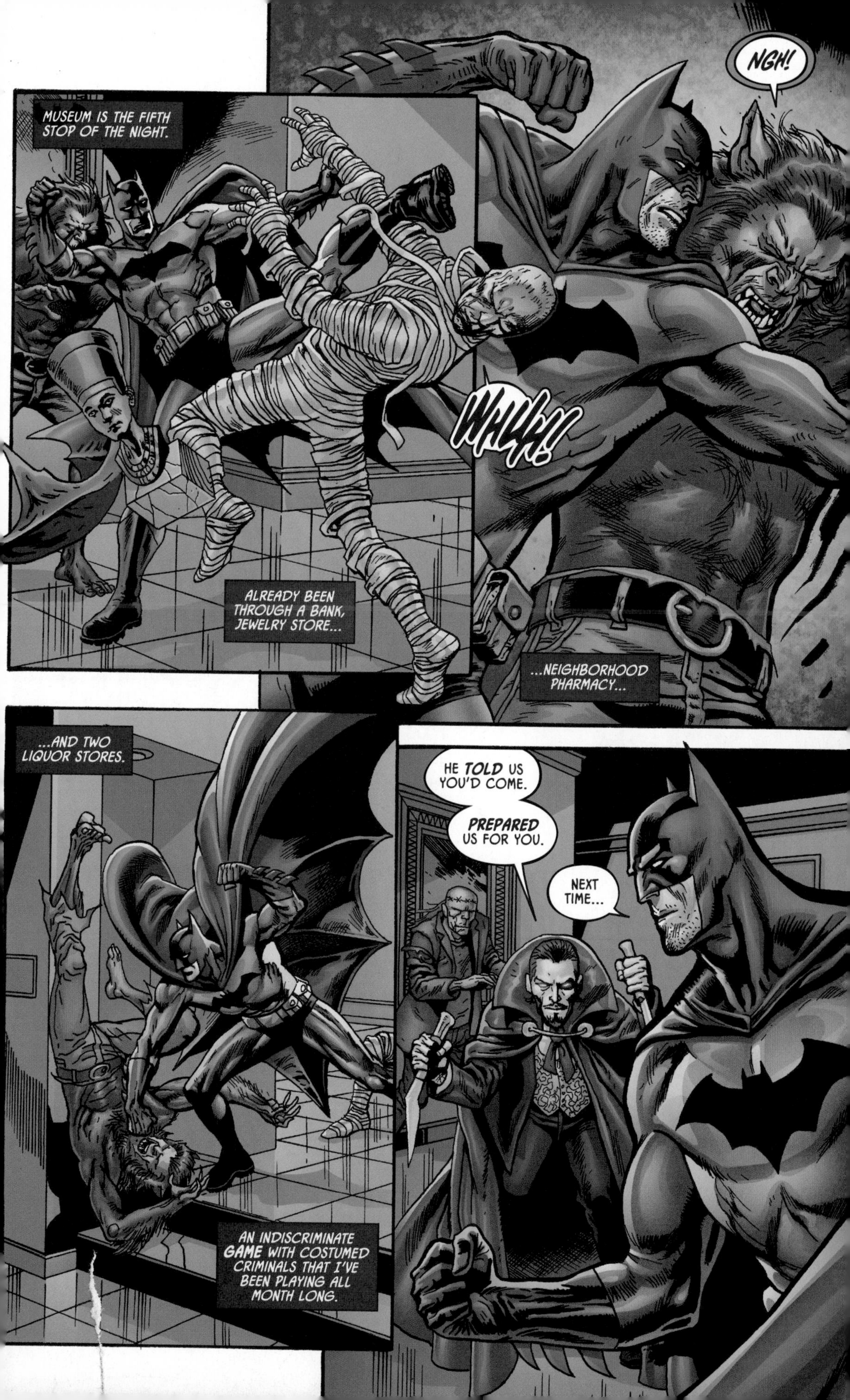
MUSEUM IS THE FIFTH STOP OF THE NIGHT.
ALREADY BEEN THROUGH A BANK, JEWELRY STORE...
NGH!
WHUD!!
...NEIGHBORHOOD PHARMACY...
...AND TWO LIQUOR STORES.
AN INDISCRIMINATE GAME WITH COSTUMED CRIMINALS THAT I'VE BEEN PLAYING ALL MONTH LONG.
HE TOLD US YOU'D COME.
PREPARED US FOR YOU.
NEXT TIME...

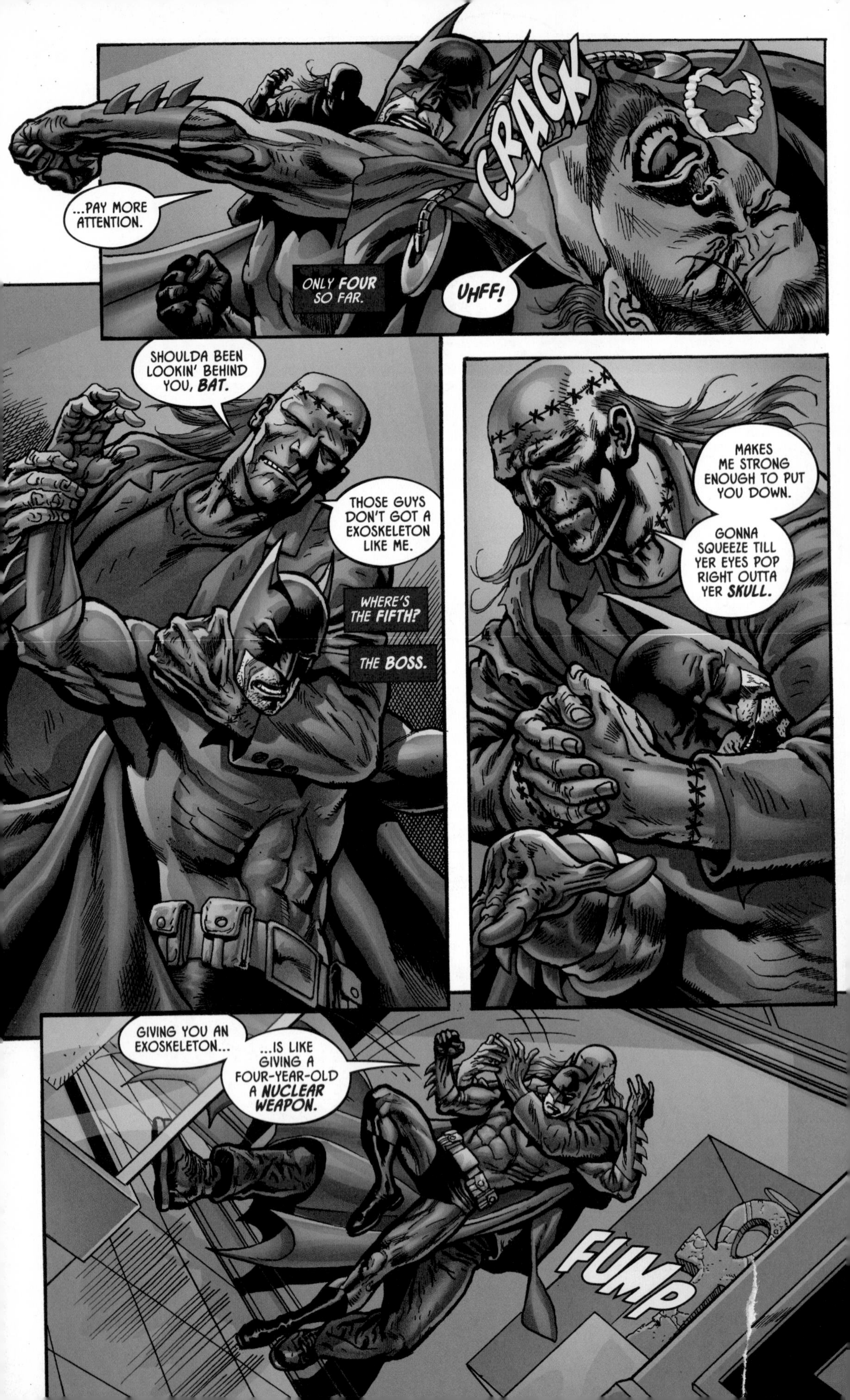

CRACK
...PAY MORE ATTENTION.
ONLY FOUR SO FAR.
UHFF!
SHOULDA BEEN LOOKIN' BEHIND YOU, BAT.
THOSE GUYS DON'T GOT A EXOSKELETON LIKE ME.
WHERE'S THE FIFTH?
THE BOSS.
MAKES ME STRONG ENOUGH TO PUT YOU DOWN.
GONNA SQUEEZE TILL YER EYES POP RIGHT OUTTA YER SKULL.
GIVING YOU AN EXOSKELETON...
...IS LIKE GIVING A FOUR-YEAR-OLD A NUCLEAR WEAPON.
FUMP

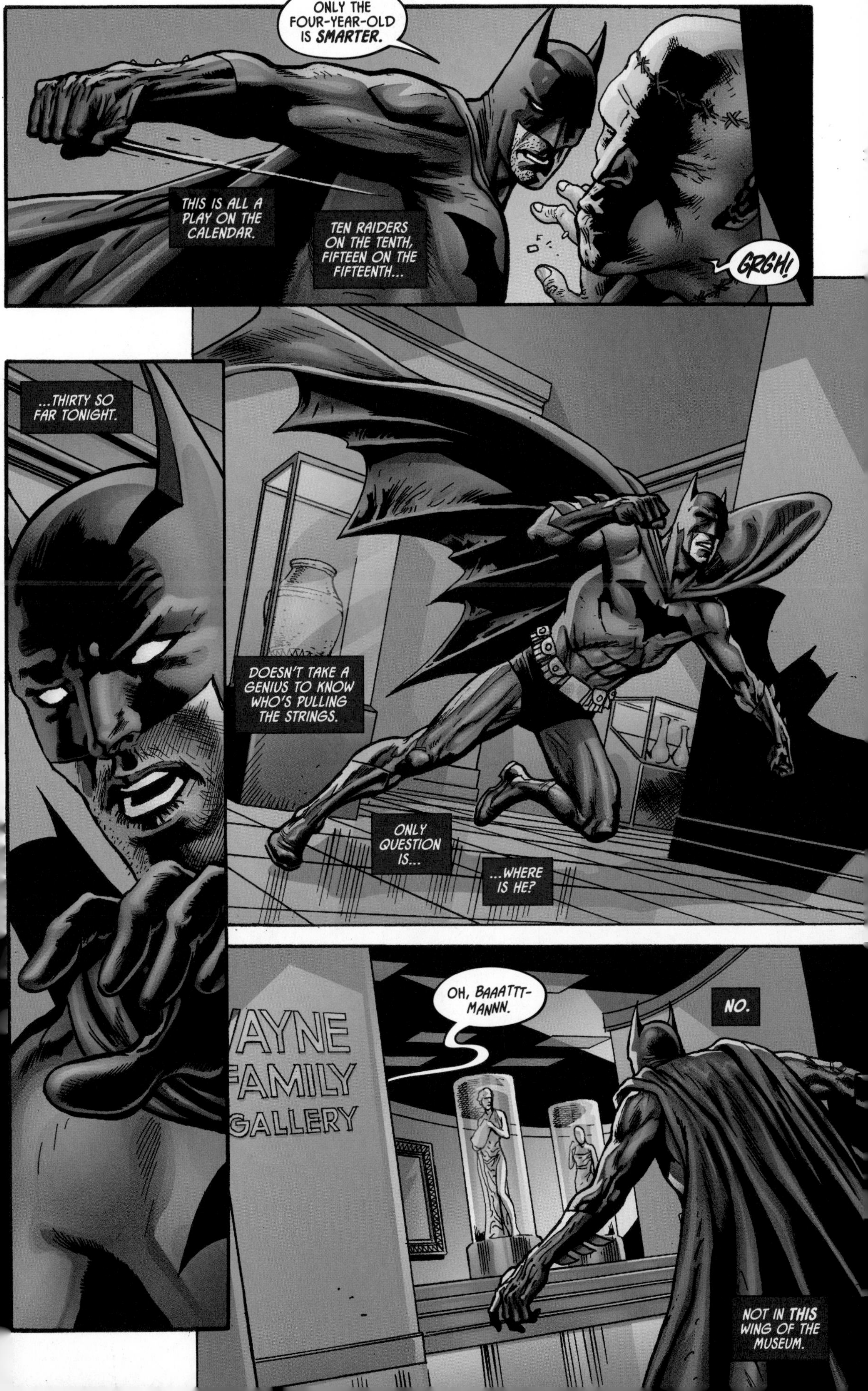

ONLY THE FOUR-YEAR-OLD IS SMARTER.
THIS IS ALL A PLAY ON THE CALENDAR.
TEN RAIDERS ON THE TENTH, FIFTEEN ON THE FIFTEENTH...
GRGH!
...THIRTY SO FAR TONIGHT.
DOESN'T TAKE A GENIUS TO KNOW WHO'S PULLING THE STRINGS.
ONLY QUESTION IS...
...WHERE IS HE?
OH, BAAATTT-MANNN.
NO.
NOT IN THIS WING OF THE MUSEUM.
VAYNE FAMILY GALLERY

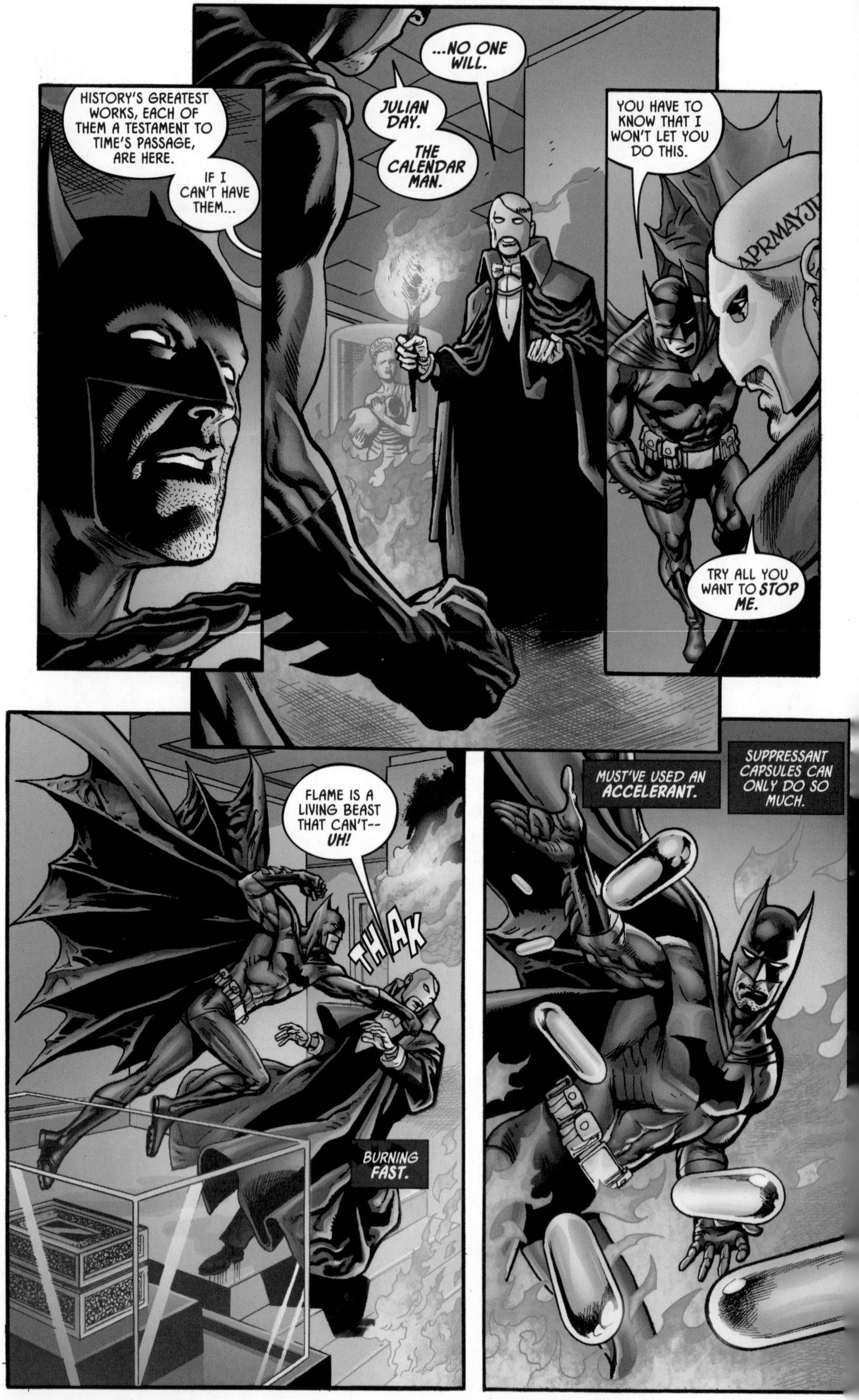
HISTORY'S GREATEST WORKS, EACH OF THEM A TESTAMENT TO TIME'S PASSAGE, ARE HERE.
IF I CAN'T HAVE THEM...
...NO ONE WILL.
JULIAN DAY.
THE CALENDAR MAN.
YOU HAVE TO KNOW THAT I WON'T LET YOU DO THIS.
APRMAYJU
TRY ALL YOU WANT TO STOP ME.
FLAME IS A LIVING BEAST THAT CAN'T-- UH!
THAK
BURNING FAST.
MUST'VE USED AN ACCELERANT.
SUPPRESSANT CAPSULES CAN ONLY DO SO MUCH.

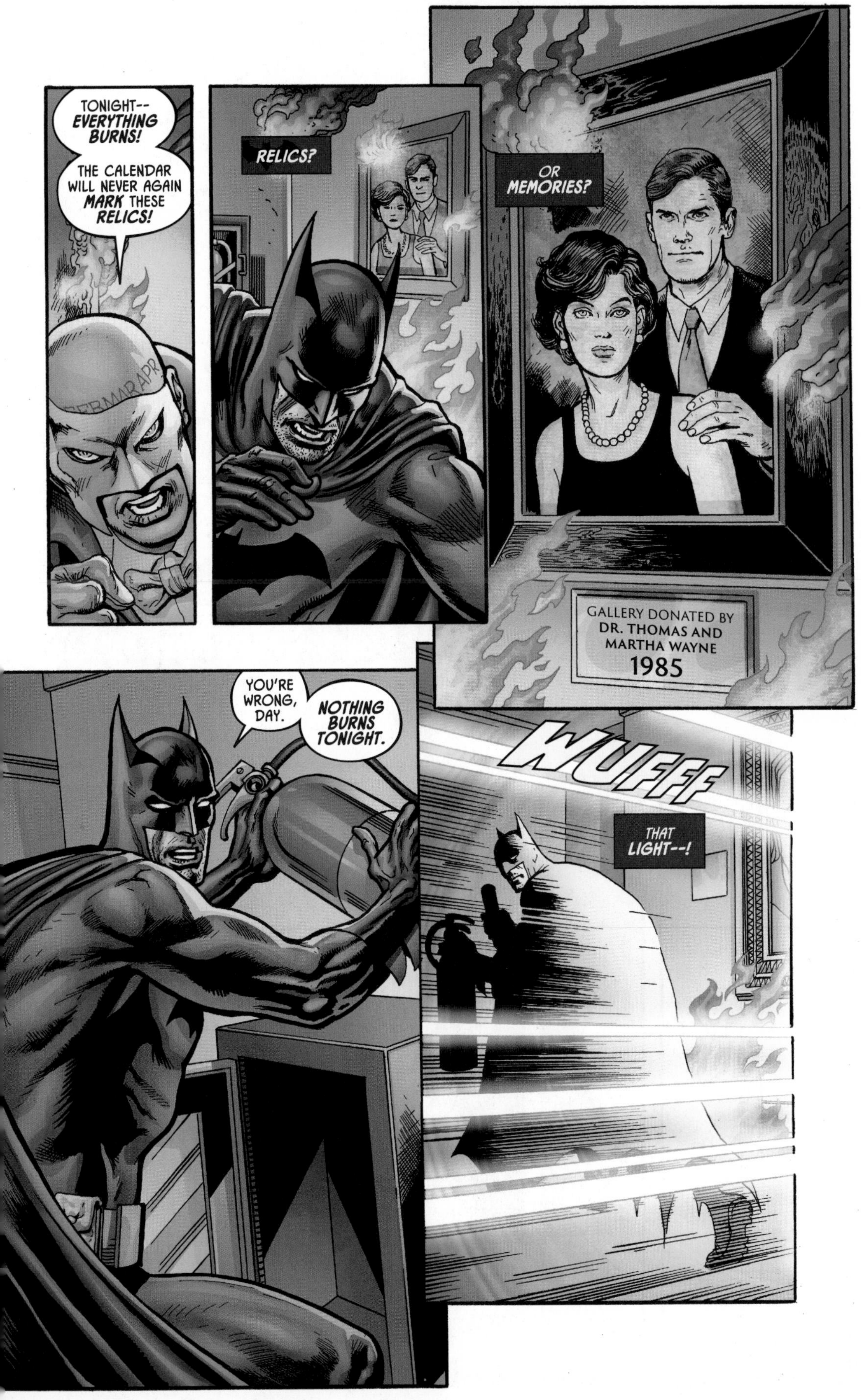

TONIGHT-- EVERYTHING BURNS!
THE CALENDAR WILL NEVER AGAIN MARK THESE RELICS!
RELICS?
OR MEMORIES?
GALLERY DONATED BY DR. THOMAS AND MARTHA WAYNE 1985
YOU'RE WRONG, DAY.
NOTHING BURNS TONIGHT.
WUFFF
THAT LIGHT--!

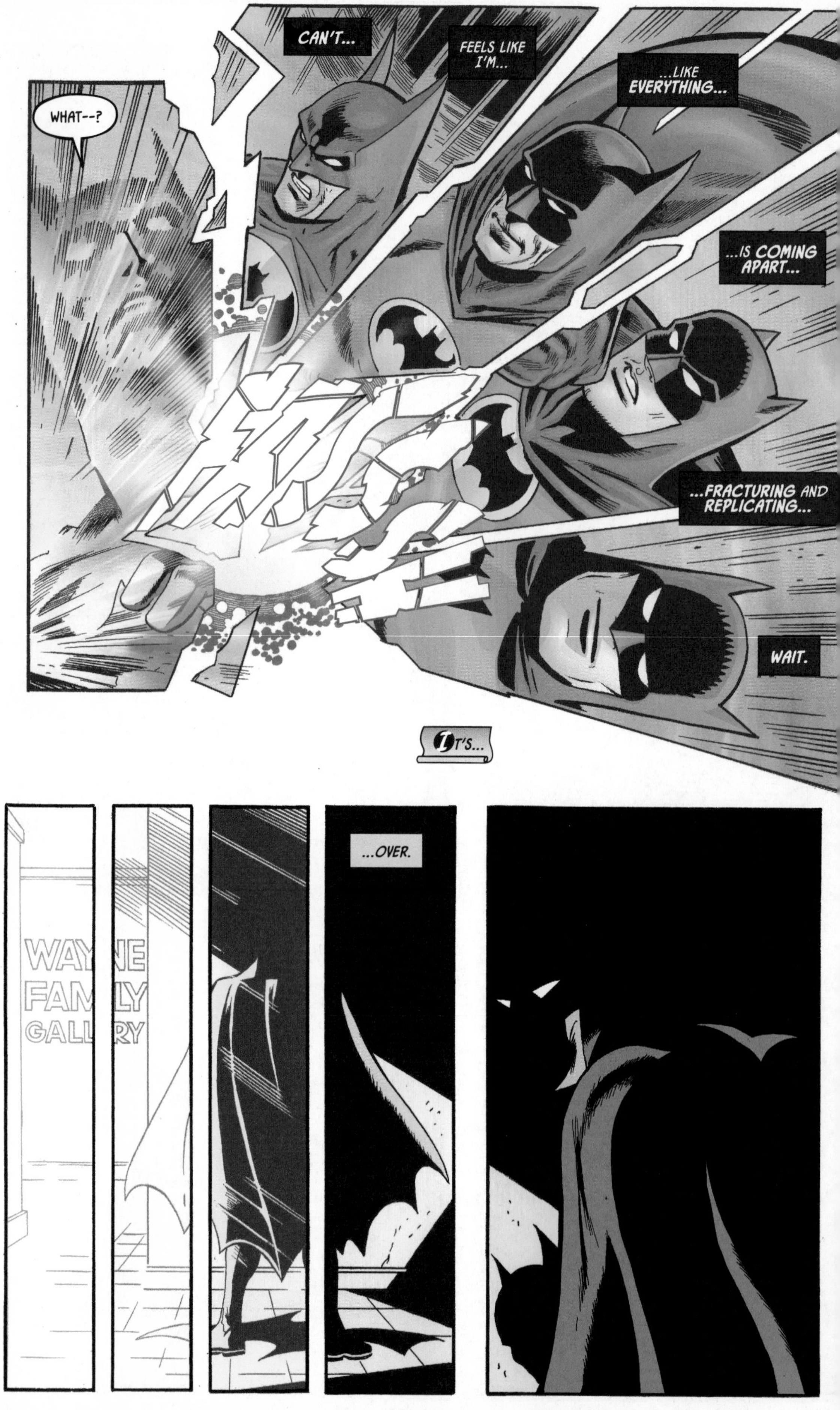
WHAT--?
CAN'T...
FEELS LIKE I'M...
...LIKE EVERYTHING...
...IS COMING APART...
...FRACTURING AND REPLICATING...
WAIT.
IT'S...
WAYNE FAMILY GALLERY
...OVER.

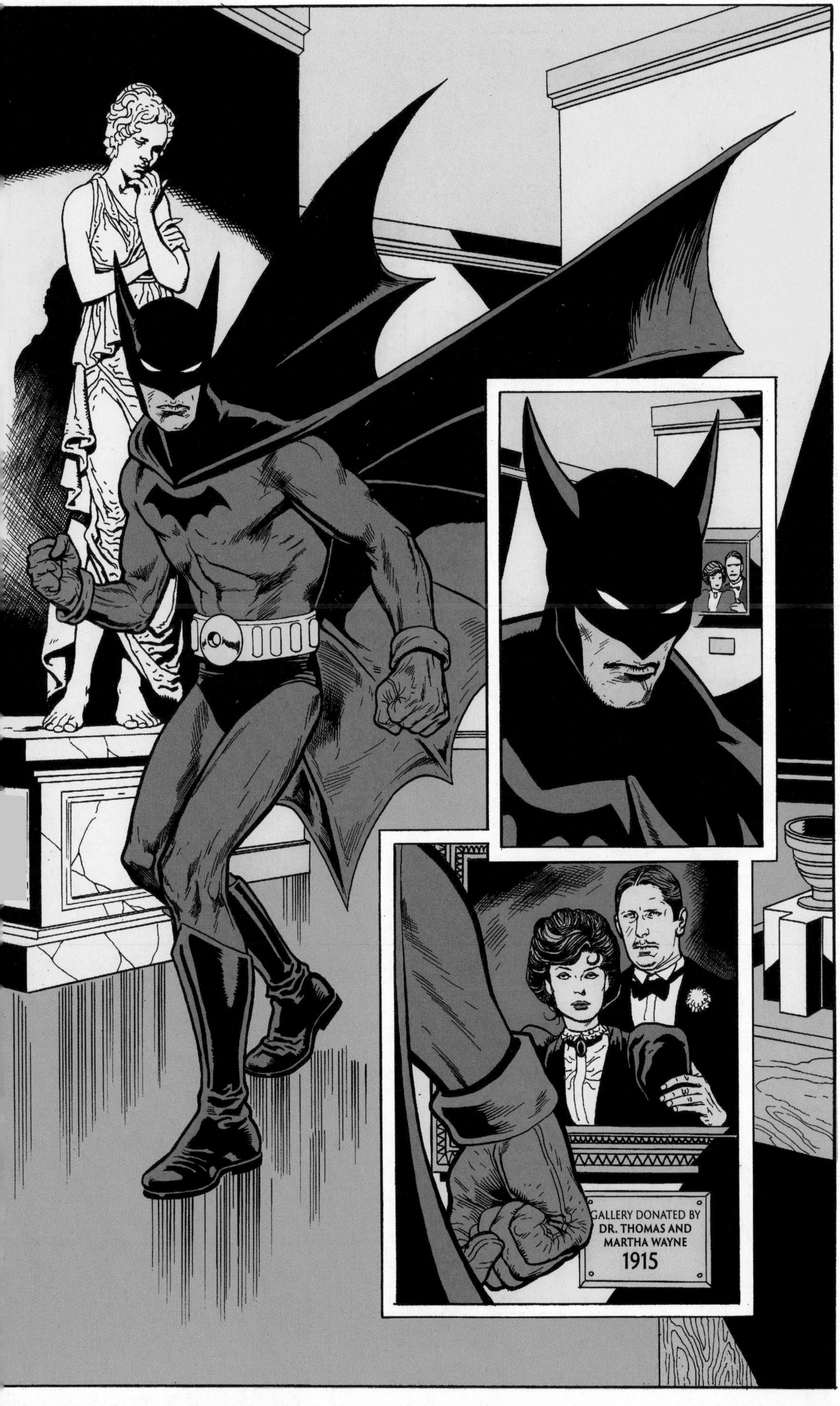
GALLERY DONATED BY
DR. THOMAS AND
MARTHA WAYNE
1915

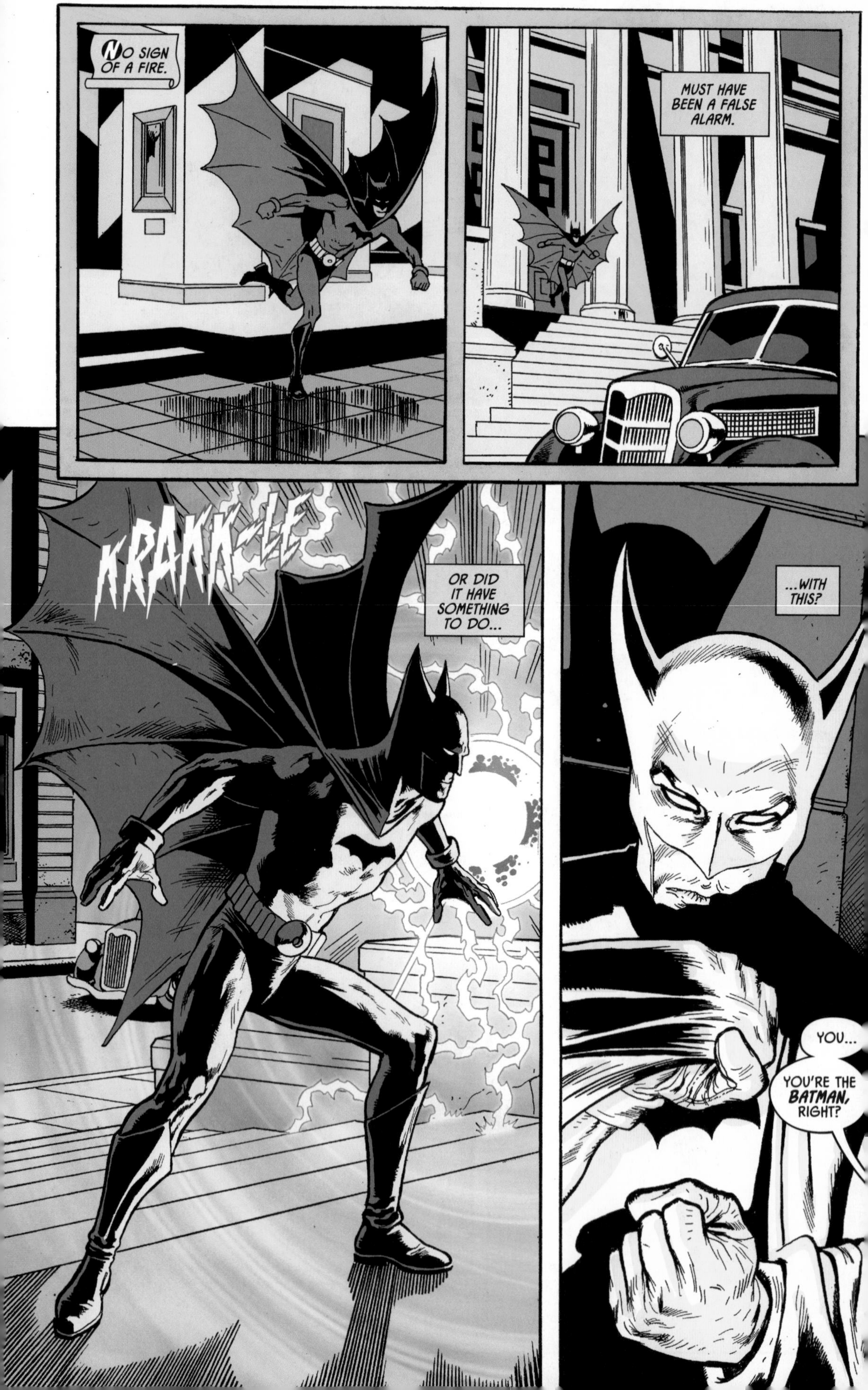
NO SIGN OF A FIRE.
MUST HAVE BEEN A FALSE ALARM.
KRAKK-LE
OR DID IT HAVE SOMETHING TO DO...
...WITH THIS?
YOU...
YOU'RE THE BATMAN, RIGHT?

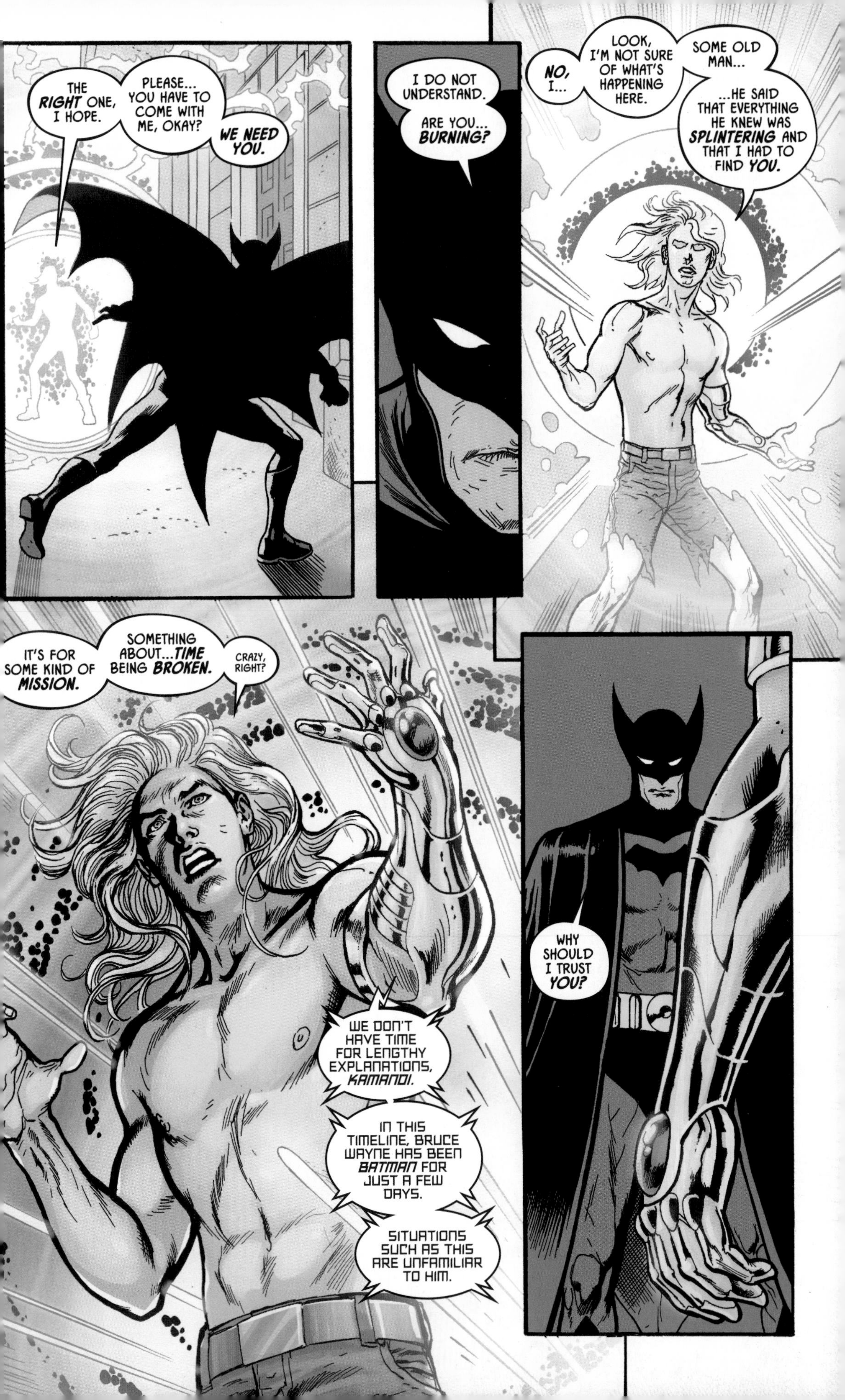
THE RIGHT ONE, I HOPE.
PLEASE... YOU HAVE TO COME WITH ME, OKAY?
WE NEED YOU.
I DO NOT UNDERSTAND.
ARE YOU... BURNING?
NO, I...
LOOK, I'M NOT SURE OF WHAT'S HAPPENING HERE.
SOME OLD MAN...
...HE SAID THAT EVERYTHING HE KNEW WAS SPLINTERING AND THAT I HAD TO FIND YOU.
IT'S FOR SOME KIND OF MISSION.
SOMETHING ABOUT...TIME BEING BROKEN.
CRAZY, RIGHT?
WHY SHOULD I TRUST YOU?
WE DON'T HAVE TIME FOR LENGTHY EXPLANATIONS, KAMANDI.
IN THIS TIMELINE, BRUCE WAYNE HAS BEEN BATMAN FOR JUST A FEW DAYS.
SITUATIONS SUCH AS THIS ARE UNFAMILIAR TO HIM.

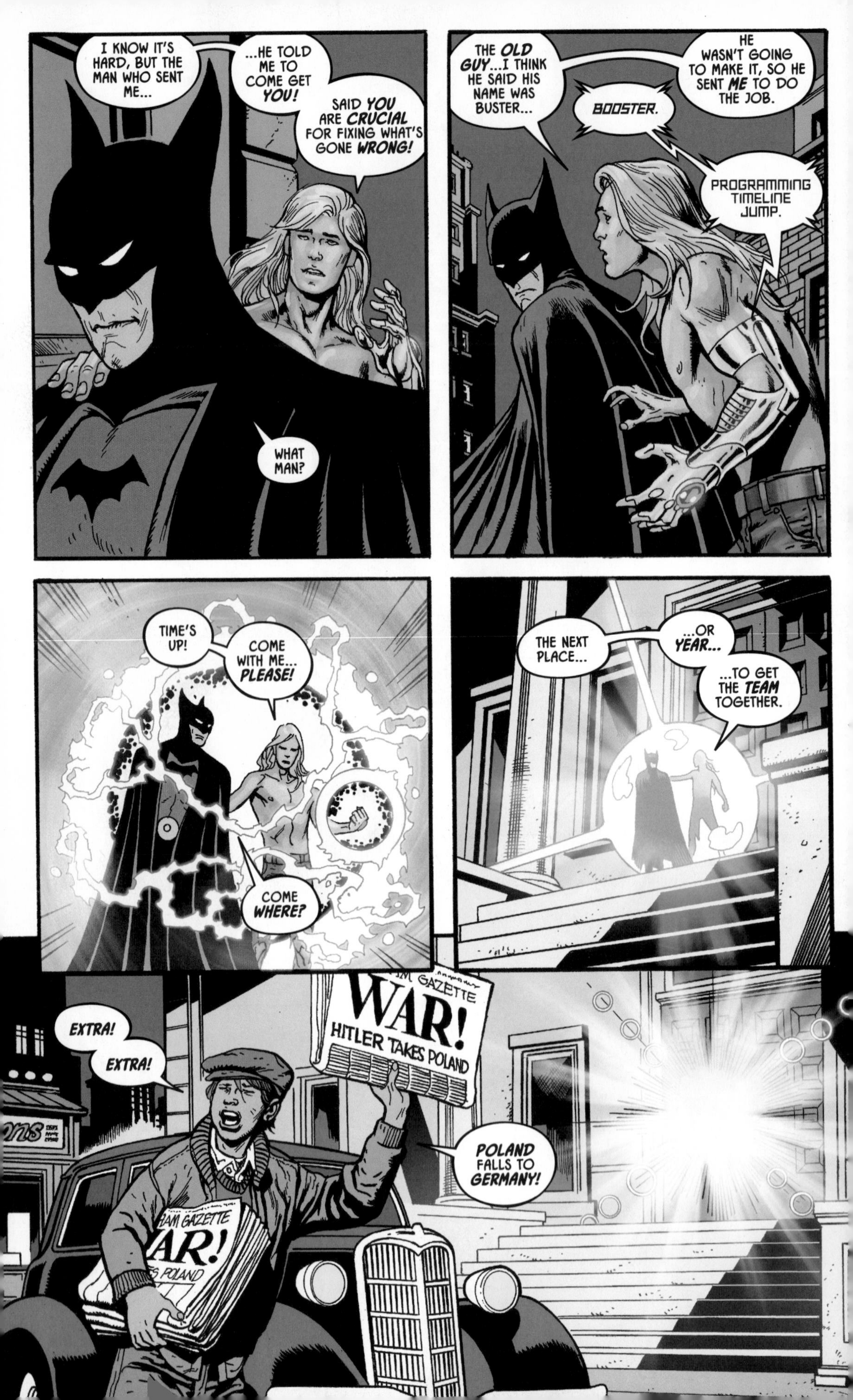
I KNOW IT'S HARD, BUT THE MAN WHO SENT ME...
...HE TOLD ME TO COME GET YOU!
SAID YOU ARE CRUCIAL FOR FIXING WHAT'S GONE WRONG!
WHAT MAN?
THE OLD GUY...I THINK HE SAID HIS NAME WAS BUSTER...
BOOSTER.
HE WASN'T GOING TO MAKE IT, SO HE SENT ME TO DO THE JOB.
PROGRAMMING TIMELINE JUMP.
TIME'S UP!
COME WITH ME... PLEASE!
COME WHERE?
THE NEXT PLACE...
...OR YEAR...
...TO GET THE TEAM TOGETHER.
WAR!
HITLER TAKES POLAND
EXTRA!
EXTRA!
POLAND FALLS TO GERMANY!

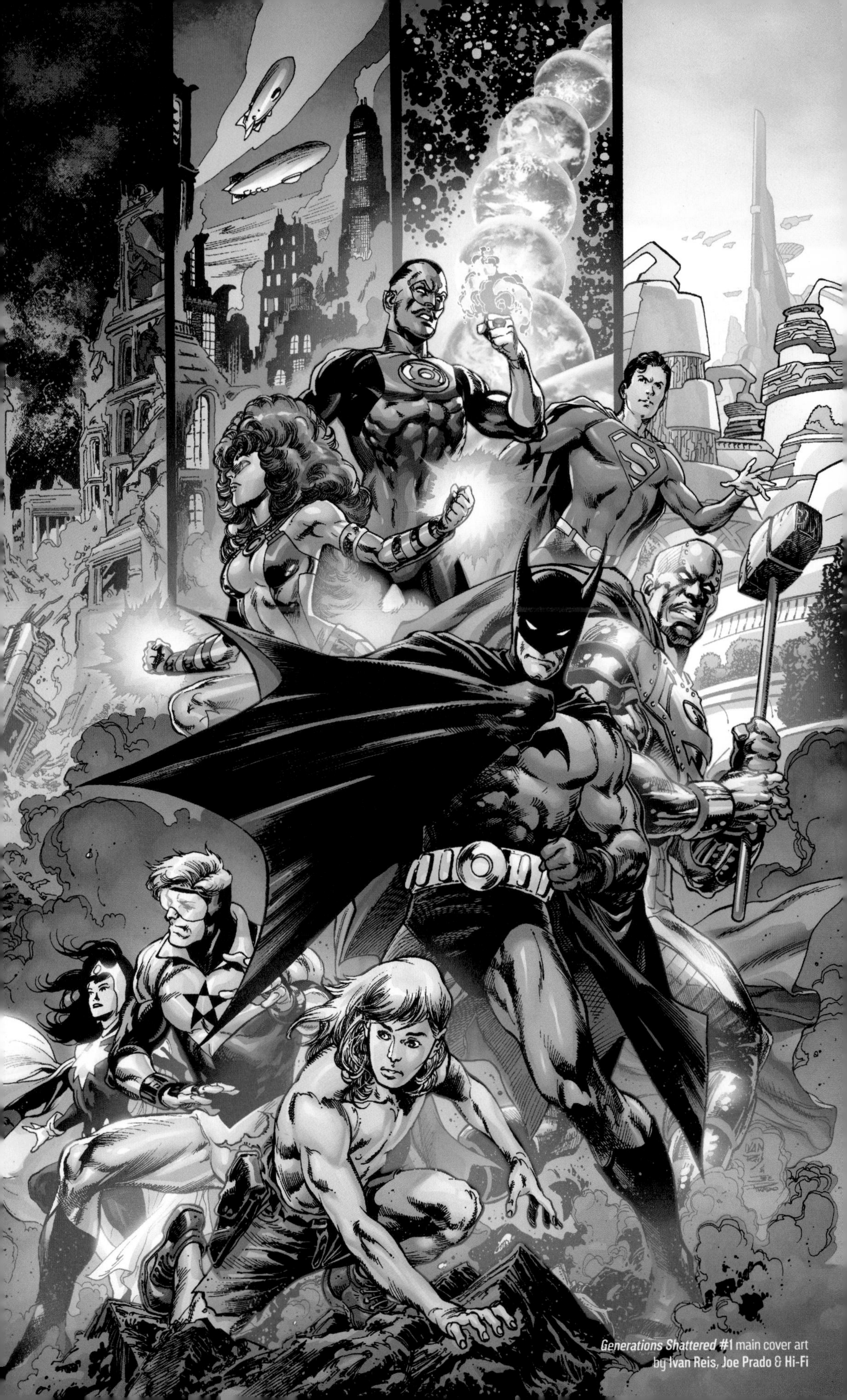

Generations Shattered #1 main cover art
by Ivan Reis, Joe Prado & Hi-Fi

CONTENTS:
GENERATIONS SHATTERED ARTISTS

IVAN REIS & JOE PRADO .... PAGES 19-26

IVAN REIS & SCOTT HANNA .... PAGES 27-34

FERNANDO PASARIN & OCLAIR ALBERT .... PAGES 35-40

AARON LOPRESTI & MATT RYAN .... PAGES 41-45

EMANUELA LUPACCHINO & WADE VON GRAWBADGER .... PAGES 46-50

BERNARD CHANG .... PAGES 51-55

YANICK PAQUETTE .... PAGES 56-60

KEVIN NOWLAN .... PAGES 61-65

DAN JURGENS & KLAUS JANSON .... PAGES 66, 92-95

PAUL PELLETIER & SANDRA HOPE .... PAGES 67-71

JOHN ROMITA JR. .... PAGES 72-79

DOUG BRAITHWAITE .... PAGES 80-85

RAGS MORALES .... PAGES 86-91

MIKE PERKINS .... PAGES 96-98

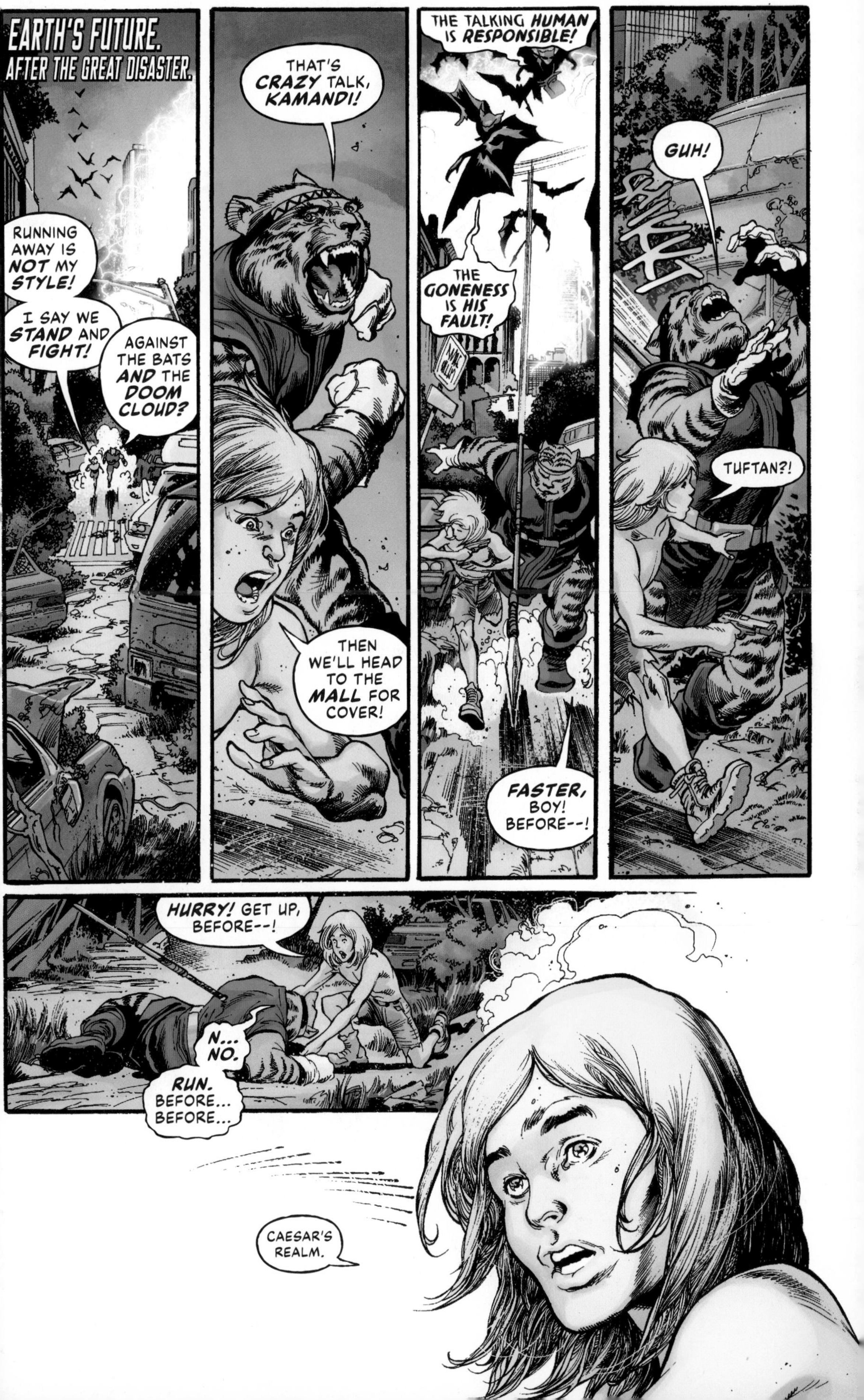
EARTH'S FUTURE.
AFTER THE GREAT DISASTER.
RUNNING AWAY IS NOT MY STYLE!
I SAY WE STAND AND FIGHT!
AGAINST THE BATS AND THE DOOM CLOUD?
THAT'S CRAZY TALK, KAMANDI!
THEN WE'LL HEAD TO THE MALL FOR COVER!
THE TALKING HUMAN IS RESPONSIBLE!
THE GONENESS IS HIS FAULT!
FASTER, BOY! BEFORE--!
GUH!
TUFTAN?!
HURRY! GET UP, BEFORE--!
N... NO.
RUN. BEFORE... BEFORE...
CAESAR'S REALM.

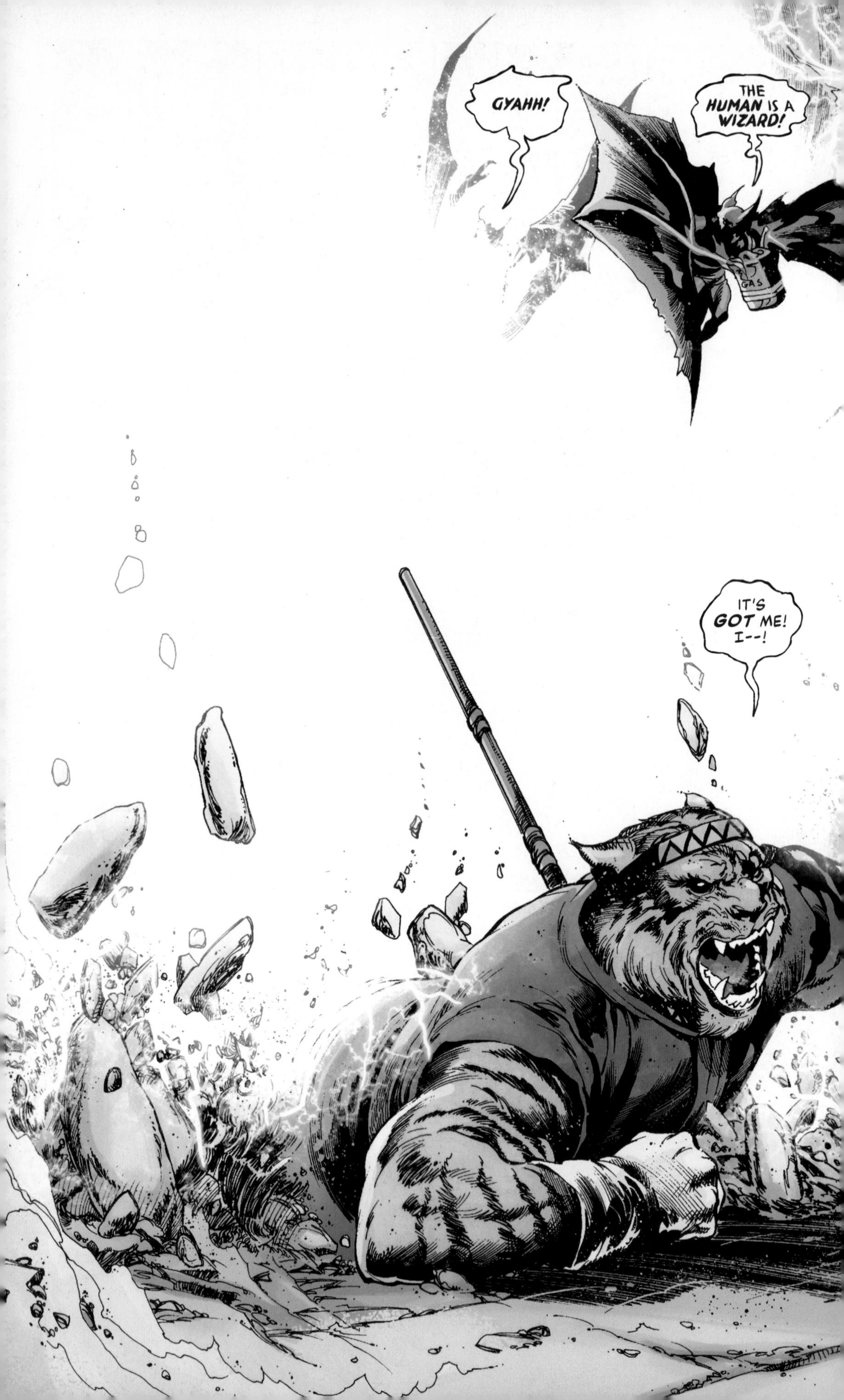
GYAHH!
THE HUMAN IS A WIZARD!
GAS
IT'S GOT ME! I--!

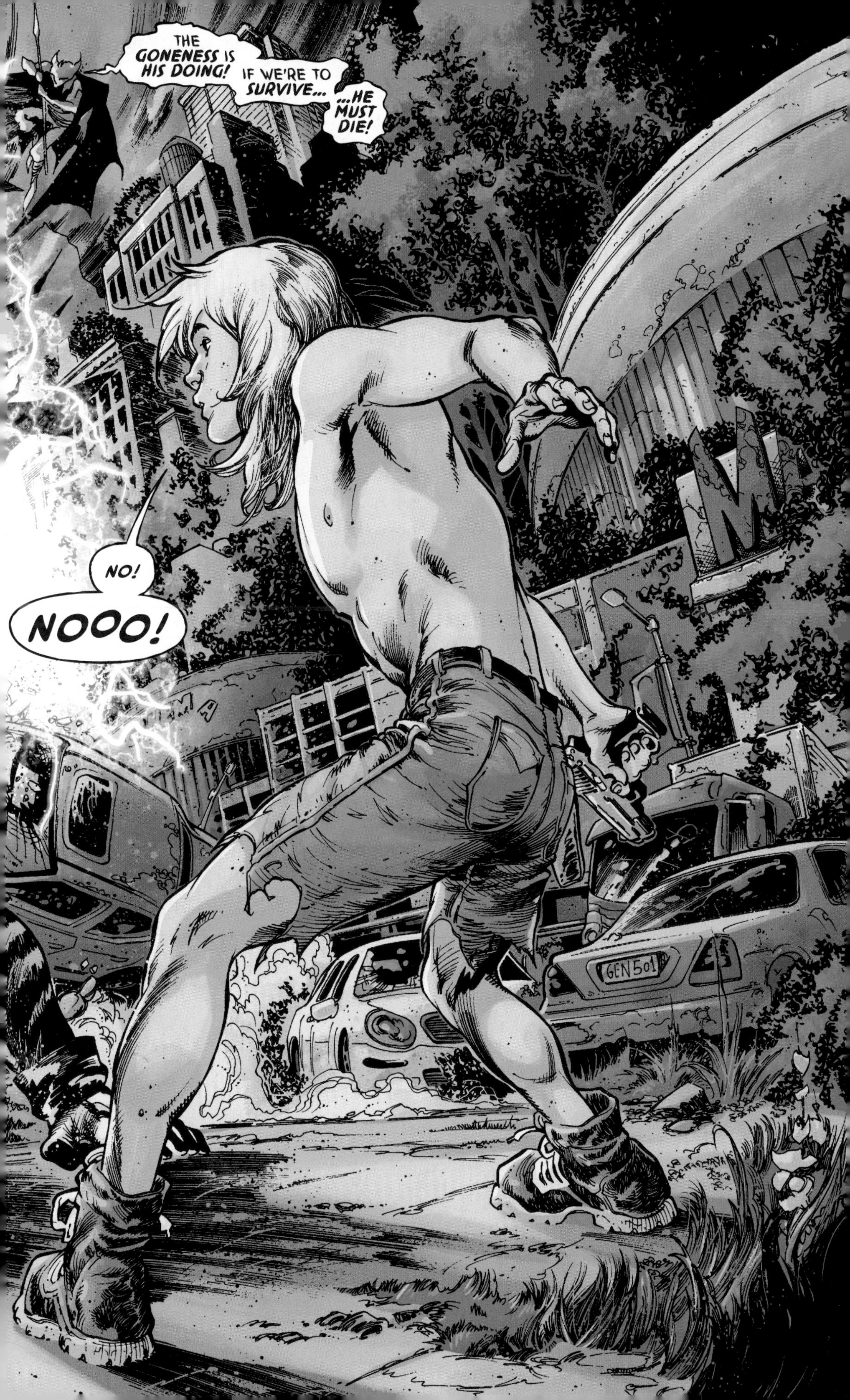
THE GONENESS IS HIS DOING!
IF WE'RE TO SURVIVE...
...HE MUST DIE!
NO!
NOOO!
GEN 501

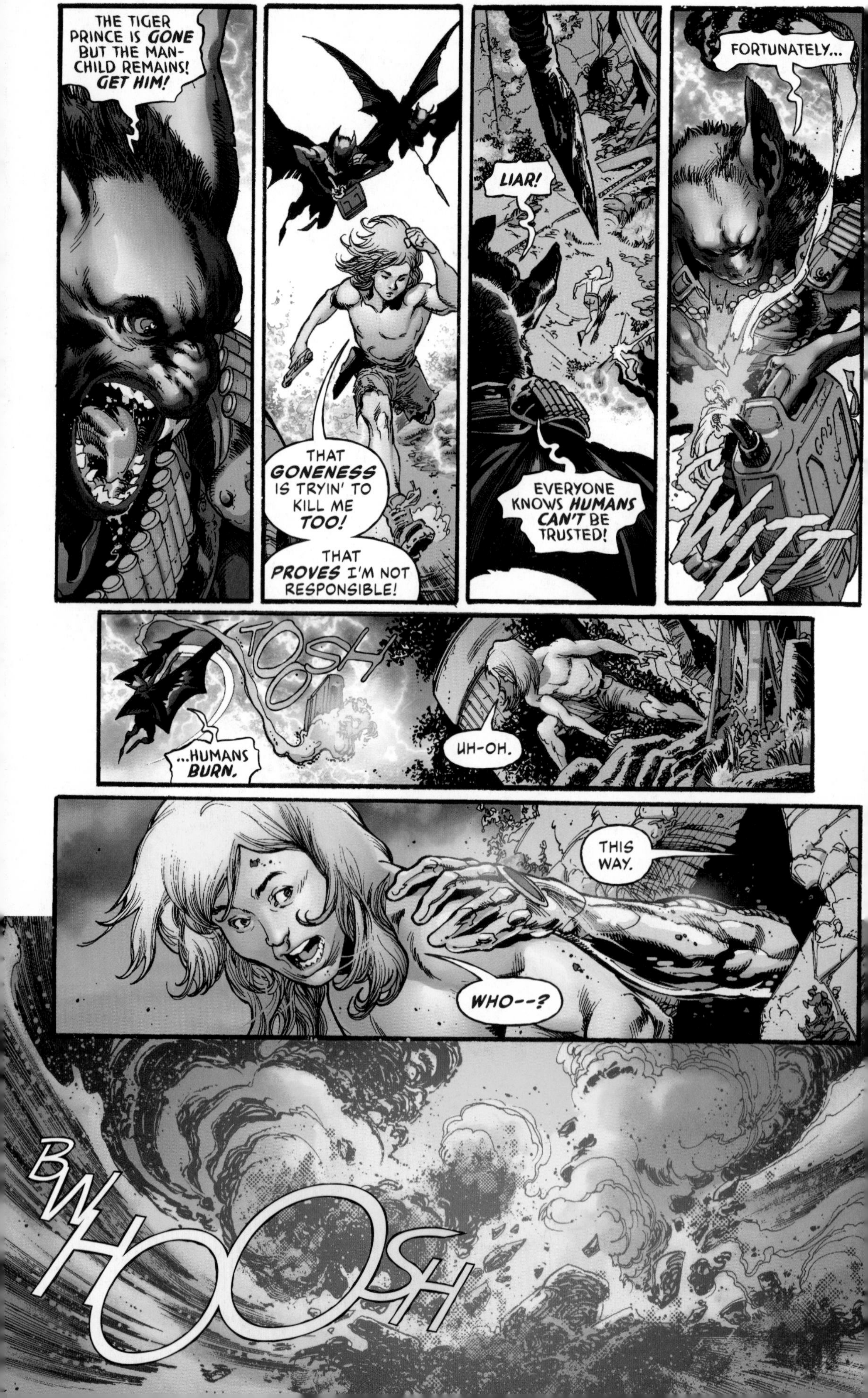
THE TIGER PRINCE IS GONE BUT THE MAN-CHILD REMAINS! GET HIM!
THAT GONENESS IS TRYIN' TO KILL ME TOO!
THAT PROVES I'M NOT RESPONSIBLE!
LIAR!
EVERYONE KNOWS HUMANS CAN'T BE TRUSTED!
FORTUNATELY...
WITT
TOOSH
...HUMANS BURN.
UH-OH.
THIS WAY.
WHO--?
BWHOOSH

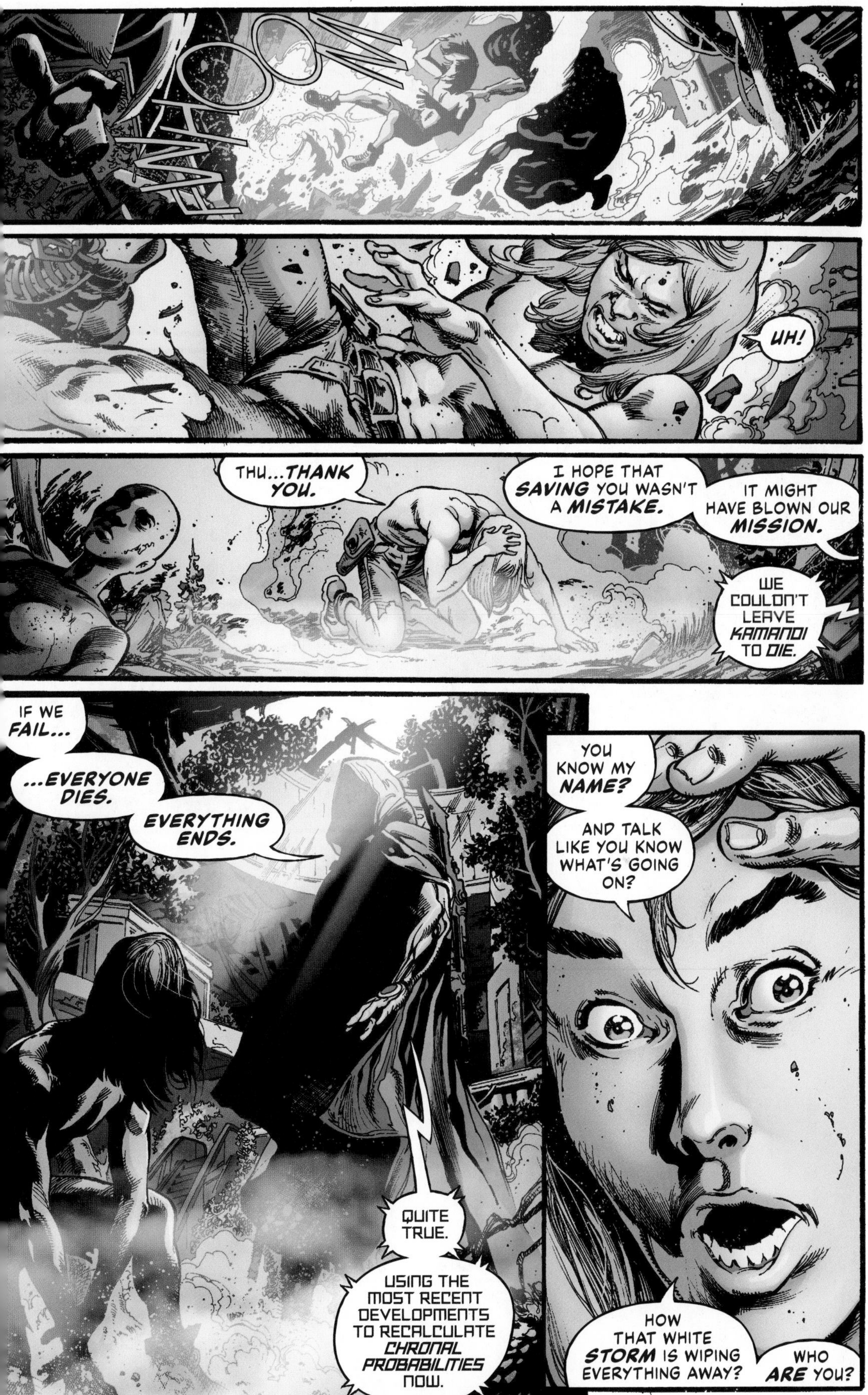
WHOOM
UH!
THU...THANK YOU.
I HOPE THAT SAVING YOU WASN'T A MISTAKE.
IT MIGHT HAVE BLOWN OUR MISSION.
WE COULDN'T LEAVE KAMANDI TO DIE.
IF WE FAIL...
...EVERYONE DIES.
EVERYTHING ENDS.
QUITE TRUE.
USING THE MOST RECENT DEVELOPMENTS TO RECALCULATE CHRONAL PROBABILITIES NOW.
YOU KNOW MY NAME?
AND TALK LIKE YOU KNOW WHAT'S GOING ON?
HOW THAT WHITE STORM IS WIPING EVERYTHING AWAY?
WHO ARE YOU?

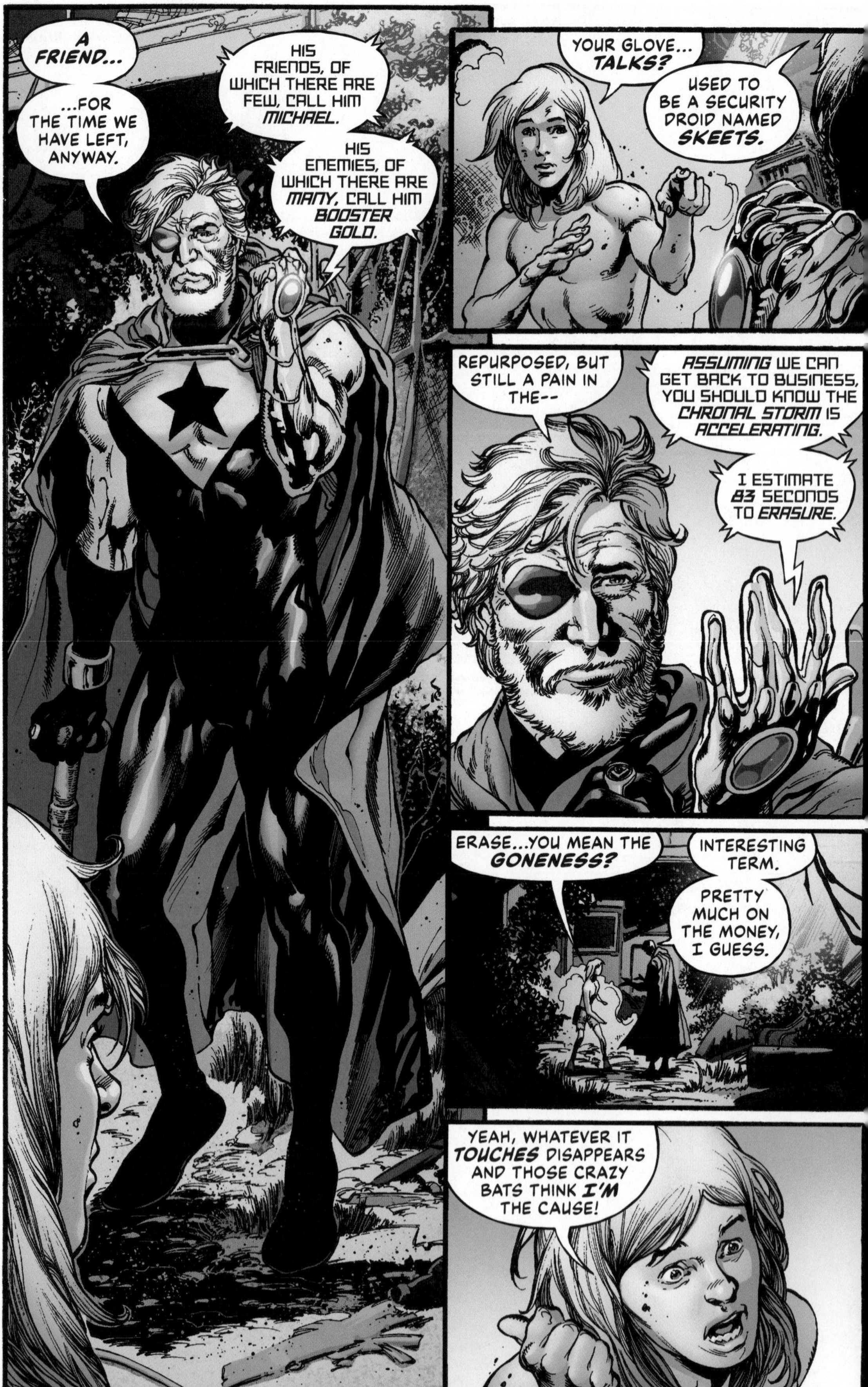
A FRIEND...
...FOR THE TIME WE HAVE LEFT, ANYWAY.
HIS FRIENDS, OF WHICH THERE ARE FEW, CALL HIM MICHAEL.
HIS ENEMIES, OF WHICH THERE ARE MANY, CALL HIM BOOSTER GOLD.
YOUR GLOVE... TALKS?
USED TO BE A SECURITY DROID NAMED SKEETS.
REPURPOSED, BUT STILL A PAIN IN THE--
ASSUMING WE CAN GET BACK TO BUSINESS, YOU SHOULD KNOW THE CHRONAL STORM IS ACCELERATING.
I ESTIMATE 83 SECONDS TO ERASURE.
ERASE...YOU MEAN THE GONENESS?
INTERESTING TERM.
PRETTY MUCH ON THE MONEY, I GUESS.
YEAH, WHATEVER IT TOUCHES DISAPPEARS AND THOSE CRAZY BATS THINK I'M THE CAUSE!

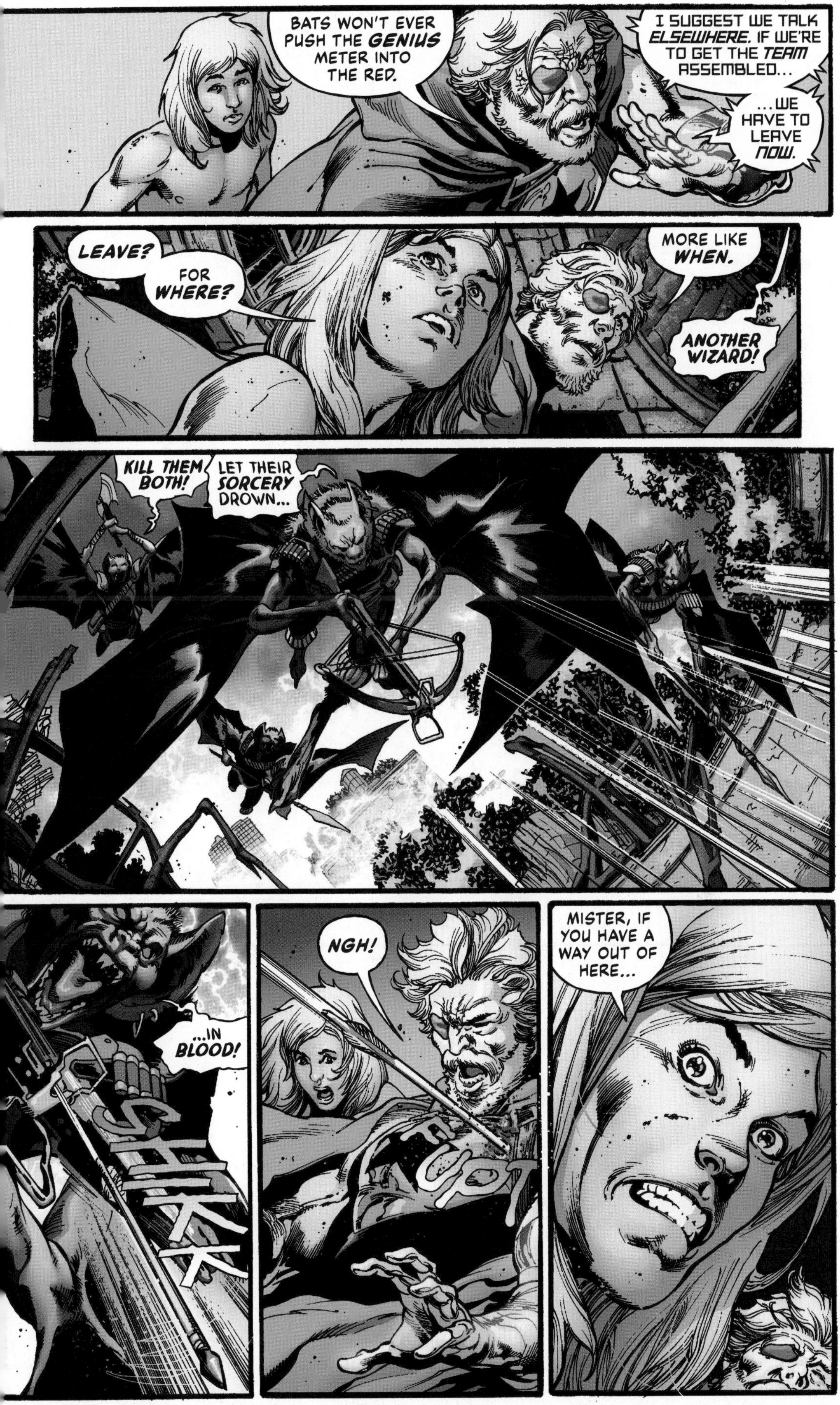
BATS WON'T EVER PUSH THE GENIUS METER INTO THE RED.
I SUGGEST WE TALK ELSEWHERE. IF WE'RE TO GET THE TEAM ASSEMBLED...
...WE HAVE TO LEAVE NOW.
LEAVE?
FOR WHERE?
MORE LIKE WHEN.
ANOTHER WIZARD!
KILL THEM BOTH!
LET THEIR SORCERY DROWN...
...IN BLOOD!
SHIKK
NGH!
THUD
MISTER, IF YOU HAVE A WAY OUT OF HERE...

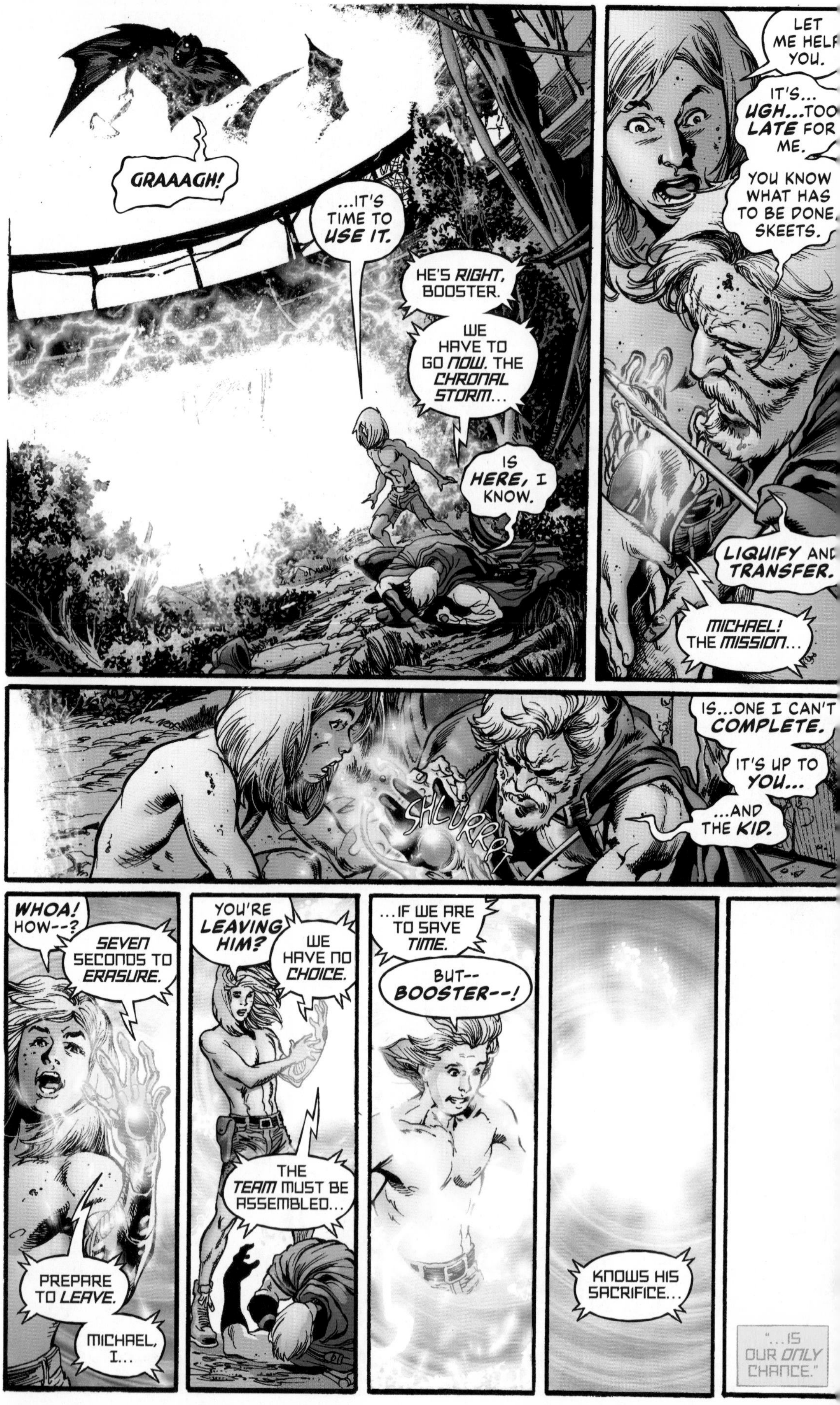
GRAAAGH!
...IT'S TIME TO USE IT.
HE'S RIGHT, BOOSTER.
WE HAVE TO GO NOW. THE CHRONAL STORM...
IS HERE, I KNOW.
LET ME HELP YOU.
IT'S... UGH...TOO LATE FOR ME.
YOU KNOW WHAT HAS TO BE DONE, SKEETS.
LIQUIFY AND TRANSFER.
MICHAEL! THE MISSION...
IS...ONE I CAN'T COMPLETE.
IT'S UP TO YOU...
...AND THE KID.
SHLURRPT
WHOA! HOW--?
SEVEN SECONDS TO ERASURE.
PREPARE TO LEAVE.
MICHAEL, I...
YOU'RE LEAVING HIM?
WE HAVE NO CHOICE.
THE TEAM MUST BE ASSEMBLED...
...IF WE ARE TO SAVE TIME.
BUT-- BOOSTER--!
KNOWS HIS SACRIFICE...
"...IS OUR ONLY CHANCE."

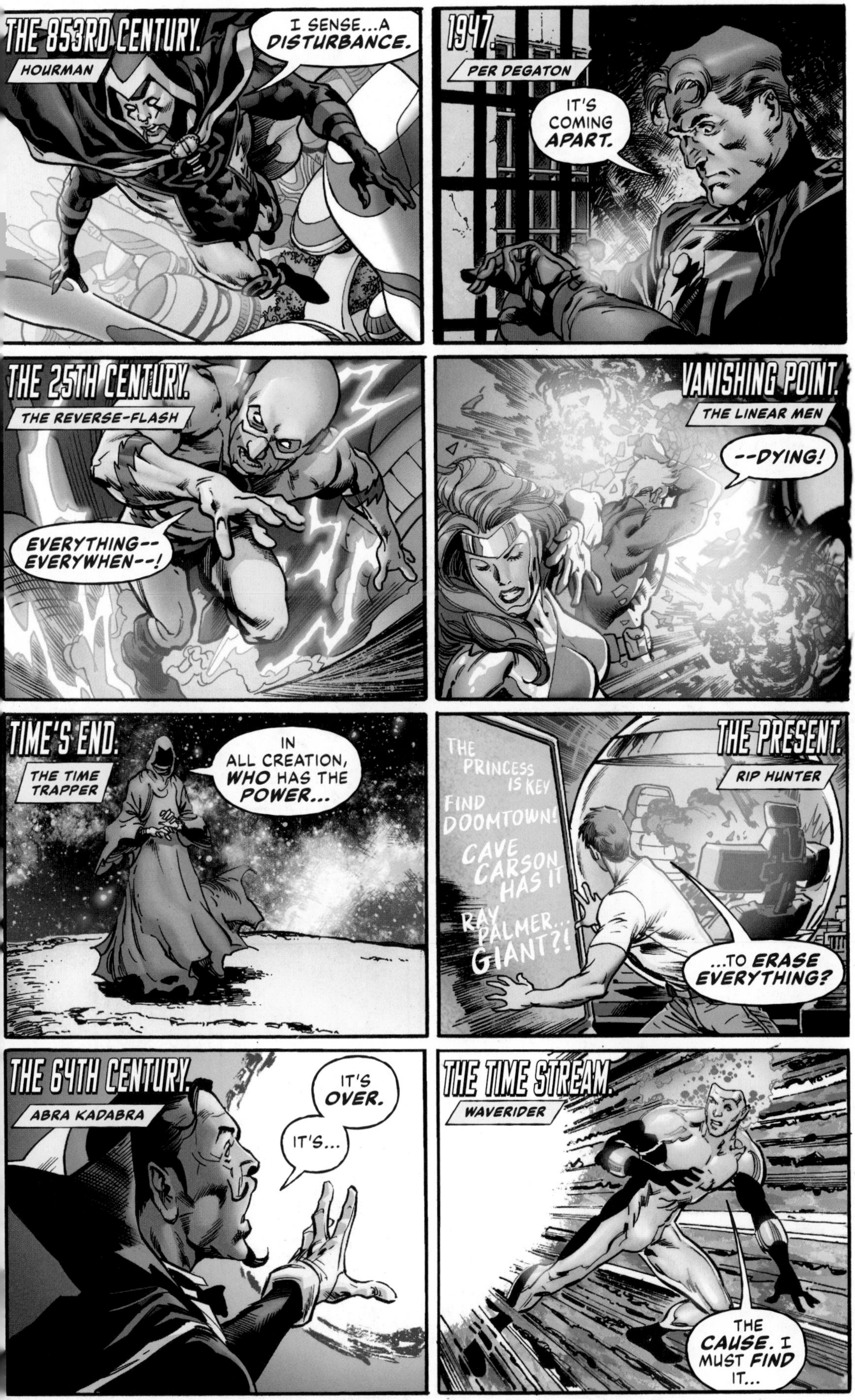
THE 853RD CENTURY.
HOURMAN
I SENSE...A DISTURBANCE.
1947.
PER DEGATON
IT'S COMING APART.
THE 25TH CENTURY.
THE REVERSE-FLASH
EVERYTHING-- EVERYWHEN--!
VANISHING POINT.
THE LINEAR MEN
--DYING!
TIME'S END.
THE TIME TRAPPER
IN ALL CREATION, WHO HAS THE POWER...
THE PRESENT.
RIP HUNTER
THE PRINCESS IS KEY
FIND DOOMTOWN!
CAVE CARSON HAS IT
RAY PALMER... GIANT?!
...TO ERASE EVERYTHING?
THE 64TH CENTURY.
ABRA KADABRA
IT'S OVER.
IT'S...
THE TIME STREAM.
WAVERIDER
THE CAUSE. I MUST FIND IT...

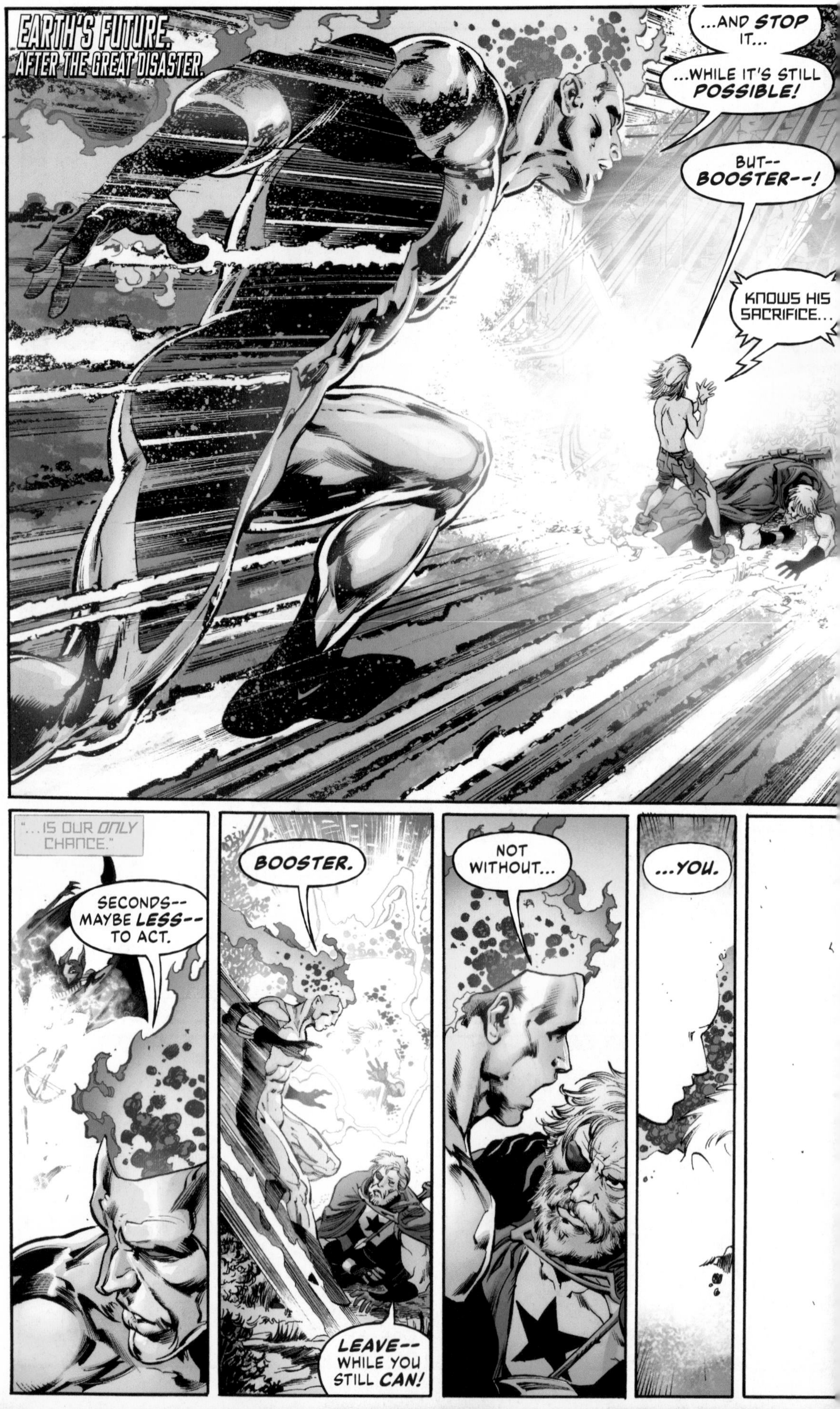
EARTH'S FUTURE.
AFTER THE GREAT DISASTER.
...AND STOP IT...
...WHILE IT'S STILL POSSIBLE!
BUT-- BOOSTER--!
KNOWS HIS SACRIFICE...
"...IS OUR ONLY CHANCE."
SECONDS-- MAYBE LESS-- TO ACT.
BOOSTER.
LEAVE-- WHILE YOU STILL CAN!
NOT WITHOUT...
...YOU.

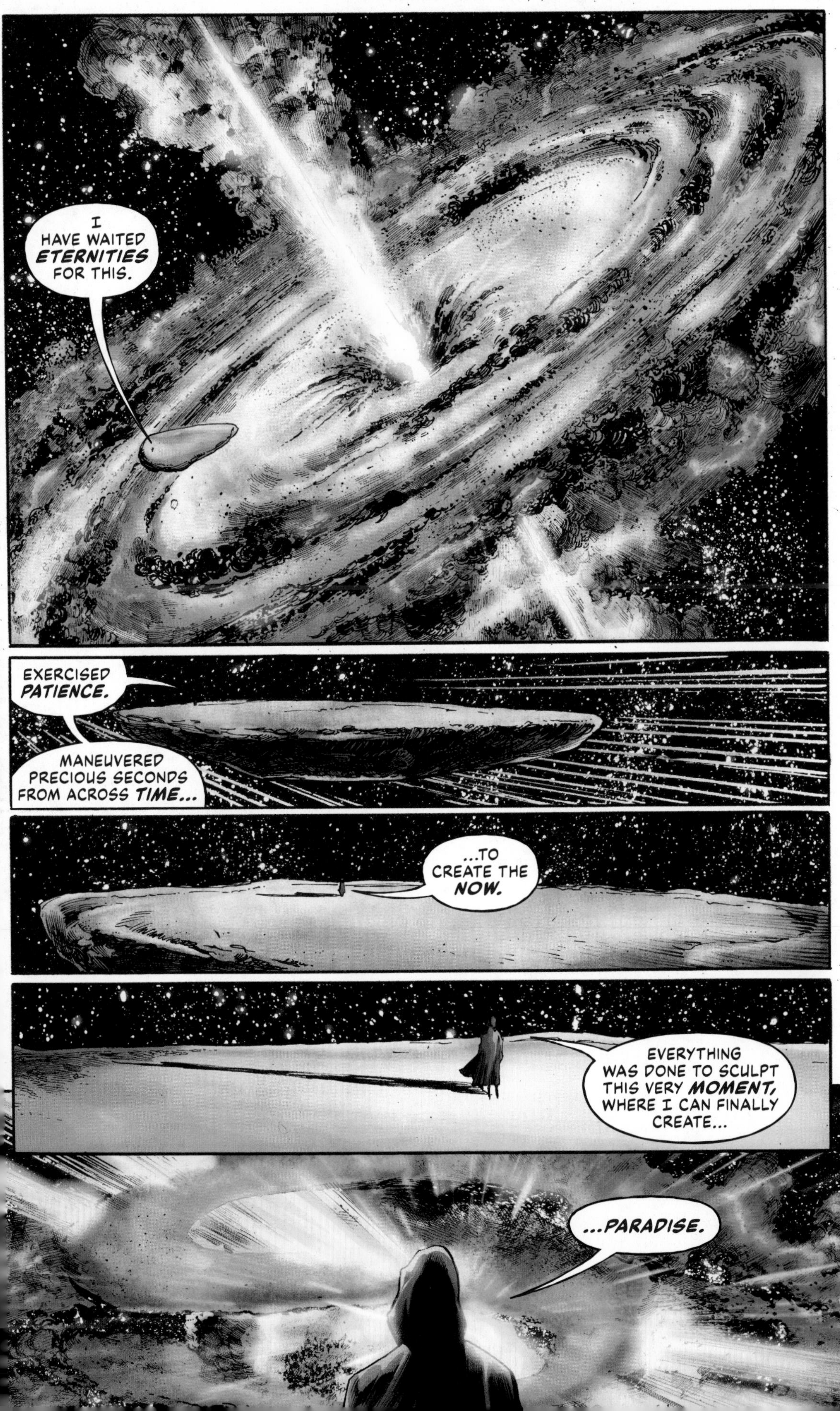
I HAVE WAITED ETERNITIES FOR THIS.
EXERCISED PATIENCE.
MANEUVERED PRECIOUS SECONDS FROM ACROSS TIME...
...TO CREATE THE NOW.
EVERYTHING WAS DONE TO SCULPT THIS VERY MOMENT, WHERE I CAN FINALLY CREATE...
...PARADISE.

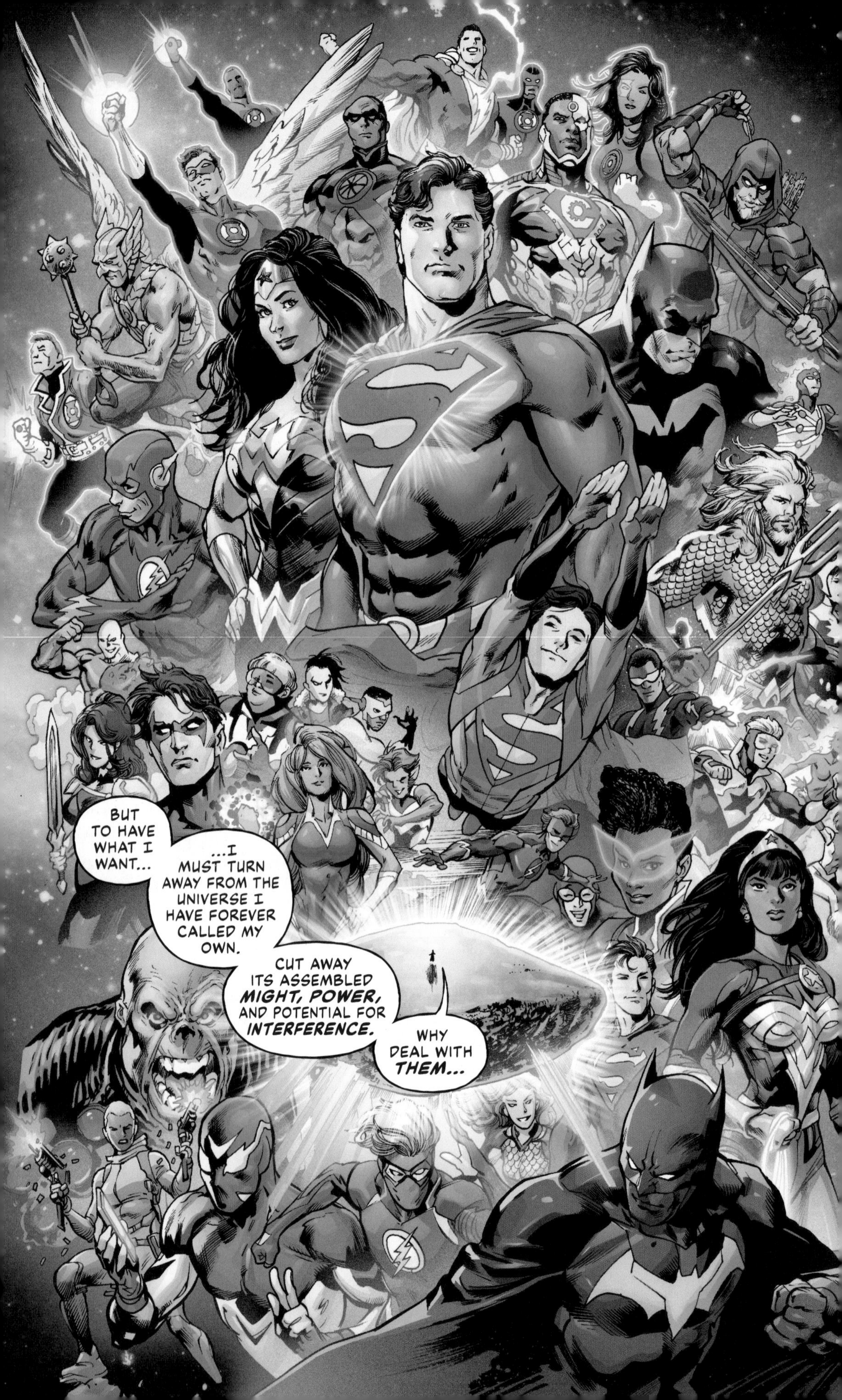
BUT TO HAVE WHAT I WANT...
...I MUST TURN AWAY FROM THE UNIVERSE I HAVE FOREVER CALLED MY OWN.
CUT AWAY ITS ASSEMBLED MIGHT, POWER, AND POTENTIAL FOR INTERFERENCE.
WHY DEAL WITH THEM...

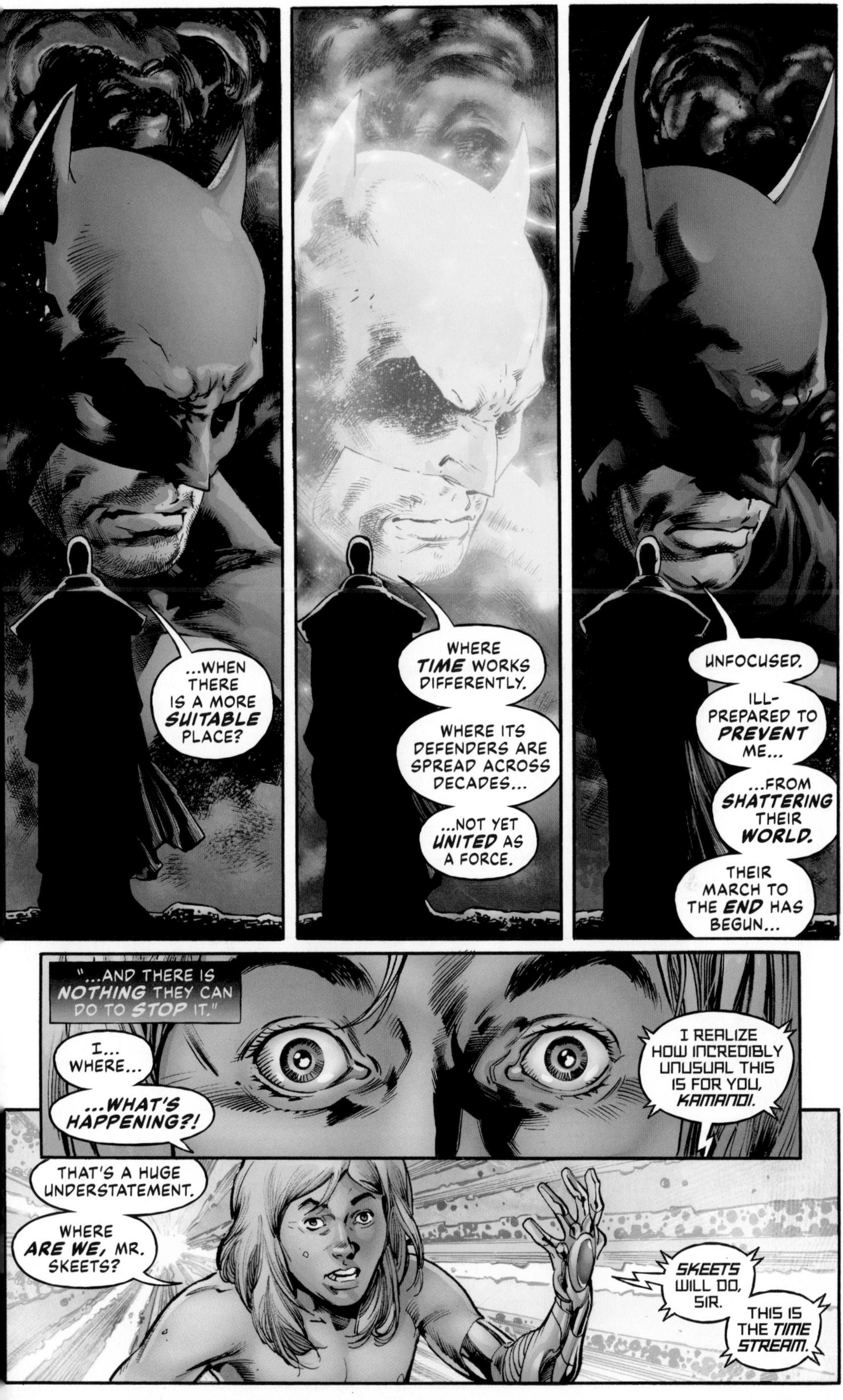
...WHEN THERE IS A MORE SUITABLE PLACE?
WHERE TIME WORKS DIFFERENTLY.
WHERE ITS DEFENDERS ARE SPREAD ACROSS DECADES...
...NOT YET UNITED AS A FORCE.
UNFOCUSED.
ILL-PREPARED TO PREVENT ME...
...FROM SHATTERING THEIR WORLD.
THEIR MARCH TO THE END HAS BEGUN...
"...AND THERE IS NOTHING THEY CAN DO TO STOP IT."
I... WHERE...
...WHAT'S HAPPENING?!
I REALIZE HOW INCREDIBLY UNUSUAL THIS IS FOR YOU, KAMANDI.
THAT'S A HUGE UNDERSTATEMENT.
WHERE ARE WE, MR. SKEETS?
SKEETS WILL DO, SIR.
THIS IS THE TIME STREAM.

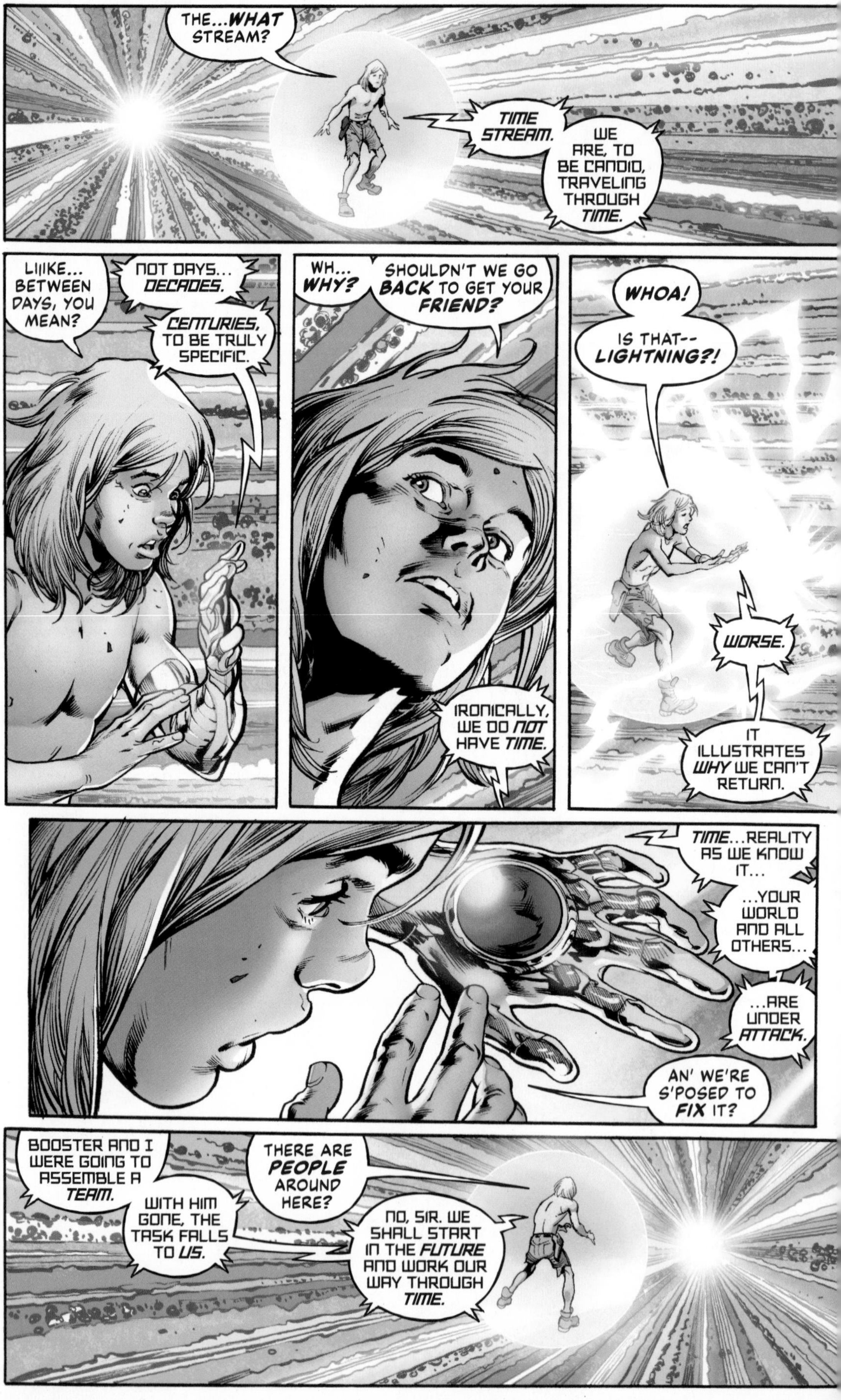

THE...WHAT STREAM?
TIME STREAM.
WE ARE, TO BE CANDID, TRAVELING THROUGH TIME.
LIIIKE... BETWEEN DAYS, YOU MEAN?
NOT DAYS... DECADES.
CENTURIES, TO BE TRULY SPECIFIC.
WH... WHY?
SHOULDN'T WE GO BACK TO GET YOUR FRIEND?
IRONICALLY, WE DO NOT HAVE TIME.
WHOA!
IS THAT--LIGHTNING?!
WORSE.
IT ILLUSTRATES WHY WE CAN'T RETURN.
TIME...REALITY AS WE KNOW IT...
...YOUR WORLD AND ALL OTHERS...
...ARE UNDER ATTACK.
AN' WE'RE S'POSED TO FIX IT?
BOOSTER AND I WERE GOING TO ASSEMBLE A TEAM.
WITH HIM GONE, THE TASK FALLS TO US.
THERE ARE PEOPLE AROUND HERE?
NO, SIR. WE SHALL START IN THE FUTURE AND WORK OUR WAY THROUGH TIME.

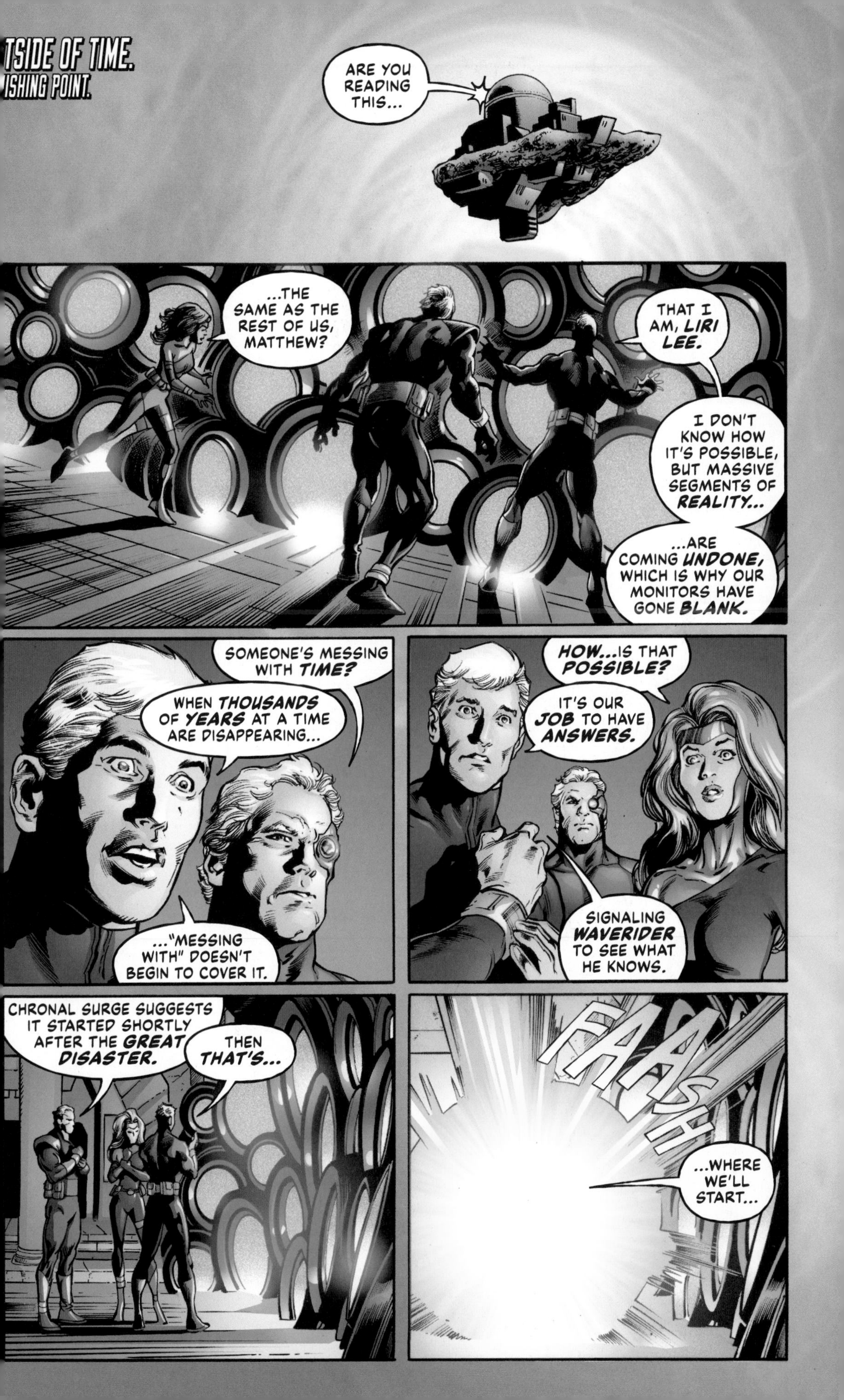
TSIDE OF TIME.
ISHING POINT.
ARE YOU READING THIS...
...THE SAME AS THE REST OF US, MATTHEW?
THAT I AM, LIRI LEE.
I DON'T KNOW HOW IT'S POSSIBLE, BUT MASSIVE SEGMENTS OF REALITY...
...ARE COMING UNDONE, WHICH IS WHY OUR MONITORS HAVE GONE BLANK.
SOMEONE'S MESSING WITH TIME?
WHEN THOUSANDS OF YEARS AT A TIME ARE DISAPPEARING...
..."MESSING WITH" DOESN'T BEGIN TO COVER IT.
HOW...IS THAT POSSIBLE?
IT'S OUR JOB TO HAVE ANSWERS.
SIGNALING WAVERIDER TO SEE WHAT HE KNOWS.
CHRONAL SURGE SUGGESTS IT STARTED SHORTLY AFTER THE GREAT DISASTER.
THEN THAT'S...
FAASH
...WHERE WE'LL START...

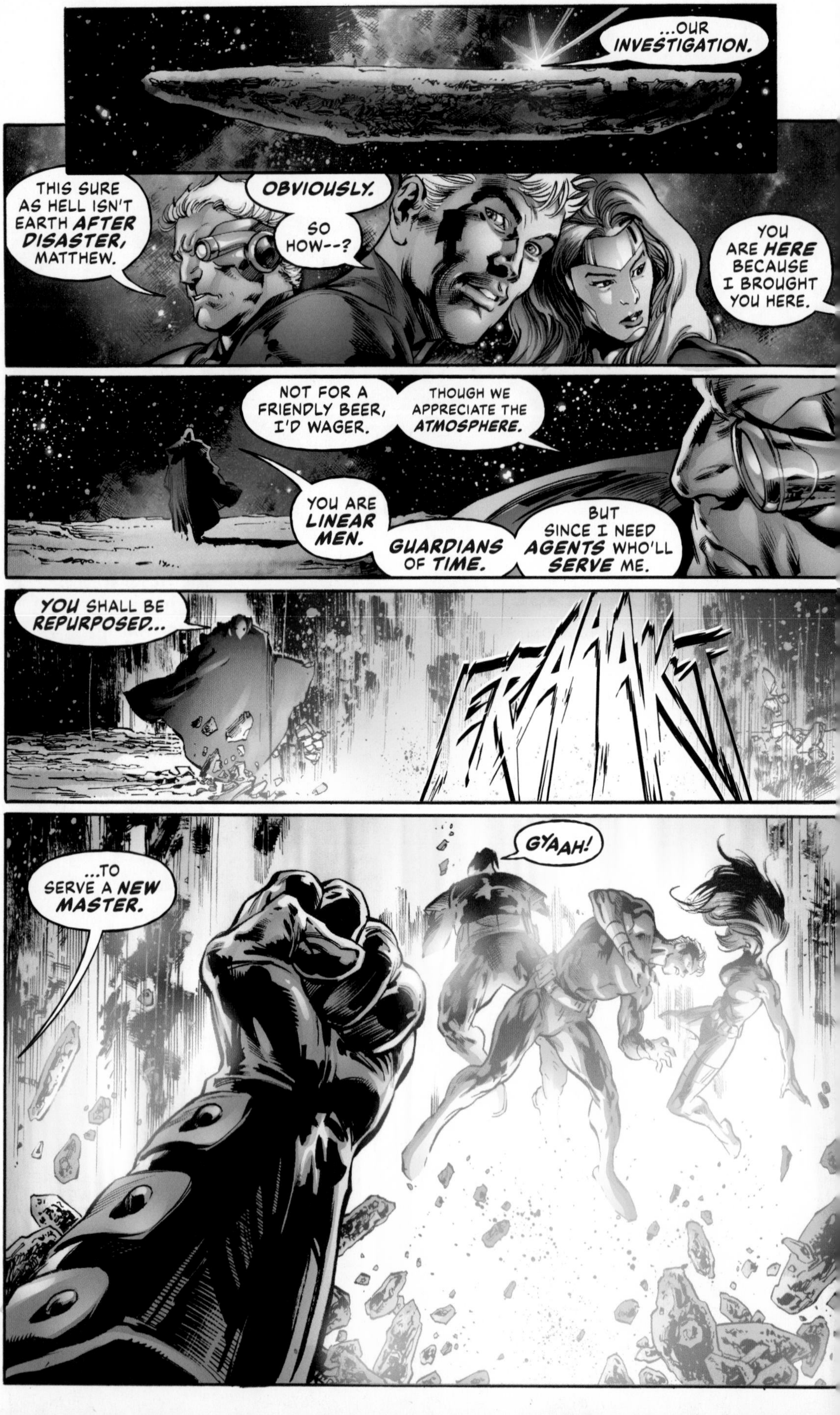

...OUR INVESTIGATION.
THIS SURE AS HELL ISN'T EARTH AFTER DISASTER, MATTHEW.
OBVIOUSLY.
SO HOW--?
YOU ARE HERE BECAUSE I BROUGHT YOU HERE.
NOT FOR A FRIENDLY BEER, I'D WAGER.
THOUGH WE APPRECIATE THE ATMOSPHERE.
YOU ARE LINEAR MEN.
GUARDIANS OF TIME.
BUT SINCE I NEED AGENTS WHO'LL SERVE ME.
YOU SHALL BE REPURPOSED...
FRAAKT
...TO SERVE A NEW MASTER.
GYAAH!

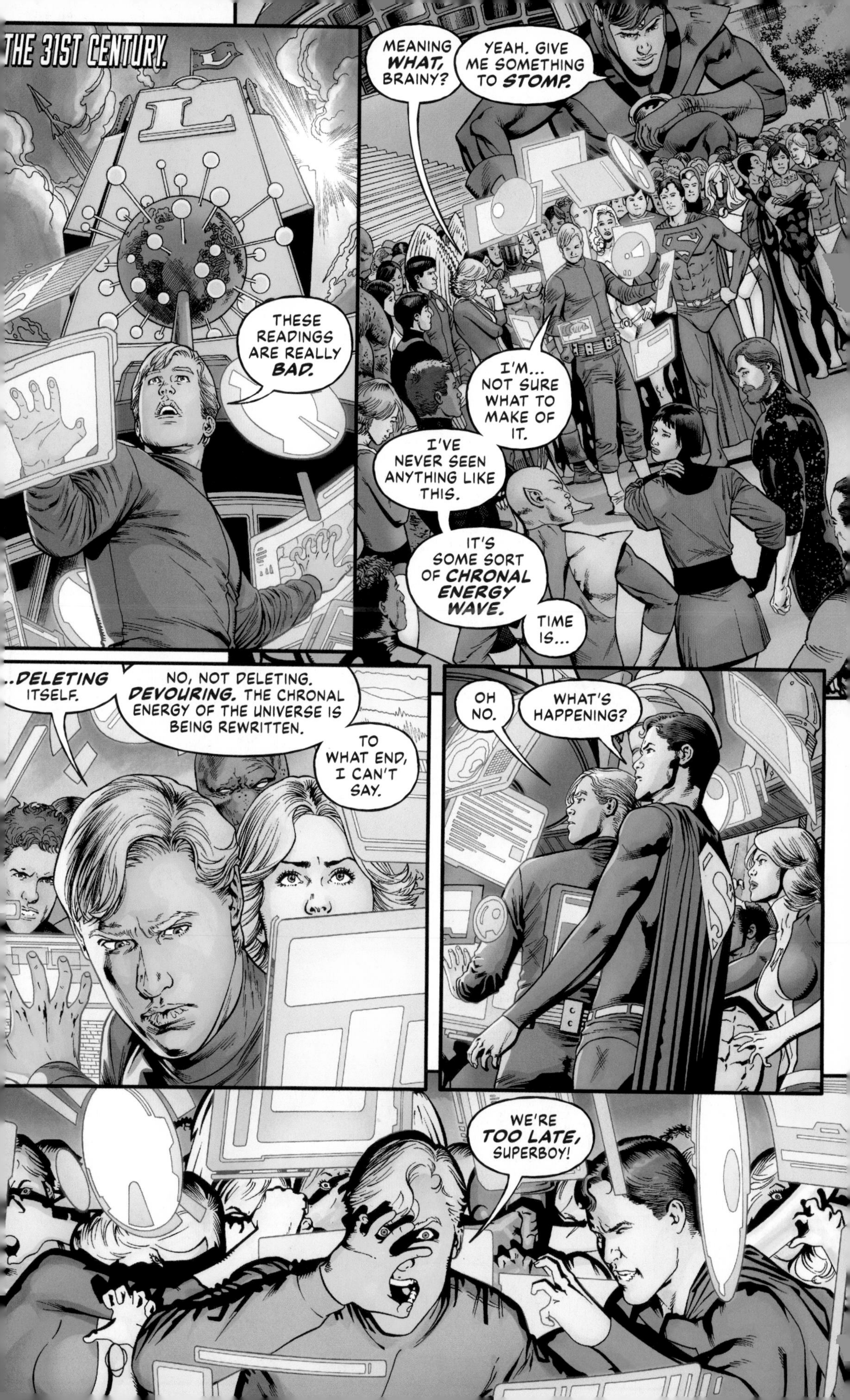
THE 31ST CENTURY.
MEANING WHAT, BRAINY?
YEAH. GIVE ME SOMETHING TO STOMP.
THESE READINGS ARE REALLY BAD.
I'M... NOT SURE WHAT TO MAKE OF IT.
I'VE NEVER SEEN ANYTHING LIKE THIS.
IT'S SOME SORT OF CHRONAL ENERGY WAVE.
TIME IS...
...DELETING ITSELF.
NO, NOT DELETING. DEVOURING. THE CHRONAL ENERGY OF THE UNIVERSE IS BEING REWRITTEN.
TO WHAT END, I CAN'T SAY.
OH NO.
WHAT'S HAPPENING?
WE'RE TOO LATE, SUPERBOY!

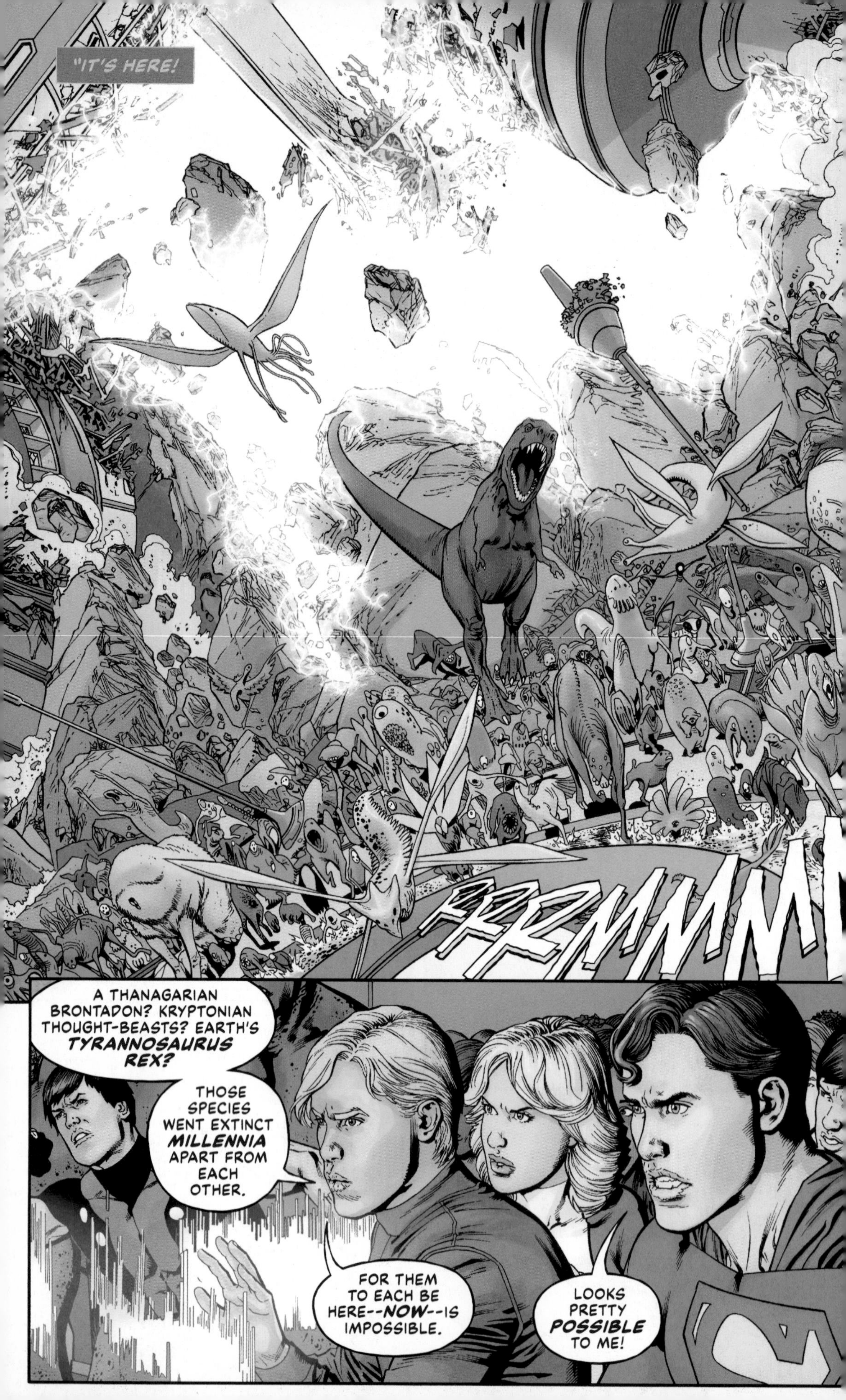
"IT'S HERE!
FRRZMMMM
A THANAGARIAN BRONTADON? KRYPTONIAN THOUGHT-BEASTS? EARTH'S TYRANNOSAURUS REX?
THOSE SPECIES WENT EXTINCT MILLENNIA APART FROM EACH OTHER.
FOR THEM TO EACH BE HERE--NOW--IS IMPOSSIBLE.
LOOKS PRETTY POSSIBLE TO ME!

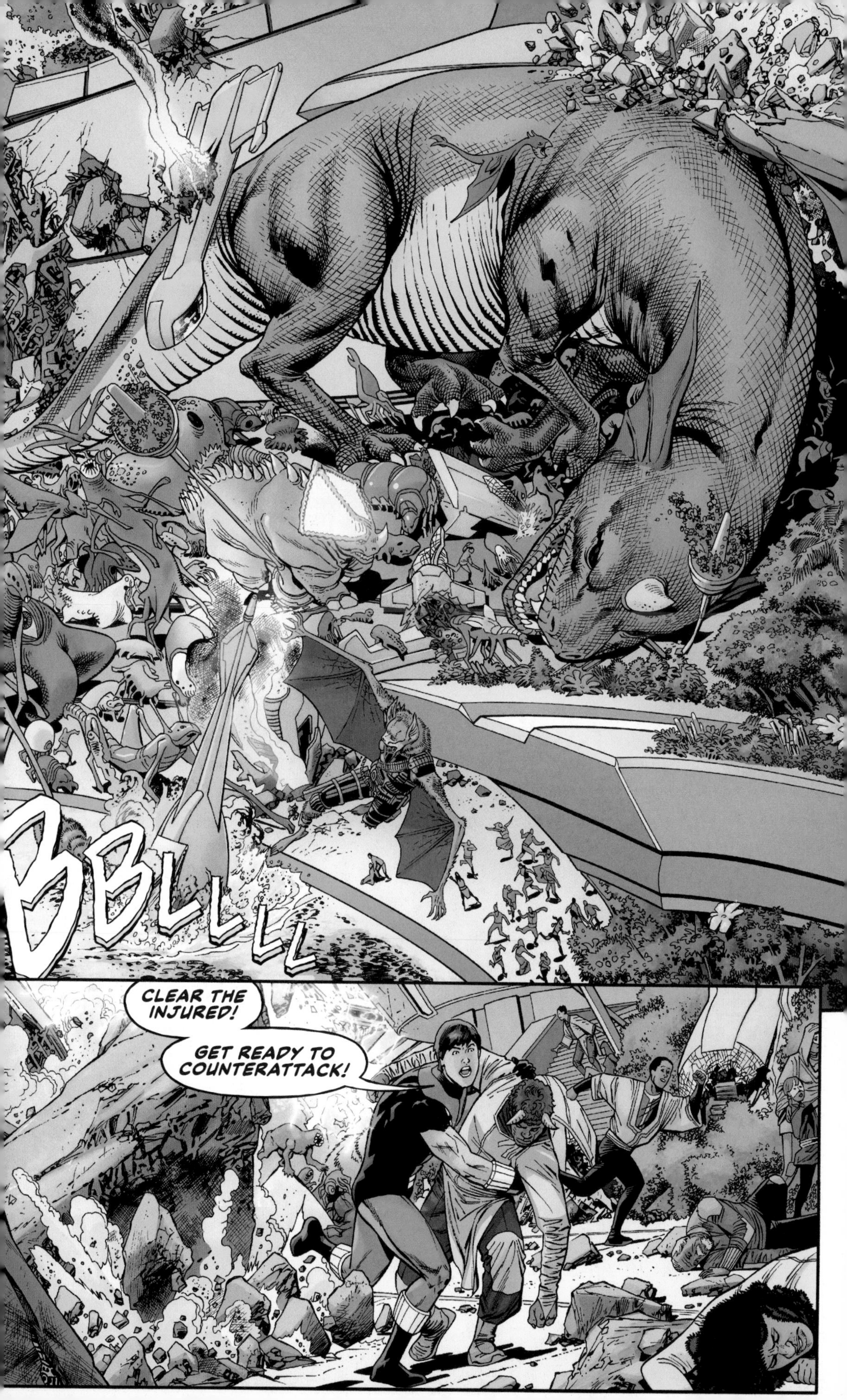
BBLLLL
CLEAR THE INJURED!
GET READY TO COUNTERATTACK!

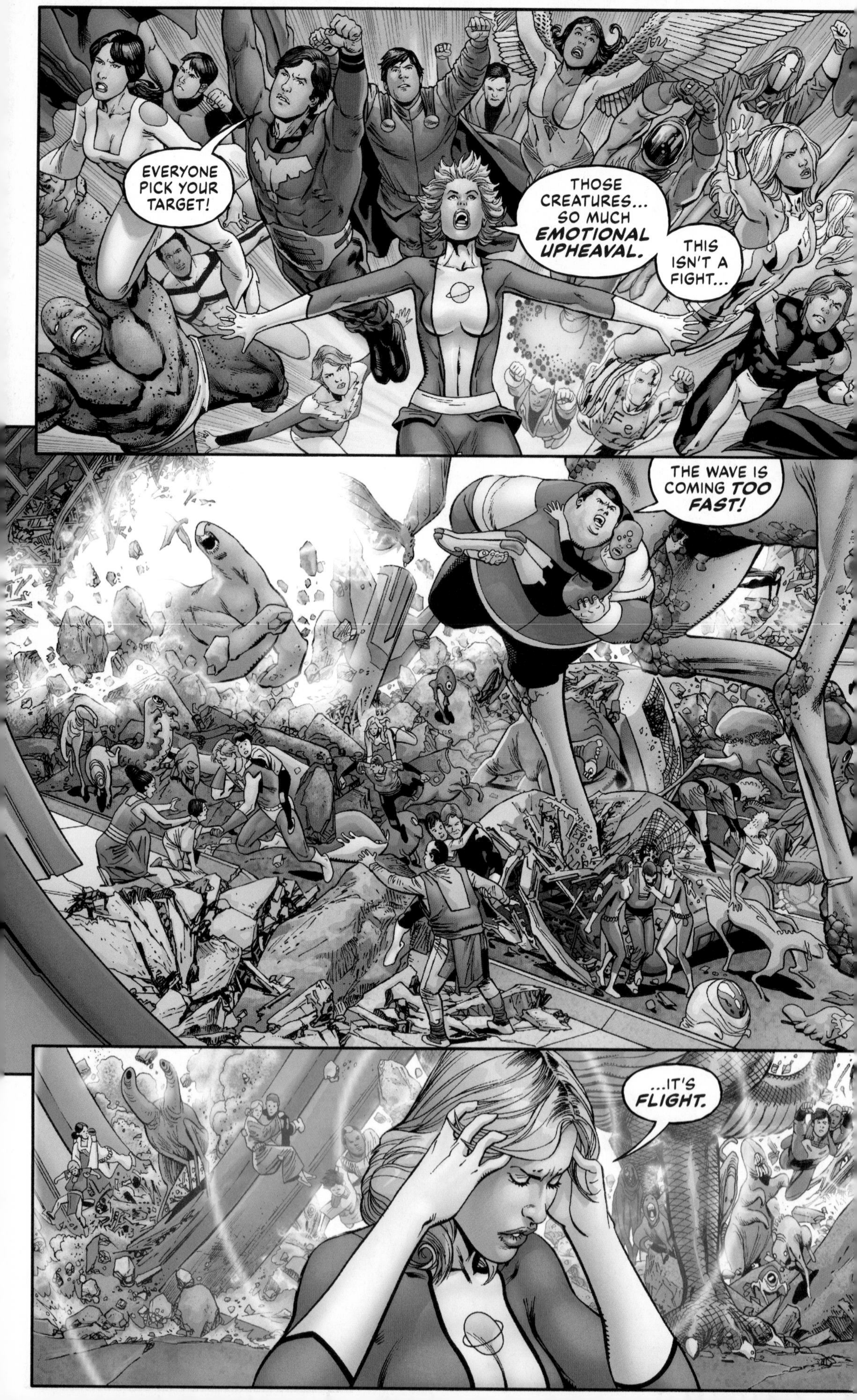
EVERYONE PICK YOUR TARGET!
THOSE CREATURES... SO MUCH EMOTIONAL UPHEAVAL.
THIS ISN'T A FIGHT...
THE WAVE IS COMING TOO FAST!
...IT'S FLIGHT.

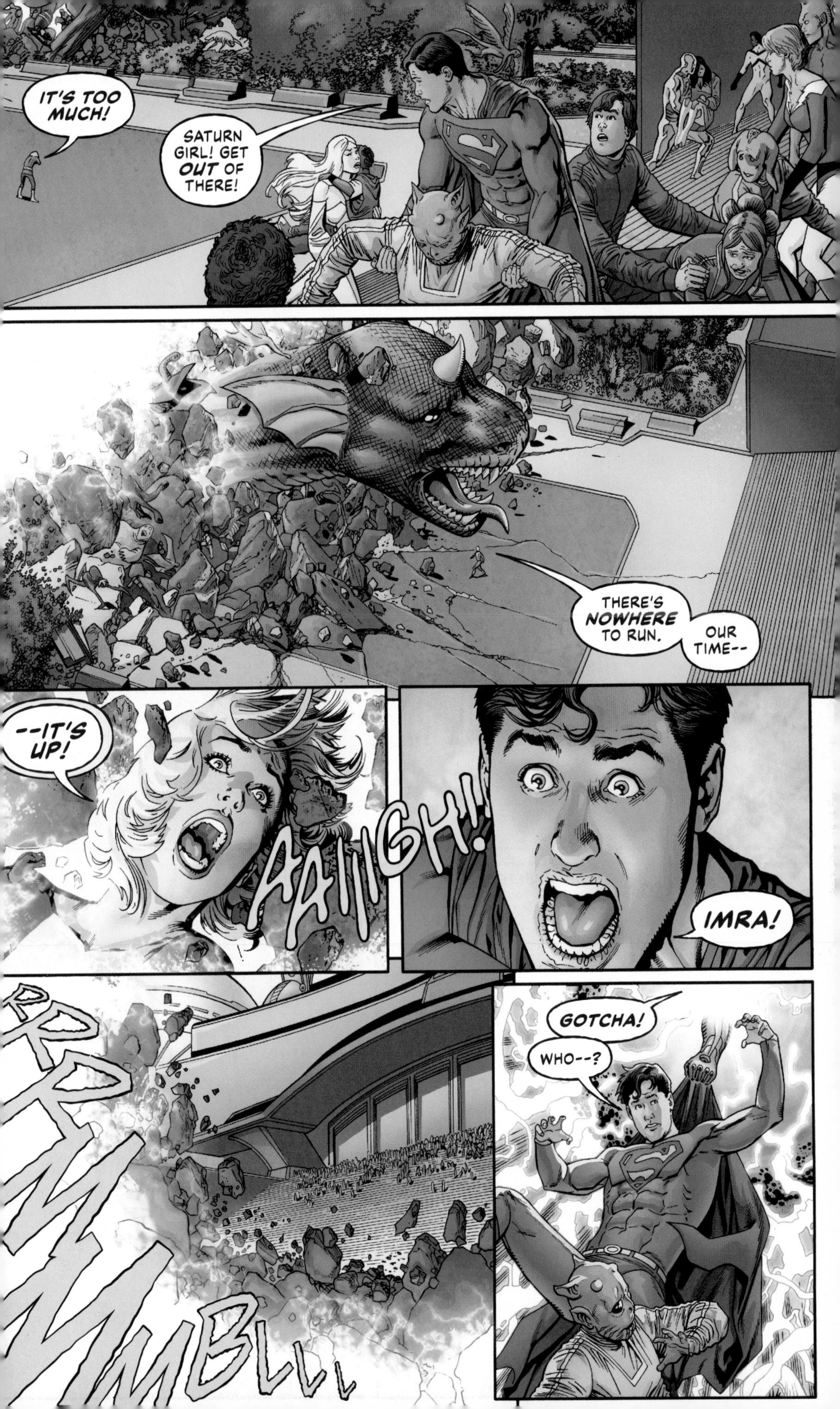

IT'S TOO MUCH!
SATURN GIRL! GET OUT OF THERE!
THERE'S NOWHERE TO RUN.
OUR TIME--
--IT'S UP!
AAIIGH!!
IMRA!
RRMMMBLLL
GOTCHA!
WHO--?

WELCOME ABOARD.

NO!

PUT ME BACK!

I HAVE TO SAVE MY FRIENDS!

WHY DID YOU TAKE ME?! THE LEGION NEEDS MY HELP!

YOU DON'T UNDERSTAND. I SAVED YOU!

YOU SAVED THE WRONG ONE, SIR.

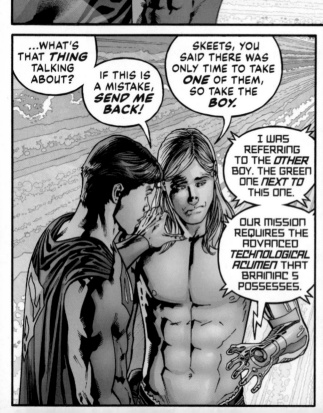

...WHAT'S THAT THING TALKING ABOUT?

IF THIS IS A MISTAKE, SEND ME BACK!

SKEETS, YOU SAID THERE WAS ONLY TIME TO TAKE ONE OF THEM, SO TAKE THE BOY.

I WAS REFERRING TO THE OTHER BOY. THE GREEN ONE NEXT TO THIS ONE.

OUR MISSION REQUIRES THE ADVANCED TECHNOLOGICAL ACUMEN THAT BRAINIAC 5 POSSESSES.

CORRECTION— POSSESSED.

WE HAVE TO HURRY NOW. THE GONENESS IS DISSOLVING ALL TIMELINES. EVERYTHING WILL UNRAVEL.

THERE'S ANOTHER GENIUS WE CAN GET—

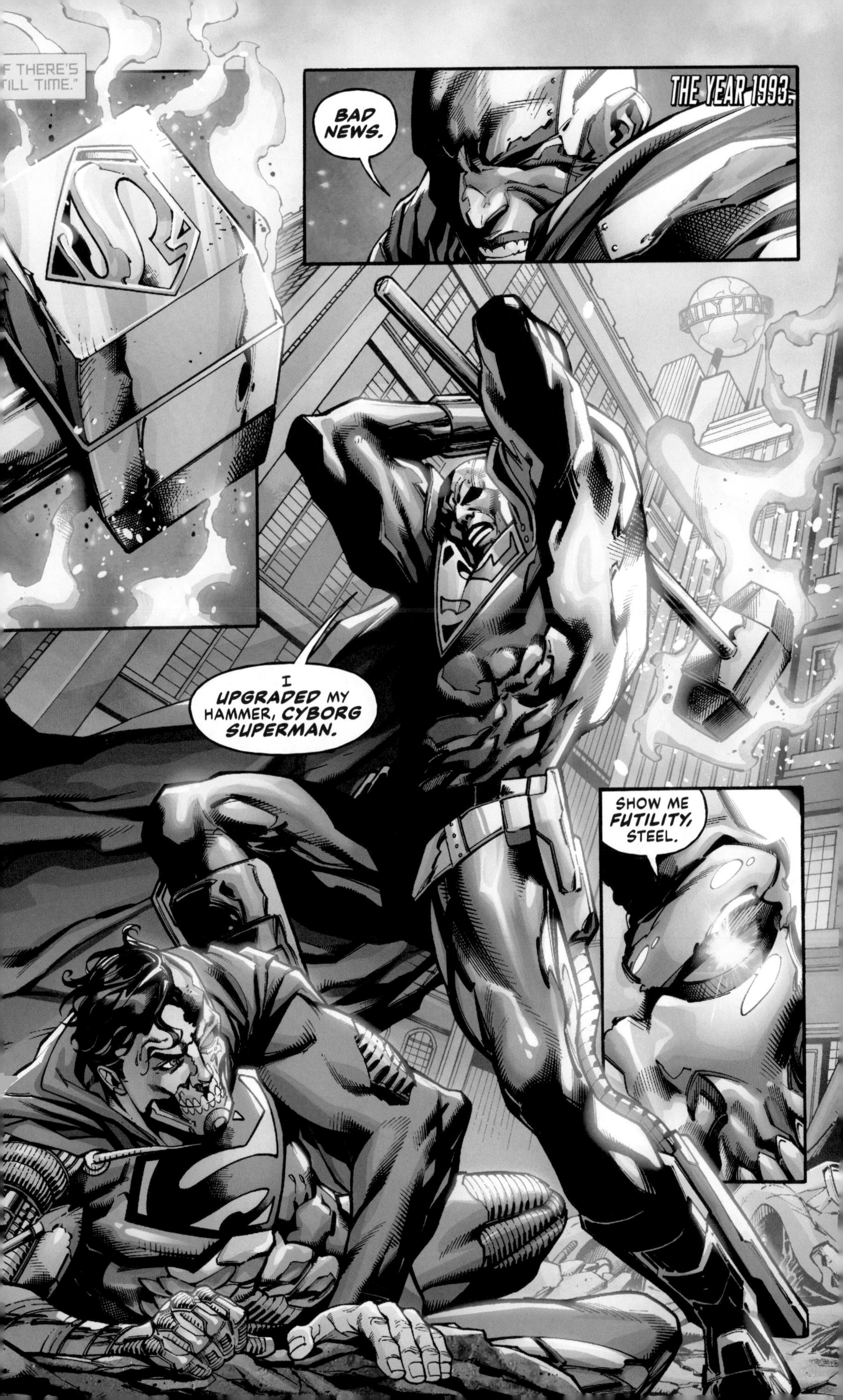
F THERE'S
TILL TIME."
THE YEAR 1993.
BAD NEWS.
I UPGRADED MY HAMMER, CYBORG SUPERMAN.
SHOW ME FUTILITY, STEEL.

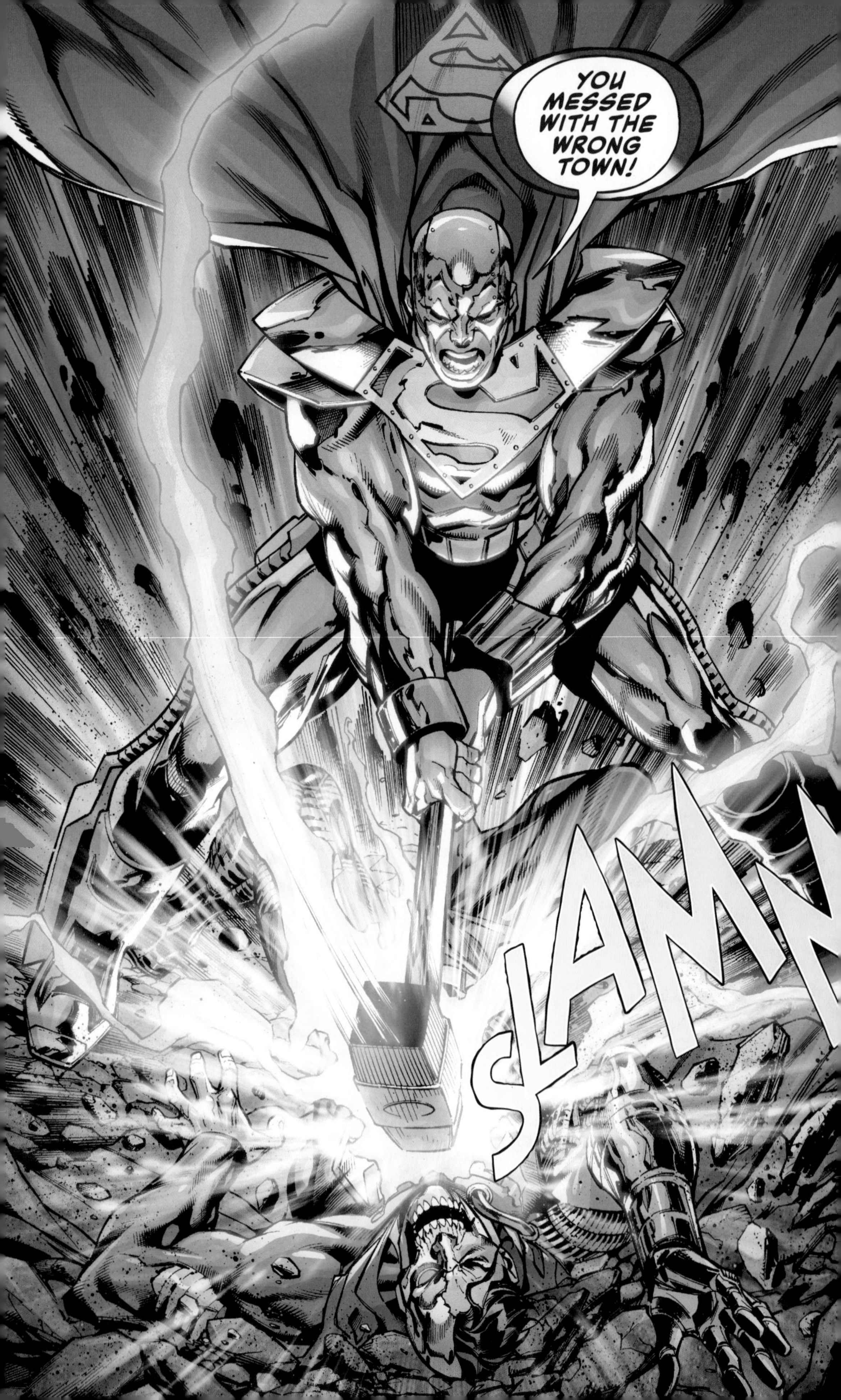
YOU MESSED WITH THE WRONG TOWN!
SLAM

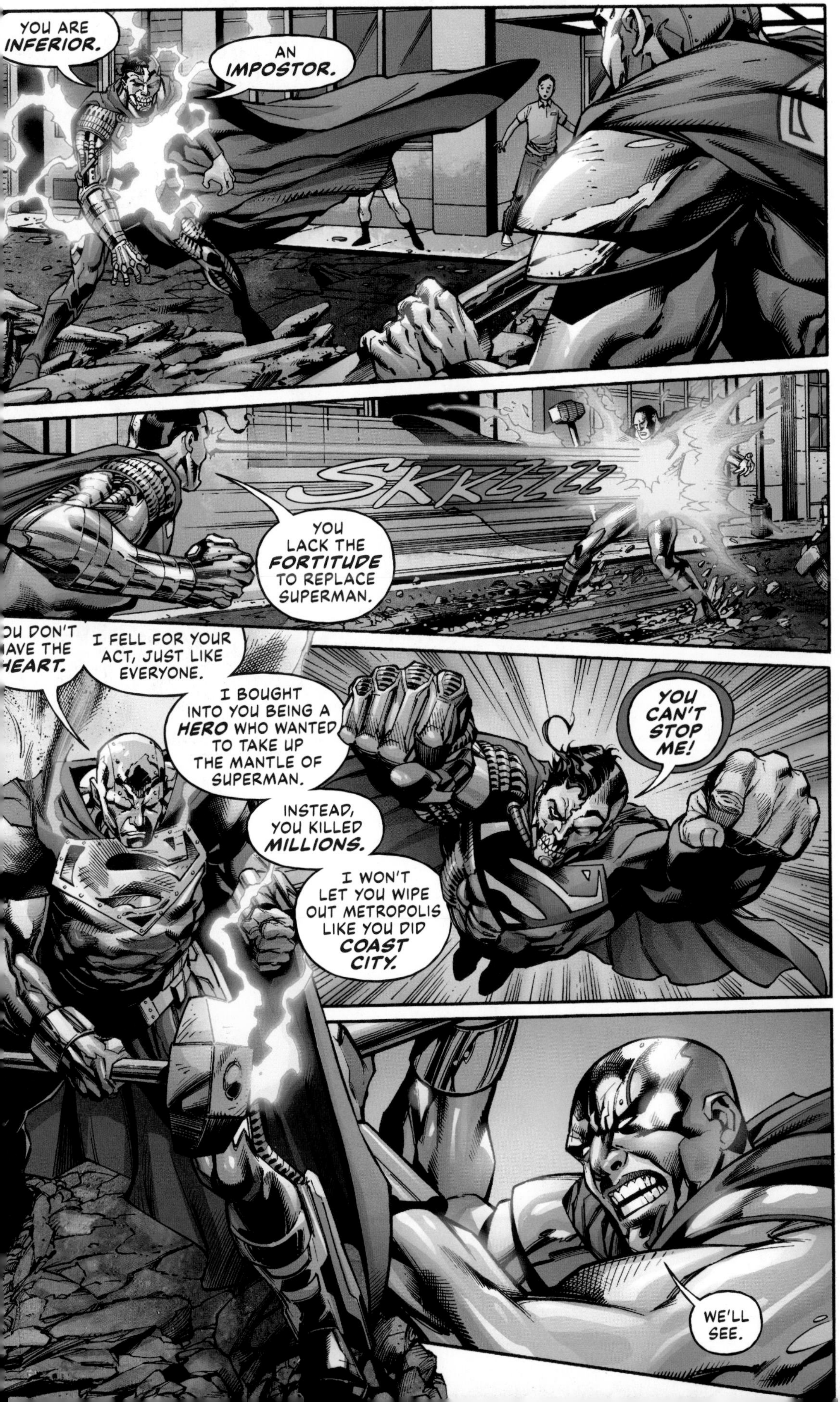

YOU ARE INFERIOR.
AN IMPOSTOR.
SKKZZZZ
YOU LACK THE FORTITUDE TO REPLACE SUPERMAN.
OU DON'T AVE THE HEART.
I FELL FOR YOUR ACT, JUST LIKE EVERYONE.
I BOUGHT INTO YOU BEING A HERO WHO WANTED TO TAKE UP THE MANTLE OF SUPERMAN.
INSTEAD, YOU KILLED MILLIONS.
I WON'T LET YOU WIPE OUT METROPOLIS LIKE YOU DID COAST CITY.
YOU CAN'T STOP ME!
WE'LL SEE.

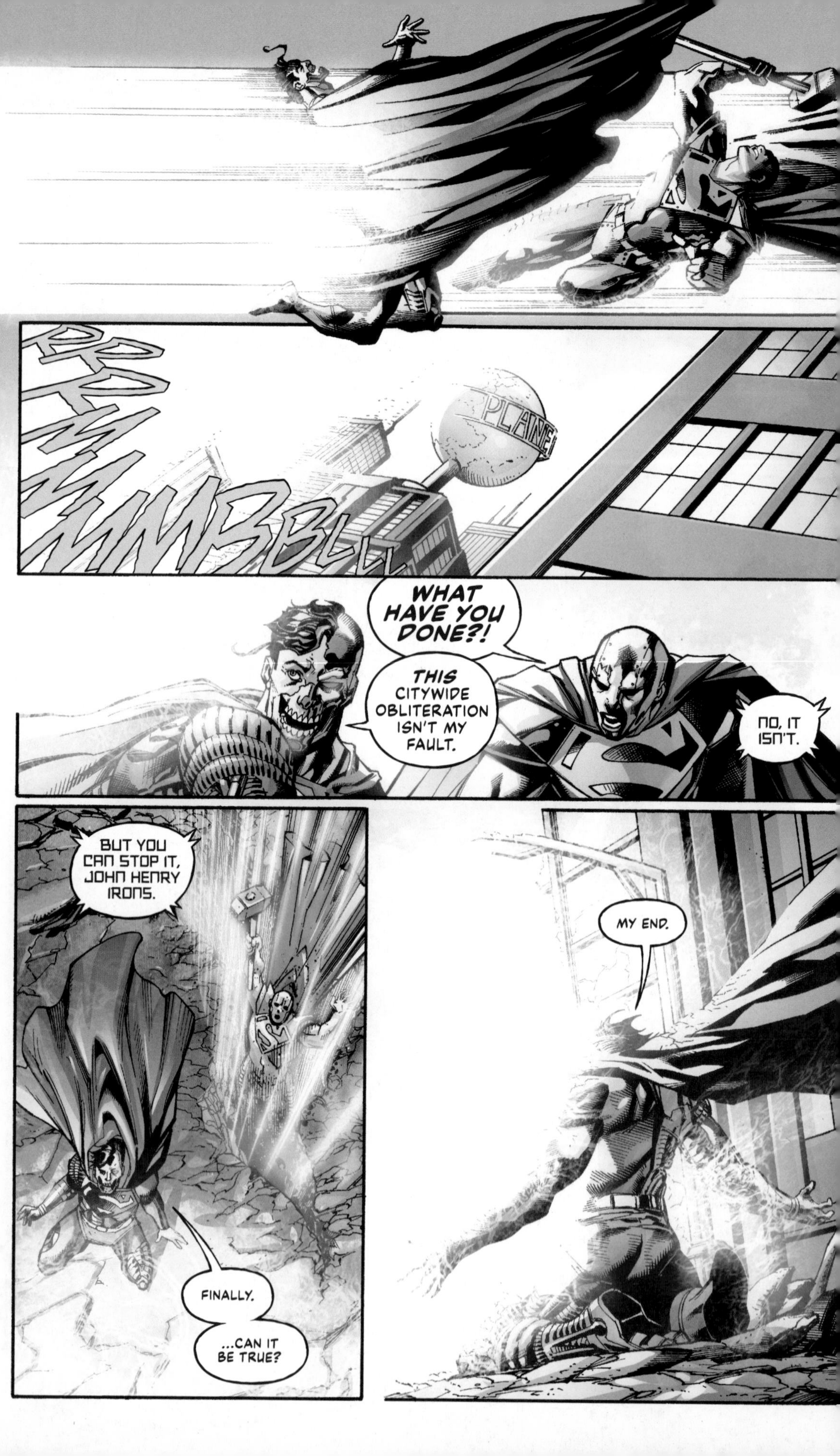

RRRMMMMBLLL
WHAT HAVE YOU DONE?!
THIS CITYWIDE OBLITERATION ISN'T MY FAULT.
NO, IT ISN'T.
BUT YOU CAN STOP IT, JOHN HENRY IRONS.
FINALLY.
...CAN IT BE TRUE?
MY END.

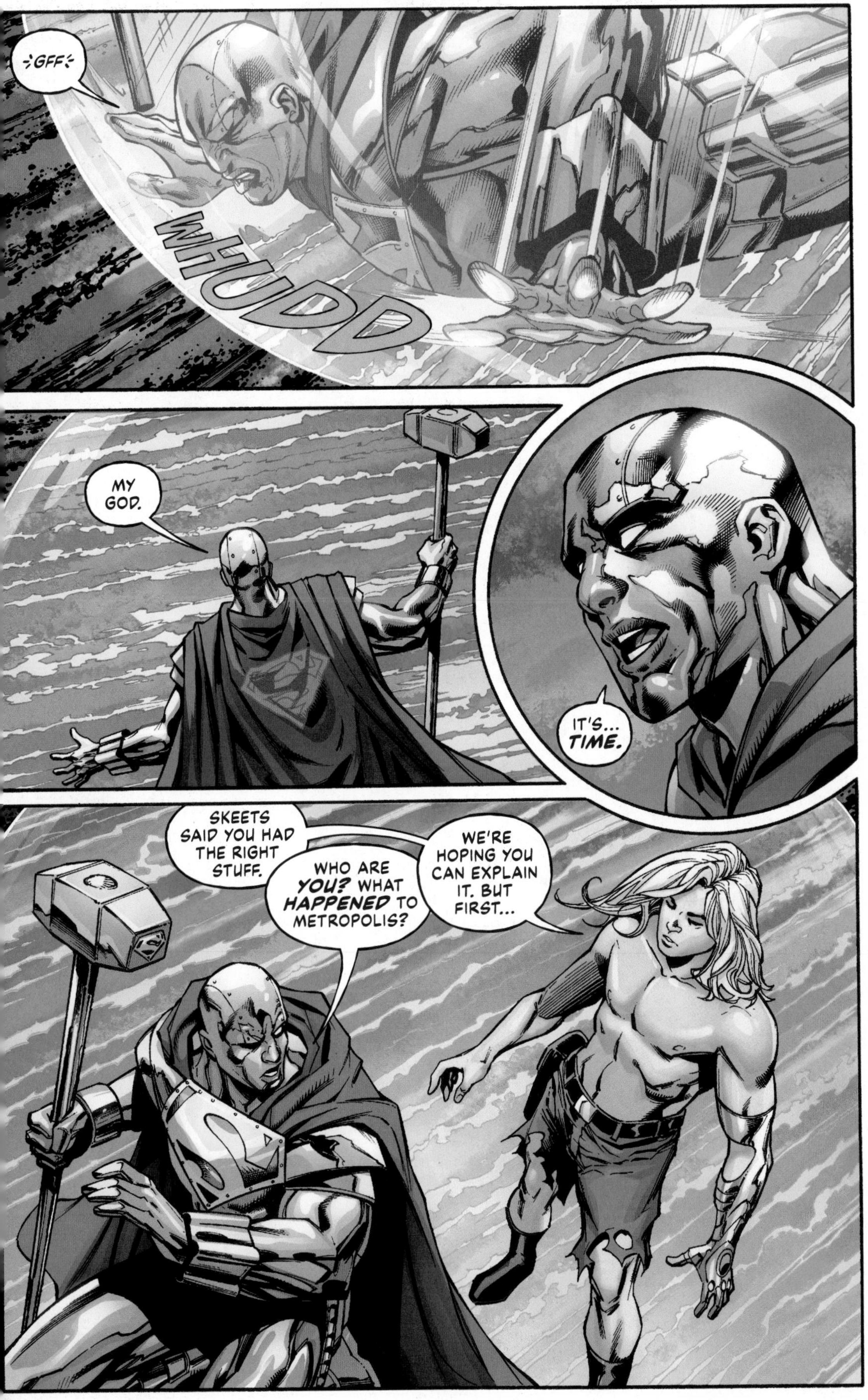
GFF
WHUDD
MY GOD.
IT'S... TIME.
SKEETS SAID YOU HAD THE RIGHT STUFF.
WHO ARE YOU? WHAT HAPPENED TO METROPOLIS?
WE'RE HOPING YOU CAN EXPLAIN IT. BUT FIRST...

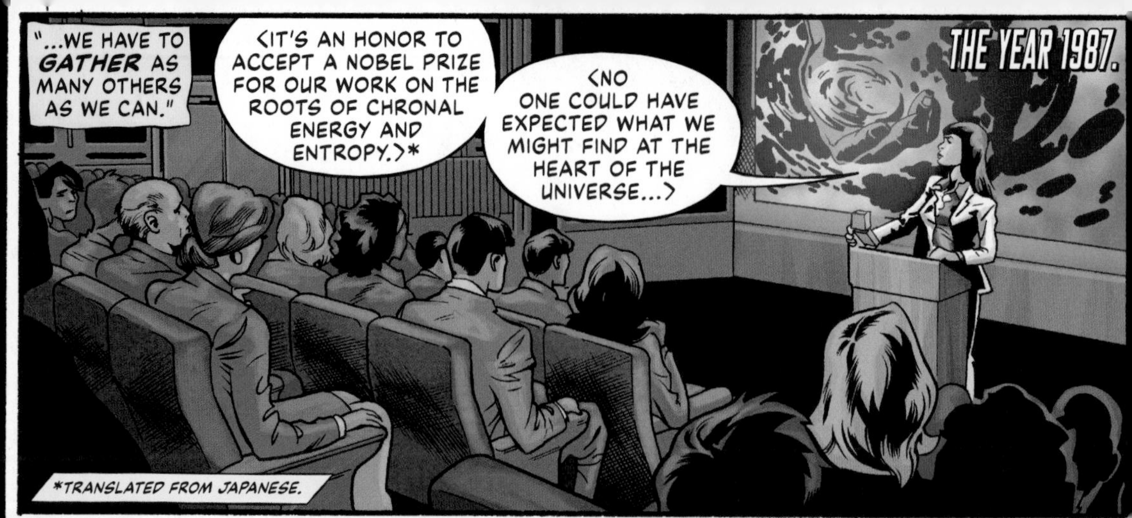
"...WE HAVE TO GATHER AS MANY OTHERS AS WE CAN."
THE YEAR 1987.
<IT'S AN HONOR TO ACCEPT A NOBEL PRIZE FOR OUR WORK ON THE ROOTS OF CHRONAL ENERGY AND ENTROPY.>*
<NO ONE COULD HAVE EXPECTED WHAT WE MIGHT FIND AT THE HEART OF THE UNIVERSE...>
*TRANSLATED FROM JAPANESE.

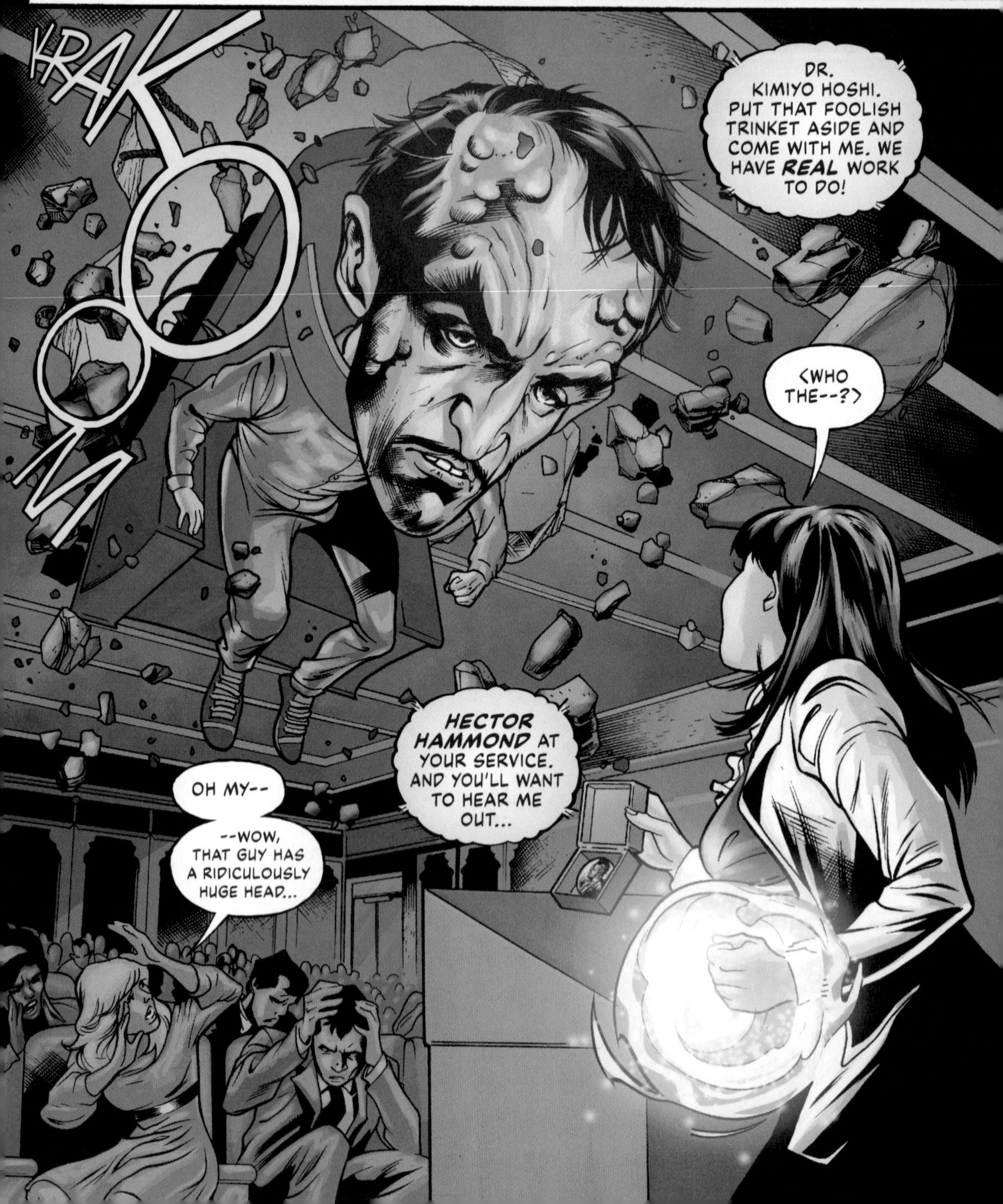
KRAKOOOM
DR. KIMIYO HOSHI. PUT THAT FOOLISH TRINKET ASIDE AND COME WITH ME. WE HAVE REAL WORK TO DO!
<WHO THE--?>
HECTOR HAMMOND AT YOUR SERVICE. AND YOU'LL WANT TO HEAR ME OUT...
OH MY--
--WOW, THAT GUY HAS A RIDICULOUSLY HUGE HEAD...

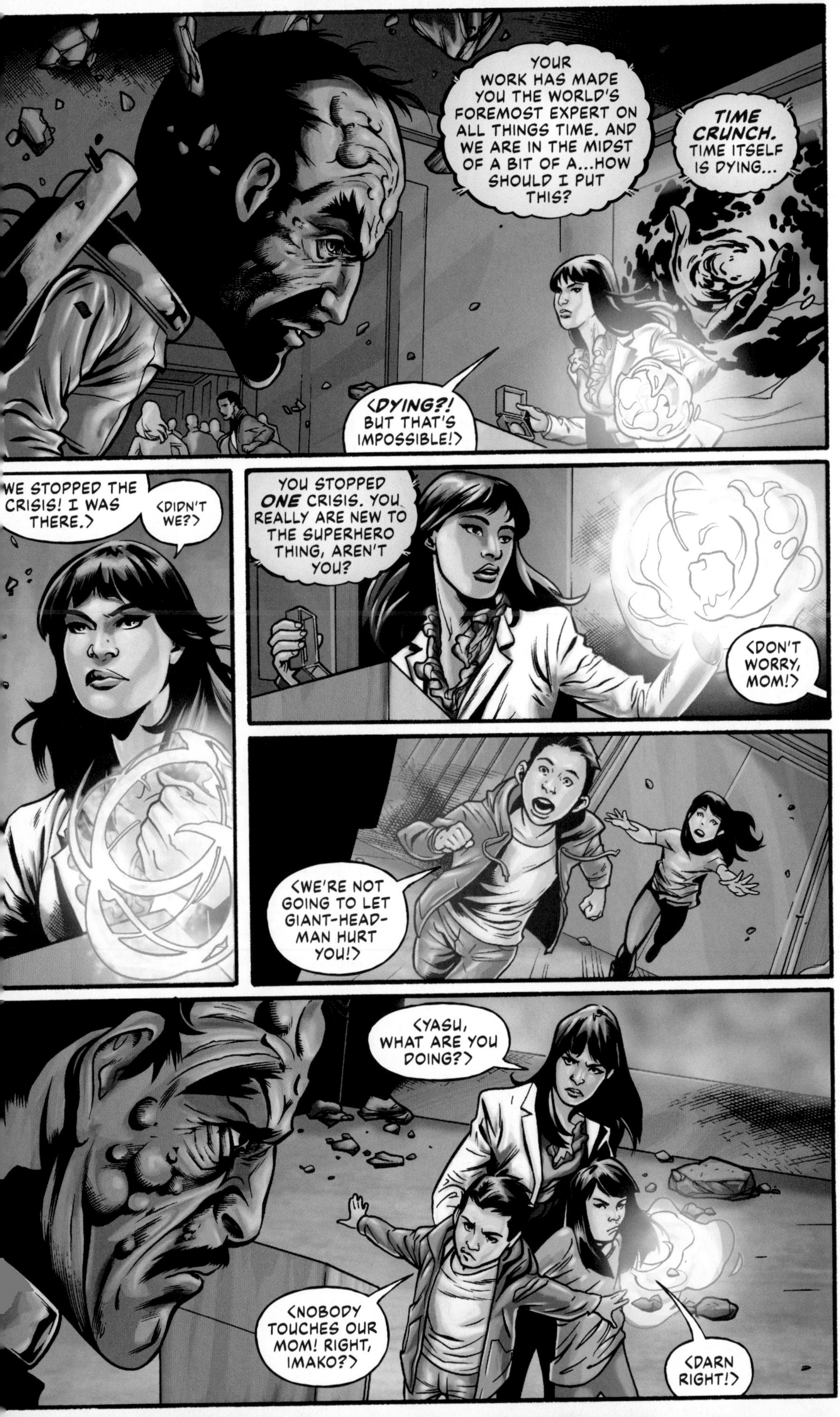
YOUR WORK HAS MADE YOU THE WORLD'S FOREMOST EXPERT ON ALL THINGS TIME. AND WE ARE IN THE MIDST OF A BIT OF A...HOW SHOULD I PUT THIS?
TIME CRUNCH. TIME ITSELF IS DYING...
<DYING?! BUT THAT'S IMPOSSIBLE!>
WE STOPPED THE CRISIS! I WAS THERE.>
<DIDN'T WE?>
YOU STOPPED ONE CRISIS. YOU REALLY ARE NEW TO THE SUPERHERO THING, AREN'T YOU?
<DON'T WORRY, MOM!>
<WE'RE NOT GOING TO LET GIANT-HEAD-MAN HURT YOU!>
<YASU, WHAT ARE YOU DOING?>
<NOBODY TOUCHES OUR MOM! RIGHT, IMAKO?>
<DARN RIGHT!>

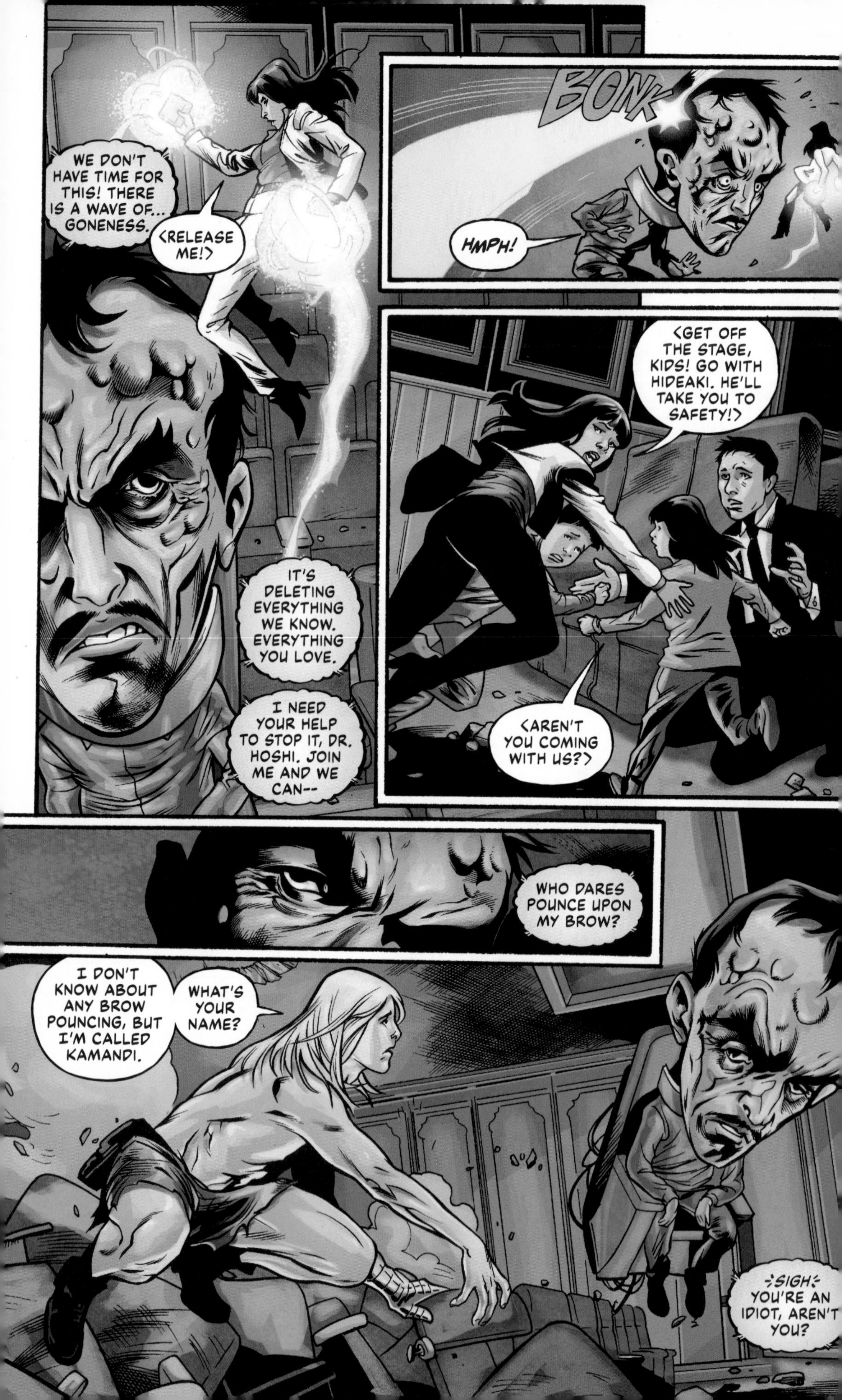
WE DON'T HAVE TIME FOR THIS! THERE IS A WAVE OF... GONENESS.
<RELEASE ME!>
BONK
HMPH!
<GET OFF THE STAGE, KIDS! GO WITH HIDEAKI. HE'LL TAKE YOU TO SAFETY!>
IT'S DELETING EVERYTHING WE KNOW. EVERYTHING YOU LOVE.
I NEED YOUR HELP TO STOP IT, DR. HOSHI. JOIN ME AND WE CAN--
<AREN'T YOU COMING WITH US?>
WHO DARES POUNCE UPON MY BROW?
I DON'T KNOW ABOUT ANY BROW POUNCING, BUT I'M CALLED KAMANDI.
WHAT'S YOUR NAME?
-SIGH- YOU'RE AN IDIOT, AREN'T YOU?

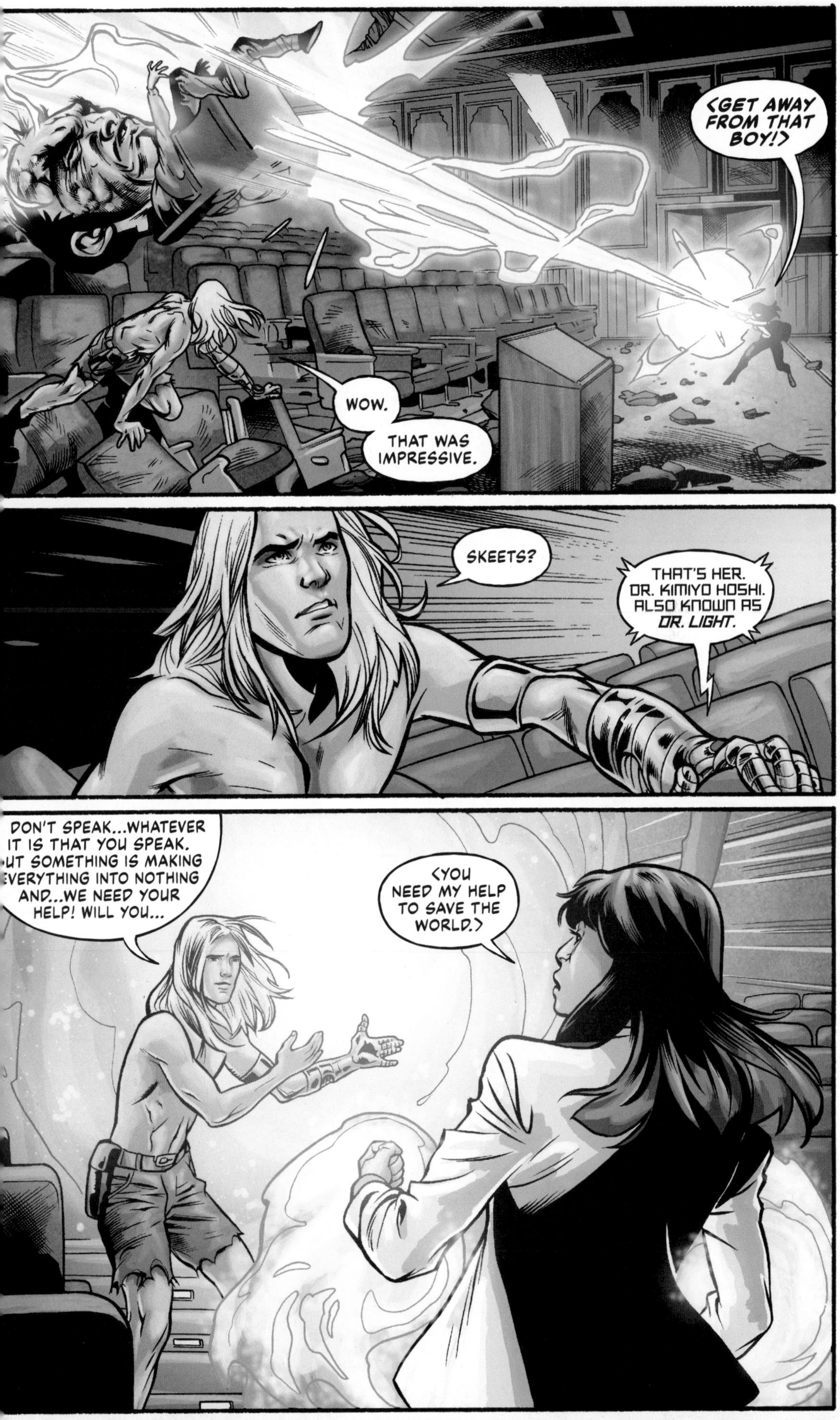
<GET AWAY FROM THAT BOY!>
WOW.
THAT WAS IMPRESSIVE.
SKEETS?
THAT'S HER. DR. KIMIYO HOSHI. ALSO KNOWN AS *DR. LIGHT*.
DON'T SPEAK...WHATEVER IT IS THAT YOU SPEAK. UT SOMETHING IS MAKING VERYTHING INTO NOTHING AND...WE NEED YOUR HELP! WILL YOU...
<YOU NEED MY HELP TO SAVE THE WORLD.>

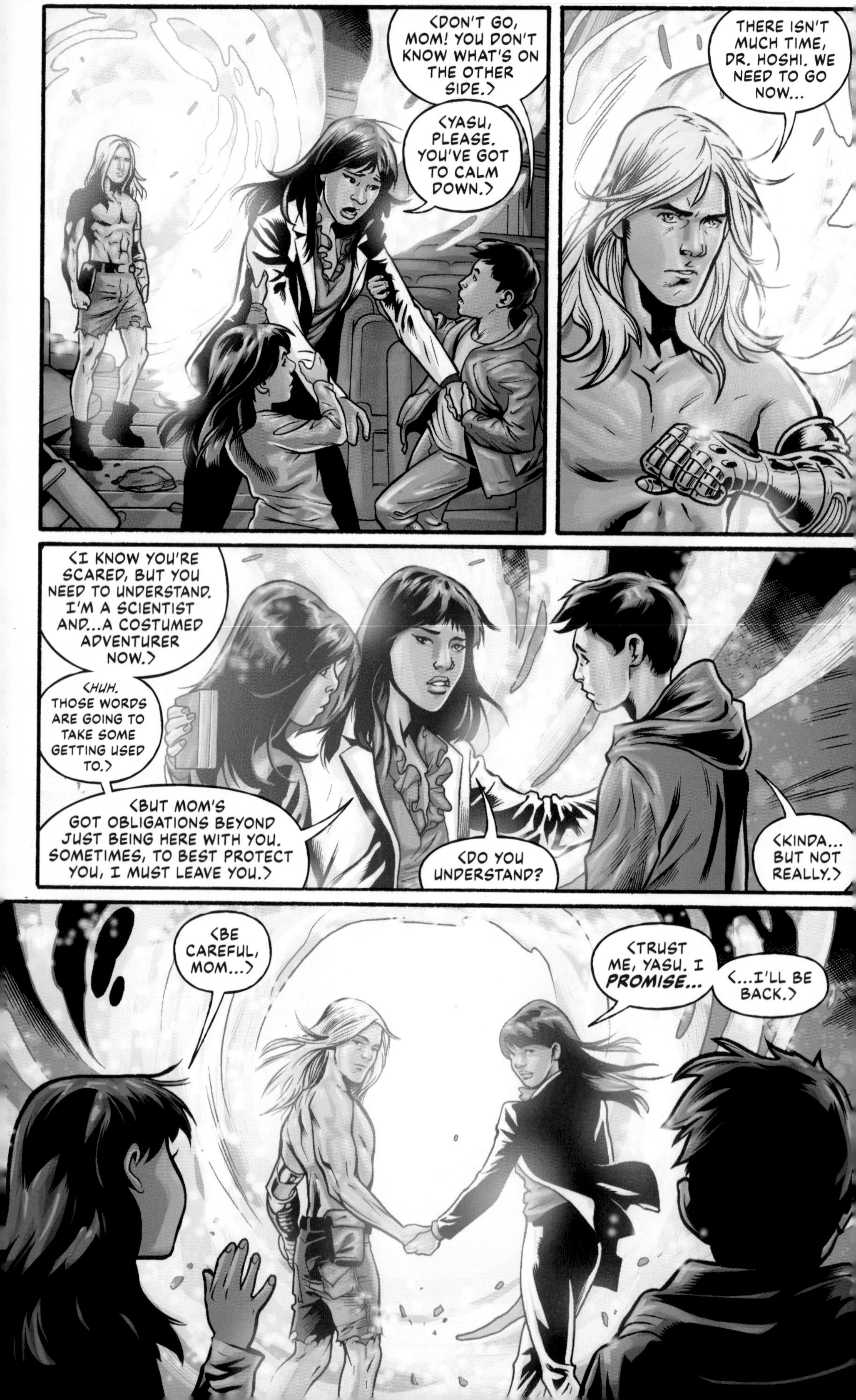

<DON'T GO, MOM! YOU DON'T KNOW WHAT'S ON THE OTHER SIDE.>
<YASU, PLEASE. YOU'VE GOT TO CALM DOWN.>
THERE ISN'T MUCH TIME, DR. HOSHI. WE NEED TO GO NOW...
<I KNOW YOU'RE SCARED, BUT YOU NEED TO UNDERSTAND. I'M A SCIENTIST AND...A COSTUMED ADVENTURER NOW.>
<*HUH.* THOSE WORDS ARE GOING TO TAKE SOME GETTING USED TO.>
<BUT MOM'S GOT OBLIGATIONS BEYOND JUST BEING HERE WITH YOU. SOMETIMES, TO BEST PROTECT YOU, I MUST LEAVE YOU.>
<DO YOU UNDERSTAND?
<KINDA... BUT NOT REALLY.>
<BE CAREFUL, MOM...>
<TRUST ME, YASU. I ***PROMISE...***
<...I'LL BE BACK.>

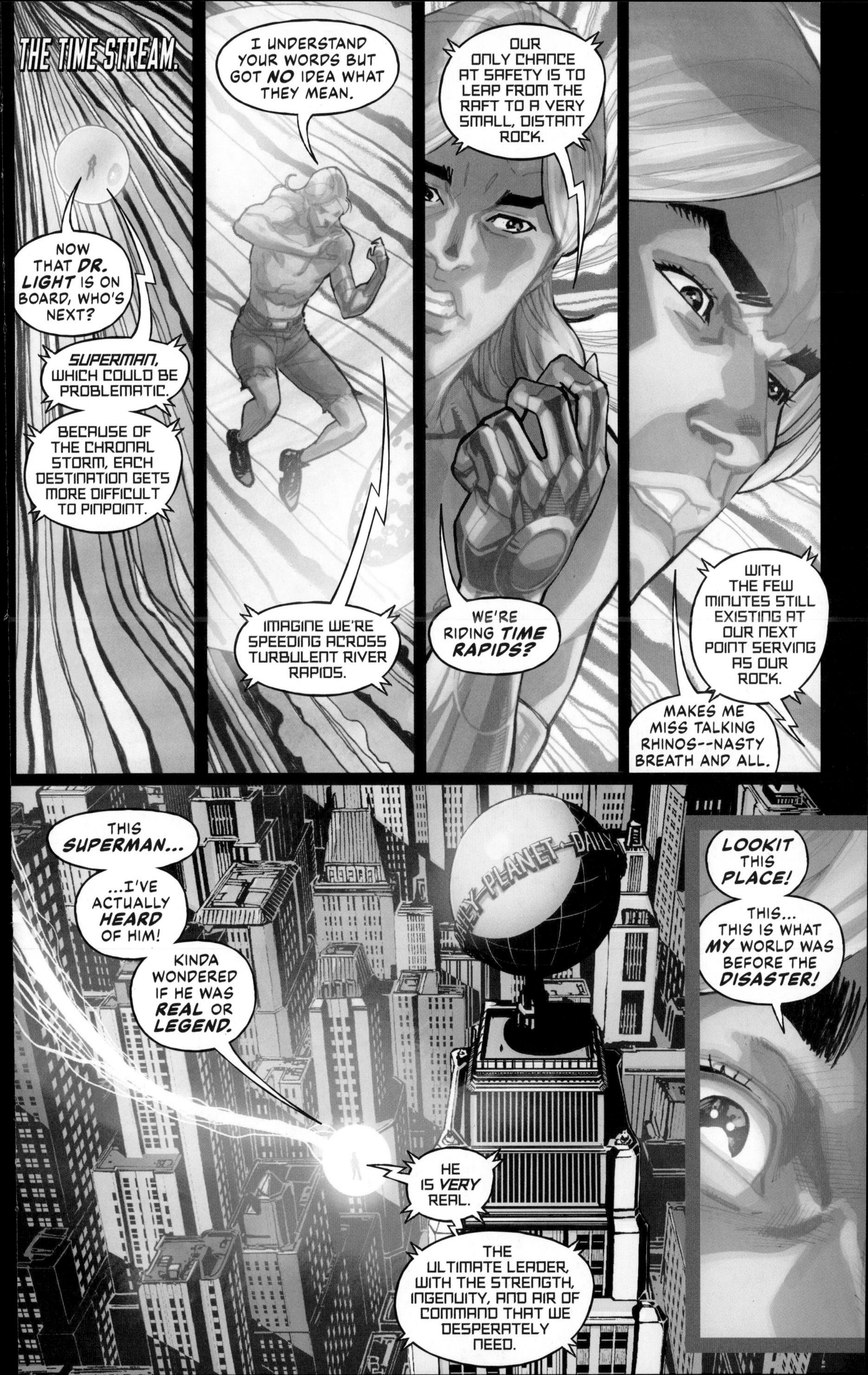
THE TIME STREAM.
NOW THAT DR. LIGHT IS ON BOARD, WHO'S NEXT?
SUPERMAN, WHICH COULD BE PROBLEMATIC.
BECAUSE OF THE CHRONAL STORM, EACH DESTINATION GETS MORE DIFFICULT TO PINPOINT.
I UNDERSTAND YOUR WORDS BUT GOT NO IDEA WHAT THEY MEAN.
IMAGINE WE'RE SPEEDING ACROSS TURBULENT RIVER RAPIDS.
OUR ONLY CHANCE AT SAFETY IS TO LEAP FROM THE RAFT TO A VERY SMALL, DISTANT ROCK.
WE'RE RIDING TIME RAPIDS?
WITH THE FEW MINUTES STILL EXISTING AT OUR NEXT POINT SERVING AS OUR ROCK.
MAKES ME MISS TALKING RHINOS--NASTY BREATH AND ALL.
THIS SUPERMAN...
...I'VE ACTUALLY HEARD OF HIM!
KINDA WONDERED IF HE WAS REAL OR LEGEND.
HE IS VERY REAL.
THE ULTIMATE LEADER, WITH THE STRENGTH, INGENUITY, AND AIR OF COMMAND THAT WE DESPERATELY NEED.
LOOKIT THIS PLACE!
THIS... THIS IS WHAT MY WORLD WAS BEFORE THE DISASTER!

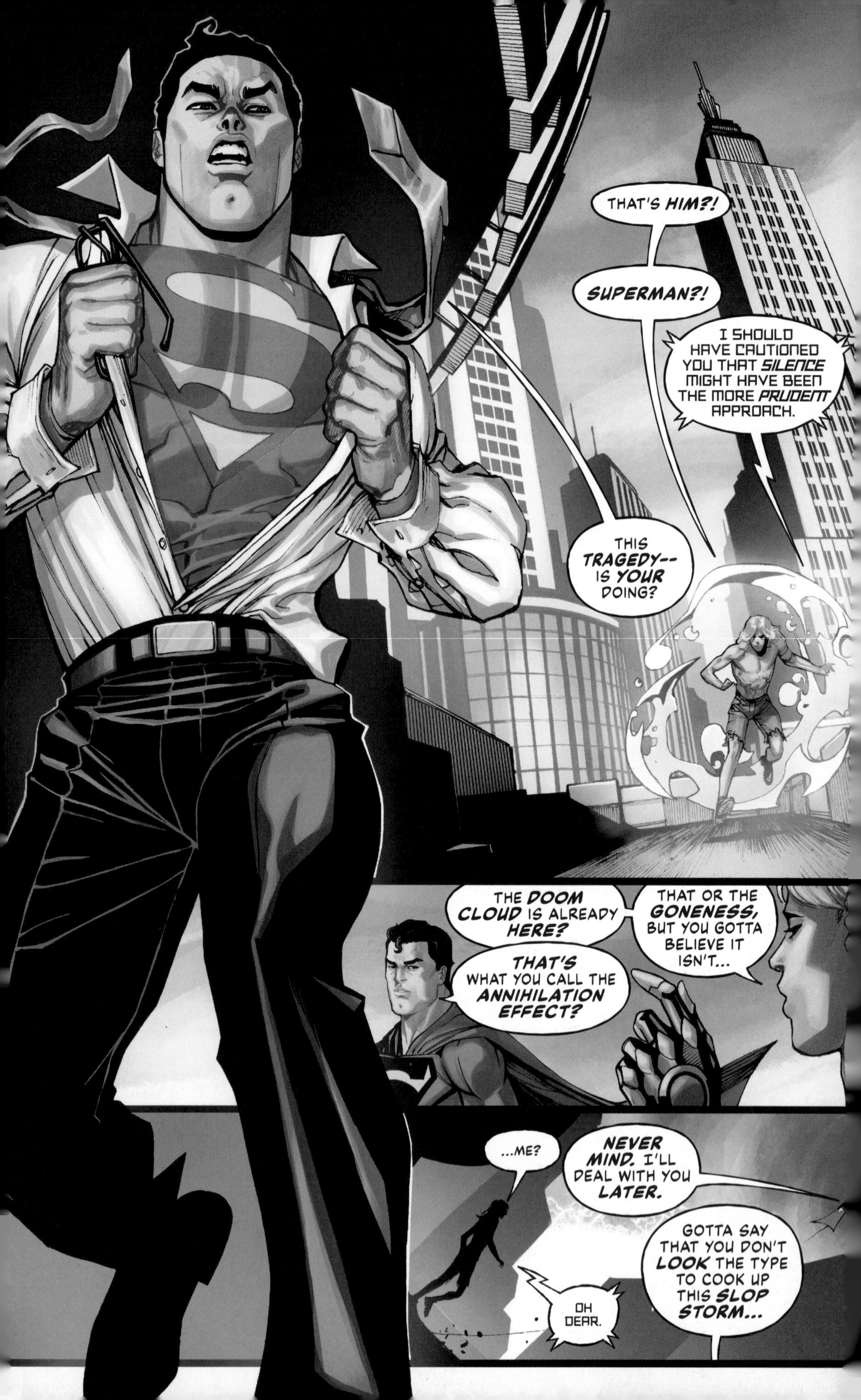
THAT'S HIM?!
SUPERMAN?!
I SHOULD HAVE CAUTIONED YOU THAT SILENCE MIGHT HAVE BEEN THE MORE PRUDENT APPROACH.
THIS TRAGEDY-- IS YOUR DOING?
THE DOOM CLOUD IS ALREADY HERE?
THAT'S WHAT YOU CALL THE ANNIHILATION EFFECT?
THAT OR THE GONENESS, BUT YOU GOTTA BELIEVE IT ISN'T...
...ME?
NEVER MIND. I'LL DEAL WITH YOU LATER.
GOTTA SAY THAT YOU DON'T LOOK THE TYPE TO COOK UP THIS SLOP STORM...
OH DEAR.

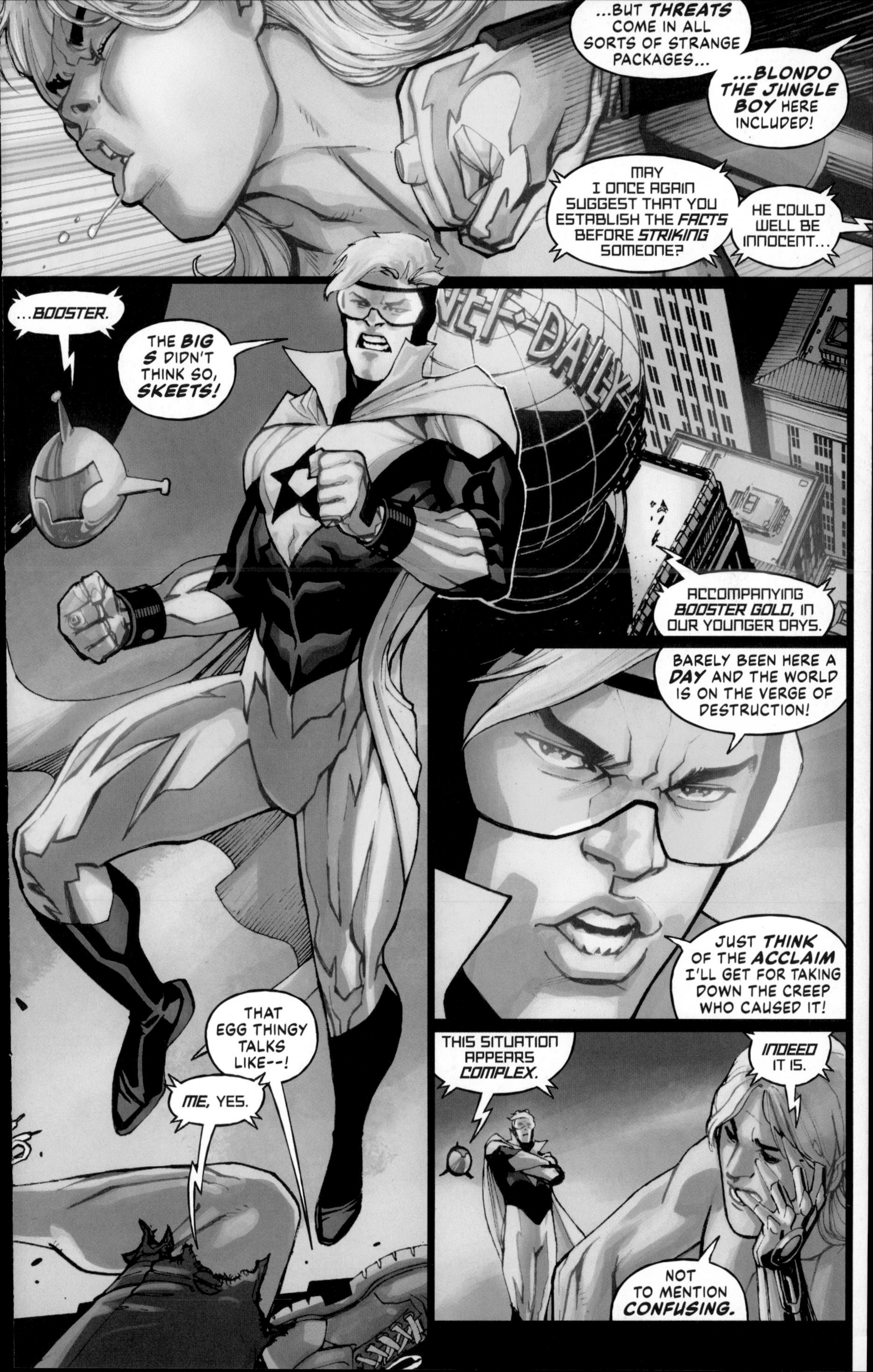
...BUT THREATS COME IN ALL SORTS OF STRANGE PACKAGES...
...BLONDO THE JUNGLE BOY HERE INCLUDED!
MAY I ONCE AGAIN SUGGEST THAT YOU ESTABLISH THE FACTS BEFORE STRIKING SOMEONE?
HE COULD WELL BE INNOCENT...
...BOOSTER.
THE BIG S DIDN'T THINK SO, SKEETS!
ACCOMPANYING BOOSTER GOLD, IN OUR YOUNGER DAYS.
BARELY BEEN HERE A DAY AND THE WORLD IS ON THE VERGE OF DESTRUCTION!
JUST THINK OF THE ACCLAIM I'LL GET FOR TAKING DOWN THE CREEP WHO CAUSED IT!
THAT EGG THINGY TALKS LIKE--!
ME, YES.
THIS SITUATION APPEARS COMPLEX.
INDEED IT IS.
NOT TO MENTION CONFUSING.

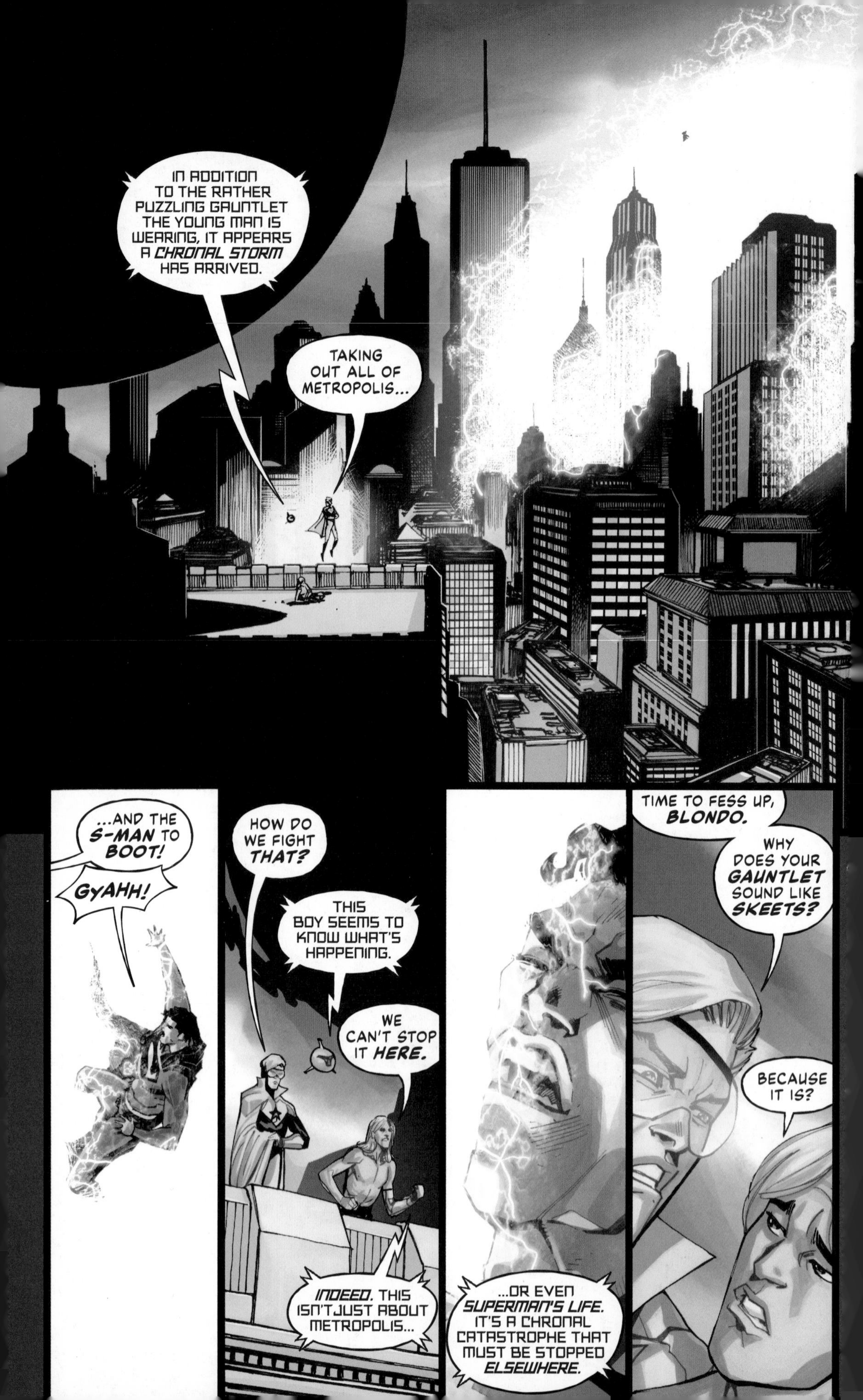
IN ADDITION TO THE RATHER PUZZLING GAUNTLET THE YOUNG MAN IS WEARING, IT APPEARS A CHRONAL STORM HAS ARRIVED.
TAKING OUT ALL OF METROPOLIS...
...AND THE S-MAN TO BOOT!
GYAHH!
HOW DO WE FIGHT THAT?
THIS BOY SEEMS TO KNOW WHAT'S HAPPENING.
WE CAN'T STOP IT HERE.
INDEED. THIS ISN'T JUST ABOUT METROPOLIS...
...OR EVEN SUPERMAN'S LIFE. IT'S A CHRONAL CATASTROPHE THAT MUST BE STOPPED ELSEWHERE.
TIME TO FESS UP, BLONDO.
WHY DOES YOUR GAUNTLET SOUND LIKE SKEETS?
BECAUSE IT IS?

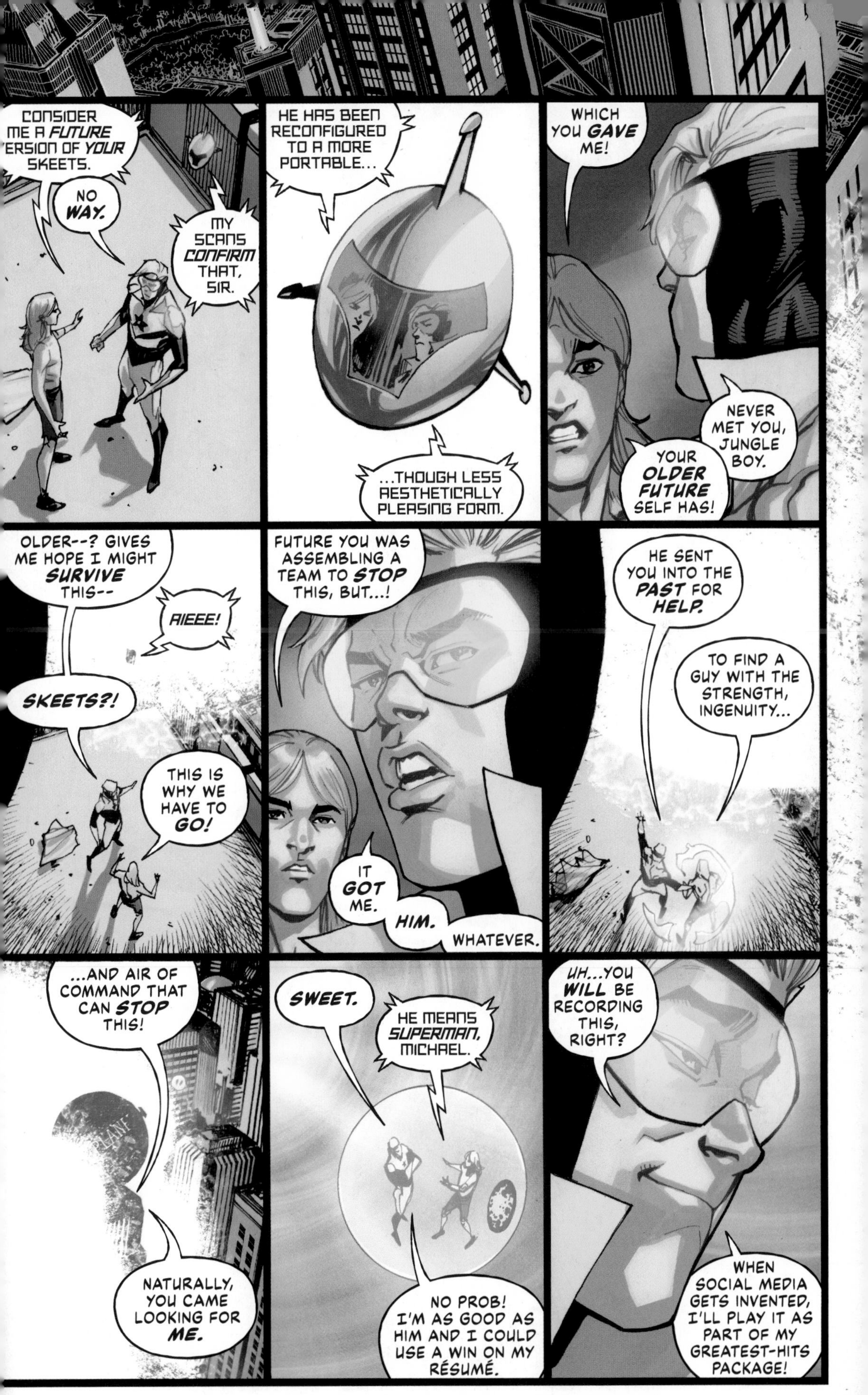

CONSIDER ME A FUTURE VERSION OF YOUR SKEETS.
NO WAY.
MY SCANS CONFIRM THAT, SIR.
HE HAS BEEN RECONFIGURED TO A MORE PORTABLE...
...THOUGH LESS AESTHETICALLY PLEASING FORM.
WHICH YOU GAVE ME!
NEVER MET YOU, JUNGLE BOY.
YOUR OLDER FUTURE SELF HAS!
OLDER--? GIVES ME HOPE I MIGHT SURVIVE THIS--
AIEEE!
SKEETS?!
THIS IS WHY WE HAVE TO GO!
FUTURE YOU WAS ASSEMBLING A TEAM TO STOP THIS, BUT...!
IT GOT ME.
HIM.
WHATEVER.
HE SENT YOU INTO THE PAST FOR HELP.
TO FIND A GUY WITH THE STRENGTH, INGENUITY...
...AND AIR OF COMMAND THAT CAN STOP THIS!
NATURALLY, YOU CAME LOOKING FOR ME.
SWEET.
HE MEANS SUPERMAN, MICHAEL.
NO PROB! I'M AS GOOD AS HIM AND I COULD USE A WIN ON MY RÉSUMÉ.
UH...YOU WILL BE RECORDING THIS, RIGHT?
WHEN SOCIAL MEDIA GETS INVENTED, I'LL PLAY IT AS PART OF MY GREATEST-HITS PACKAGE!

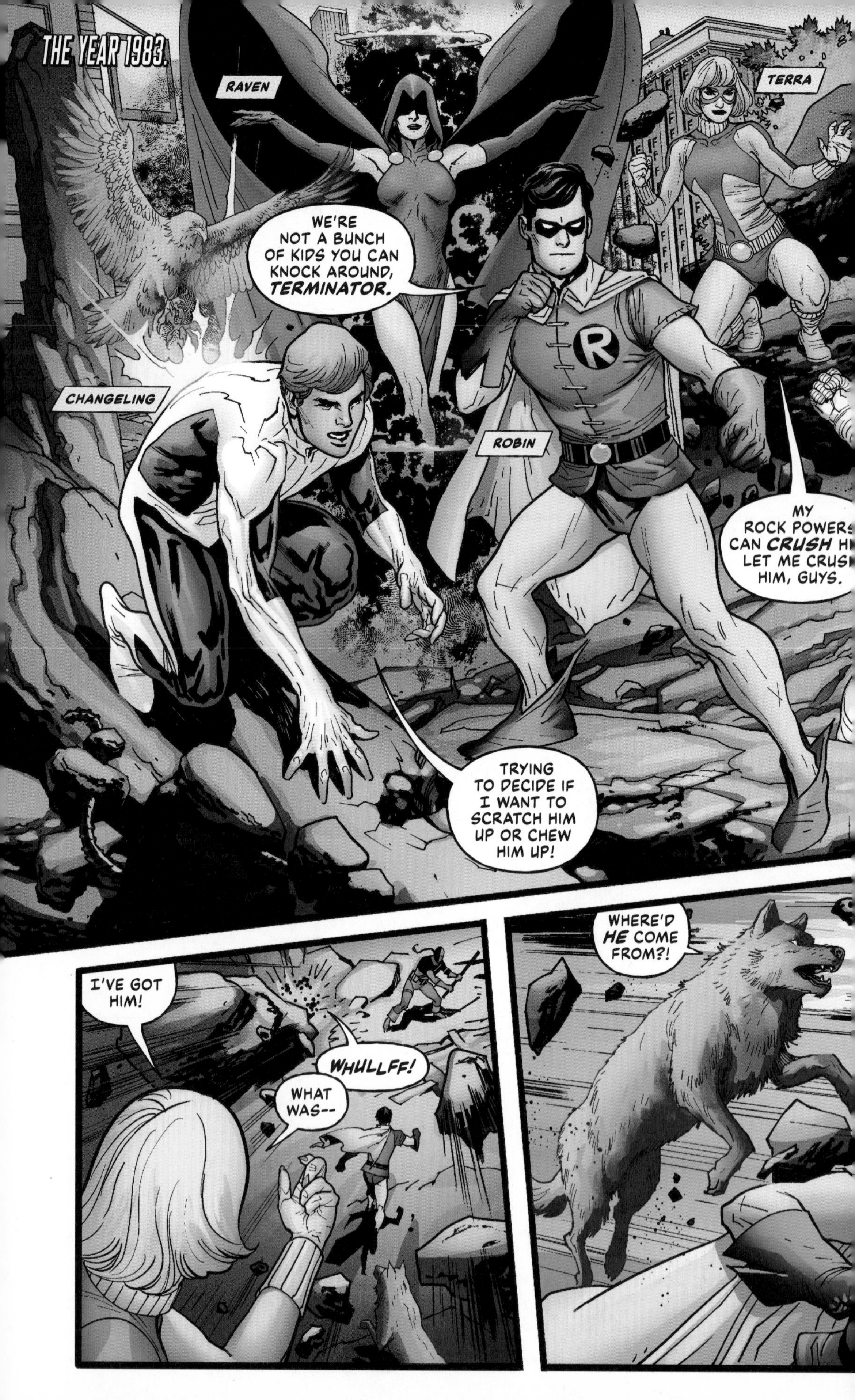
THE YEAR 1983.
RAVEN
TERRA
WE'RE NOT A BUNCH OF KIDS YOU CAN KNOCK AROUND, TERMINATOR.
CHANGELING
ROBIN
MY ROCK POWERS CAN CRUSH HI LET ME CRUS HIM, GUYS.
TRYING TO DECIDE IF I WANT TO SCRATCH HIM UP OR CHEW HIM UP!
I'VE GOT HIM!
WHULLFF!
WHAT WAS--
WHERE'D HE COME FROM?!

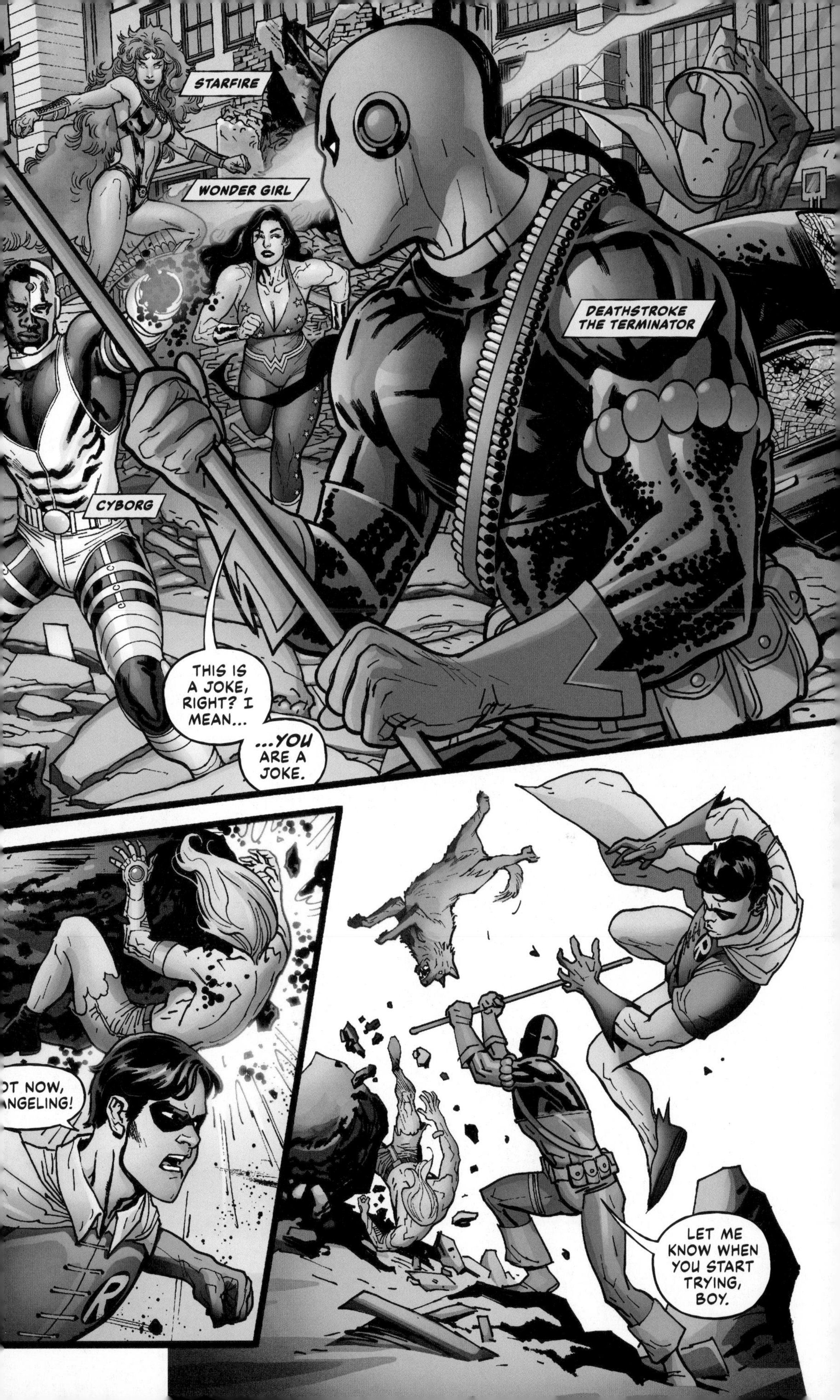
STARFIRE
WONDER GIRL
DEATHSTROKE THE TERMINATOR
CYBORG
THIS IS A JOKE, RIGHT? I MEAN...
...YOU ARE A JOKE.
NGELING!
LET ME KNOW WHEN YOU START TRYING, BOY.

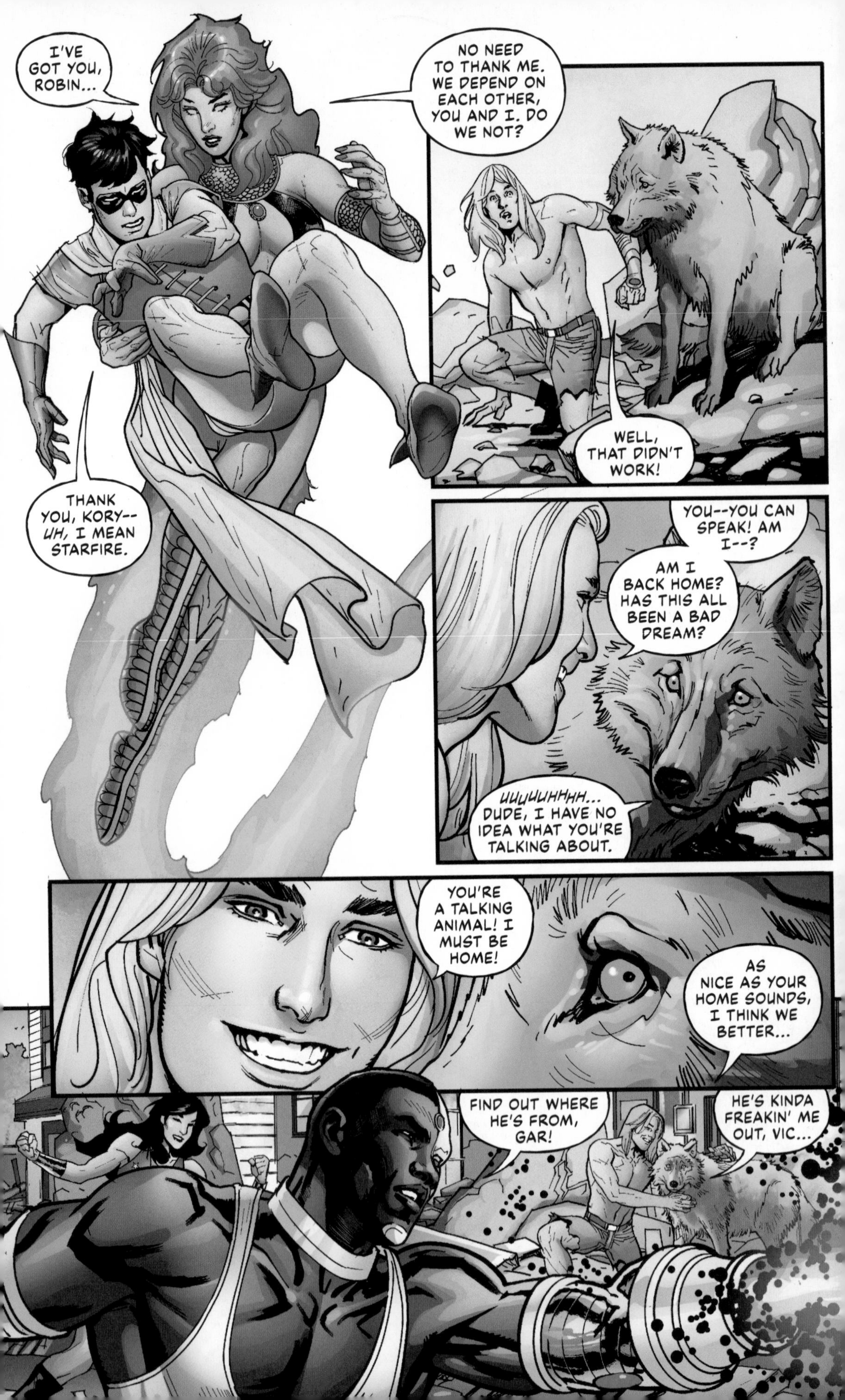
I'VE GOT YOU, ROBIN...
NO NEED TO THANK ME. WE DEPEND ON EACH OTHER, YOU AND I. DO WE NOT?
THANK YOU, KORY-- UH, I MEAN STARFIRE.
WELL, THAT DIDN'T WORK!
YOU--YOU CAN SPEAK! AM I--?
AM I BACK HOME? HAS THIS ALL BEEN A BAD DREAM?
UUUUUHHHH... DUDE, I HAVE NO IDEA WHAT YOU'RE TALKING ABOUT.
YOU'RE A TALKING ANIMAL! I MUST BE HOME!
AS NICE AS YOUR HOME SOUNDS, I THINK WE BETTER...
FIND OUT WHERE HE'S FROM, GAR!
HE'S KINDA FREAKIN' ME OUT, VIC...

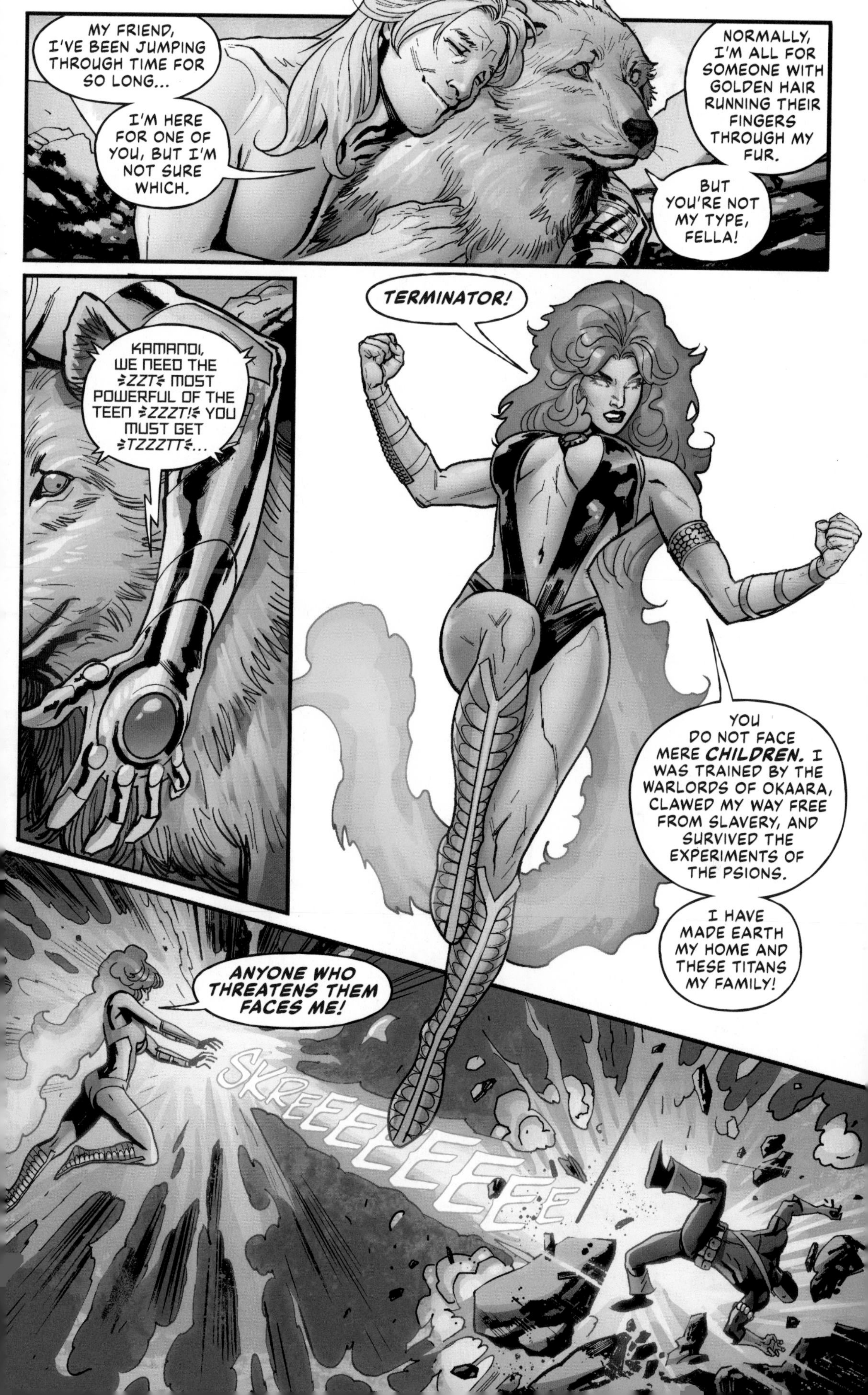
MY FRIEND, I'VE BEEN JUMPING THROUGH TIME FOR SO LONG...
I'M HERE FOR ONE OF YOU, BUT I'M NOT SURE WHICH.
NORMALLY, I'M ALL FOR SOMEONE WITH GOLDEN HAIR RUNNING THEIR FINGERS THROUGH MY FUR.
BUT YOU'RE NOT MY TYPE, FELLA!
KAMANDI, WE NEED THE ZZT MOST POWERFUL OF THE TEEN ZZZT! YOU MUST GET TZZZTT...
TERMINATOR!
YOU DO NOT FACE MERE CHILDREN. I WAS TRAINED BY THE WARLORDS OF OKAARA, CLAWED MY WAY FREE FROM SLAVERY, AND SURVIVED THE EXPERIMENTS OF THE PSIONS.
I HAVE MADE EARTH MY HOME AND THESE TITANS MY FAMILY!
ANYONE WHO THREATENS THEM FACES ME!
SKREEEEEEEEEE

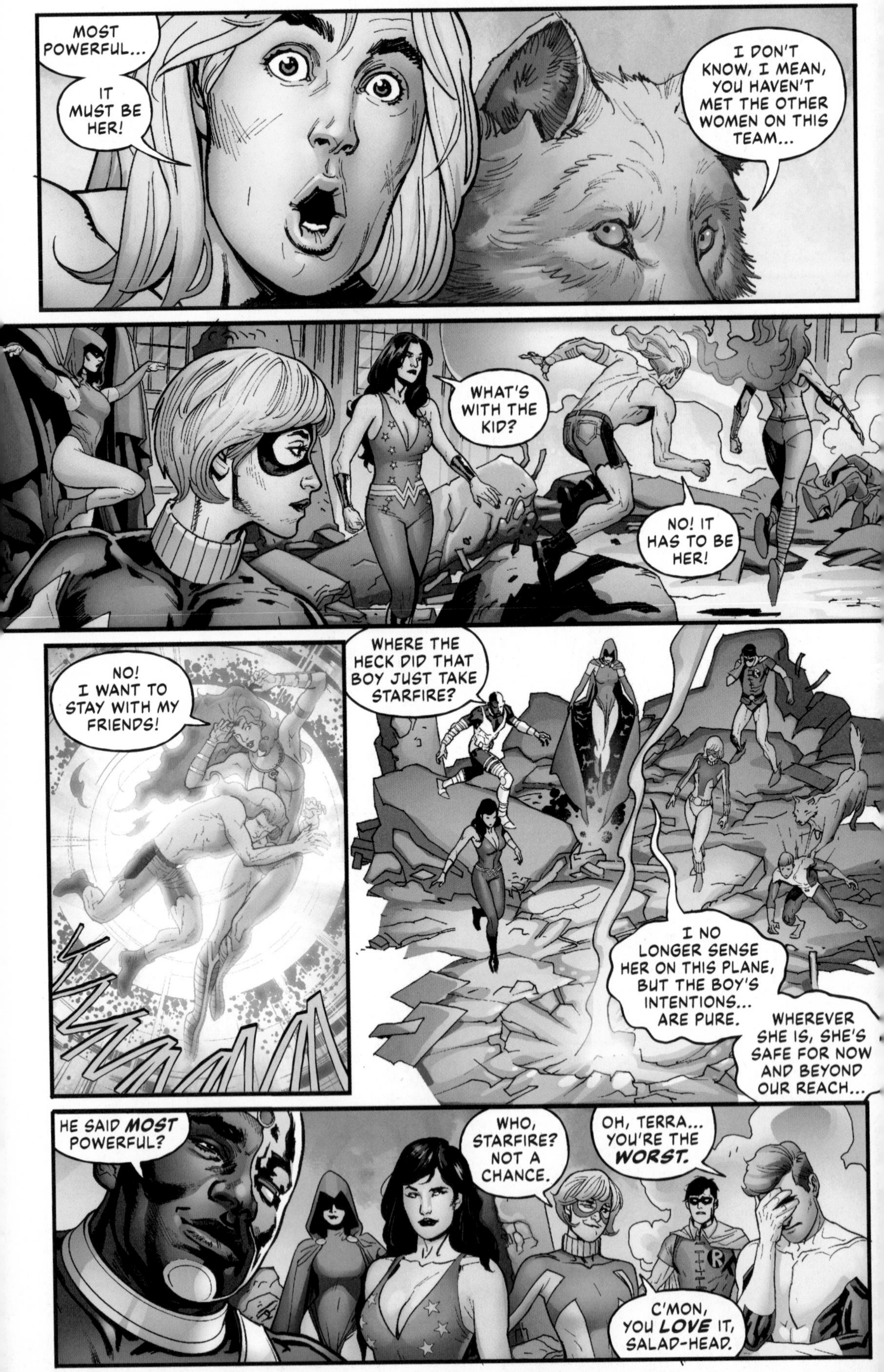
MOST POWERFUL...
IT MUST BE HER!
I DON'T KNOW, I MEAN, YOU HAVEN'T MET THE OTHER WOMEN ON THIS TEAM...
WHAT'S WITH THE KID?
NO! IT HAS TO BE HER!
NO! I WANT TO STAY WITH MY FRIENDS!
WHERE THE HECK DID THAT BOY JUST TAKE STARFIRE?
I NO LONGER SENSE HER ON THIS PLANE, BUT THE BOY'S INTENTIONS... ARE PURE.
WHEREVER SHE IS, SHE'S SAFE FOR NOW AND BEYOND OUR REACH...
HE SAID MOST POWERFUL?
WHO, STARFIRE? NOT A CHANCE.
OH, TERRA... YOU'RE THE WORST.
C'MON, YOU LOVE IT, SALAD-HEAD.

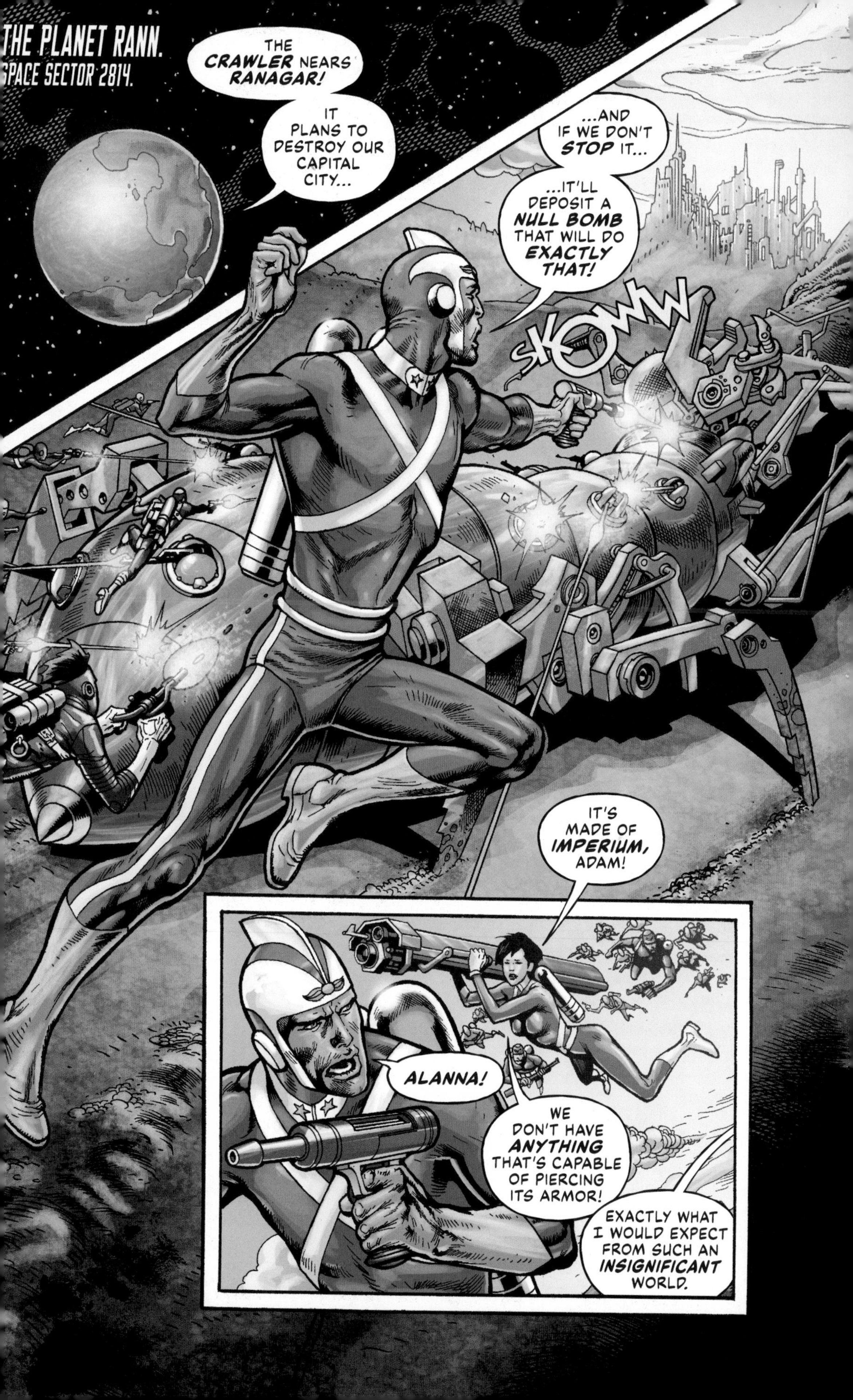
THE PLANET RANN.
SPACE SECTOR 2814.
THE CRAWLER NEARS RANAGAR!
IT PLANS TO DESTROY OUR CAPITAL CITY...
...AND IF WE DON'T STOP IT...
...IT'LL DEPOSIT A NULL BOMB THAT WILL DO EXACTLY THAT!
SKOWW
IT'S MADE OF IMPERIUM, ADAM!
ALANNA!
WE DON'T HAVE ANYTHING THAT'S CAPABLE OF PIERCING ITS ARMOR!
EXACTLY WHAT I WOULD EXPECT FROM SUCH AN INSIGNIFICANT WORLD.

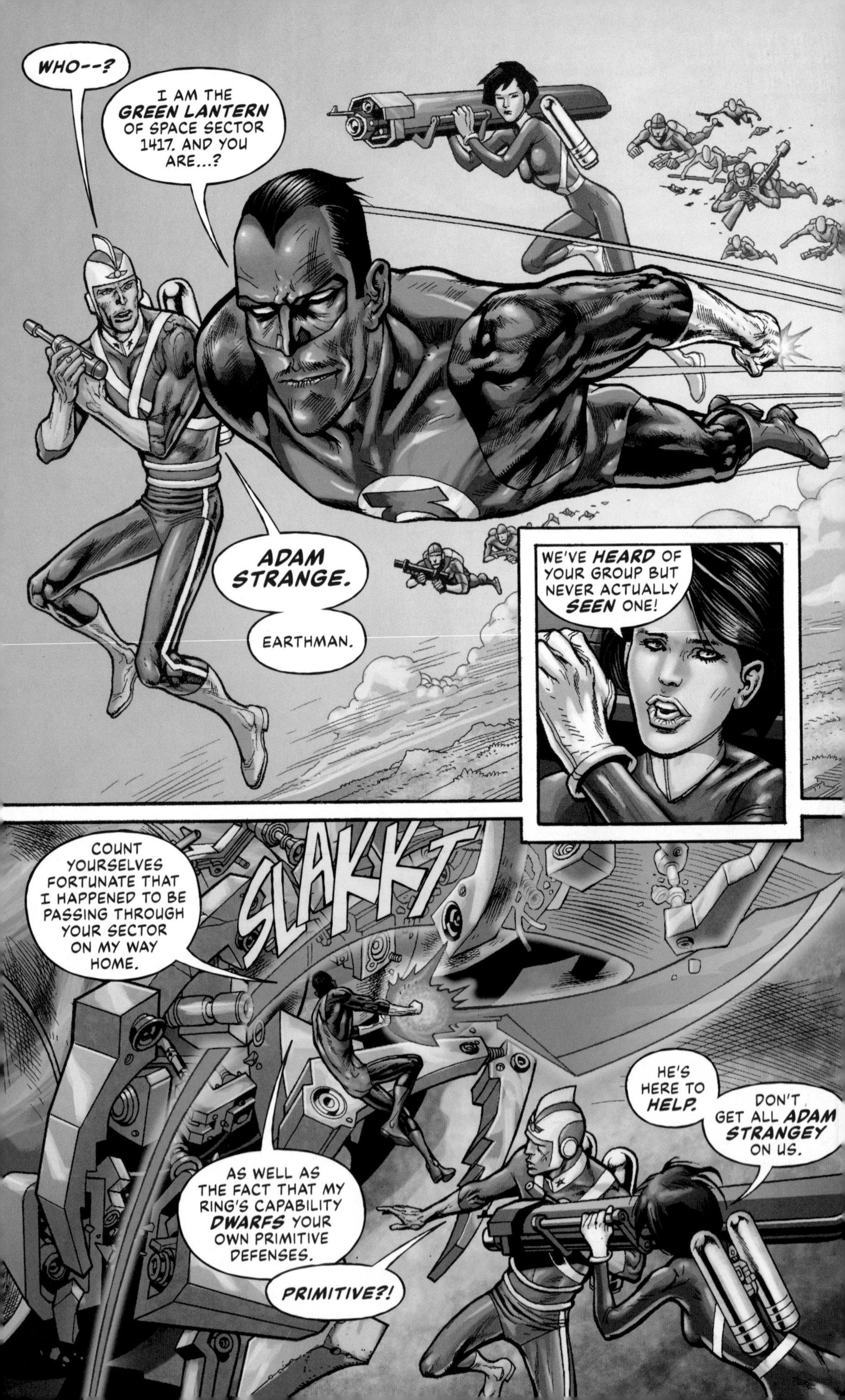
WHO--?
I AM THE GREEN LANTERN OF SPACE SECTOR 1417. AND YOU ARE...?
ADAM STRANGE.
EARTHMAN.
WE'VE HEARD OF YOUR GROUP BUT NEVER ACTUALLY SEEN ONE!
SLAKKT
COUNT YOURSELVES FORTUNATE THAT I HAPPENED TO BE PASSING THROUGH YOUR SECTOR ON MY WAY HOME.
AS WELL AS THE FACT THAT MY RING'S CAPABILITY DWARFS YOUR OWN PRIMITIVE DEFENSES.
PRIMITIVE?!
HE'S HERE TO HELP.
DON'T GET ALL ADAM STRANGEY ON US.

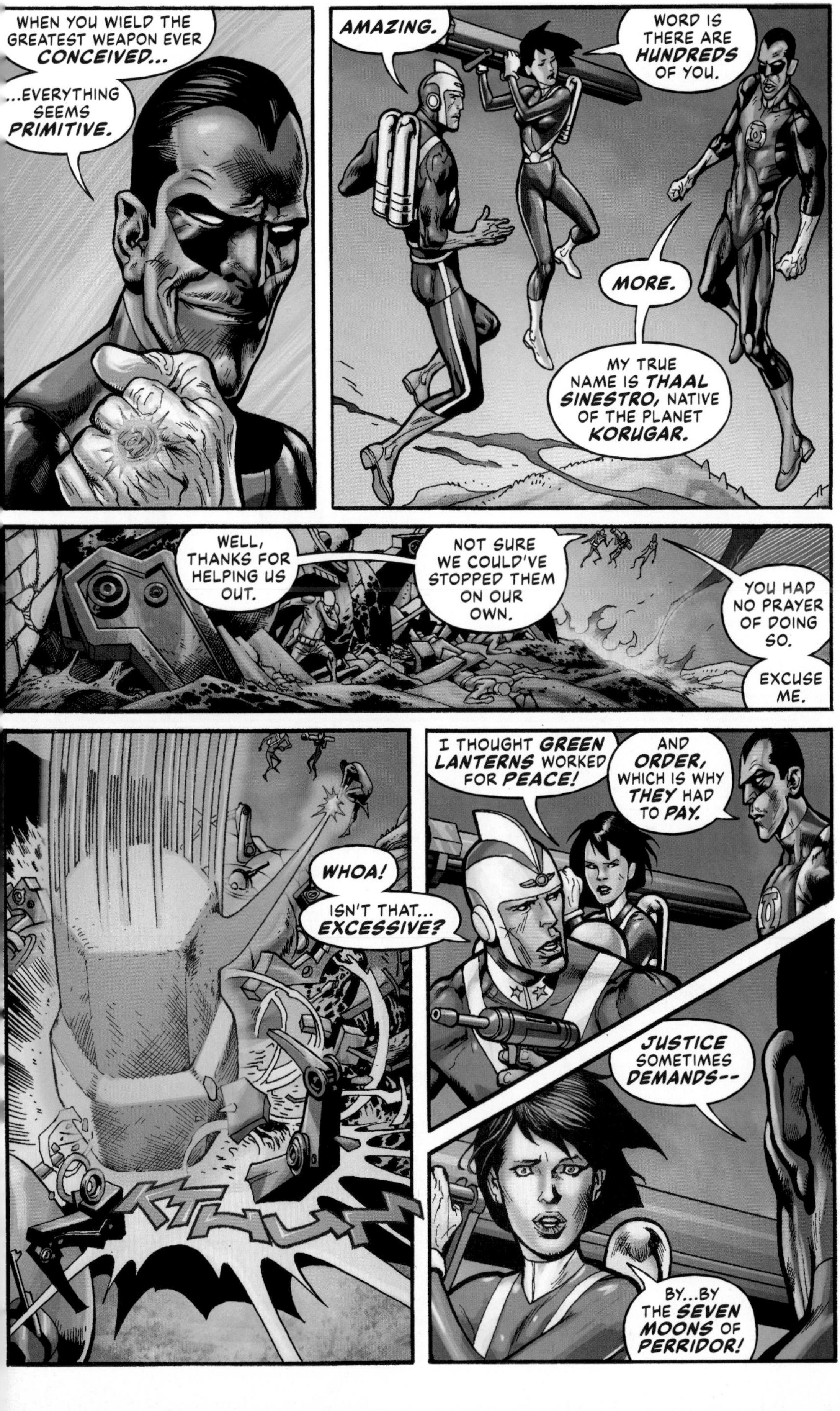
WHEN YOU WIELD THE GREATEST WEAPON EVER CONCEIVED...
...EVERYTHING SEEMS PRIMITIVE.
AMAZING.
WORD IS THERE ARE HUNDREDS OF YOU.
MORE.
MY TRUE NAME IS THAAL SINESTRO, NATIVE OF THE PLANET KORUGAR.
WELL, THANKS FOR HELPING US OUT.
NOT SURE WE COULD'VE STOPPED THEM ON OUR OWN.
YOU HAD NO PRAYER OF DOING SO.
EXCUSE ME.
WHOA!
ISN'T THAT... EXCESSIVE?
KTHUM
I THOUGHT GREEN LANTERNS WORKED FOR PEACE!
AND ORDER, WHICH IS WHY THEY HAD TO PAY.
JUSTICE SOMETIMES DEMANDS--
BY...BY THE SEVEN MOONS OF PERRIDOR!

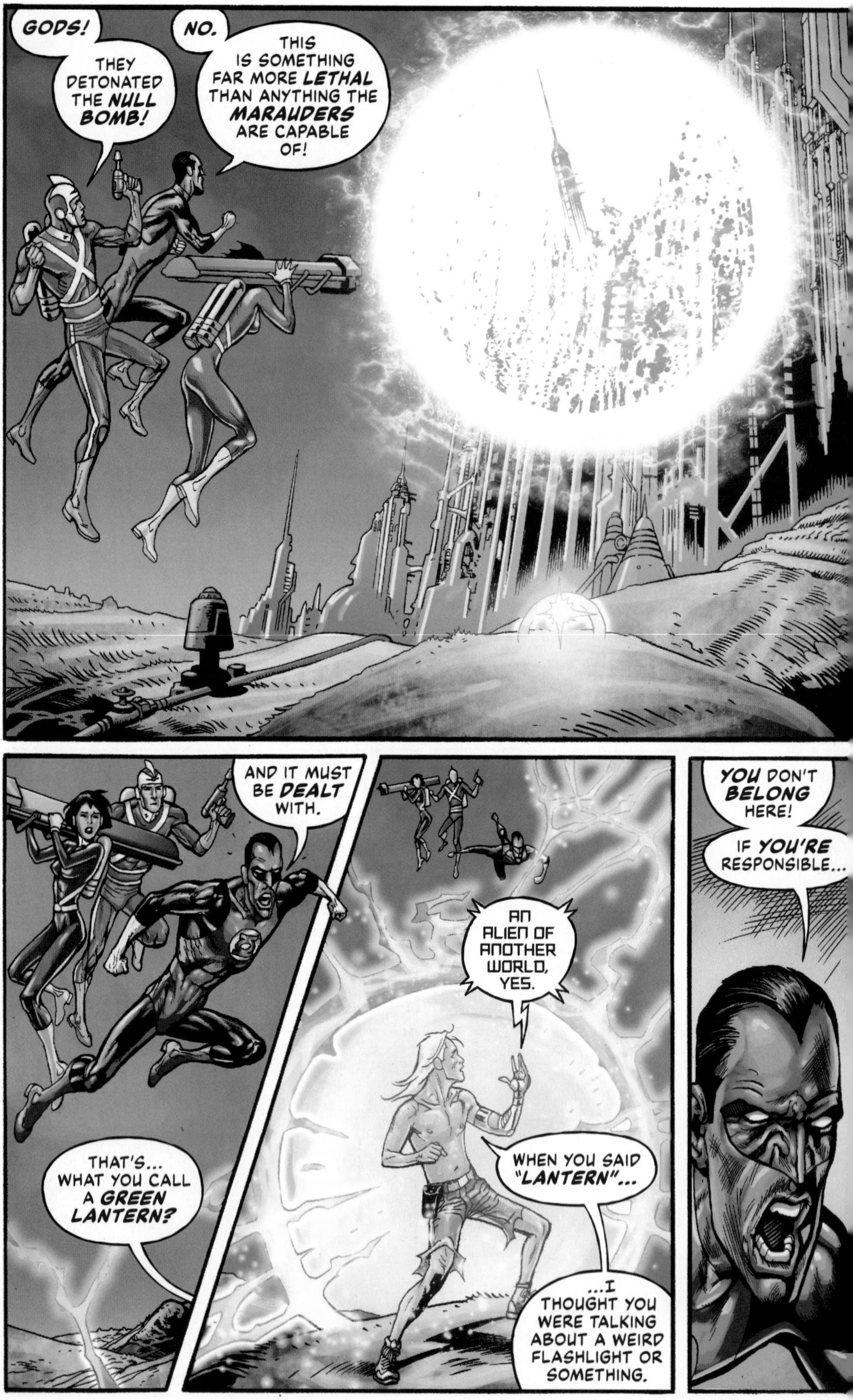
GODS!
THEY DETONATED THE NULL BOMB!
NO.
THIS IS SOMETHING FAR MORE LETHAL THAN ANYTHING THE MARAUDERS ARE CAPABLE OF!
AND IT MUST BE DEALT WITH.
THAT'S... WHAT YOU CALL A GREEN LANTERN?
AN ALIEN OF ANOTHER WORLD, YES.
WHEN YOU SAID "LANTERN"...
...I THOUGHT YOU WERE TALKING ABOUT A WEIRD FLASHLIGHT OR SOMETHING.
YOU DON'T BELONG HERE!
IF YOU'RE RESPONSIBLE...

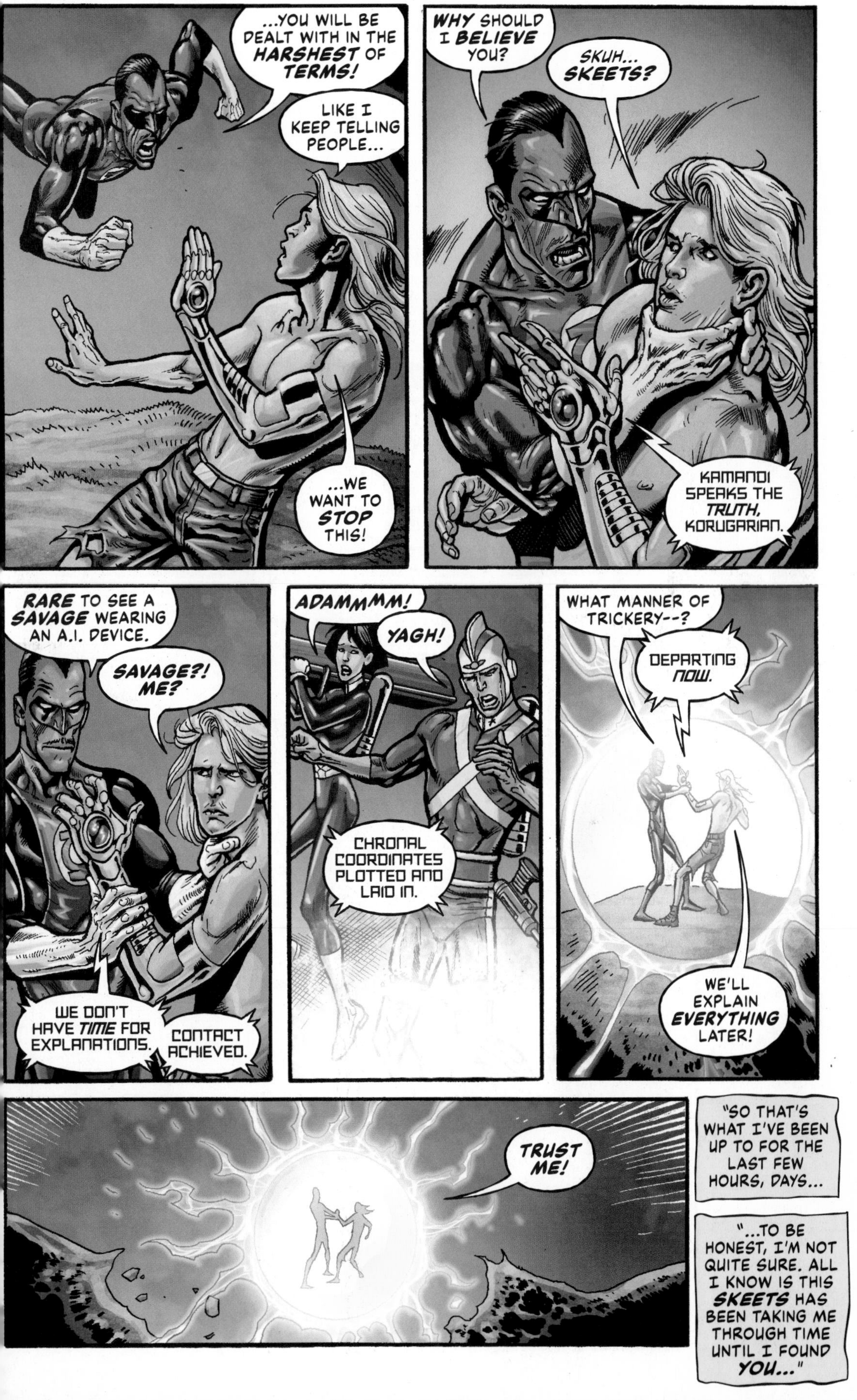
...YOU WILL BE DEALT WITH IN THE HARSHEST OF TERMS!
LIKE I KEEP TELLING PEOPLE...
...WE WANT TO STOP THIS!
WHY SHOULD I BELIEVE YOU?
SKUH... SKEETS?
KAMANDI SPEAKS THE TRUTH, KORUGARIAN.
RARE TO SEE A SAVAGE WEARING AN A.I. DEVICE.
SAVAGE?! ME?
WE DON'T HAVE TIME FOR EXPLANATIONS.
CONTACT ACHIEVED.
ADAMMMM!
YAGH!
CHRONAL COORDINATES PLOTTED AND LAID IN.
WHAT MANNER OF TRICKERY--?
DEPARTING NOW.
WE'LL EXPLAIN EVERYTHING LATER!
TRUST ME!
"SO THAT'S WHAT I'VE BEEN UP TO FOR THE LAST FEW HOURS, DAYS...
"...TO BE HONEST, I'M NOT QUITE SURE. ALL I KNOW IS THIS SKEETS HAS BEEN TAKING ME THROUGH TIME UNTIL I FOUND YOU..."

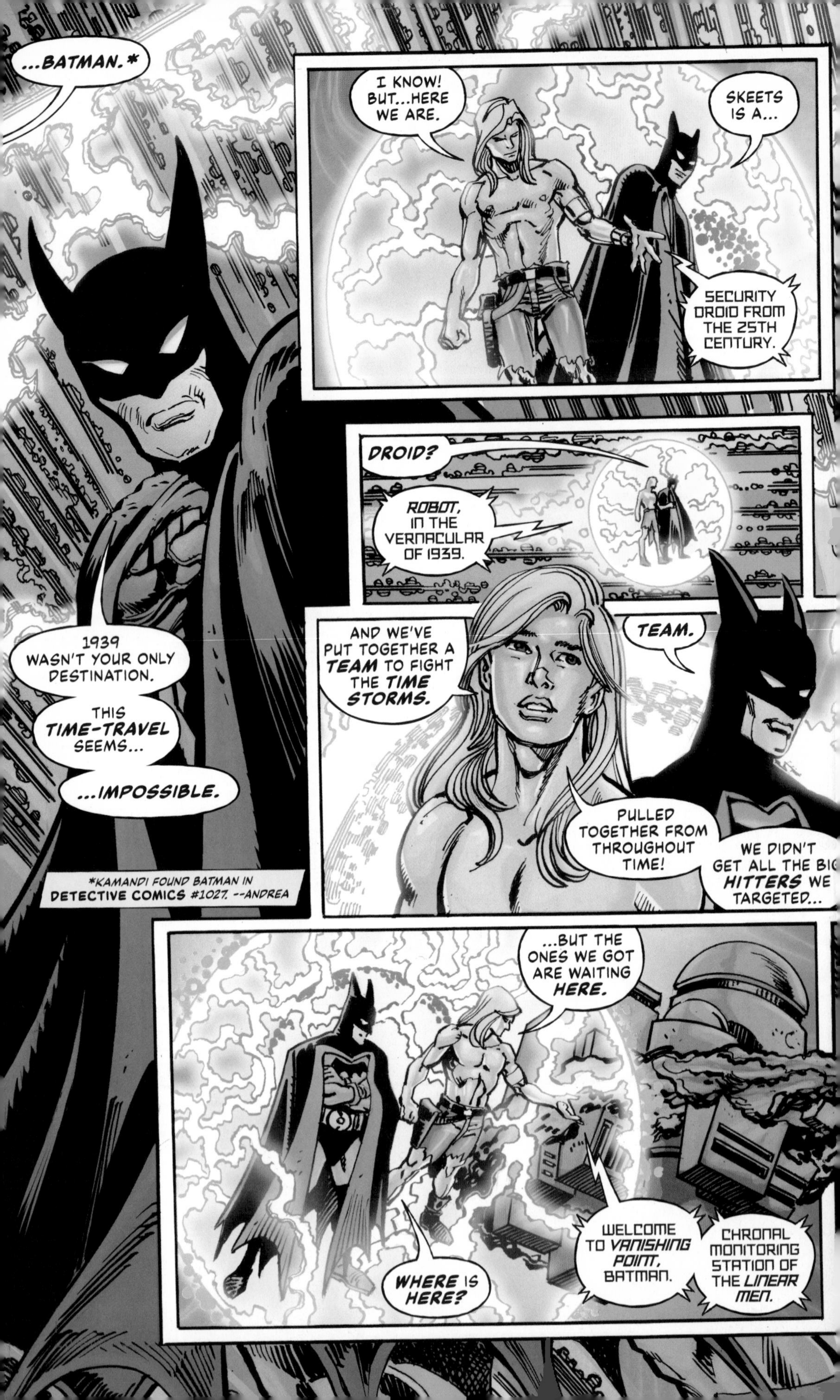
...BATMAN.*
I KNOW! BUT...HERE WE ARE.
SKEETS IS A...
SECURITY DROID FROM THE 25TH CENTURY.
DROID?
ROBOT, IN THE VERNACULAR OF 1939.
1939 WASN'T YOUR ONLY DESTINATION.
THIS TIME-TRAVEL SEEMS...
...IMPOSSIBLE.
*KAMANDI FOUND BATMAN IN DETECTIVE COMICS #1027. --ANDREA
AND WE'VE PUT TOGETHER A TEAM TO FIGHT THE TIME STORMS.
TEAM.
PULLED TOGETHER FROM THROUGHOUT TIME!
WE DIDN'T GET ALL THE BIG HITTERS WE TARGETED...
...BUT THE ONES WE GOT ARE WAITING HERE.
WHERE IS HERE?
WELCOME TO VANISHING POINT, BATMAN.
CHRONAL MONITORING STATION OF THE LINEAR MEN.

EXPLAIN.

WELL, FROM WHAT SKEETS HAS SAID, THE *VANISHING POINT* IS KIND OF A TIME-MONITORING OUTPOST.

AS FOR THESE PEOPLE, I JUST MET THEM, SAME AS YOU.

PICKED THEM UP FROM DIFFERENT ERAS, THANKS TO SKEETS' GUIDANCE.

ALL I KNOW IS THAT WE SEEM TO BE ALL THAT STANDS BETWEEN, WELL...

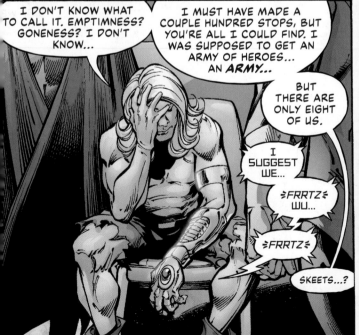

I DON'T KNOW WHAT TO CALL IT. EMPTIMNESS? GONENESS? I DON'T KNOW...

I MUST HAVE MADE A COUPLE HUNDRED STOPS, BUT YOU'RE ALL I COULD FIND. I WAS SUPPOSED TO GET AN ARMY OF HEROES... AN *ARMY*...

BUT THERE ARE ONLY EIGHT OF US.

I SUGGEST WE...

≠FRRTZ≠ WU...

≠FRRTZ≠

SKEETS...?

WE SHOULD SUFFICE, BOY.

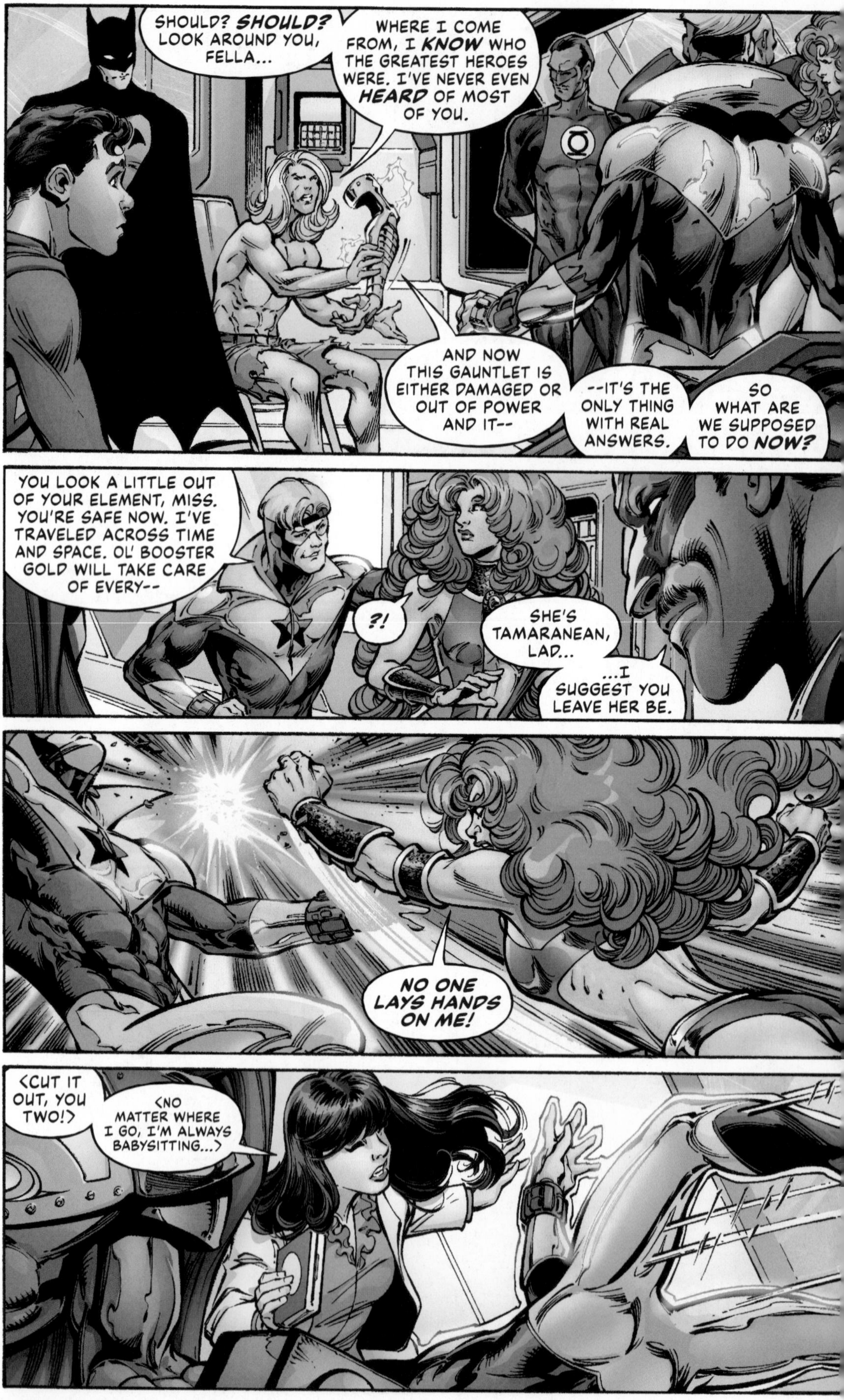
SHOULD? SHOULD? LOOK AROUND YOU, FELLA...
WHERE I COME FROM, I KNOW WHO THE GREATEST HEROES WERE. I'VE NEVER EVEN HEARD OF MOST OF YOU.
AND NOW THIS GAUNTLET IS EITHER DAMAGED OR OUT OF POWER AND IT--
--IT'S THE ONLY THING WITH REAL ANSWERS.
SO WHAT ARE WE SUPPOSED TO DO NOW?
YOU LOOK A LITTLE OUT OF YOUR ELEMENT, MISS. YOU'RE SAFE NOW. I'VE TRAVELED ACROSS TIME AND SPACE. OL' BOOSTER GOLD WILL TAKE CARE OF EVERY--
?!
SHE'S TAMARANEAN, LAD...
...I SUGGEST YOU LEAVE HER BE.
NO ONE LAYS HANDS ON ME!
<CUT IT OUT, YOU TWO!>
<NO MATTER WHERE I GO, I'M ALWAYS BABYSITTING...>

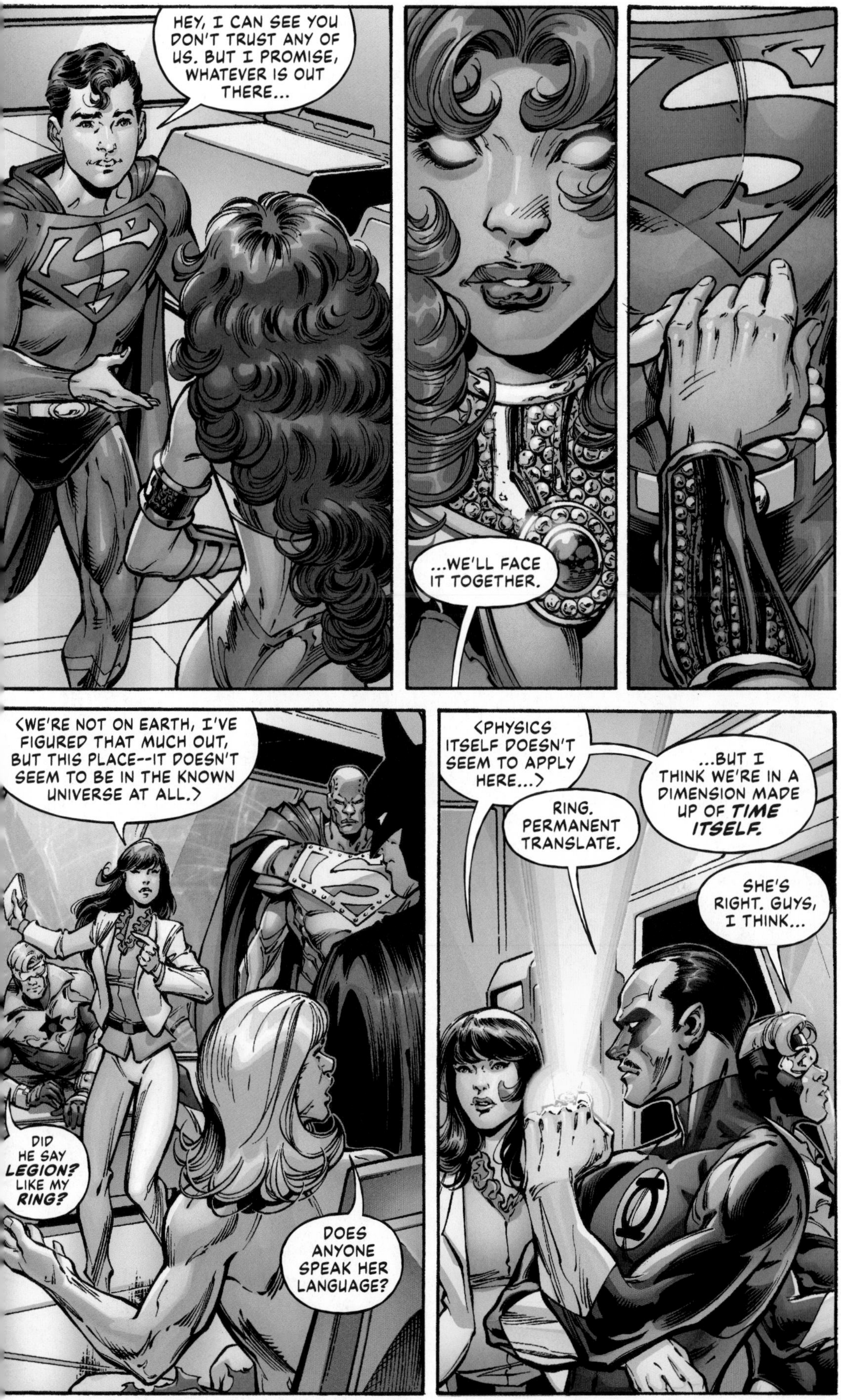
HEY, I CAN SEE YOU DON'T TRUST ANY OF US. BUT I PROMISE, WHATEVER IS OUT THERE...
...WE'LL FACE IT TOGETHER.
<WE'RE NOT ON EARTH, I'VE FIGURED THAT MUCH OUT, BUT THIS PLACE--IT DOESN'T SEEM TO BE IN THE KNOWN UNIVERSE AT ALL.>
DID HE SAY LEGION? LIKE MY RING?
DOES ANYONE SPEAK HER LANGUAGE?
<PHYSICS ITSELF DOESN'T SEEM TO APPLY HERE...>
RING. PERMANENT TRANSLATE.
...BUT I THINK WE'RE IN A DIMENSION MADE UP OF TIME ITSELF.
SHE'S RIGHT. GUYS, I THINK...

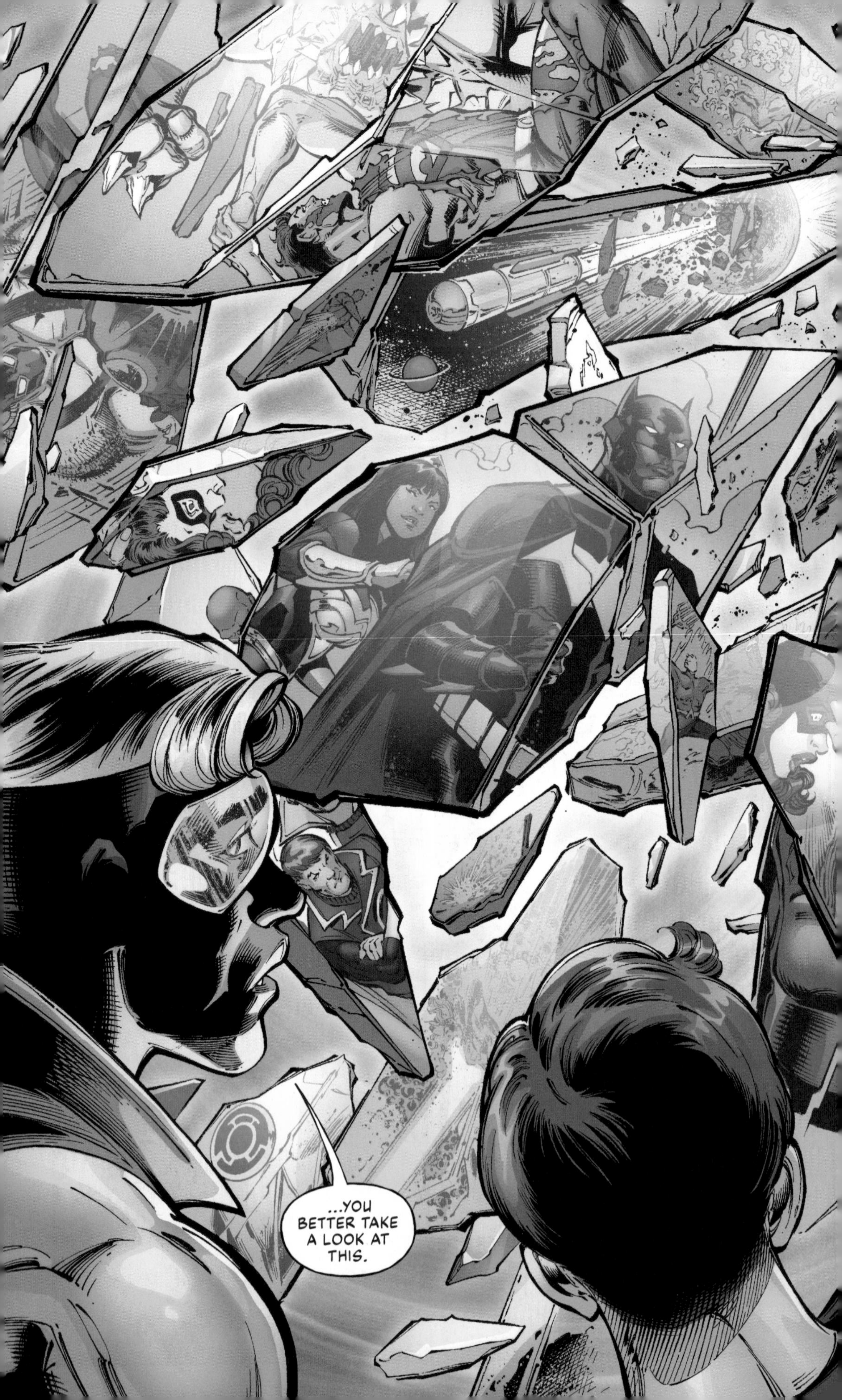
...YOU BETTER TAKE A LOOK AT THIS.

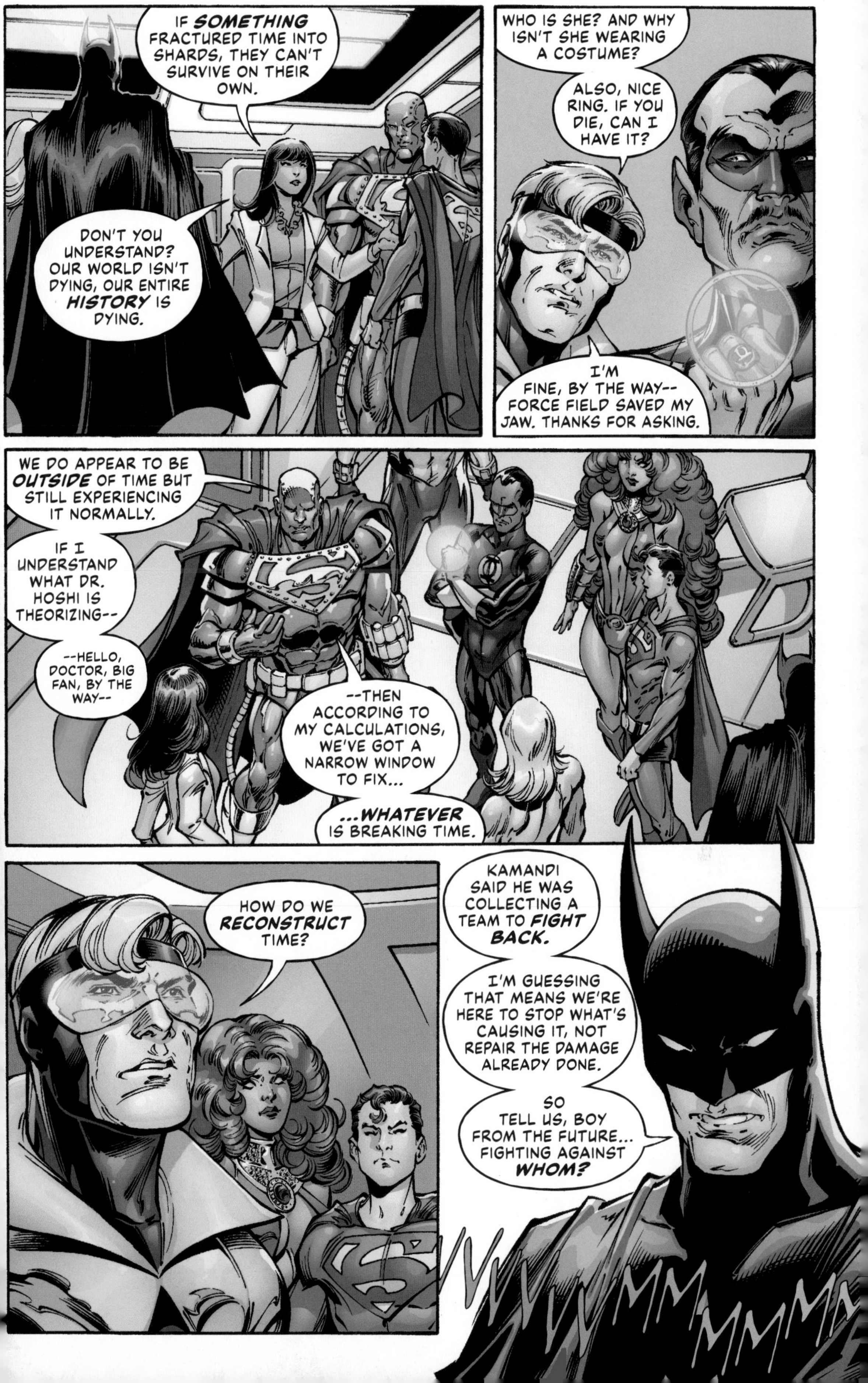
IF SOMETHING FRACTURED TIME INTO SHARDS, THEY CAN'T SURVIVE ON THEIR OWN.
DON'T YOU UNDERSTAND? OUR WORLD ISN'T DYING, OUR ENTIRE HISTORY IS DYING.
WHO IS SHE? AND WHY ISN'T SHE WEARING A COSTUME?
ALSO, NICE RING. IF YOU DIE, CAN I HAVE IT?
I'M FINE, BY THE WAY-- FORCE FIELD SAVED MY JAW. THANKS FOR ASKING.
WE DO APPEAR TO BE OUTSIDE OF TIME BUT STILL EXPERIENCING IT NORMALLY.
IF I UNDERSTAND WHAT DR. HOSHI IS THEORIZING--
--HELLO, DOCTOR, BIG FAN, BY THE WAY--
--THEN ACCORDING TO MY CALCULATIONS, WE'VE GOT A NARROW WINDOW TO FIX...
...WHATEVER IS BREAKING TIME.
HOW DO WE RECONSTRUCT TIME?
KAMANDI SAID HE WAS COLLECTING A TEAM TO FIGHT BACK.
I'M GUESSING THAT MEANS WE'RE HERE TO STOP WHAT'S CAUSING IT, NOT REPAIR THE DAMAGE ALREADY DONE.
SO TELL US, BOY FROM THE FUTURE... FIGHTING AGAINST WHOM?
VVVMMMMMM

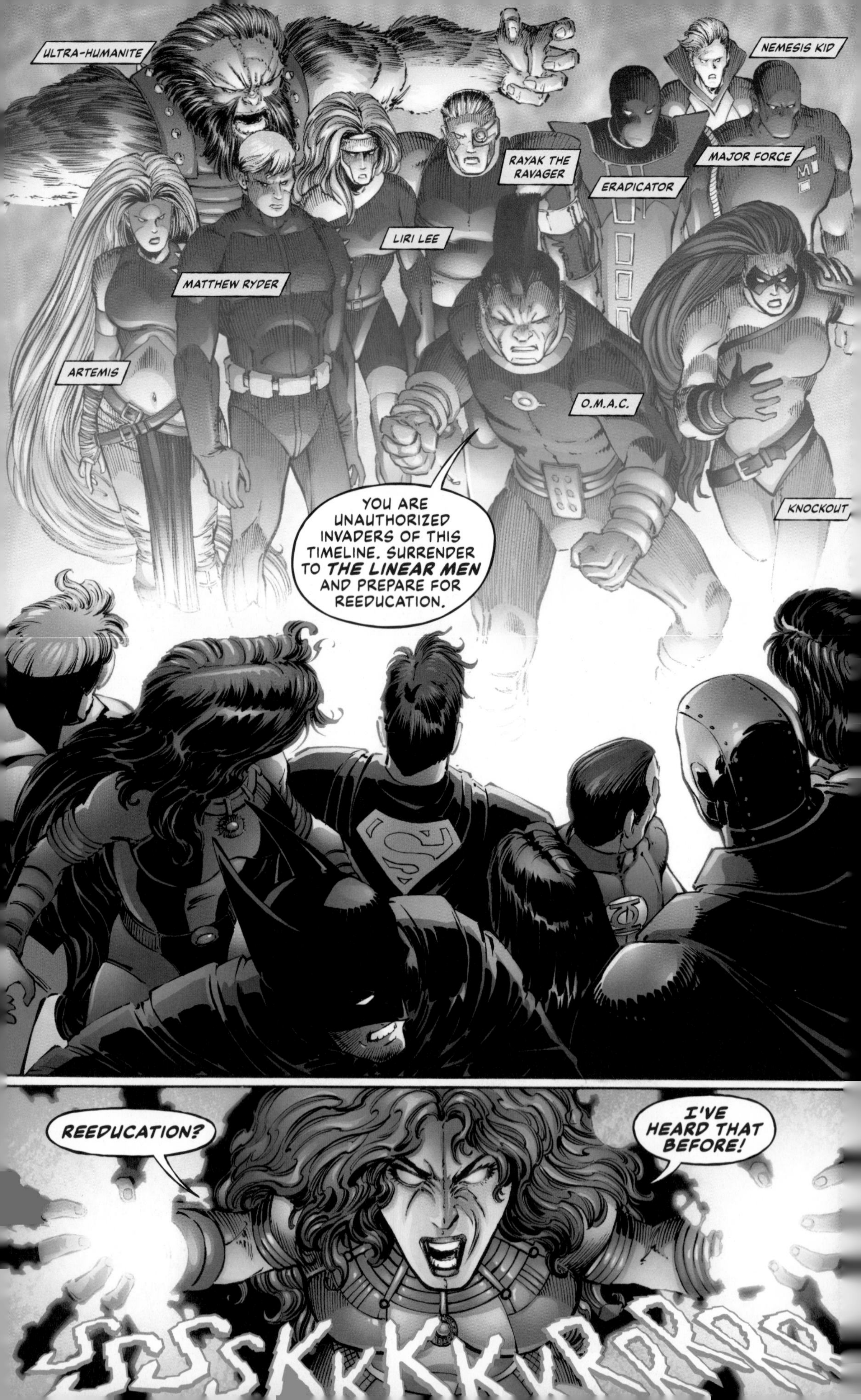
ULTRA-HUMANITE
NEMESIS KID
RAYAK THE RAVAGER
ERADICATOR
MAJOR FORCE
LIRI LEE
MATTHEW RYDER
ARTEMIS
O.M.A.C.
KNOCKOUT
YOU ARE UNAUTHORIZED INVADERS OF THIS TIMELINE. SURRENDER TO ***THE LINEAR MEN*** AND PREPARE FOR REEDUCATION.
REEDUCATION?
I'VE HEARD THAT BEFORE!
SSSSKKKKVRRRR

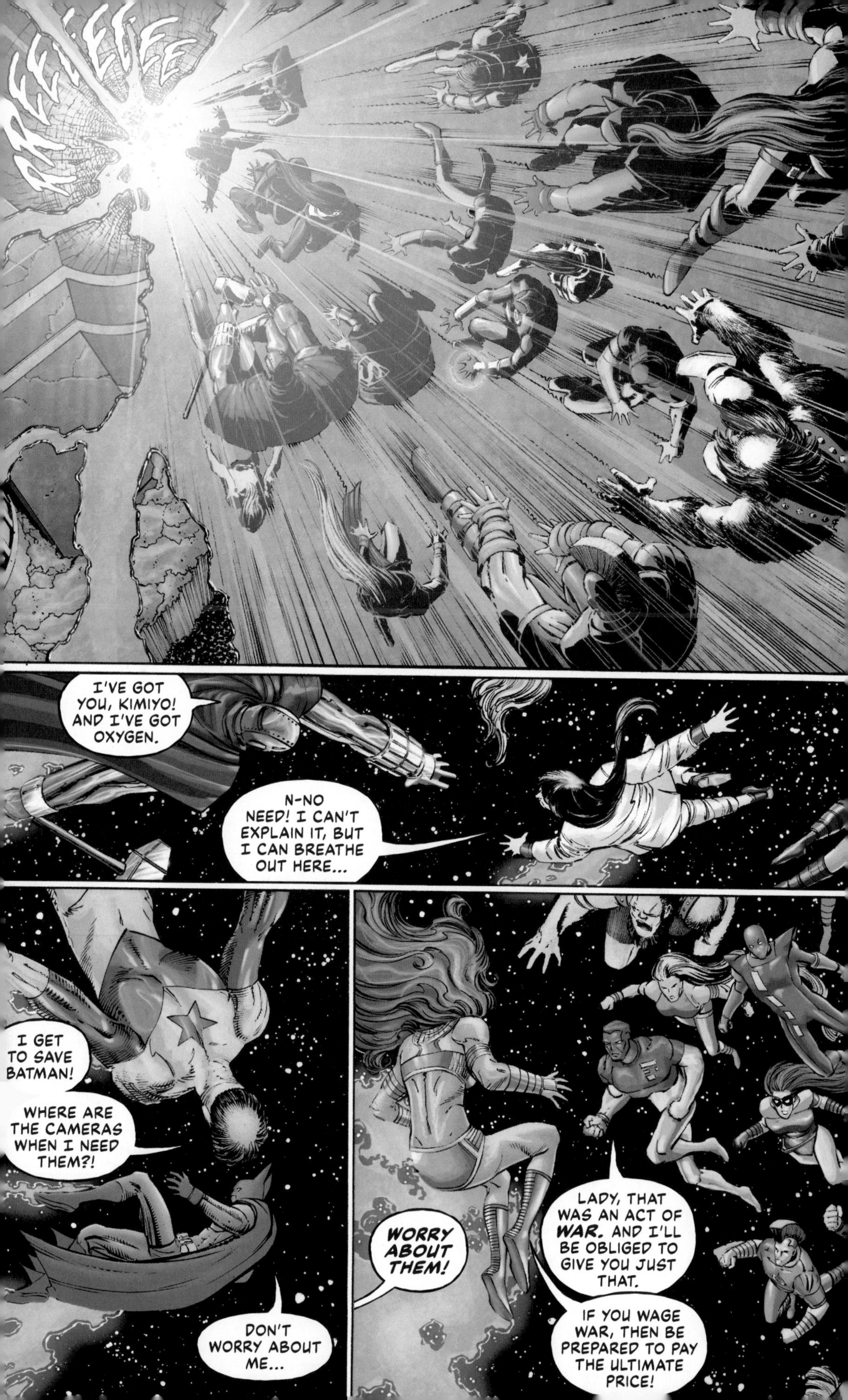

FFEEEEE
I'VE GOT YOU, KIMIYO! AND I'VE GOT OXYGEN.
N-NO NEED! I CAN'T EXPLAIN IT, BUT I CAN BREATHE OUT HERE...
I GET TO SAVE BATMAN!
WHERE ARE THE CAMERAS WHEN I NEED THEM?!
DON'T WORRY ABOUT ME...
WORRY ABOUT THEM!
LADY, THAT WAS AN ACT OF WAR. AND I'LL BE OBLIGED TO GIVE YOU JUST THAT.
IF YOU WAGE WAR, THEN BE PREPARED TO PAY THE ULTIMATE PRICE!

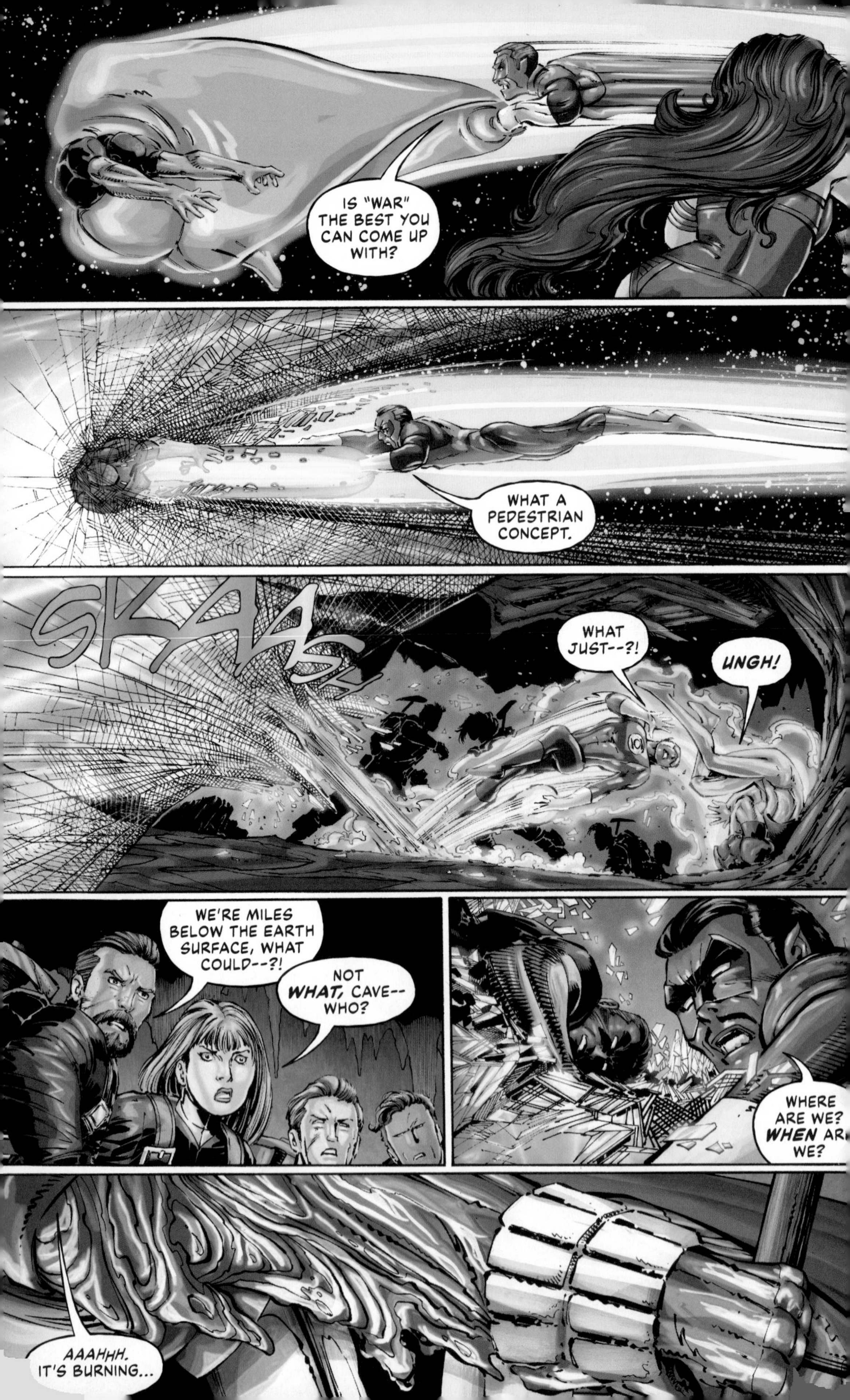

IS "WAR" THE BEST YOU CAN COME UP WITH?
WHAT A PEDESTRIAN CONCEPT.
SKAASH
WHAT JUST--?!
UNGH!
WE'RE MILES BELOW THE EARTH SURFACE, WHAT COULD--?!
NOT WHAT, CAVE-- WHO?
WHERE ARE WE? WHEN AR WE?
AAAHHH. IT'S BURNING...

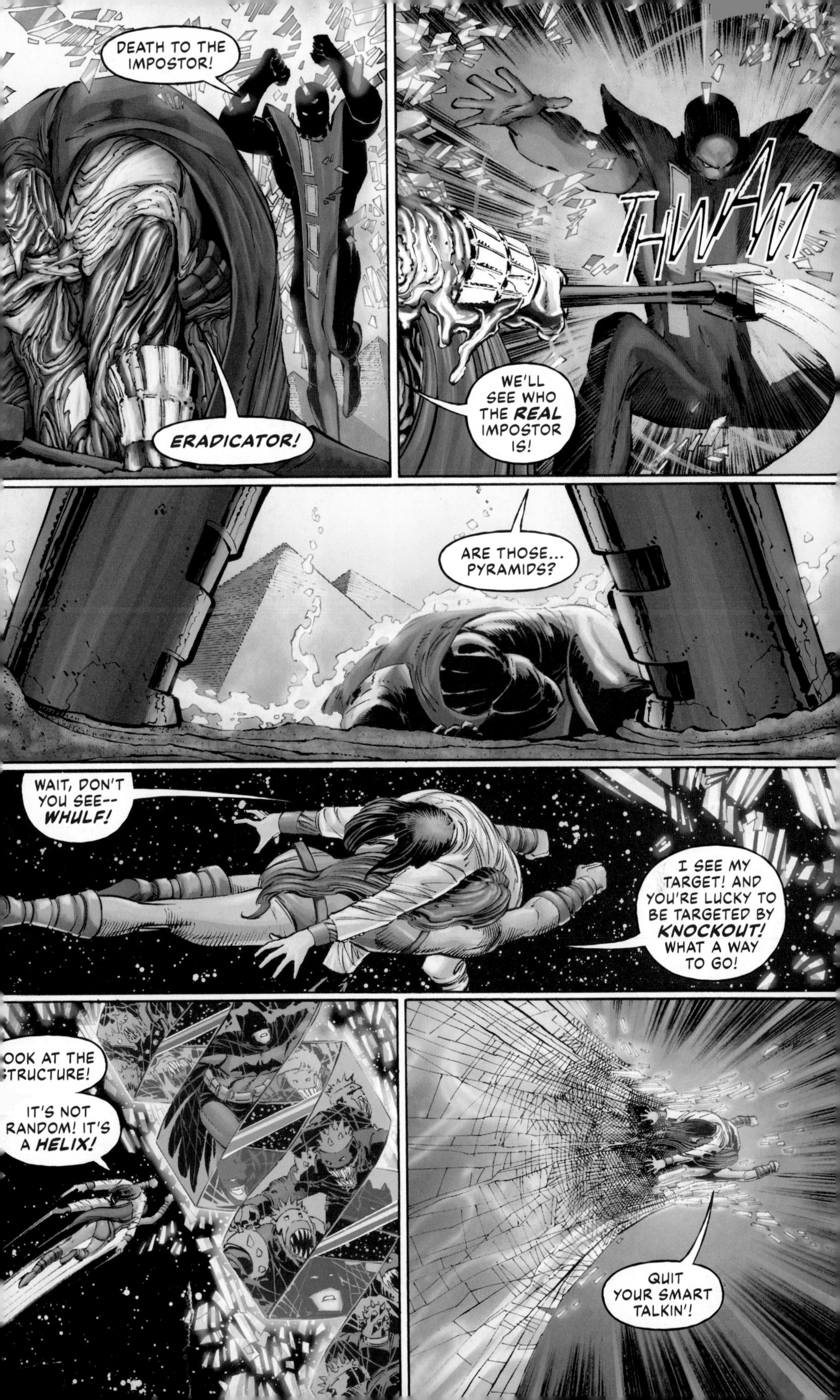
DEATH TO THE IMPOSTOR!
ERADICATOR!
THWAM
WE'LL SEE WHO THE REAL IMPOSTOR IS!
ARE THOSE... PYRAMIDS?
WAIT, DON'T YOU SEE-- WHULF!
I SEE MY TARGET! AND YOU'RE LUCKY TO BE TARGETED BY KNOCKOUT! WHAT A WAY TO GO!
IT'S NOT RANDOM! IT'S A HELIX!
QUIT YOUR SMART TALKIN'!

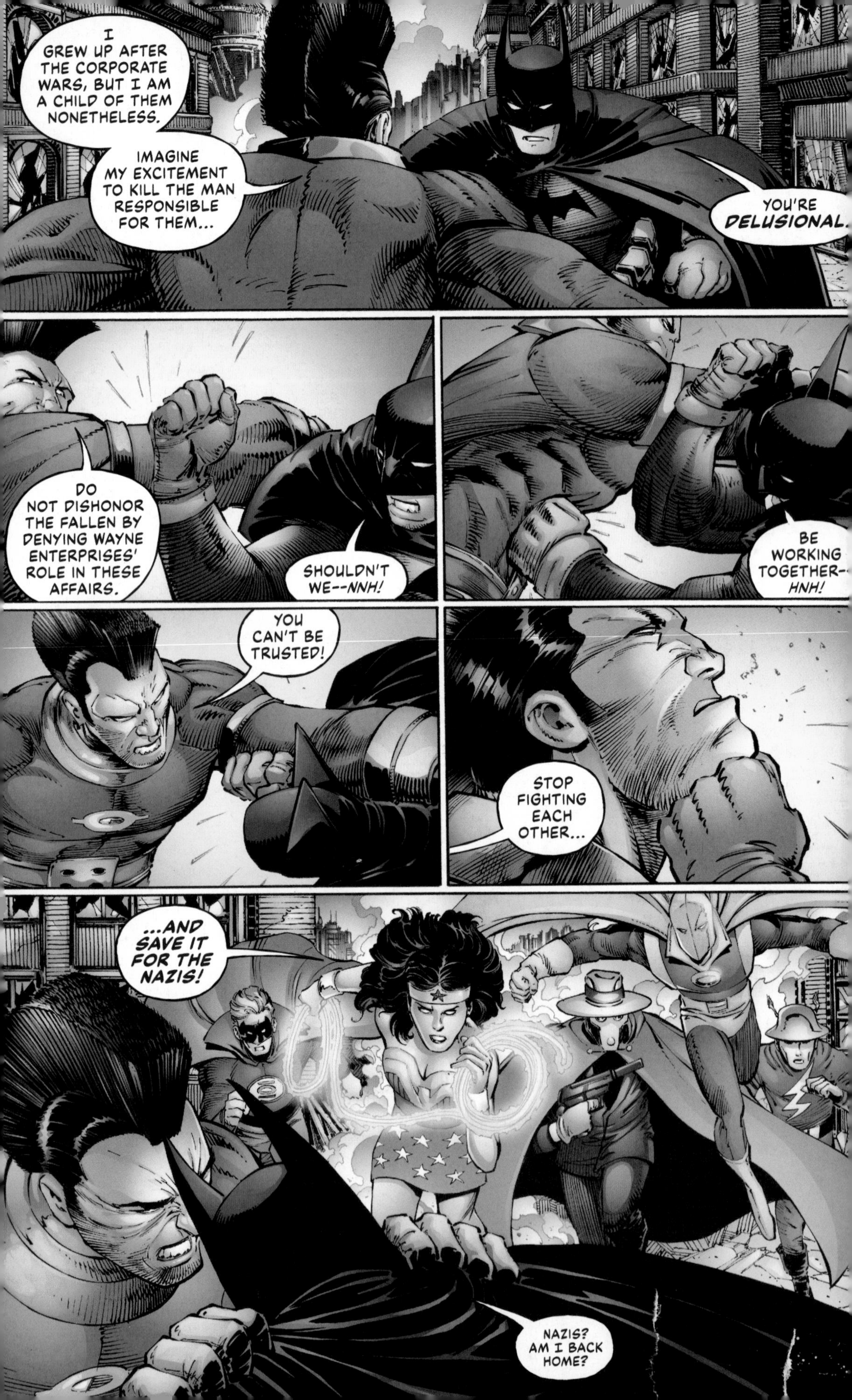
I GREW UP AFTER THE CORPORATE WARS, BUT I AM A CHILD OF THEM NONETHELESS.
IMAGINE MY EXCITEMENT TO KILL THE MAN RESPONSIBLE FOR THEM...
YOU'RE *DELUSIONAL.*
DO NOT DISHONOR THE FALLEN BY DENYING WAYNE ENTERPRISES' ROLE IN THESE AFFAIRS.
SHOULDN'T WE--*NNH!*
BE WORKING TOGETHER--*HNH!*
YOU CAN'T BE TRUSTED!
STOP FIGHTING EACH OTHER...
...AND SAVE IT FOR THE NAZIS!
NAZIS? AM I BACK HOME?

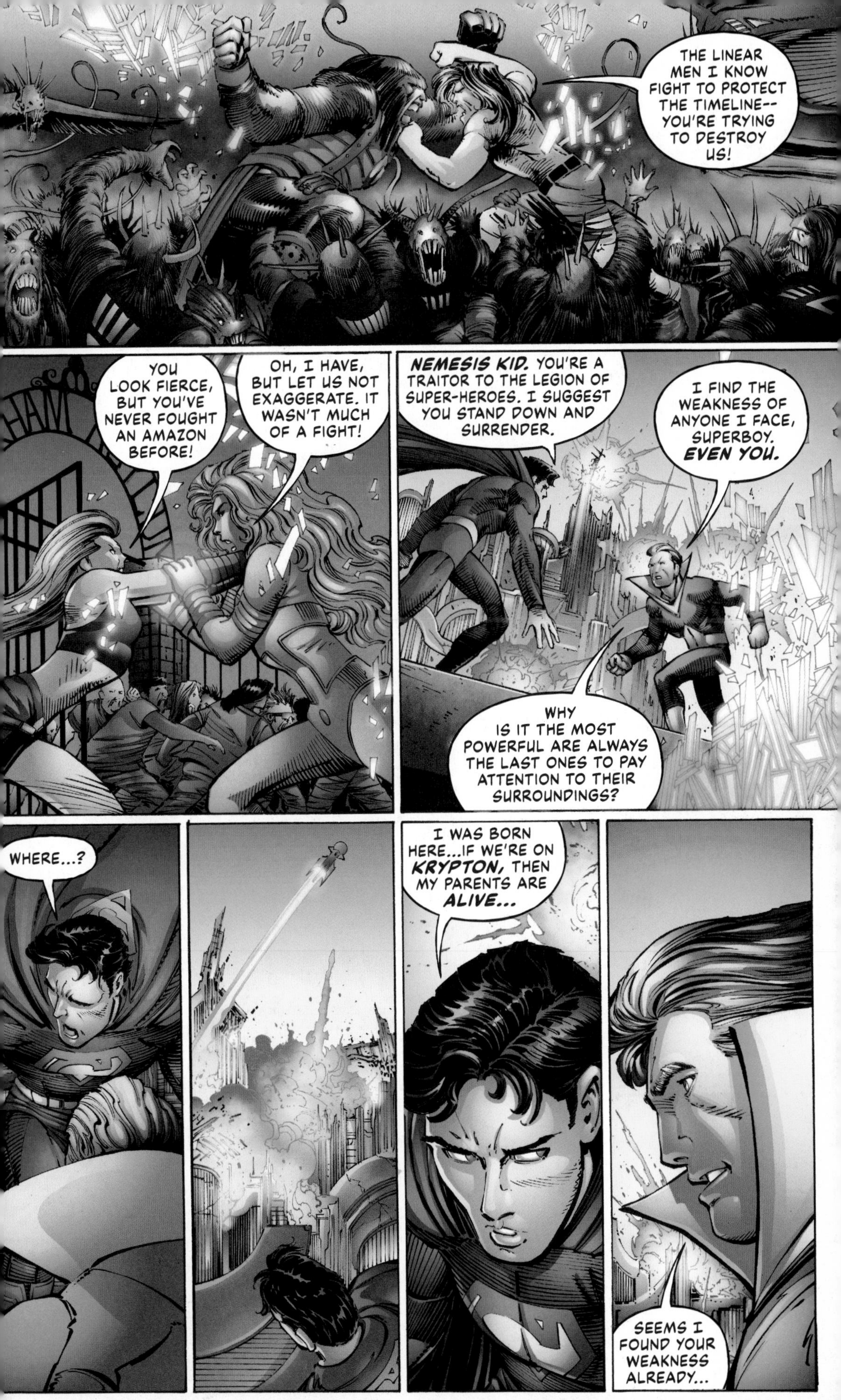
THE LINEAR MEN I KNOW FIGHT TO PROTECT THE TIMELINE-- YOU'RE TRYING TO DESTROY US!
YOU LOOK FIERCE, BUT YOU'VE NEVER FOUGHT AN AMAZON BEFORE!
OH, I HAVE, BUT LET US NOT EXAGGERATE. IT WASN'T MUCH OF A FIGHT!
NEMESIS KID. YOU'RE A TRAITOR TO THE LEGION OF SUPER-HEROES. I SUGGEST YOU STAND DOWN AND SURRENDER.
I FIND THE WEAKNESS OF ANYONE I FACE, SUPERBOY. EVEN YOU.
WHY IS IT THE MOST POWERFUL ARE ALWAYS THE LAST ONES TO PAY ATTENTION TO THEIR SURROUNDINGS?
WHERE...?
I WAS BORN HERE...IF WE'RE ON KRYPTON, THEN MY PARENTS ARE ALIVE...
SEEMS I FOUND YOUR WEAKNESS ALREADY...

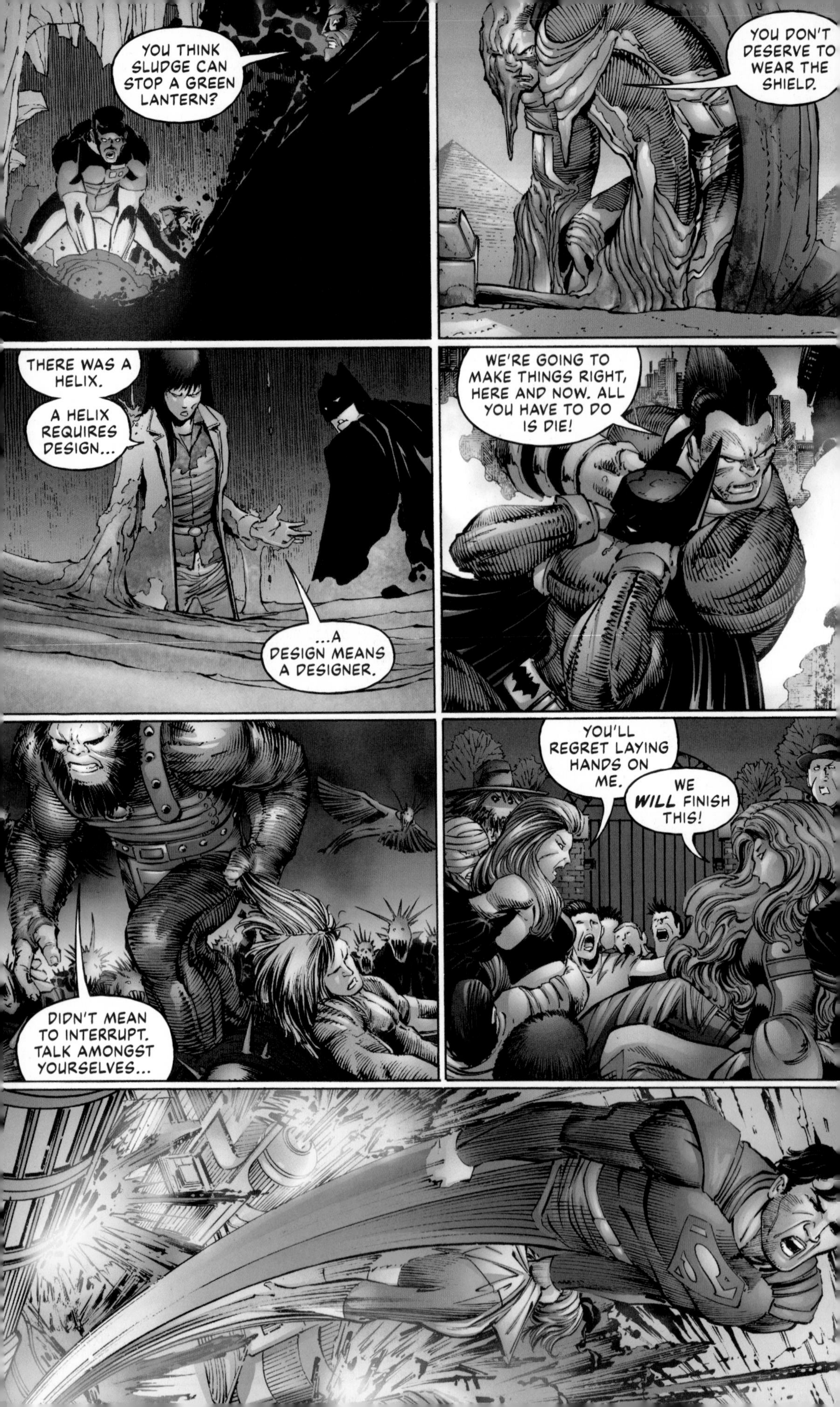

YOU THINK SLUDGE CAN STOP A GREEN LANTERN?
YOU DON'T DESERVE TO WEAR THE SHIELD.
THERE WAS A HELIX.
A HELIX REQUIRES DESIGN...
...A DESIGN MEANS A DESIGNER.
WE'RE GOING TO MAKE THINGS RIGHT, HERE AND NOW. ALL YOU HAVE TO DO IS DIE!
DIDN'T MEAN TO INTERRUPT. TALK AMONGST YOURSELVES...
YOU'LL REGRET LAYING HANDS ON ME.
WE **WILL** FINISH THIS!

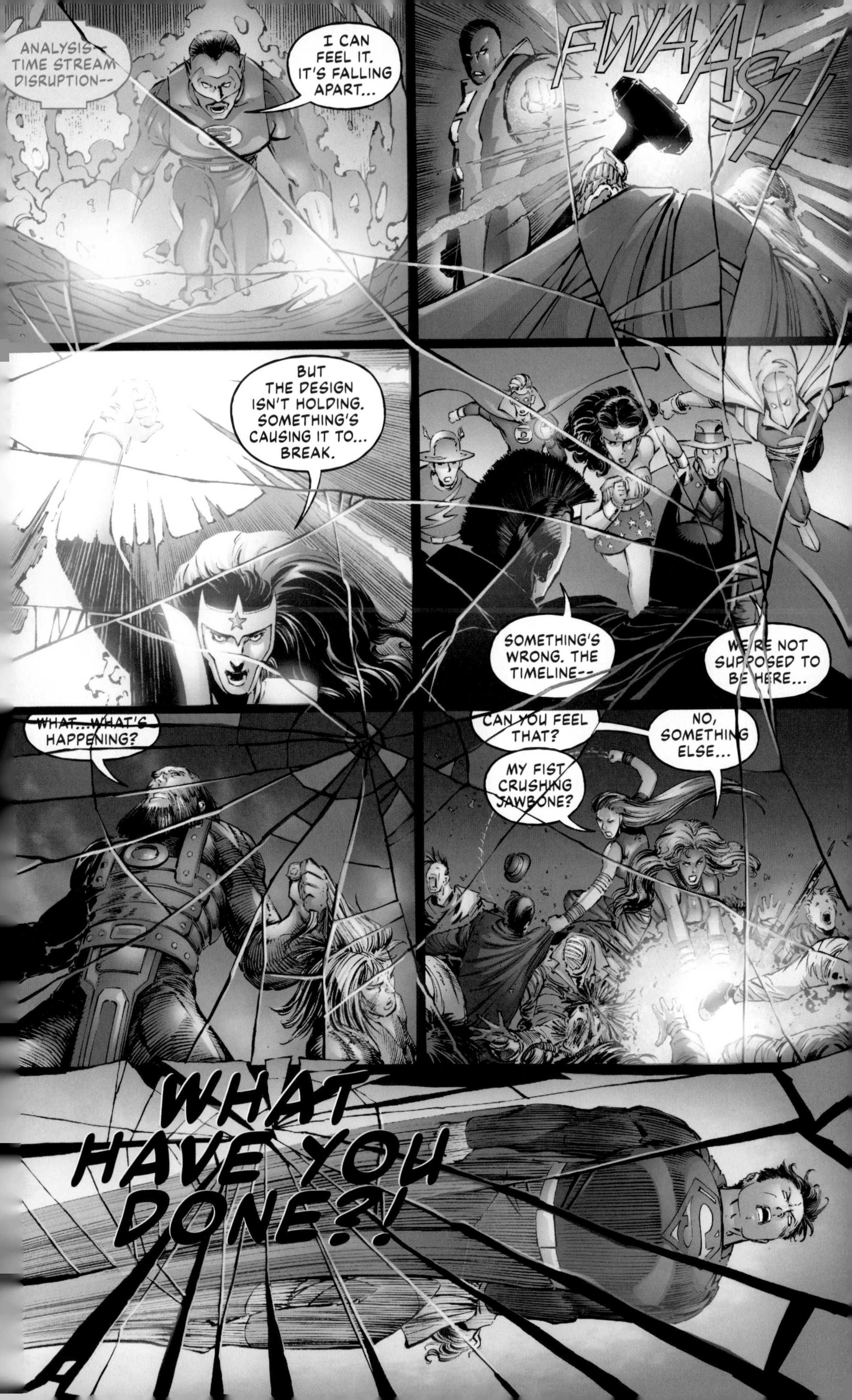
ANALYSIS-- TIME STREAM DISRUPTION--
I CAN FEEL IT. IT'S FALLING APART...
FWAAASH
BUT THE DESIGN ISN'T HOLDING. SOMETHING'S CAUSING IT TO... BREAK.
SOMETHING'S WRONG. THE TIMELINE--
WE'RE NOT SUPPOSED TO BE HERE...
WHAT...WHAT'S HAPPENING?
CAN YOU FEEL THAT?
MY FIST CRUSHING JAWBONE?
NO, SOMETHING ELSE...
WHAT HAVE YOU DONE?!

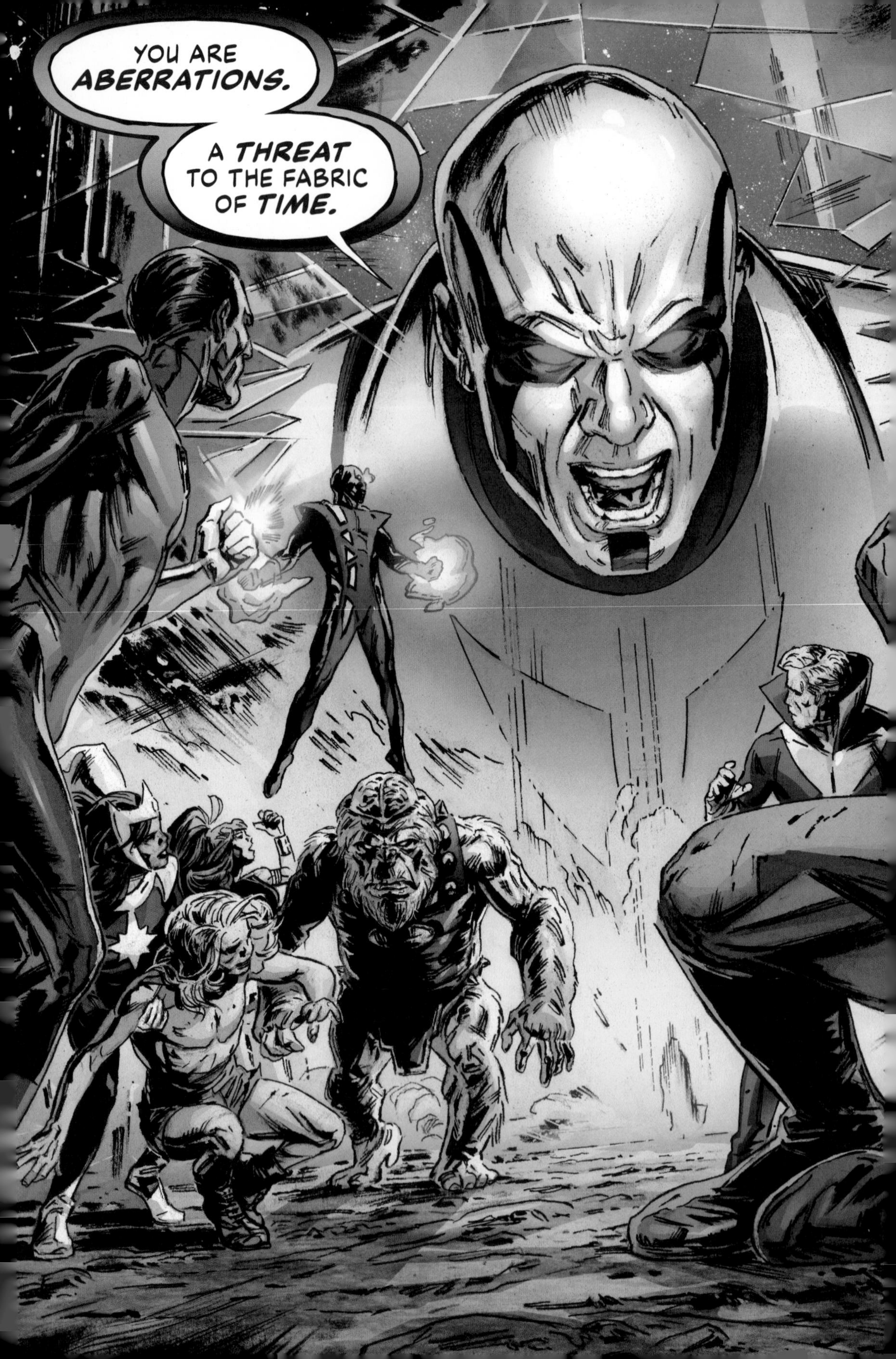
YOU ARE ABERRATIONS.
A THREAT TO THE FABRIC OF TIME.

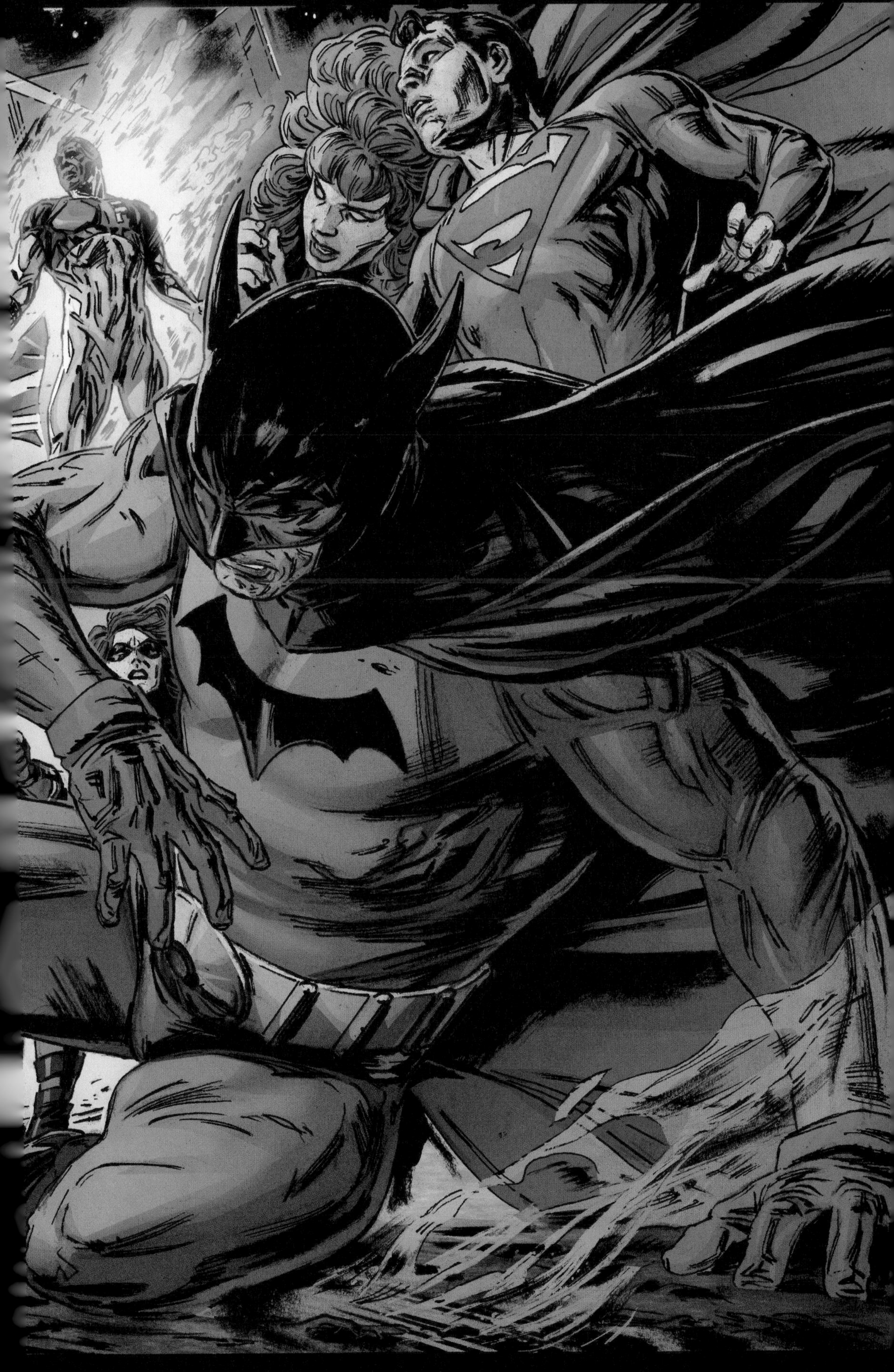

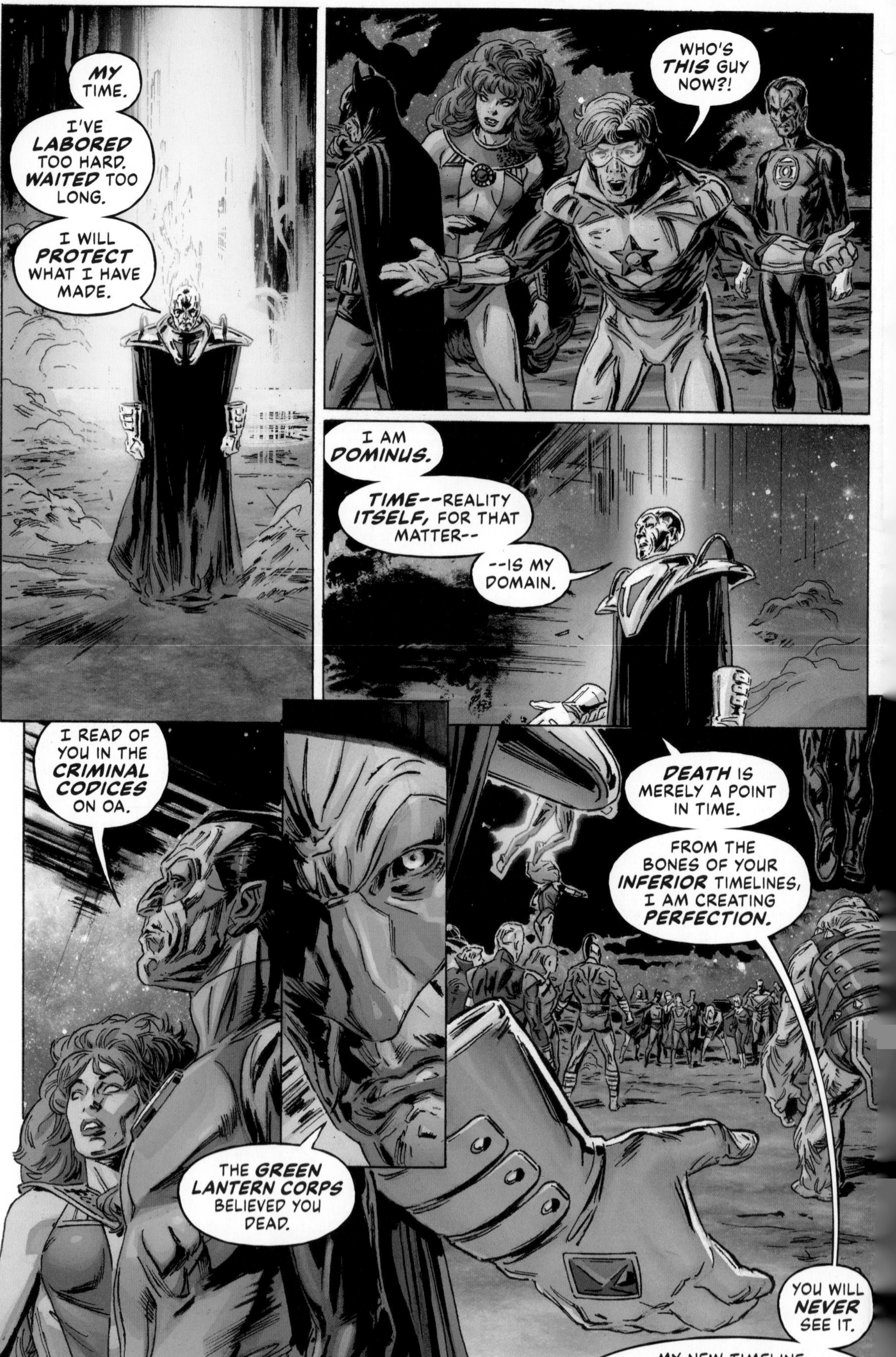
MY TIME.
I'VE LABORED TOO HARD. WAITED TOO LONG.
I WILL PROTECT WHAT I HAVE MADE.
WHO'S THIS GUY NOW?!
I AM DOMINUS.
TIME--REALITY ITSELF, FOR THAT MATTER--
--IS MY DOMAIN.
I READ OF YOU IN THE CRIMINAL CODICES ON OA.
THE GREEN LANTERN CORPS BELIEVED YOU DEAD.
DEATH IS MERELY A POINT IN TIME.
FROM THE BONES OF YOUR INFERIOR TIMELINES, I AM CREATING PERFECTION.
YOU WILL NEVER SEE IT.
MY NEW TIMELINE IS BEING SOLIDIFIED BY THE DESTRUCTION OF ALL OTHERS. LONG BEFORE THEN, YOU WILL BE GONE.

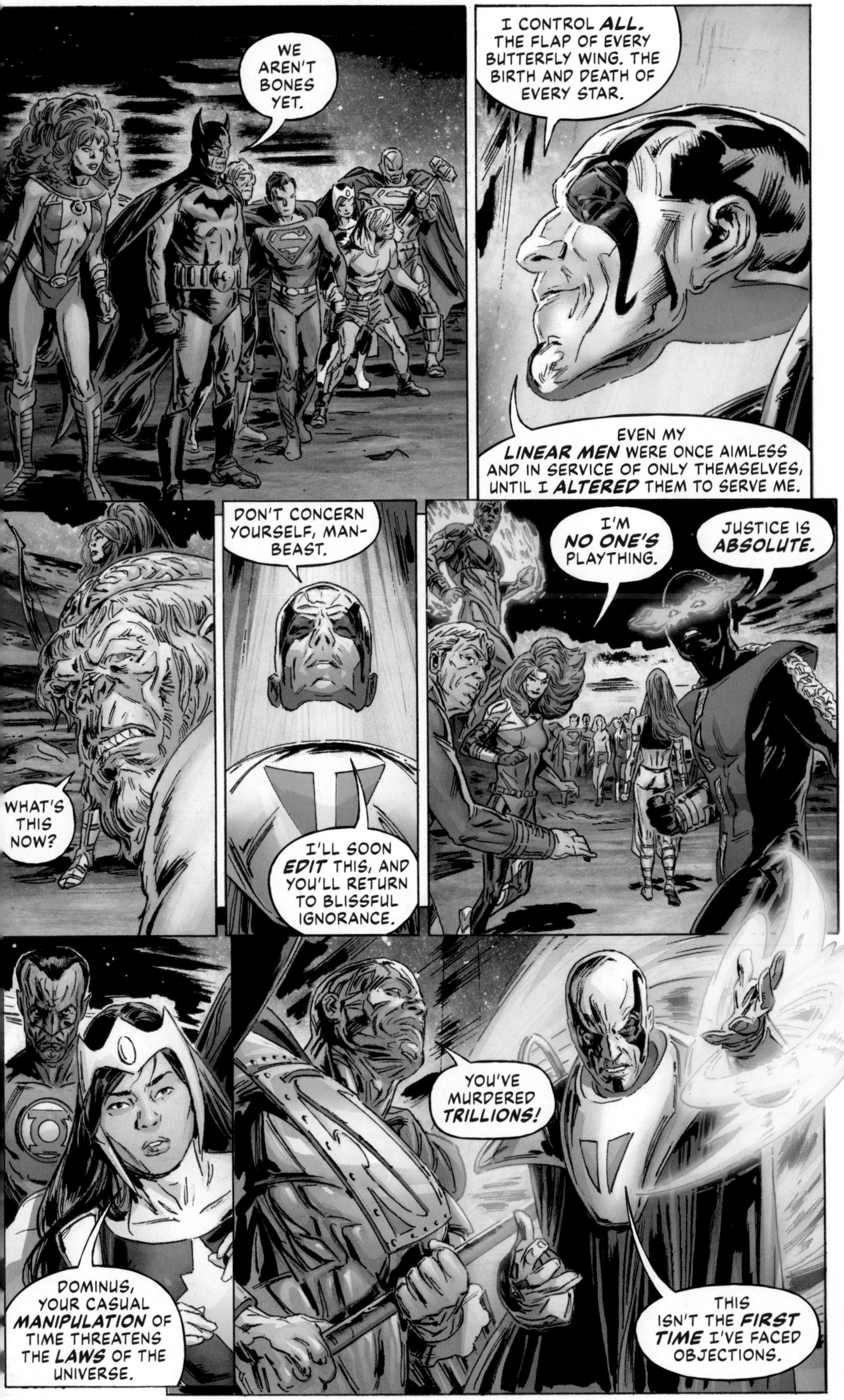

WE AREN'T BONES YET.
I CONTROL ALL. THE FLAP OF EVERY BUTTERFLY WING. THE BIRTH AND DEATH OF EVERY STAR.
EVEN MY LINEAR MEN WERE ONCE AIMLESS AND IN SERVICE OF ONLY THEMSELVES, UNTIL I ALTERED THEM TO SERVE ME.
WHAT'S THIS NOW?
DON'T CONCERN YOURSELF, MAN-BEAST.
I'LL SOON EDIT THIS, AND YOU'LL RETURN TO BLISSFUL IGNORANCE.
I'M NO ONE'S PLAYTHING.
JUSTICE IS ABSOLUTE.
DOMINUS, YOUR CASUAL MANIPULATION OF TIME THREATENS THE LAWS OF THE UNIVERSE.
YOU'VE MURDERED TRILLIONS!
THIS ISN'T THE FIRST TIME I'VE FACED OBJECTIONS.

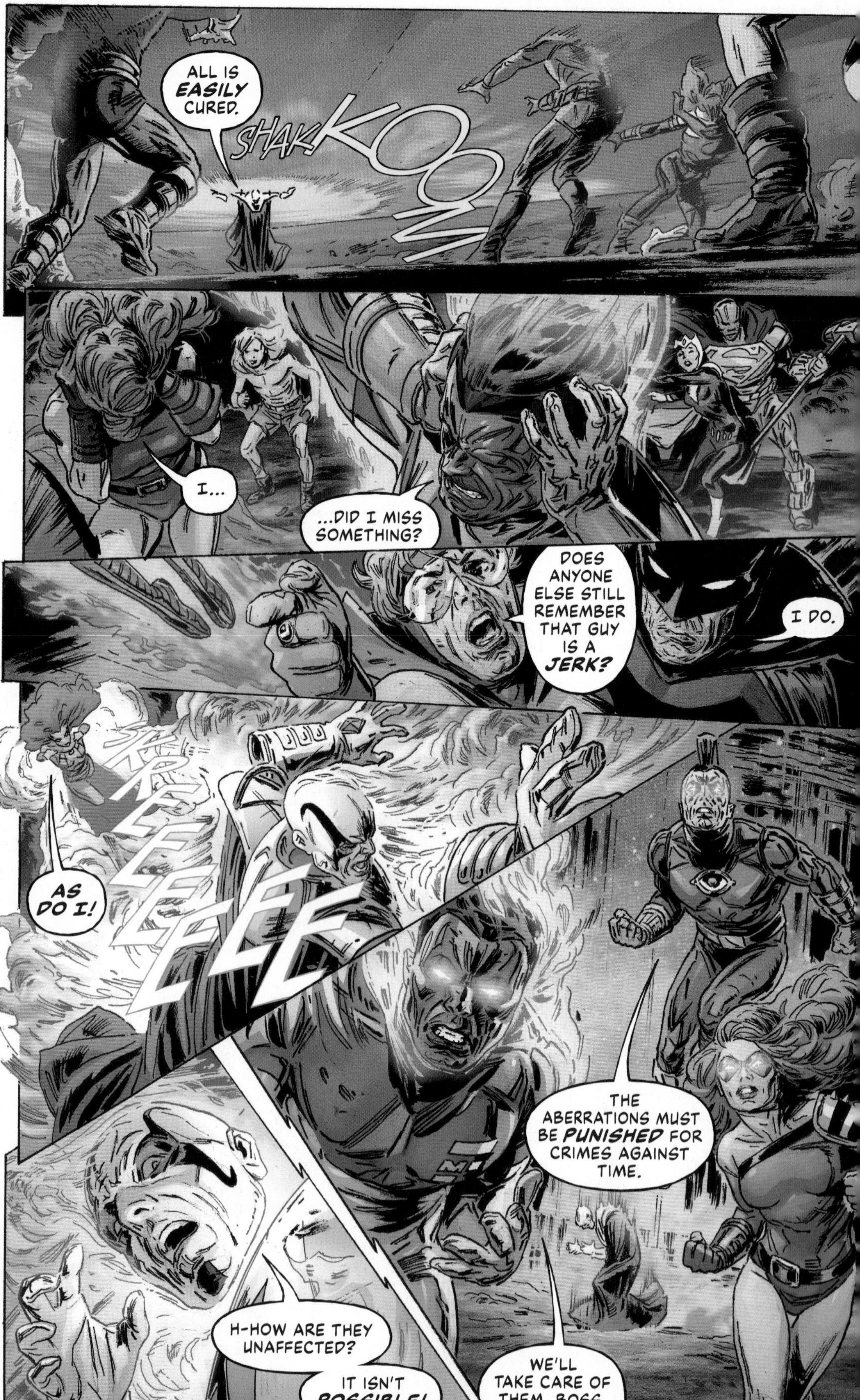
ALL IS EASILY CURED.
SHAKKOOM!
I...
...DID I MISS SOMETHING?
DOES ANYONE ELSE STILL REMEMBER THAT GUY IS A JERK?
I DO.
AS DO I!
SKREEEEEEE
THE ABERRATIONS MUST BE PUNISHED FOR CRIMES AGAINST TIME.
H-HOW ARE THEY UNAFFECTED?
IT ISN'T POSSIBLE!
WE'LL TAKE CARE OF THEM, BOSS.

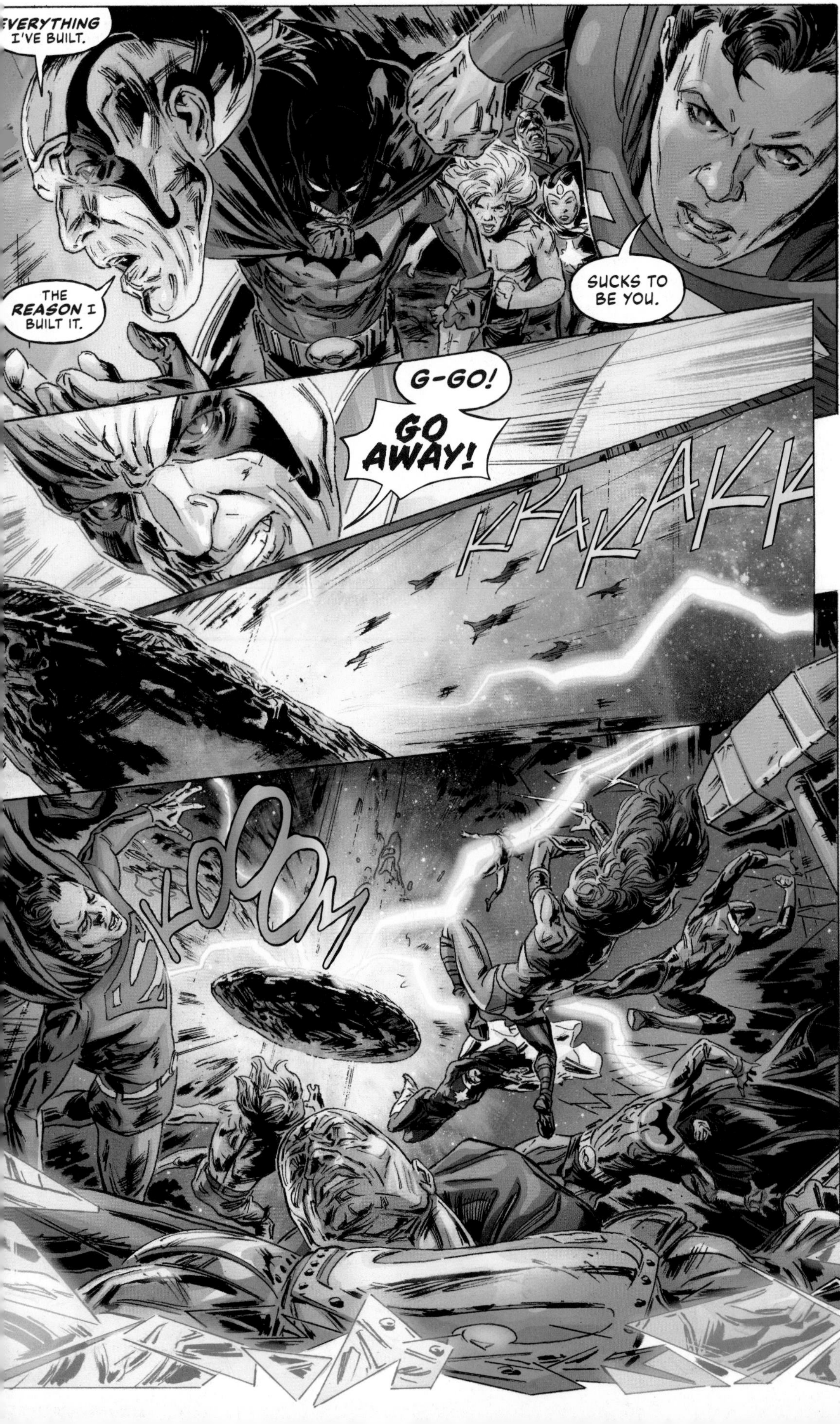

EVERYTHING I'VE BUILT.
THE REASON I BUILT IT.
SUCKS TO BE YOU.
G-GO!
GO AWAY!
KRAKAKK
KOOOM

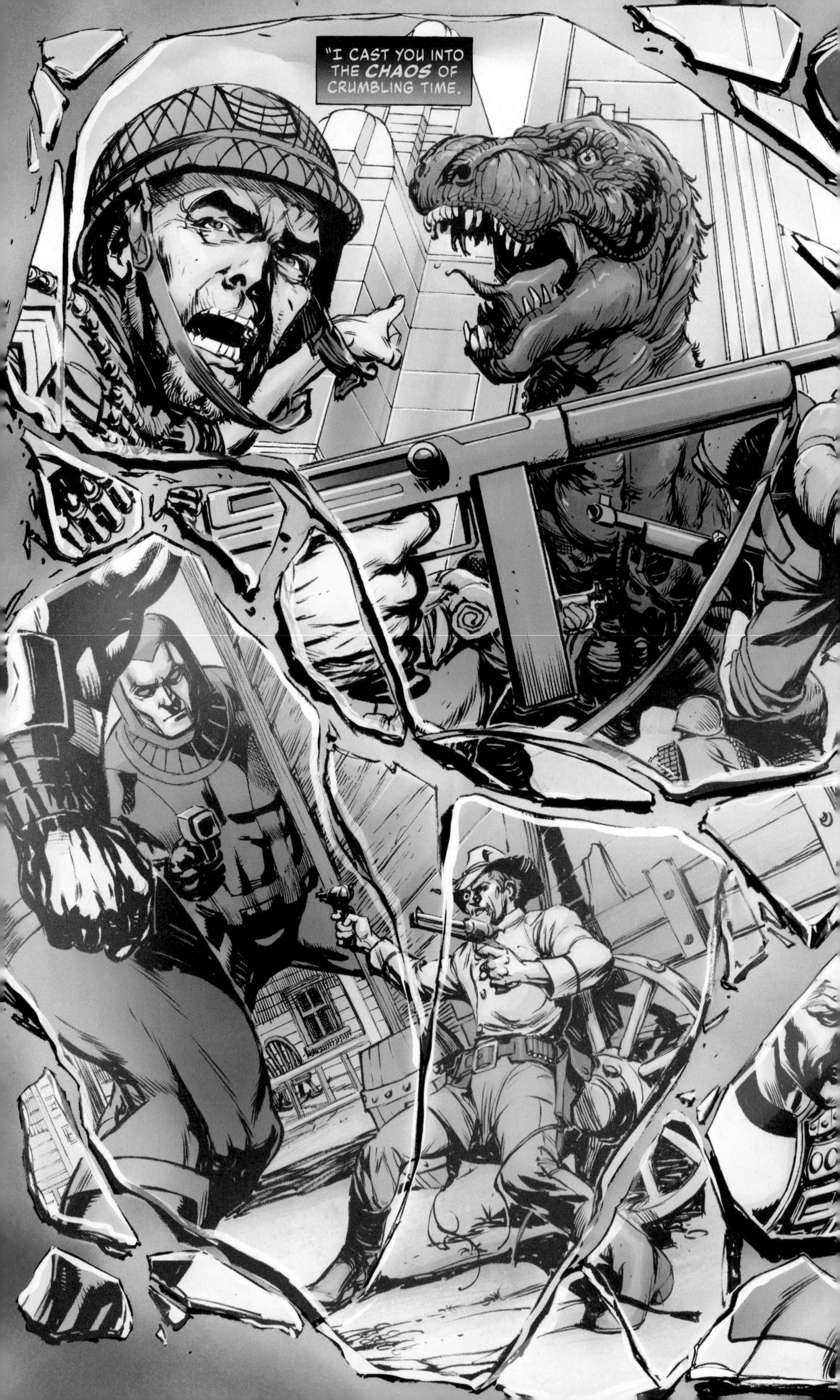
"I CAST YOU INTO THE CHAOS OF CRUMBLING TIME.

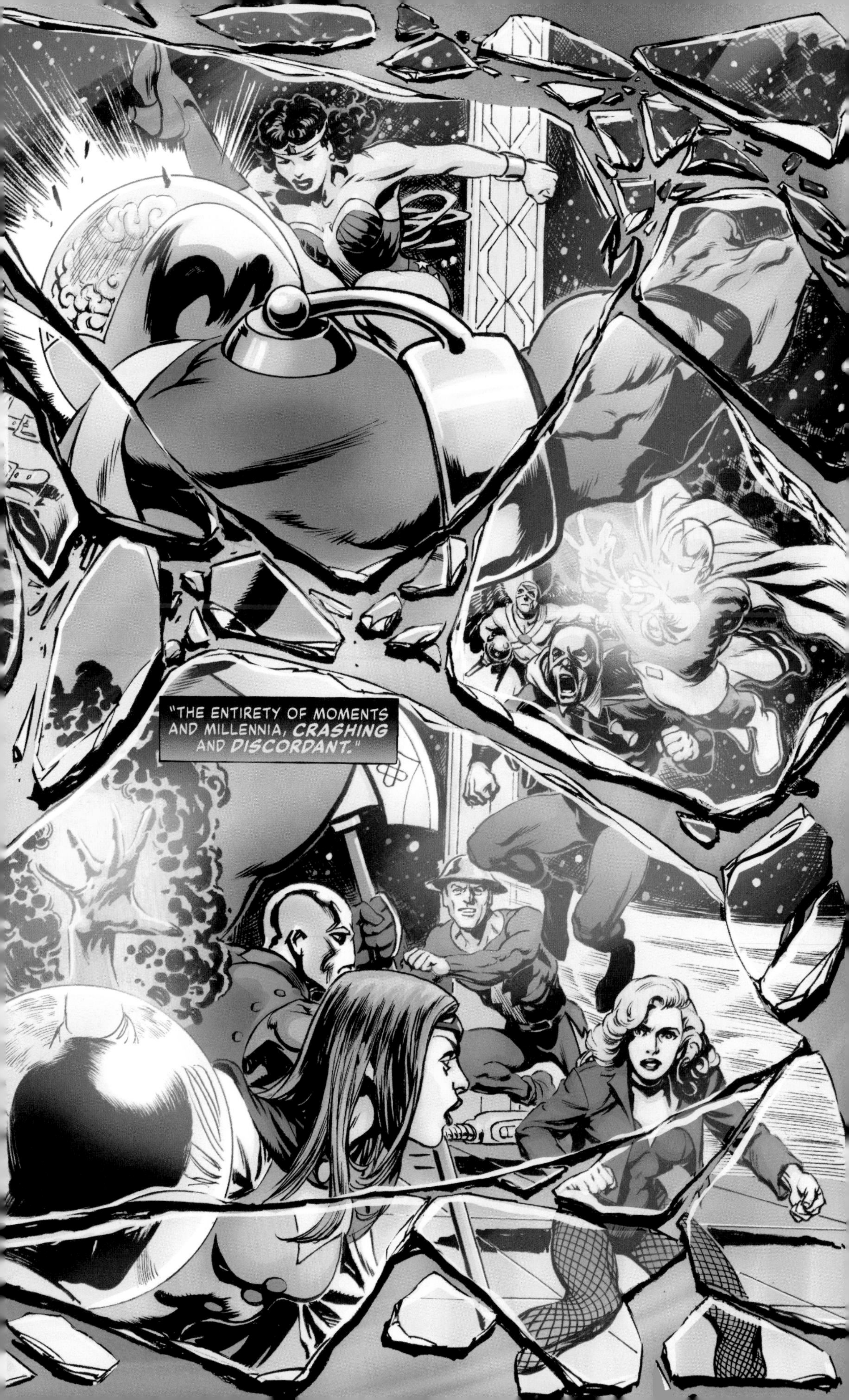
"THE ENTIRETY OF MOMENTS AND MILLENNIA, *CRASHING* AND *DISCORDANT.*"

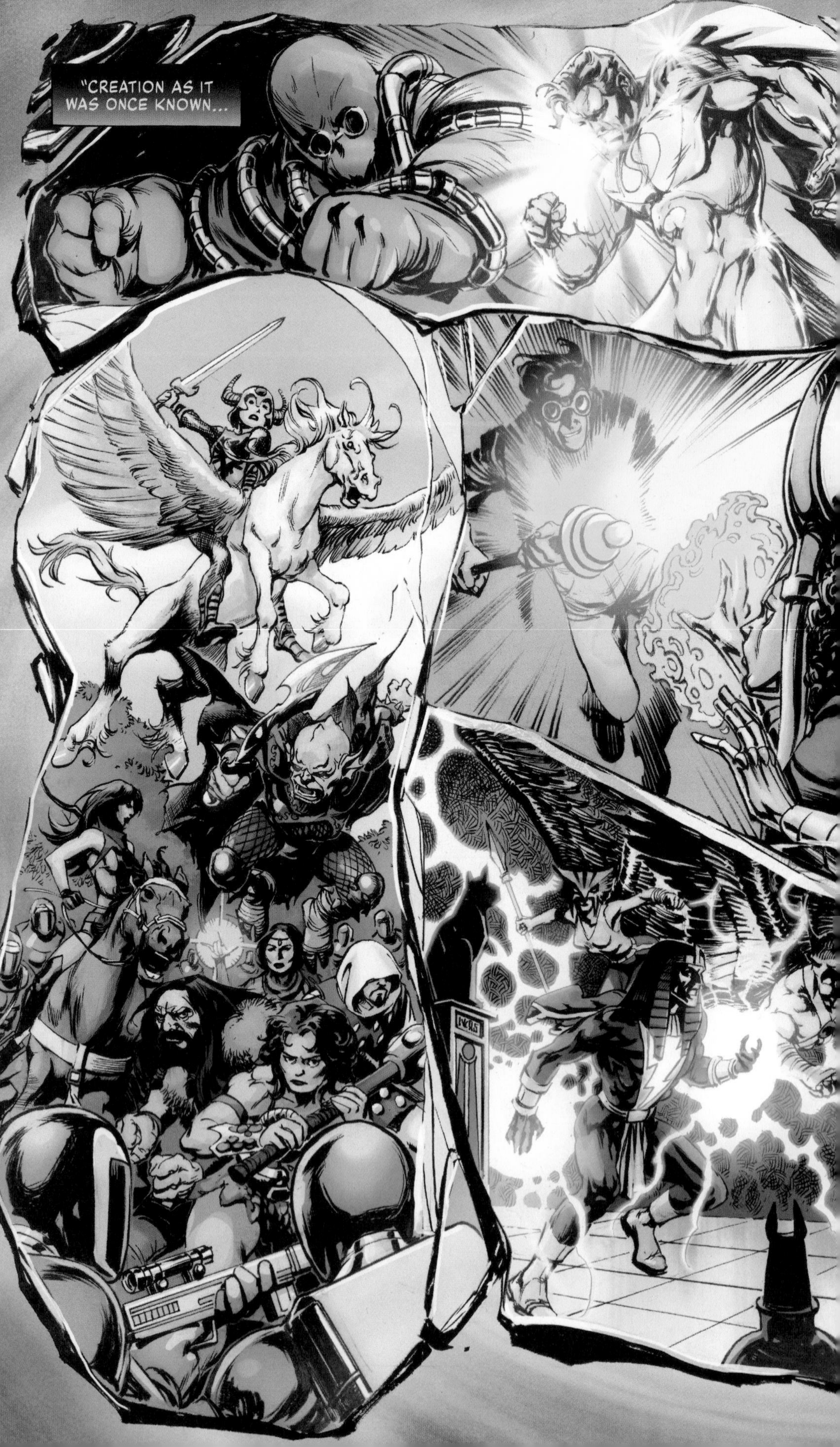
"CREATION AS IT WAS ONCE KNOWN...

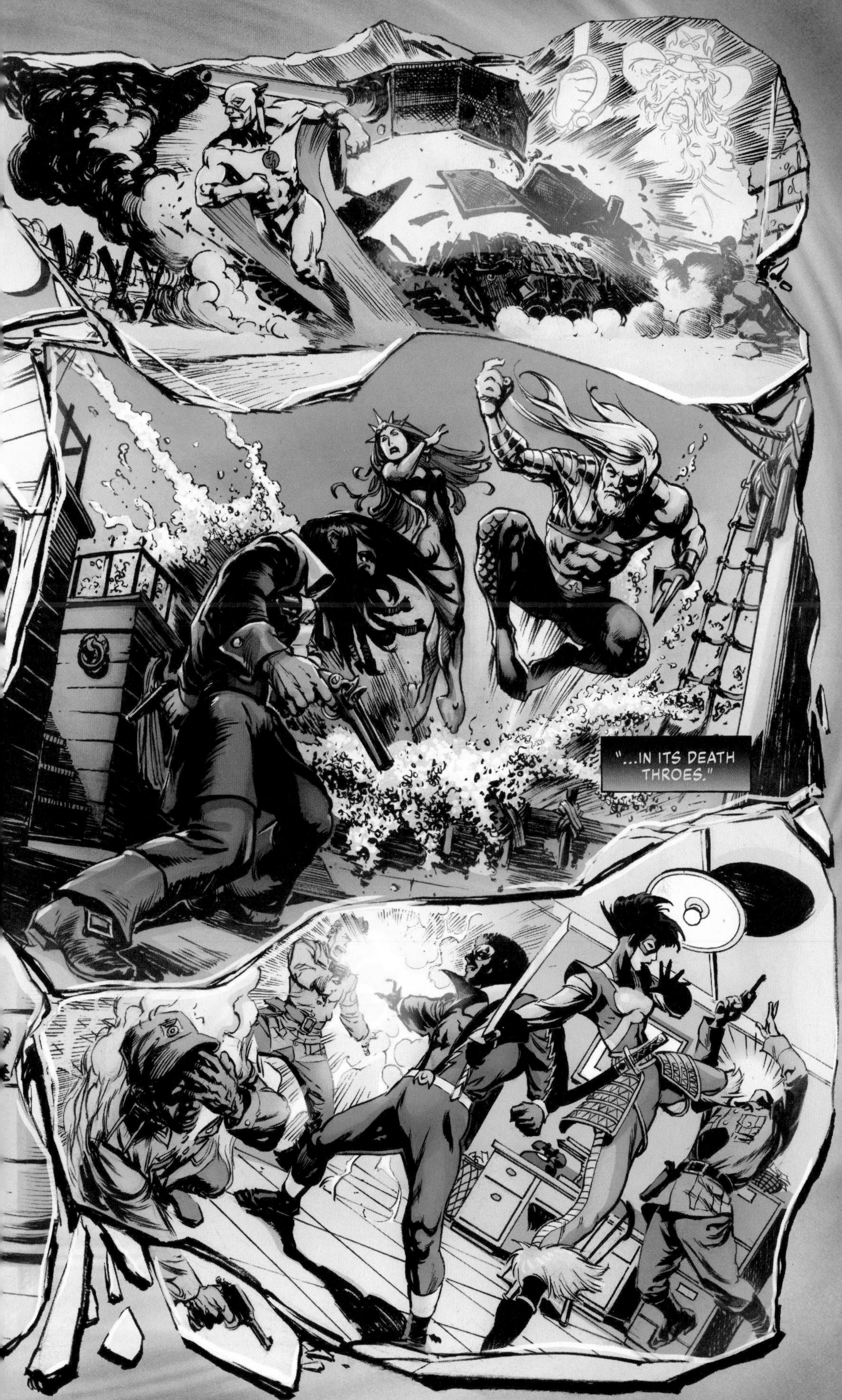
"...IN ITS DEATH THROES."

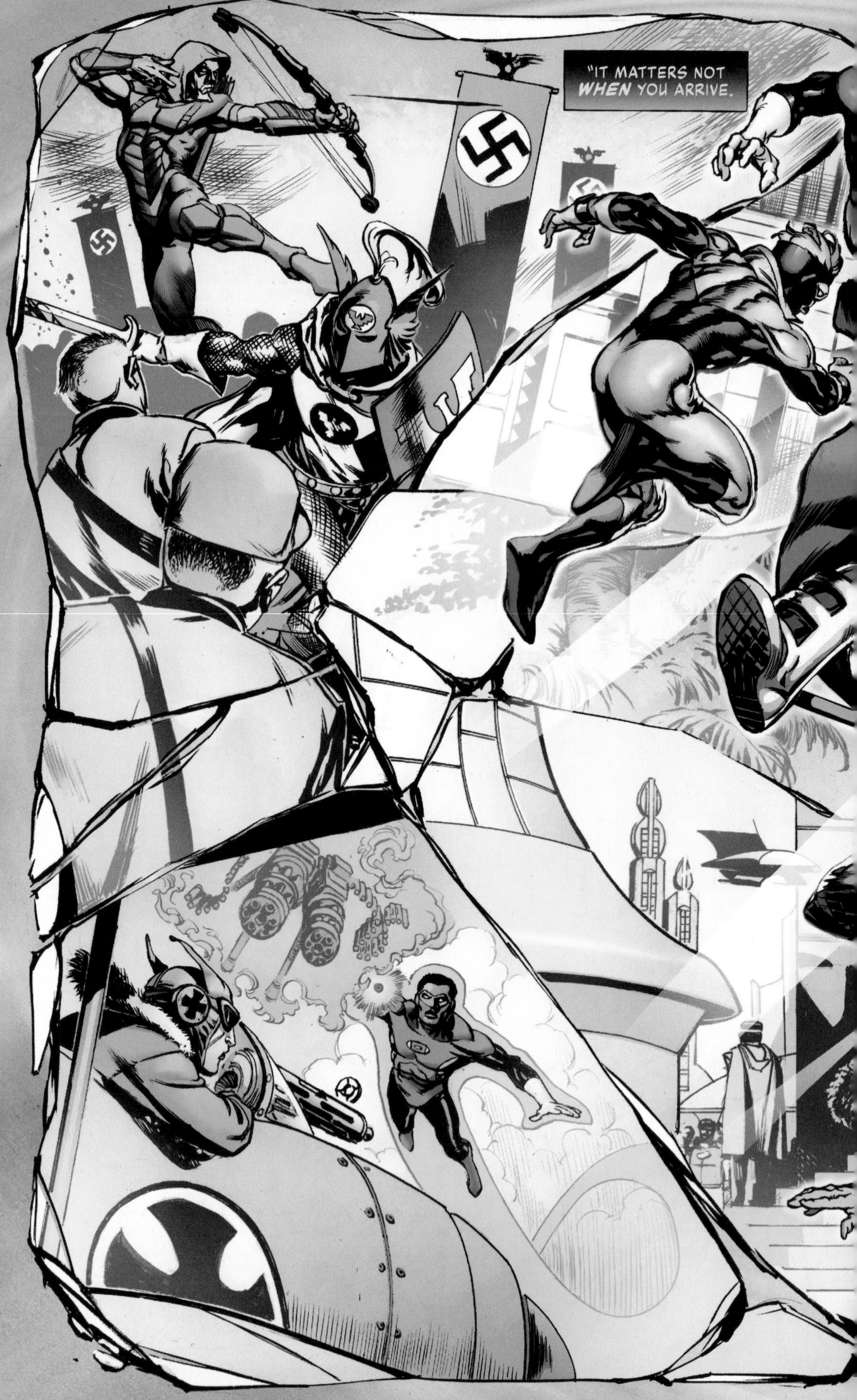
"IT MATTERS NOT
WHEN YOU ARRIVE.

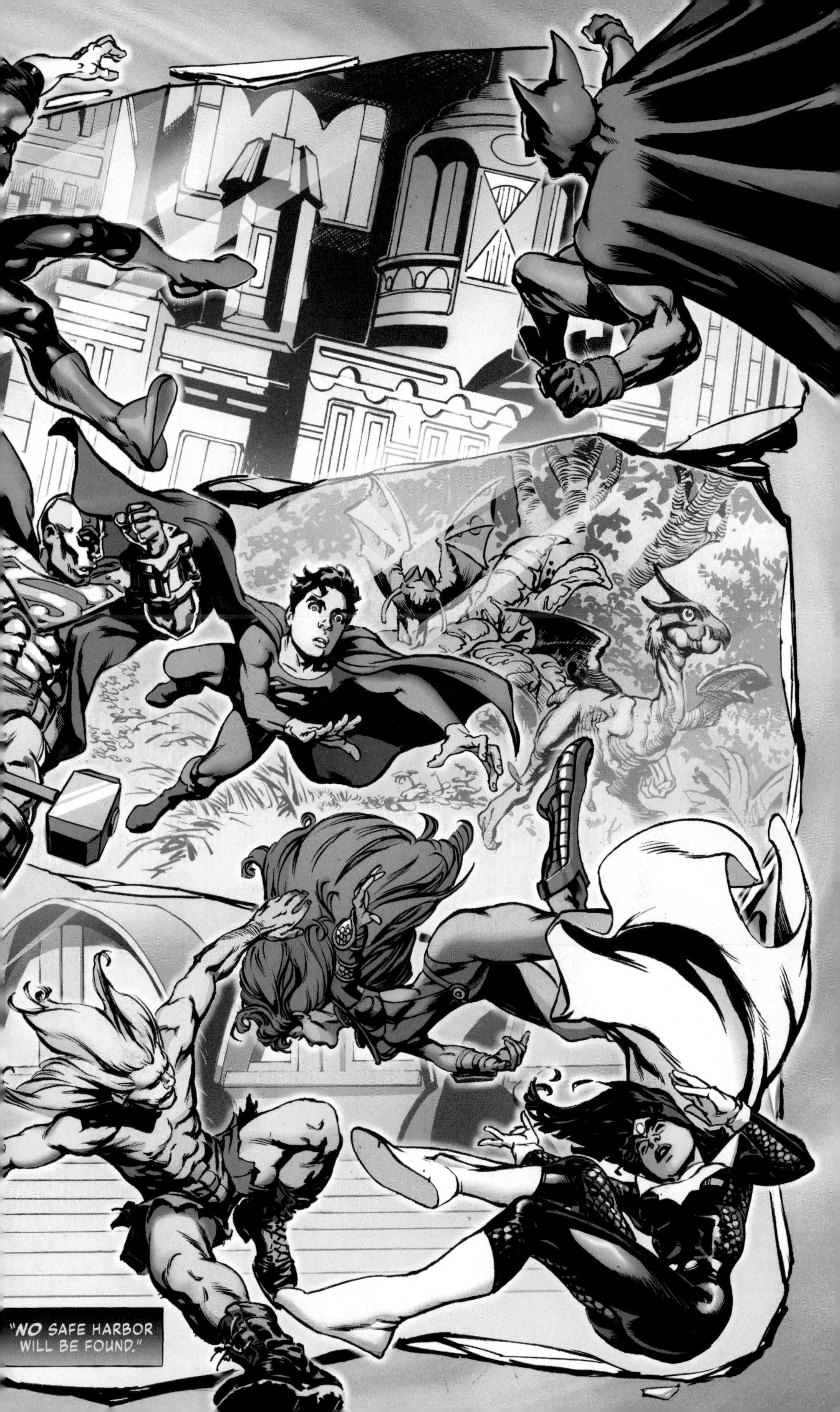
"NO SAFE HARBOR WILL BE FOUND."

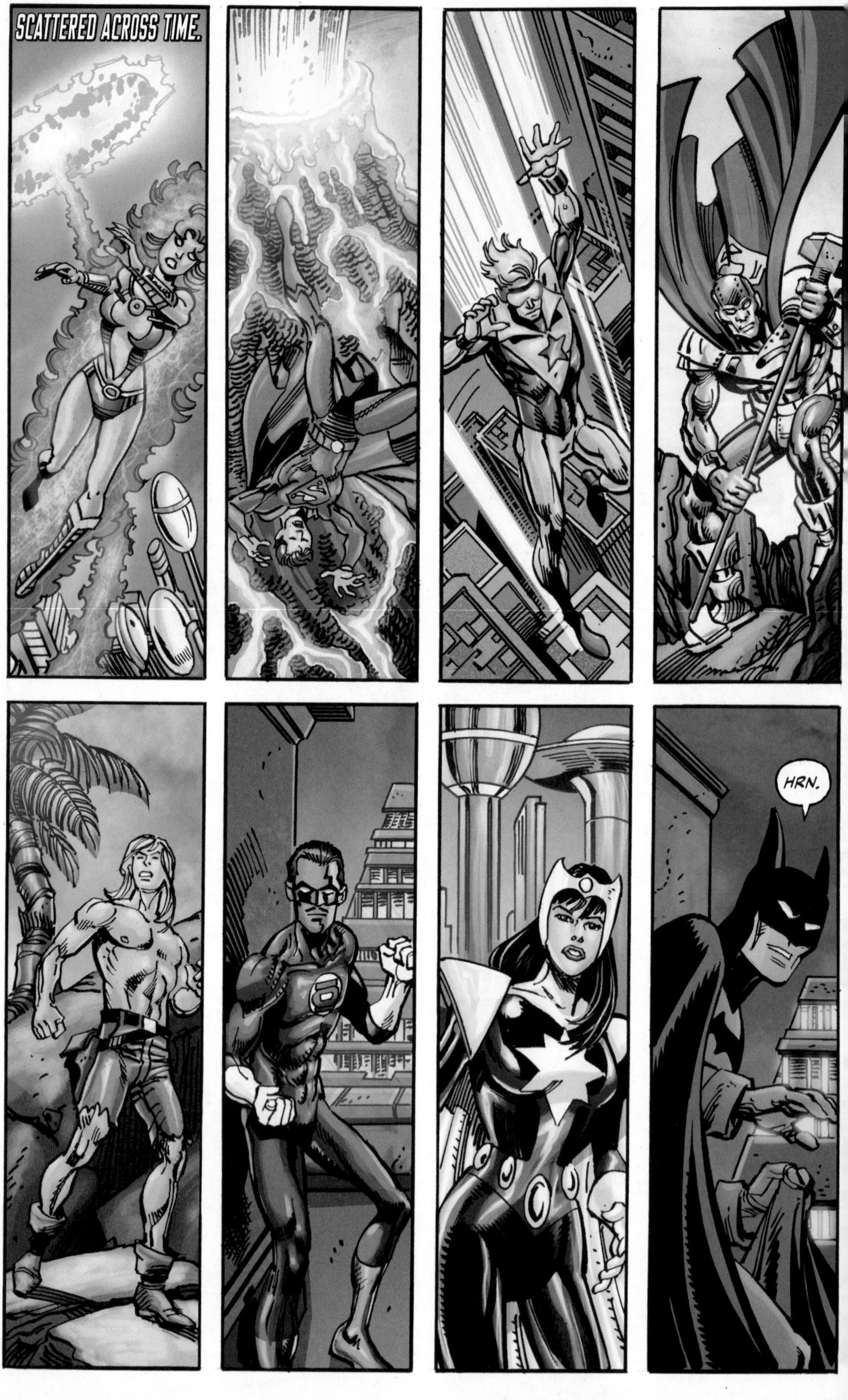
SCATTERED ACROSS TIME.
HRN.

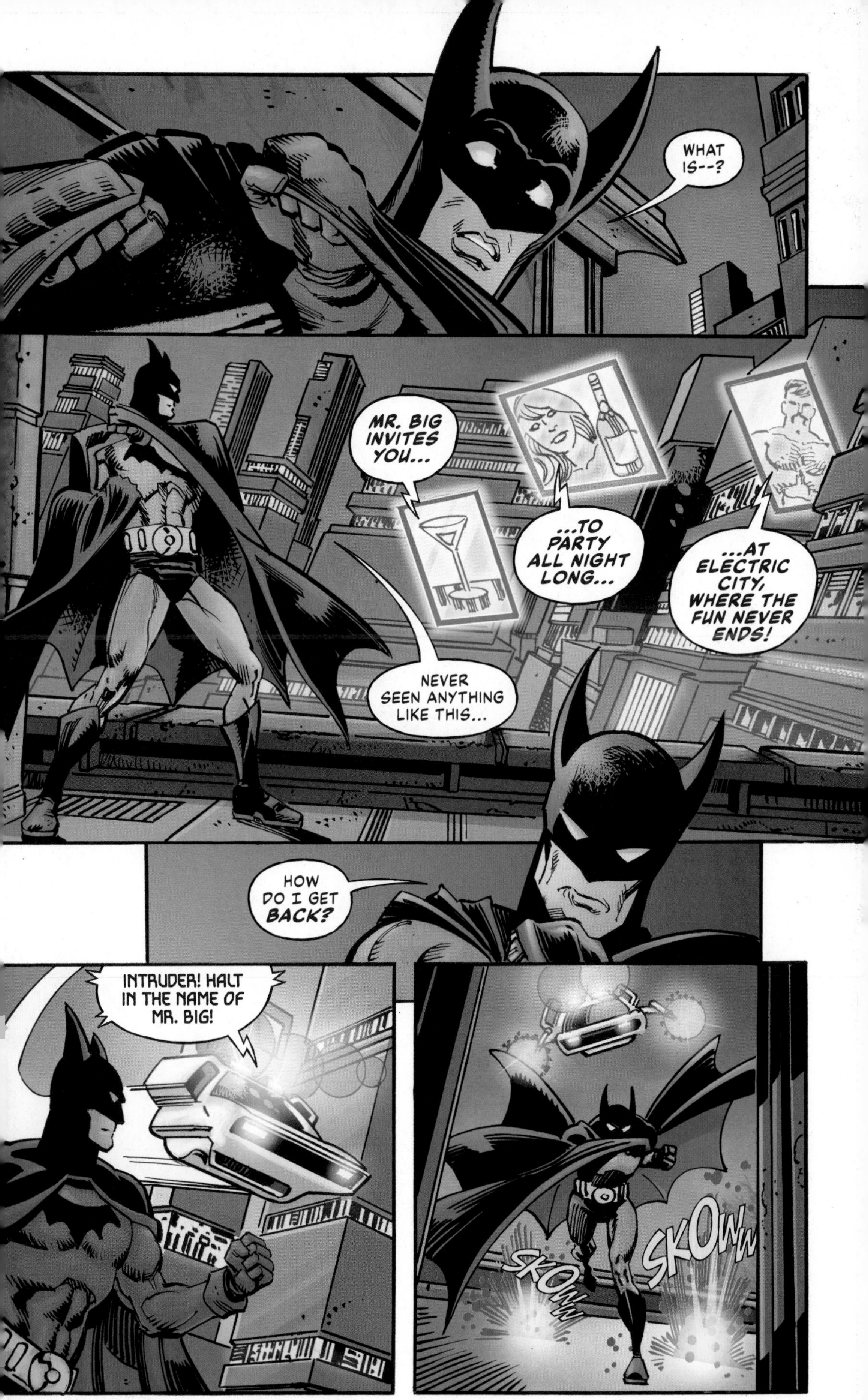
WHAT IS--?
MR. BIG INVITES YOU...
...TO PARTY ALL NIGHT LONG...
...AT ELECTRIC CITY, WHERE THE FUN NEVER ENDS!
NEVER SEEN ANYTHING LIKE THIS...
HOW DO I GET BACK?
INTRUDER! HALT IN THE NAME OF MR. BIG!
SKOWW
SKOWW

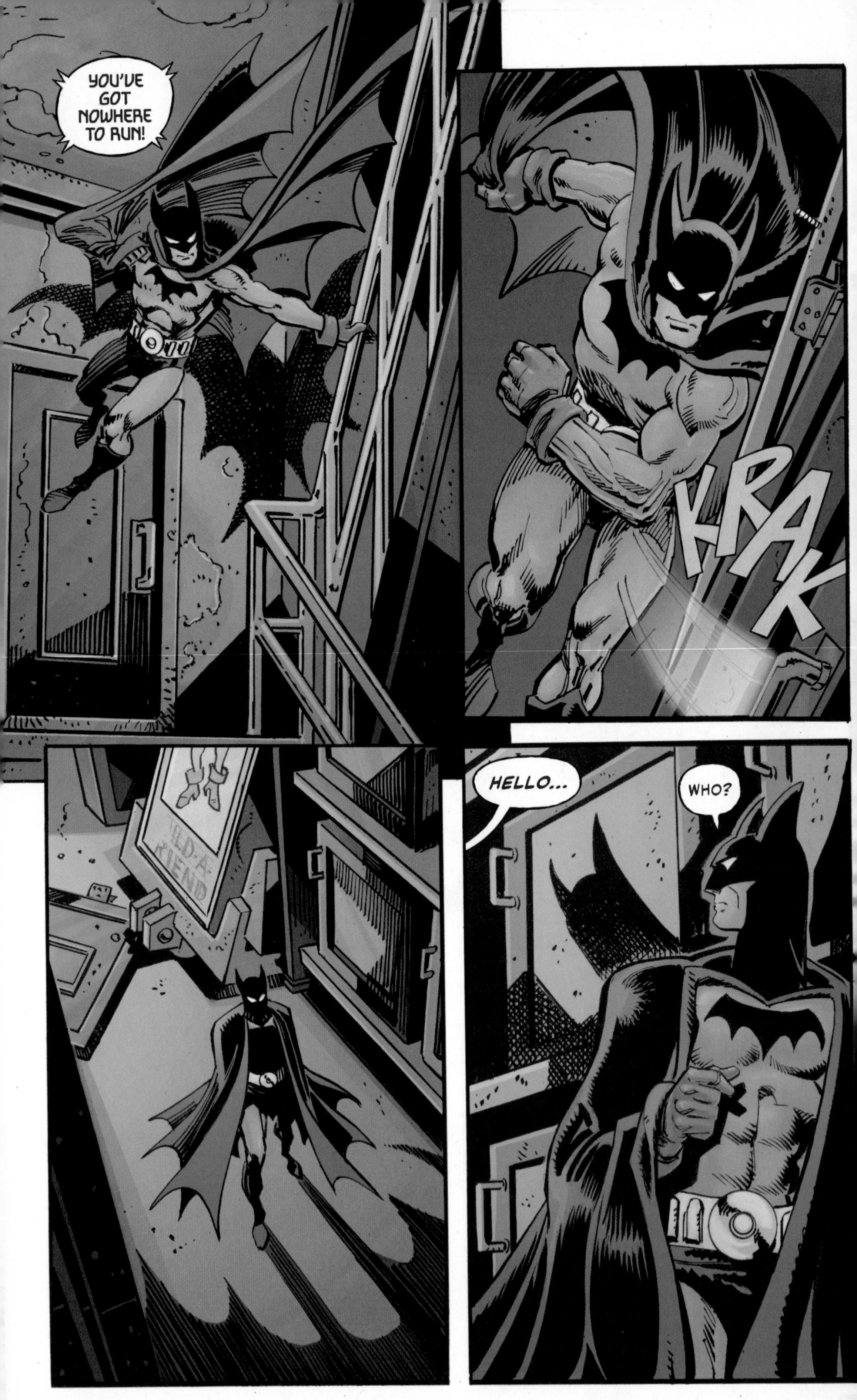
YOU'VE GOT NOWHERE TO RUN!
KRAK
HELLO...
WHO?

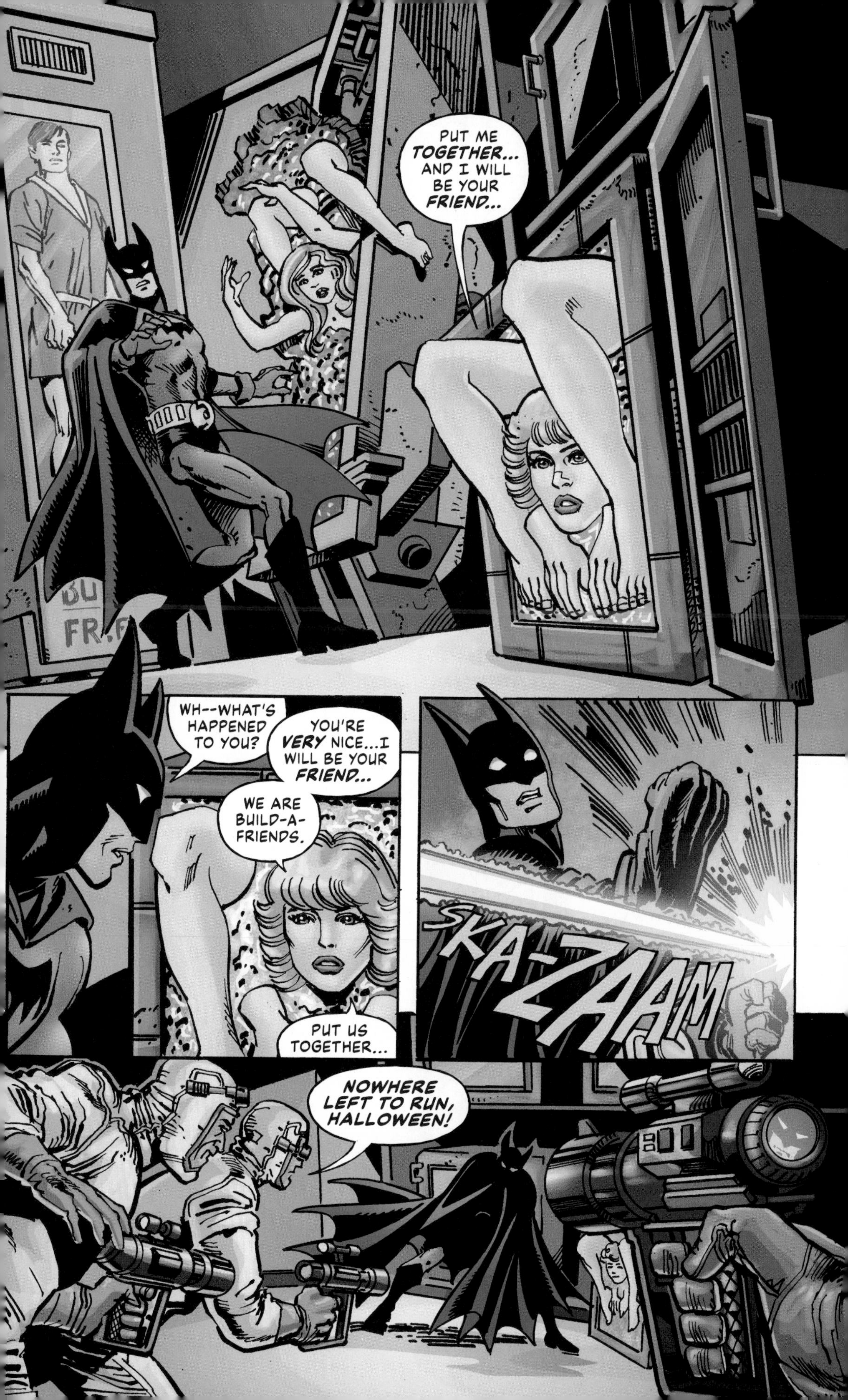
PUT ME TOGETHER... AND I WILL BE YOUR FRIEND...
WH--WHAT'S HAPPENED TO YOU?
YOU'RE VERY NICE...I WILL BE YOUR FRIEND...
WE ARE BUILD-A-FRIENDS.
PUT US TOGETHER...
SKA-ZAAM
NOWHERE LEFT TO RUN, HALLOWEEN!

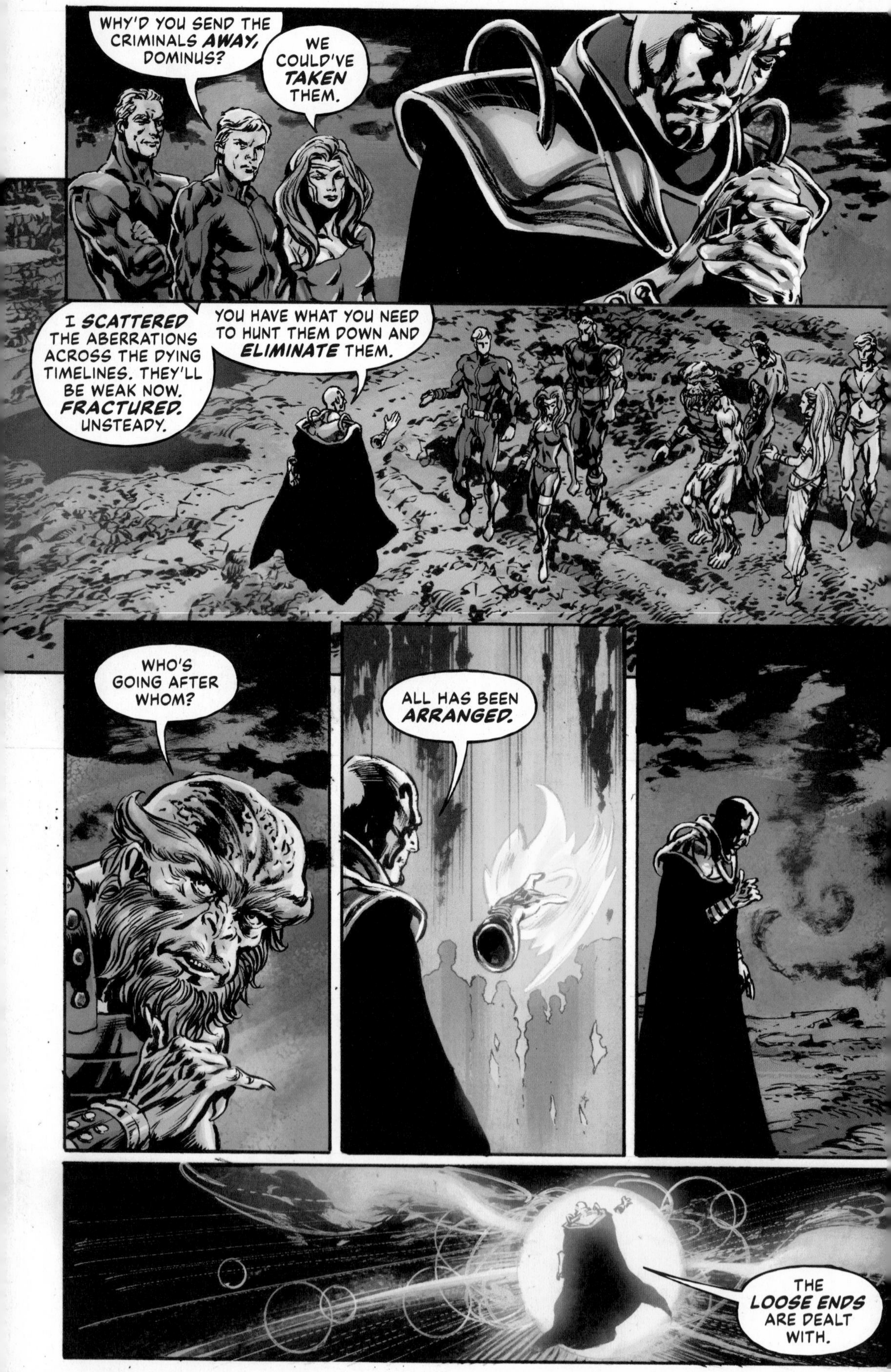

WHY'D YOU SEND THE CRIMINALS AWAY, DOMINUS?
WE COULD'VE TAKEN THEM.
I SCATTERED THE ABERRATIONS ACROSS THE DYING TIMELINES. THEY'LL BE WEAK NOW. FRACTURED. UNSTEADY.
YOU HAVE WHAT YOU NEED TO HUNT THEM DOWN AND ELIMINATE THEM.
WHO'S GOING AFTER WHOM?
ALL HAS BEEN ARRANGED.
THE LOOSE ENDS ARE DEALT WITH.

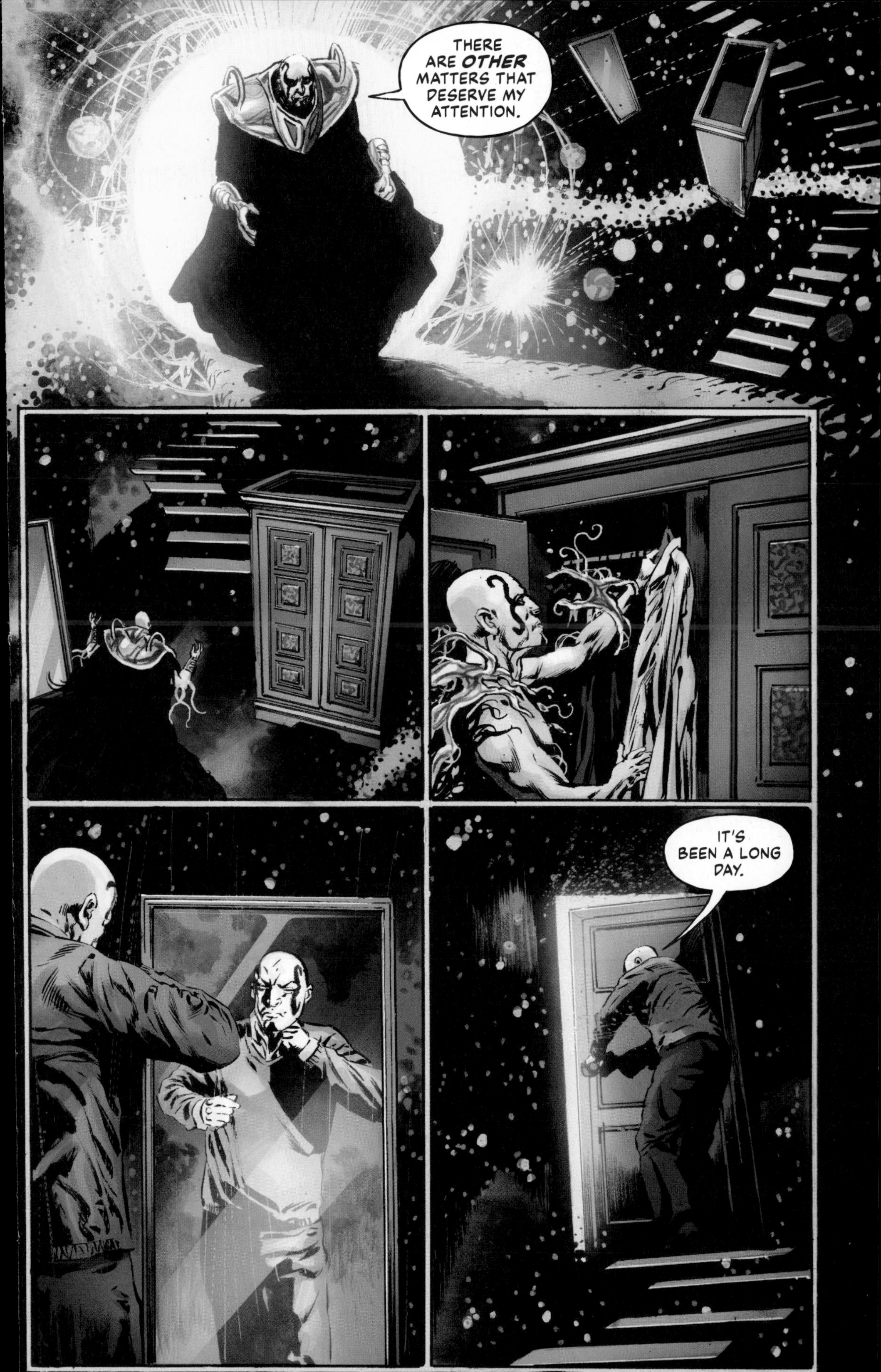
THERE ARE *OTHER* MATTERS THAT DESERVE MY ATTENTION.
IT'S BEEN A LONG DAY.

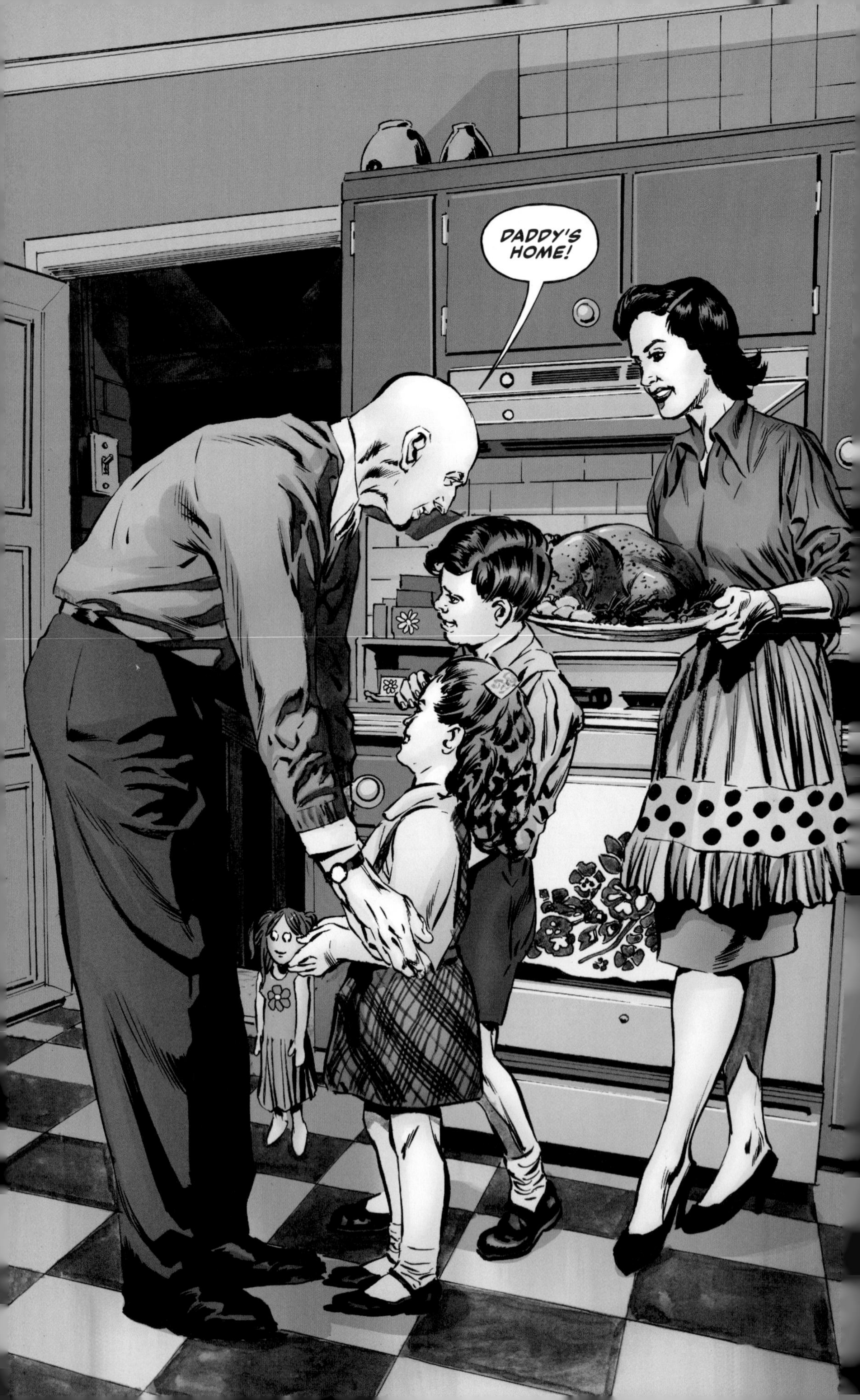
DADDY'S HOME!

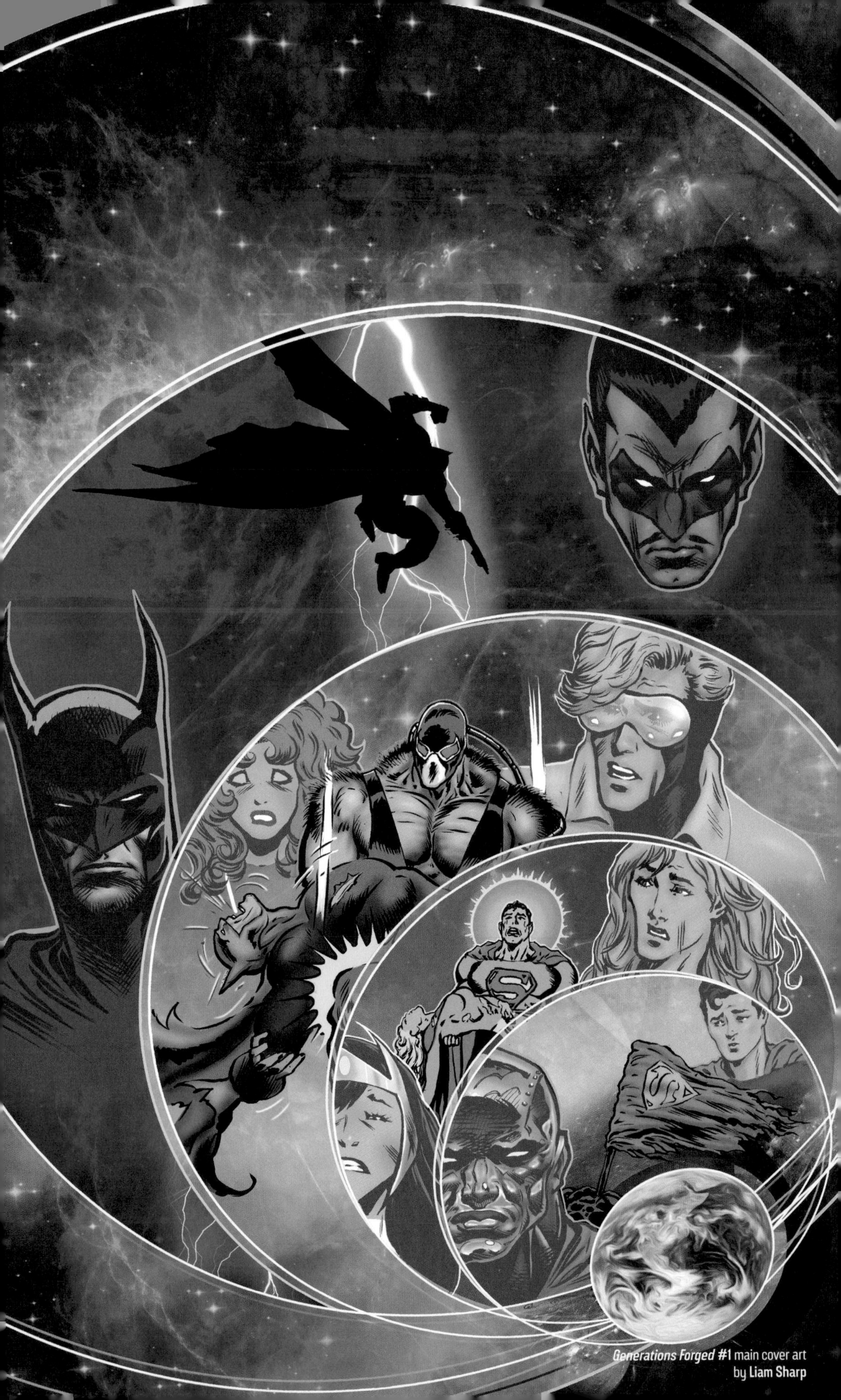

Generations Forged #1 main cover art
by Liam Sharp

CONTENTS:
GENERATIONS FORGED ARTISTS

MIKE PERKINS .... PAGES 101-104, 121, 158-159

MARCO SANTUCCI .... PAGES 105-110, 132-134, 137-138

PAUL PELLETIER & NORM RAPMUND .... PAGES 111-120, 140-145

BERNARD CHANG .... PAGES 122-129, 146-153

JOE PRADO .... PAGES 130-131, 135-136, 139

COLLEEN DORAN .... PAGES 154-157

BRYAN HITCH .... PAGES 160-174

DAN JURGENS & KEVIN NOWLAN .... PAGES 175-180

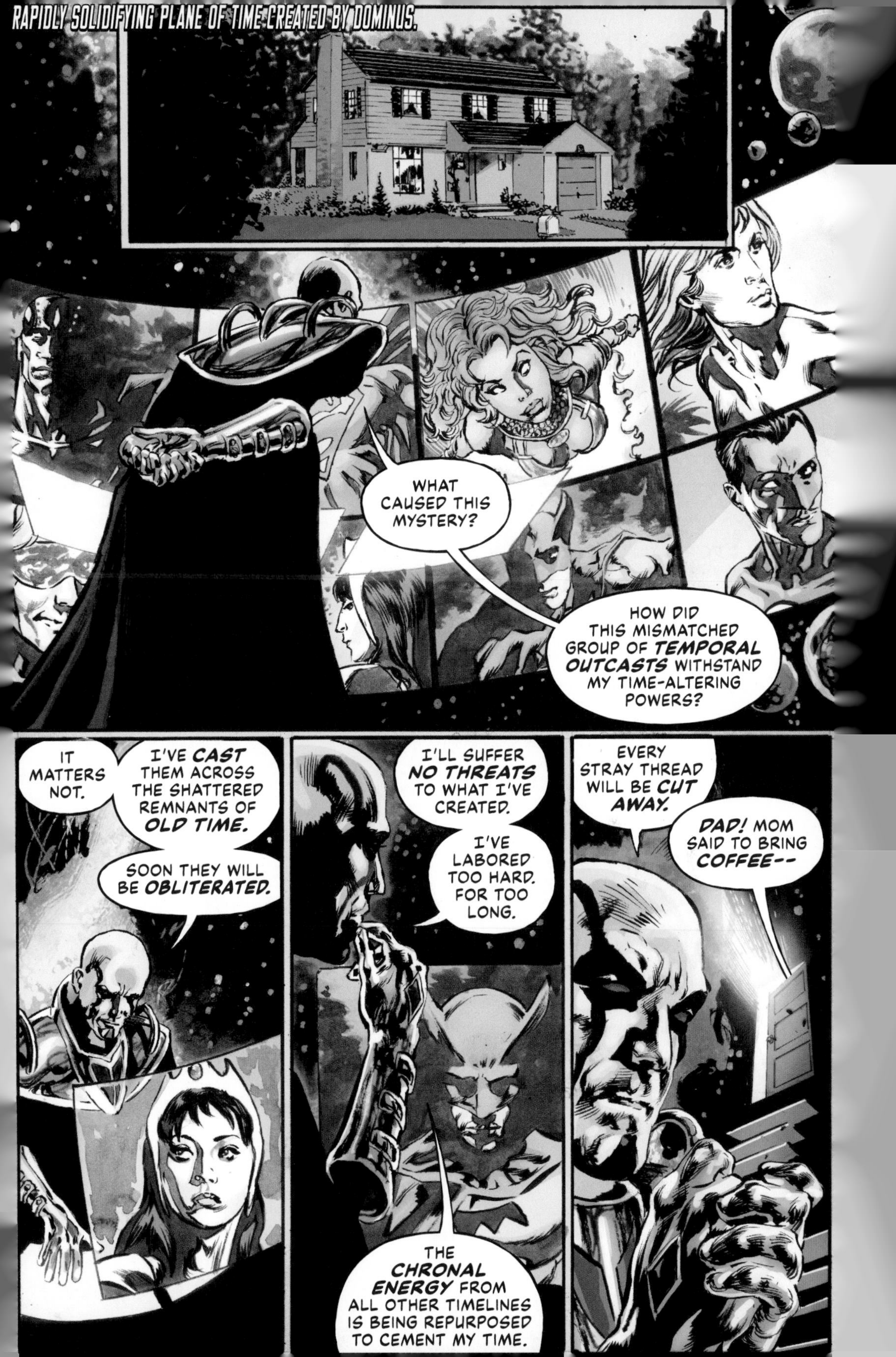
RAPIDLY SOLIDIFYING PLANE OF TIME CREATED BY DOMINUS.
WHAT CAUSED THIS MYSTERY?
HOW DID THIS MISMATCHED GROUP OF TEMPORAL OUTCASTS WITHSTAND MY TIME-ALTERING POWERS?
IT MATTERS NOT.
I'VE CAST THEM ACROSS THE SHATTERED REMNANTS OF OLD TIME.
SOON THEY WILL BE OBLITERATED.
I'LL SUFFER NO THREATS TO WHAT I'VE CREATED.
I'VE LABORED TOO HARD. FOR TOO LONG.
THE CHRONAL ENERGY FROM ALL OTHER TIMELINES IS BEING REPURPOSED TO CEMENT MY TIME.
EVERY STRAY THREAD WILL BE CUT AWAY.
DAD! MOM SAID TO BRING COFFEE--

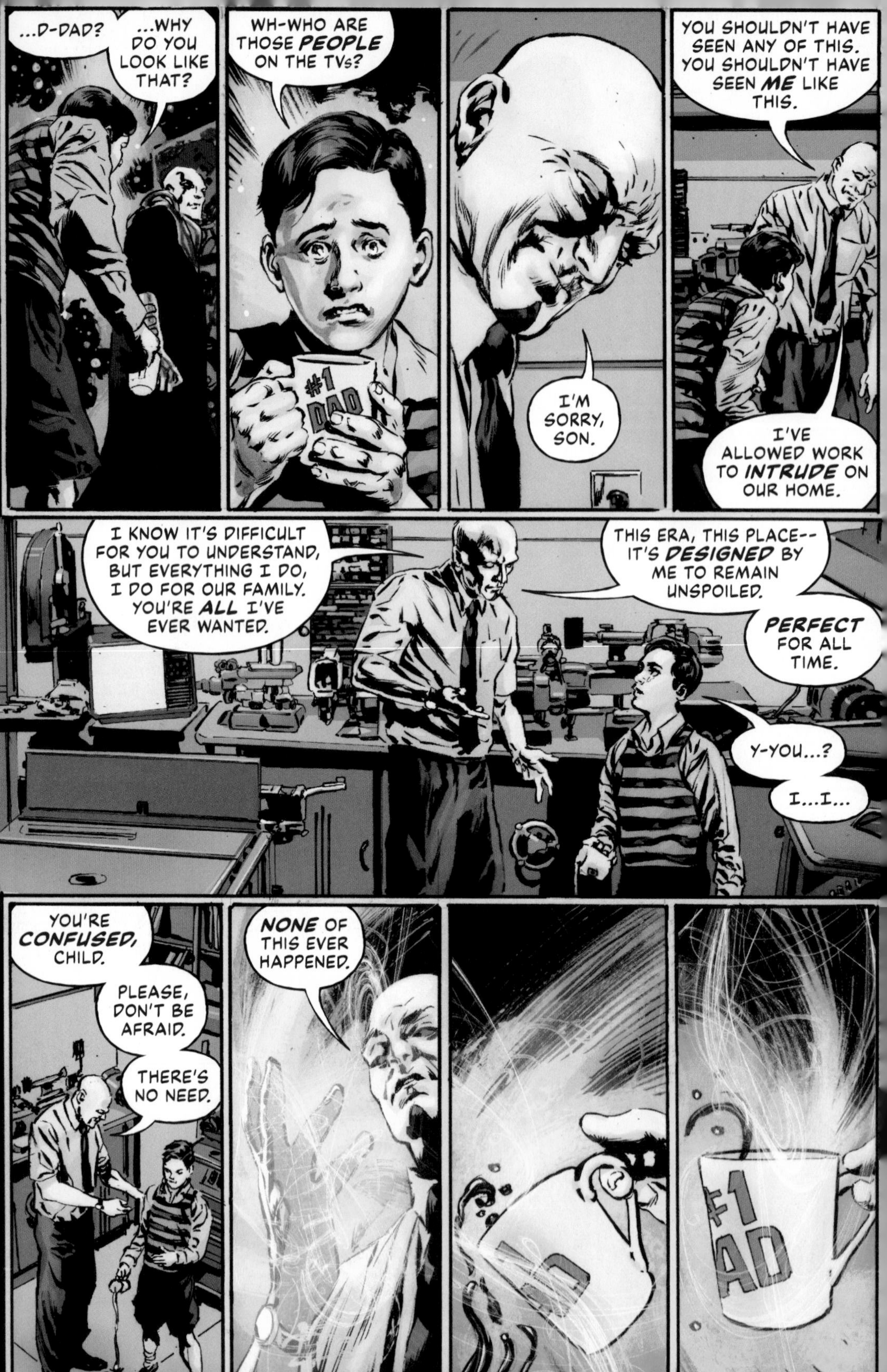
...D-DAD?
...WHY DO YOU LOOK LIKE THAT?
WH-WHO ARE THOSE PEOPLE ON THE TVs?
#1 DAD
I'M SORRY, SON.
YOU SHOULDN'T HAVE SEEN ANY OF THIS. YOU SHOULDN'T HAVE SEEN ME LIKE THIS.
I'VE ALLOWED WORK TO INTRUDE ON OUR HOME.
I KNOW IT'S DIFFICULT FOR YOU TO UNDERSTAND, BUT EVERYTHING I DO, I DO FOR OUR FAMILY. YOU'RE ALL I'VE EVER WANTED.
THIS ERA, THIS PLACE--IT'S DESIGNED BY ME TO REMAIN UNSPOILED.
PERFECT FOR ALL TIME.
Y-YOU...?
I...I...
YOU'RE CONFUSED, CHILD.
PLEASE, DON'T BE AFRAID.
THERE'S NO NEED.
SP LT
NONE OF THIS EVER HAPPENED.

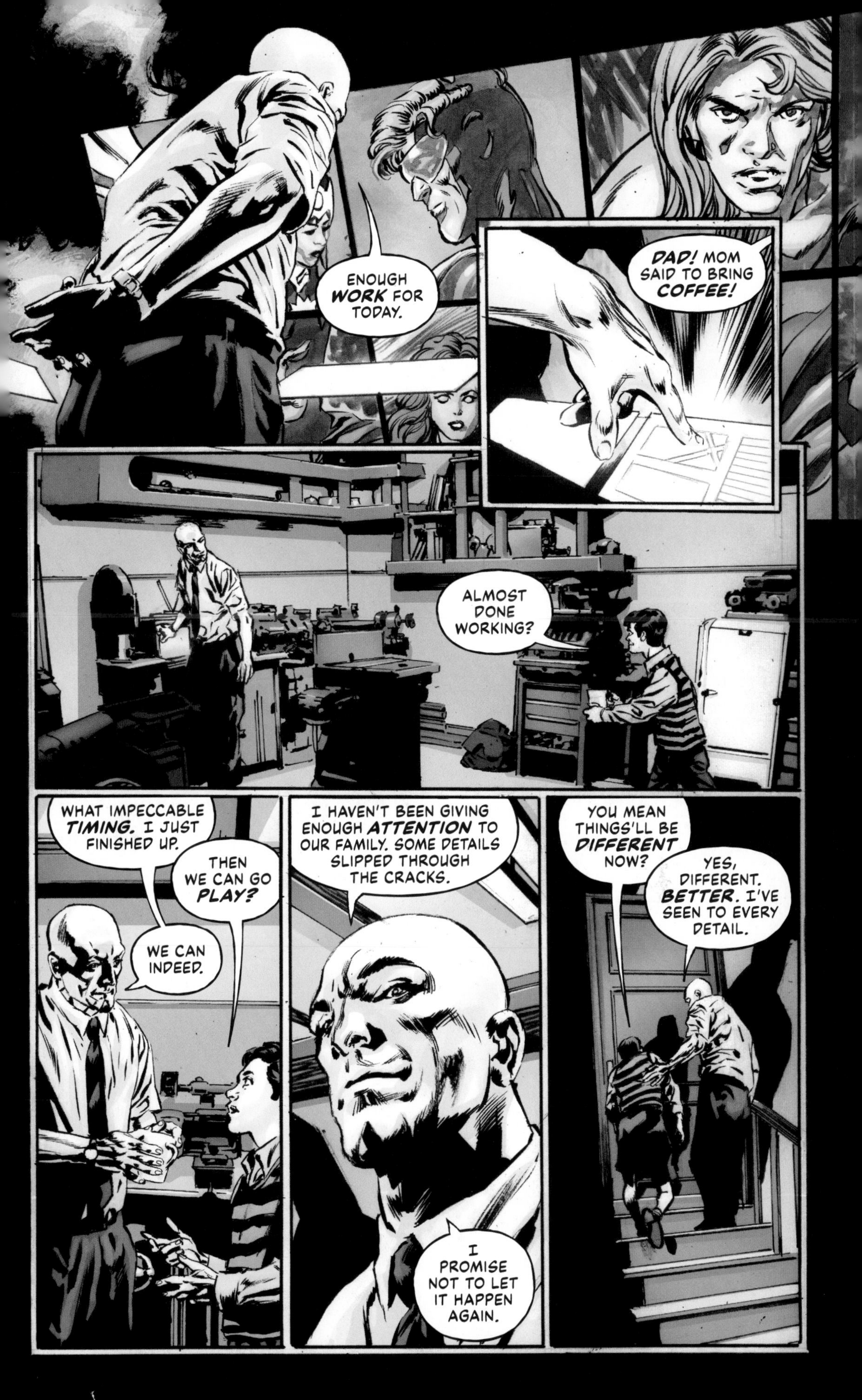
ENOUGH WORK FOR TODAY.
DAD! MOM SAID TO BRING COFFEE!
ALMOST DONE WORKING?
WHAT IMPECCABLE TIMING. I JUST FINISHED UP.
THEN WE CAN GO PLAY?
WE CAN INDEED.
I HAVEN'T BEEN GIVING ENOUGH ATTENTION TO OUR FAMILY. SOME DETAILS SLIPPED THROUGH THE CRACKS.
I PROMISE NOT TO LET IT HAPPEN AGAIN.
YOU MEAN THINGS'LL BE DIFFERENT NOW?
YES, DIFFERENT. BETTER. I'VE SEEN TO EVERY DETAIL.

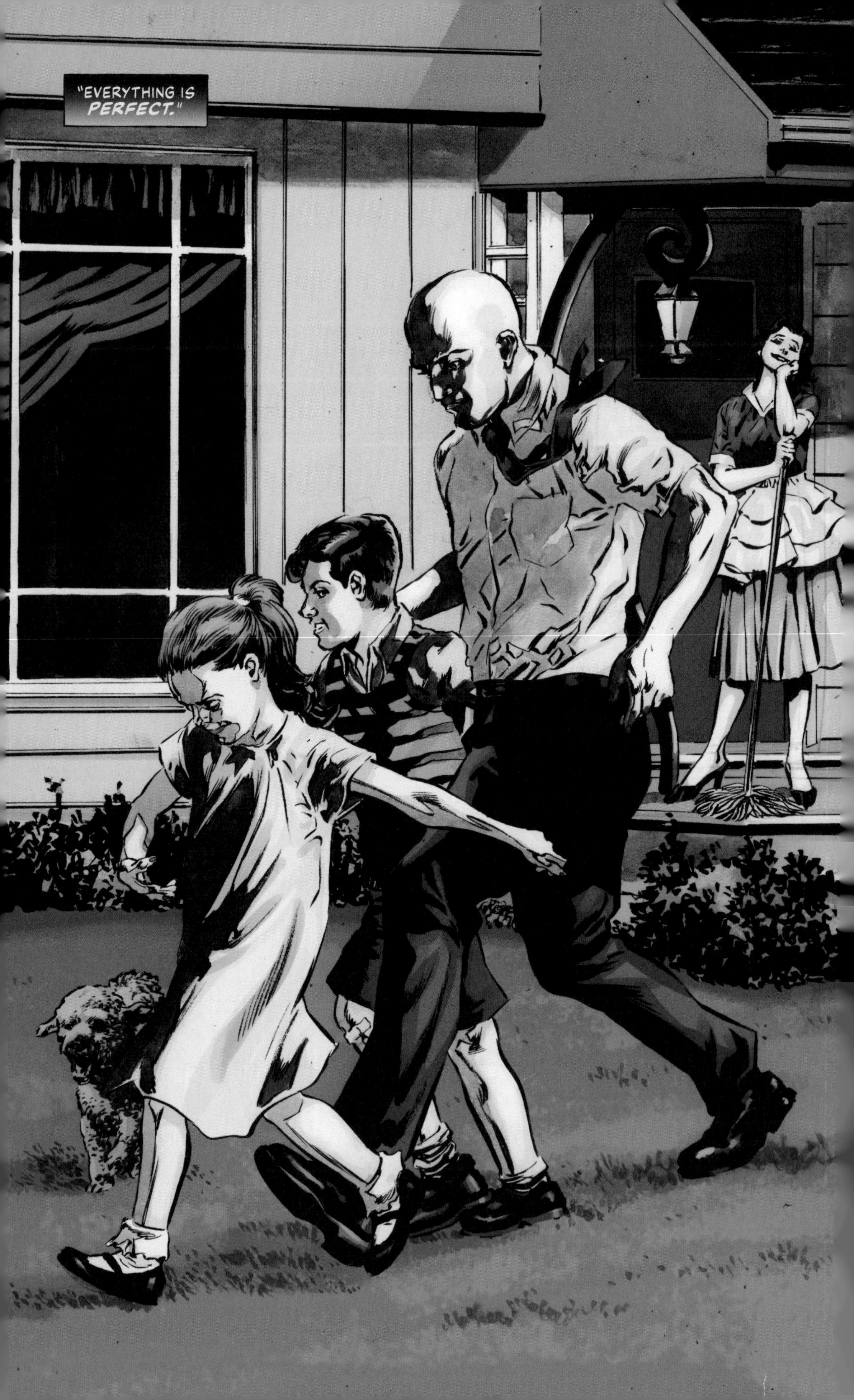
"EVERYTHING IS PERFECT."

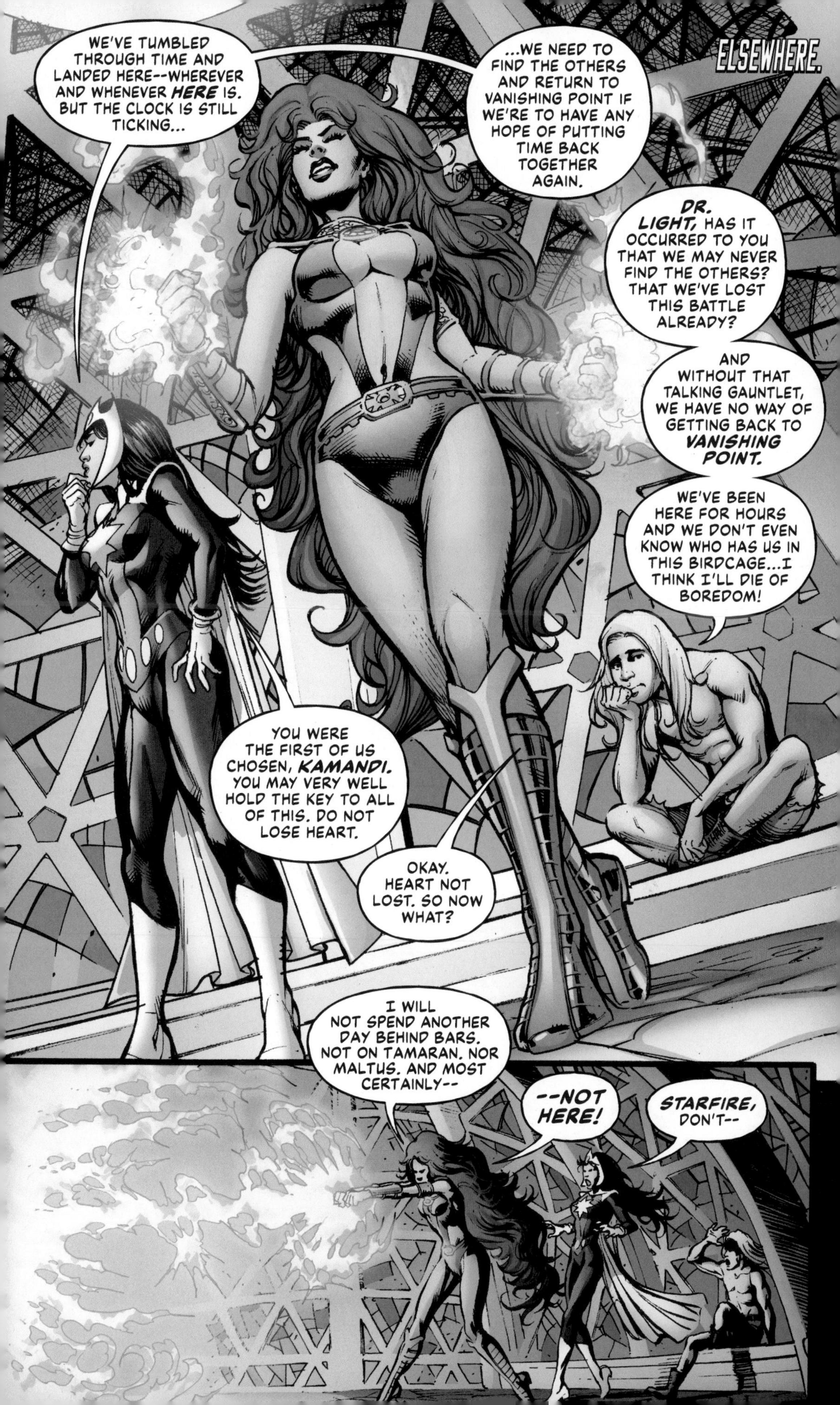
ELSEWHERE.
WE'VE TUMBLED THROUGH TIME AND LANDED HERE--WHEREVER AND WHENEVER *HERE* IS. BUT THE CLOCK IS STILL TICKING...
...WE NEED TO FIND THE OTHERS AND RETURN TO VANISHING POINT IF WE'RE TO HAVE ANY HOPE OF PUTTING TIME BACK TOGETHER AGAIN.
DR. LIGHT, HAS IT OCCURRED TO YOU THAT WE MAY NEVER FIND THE OTHERS? THAT WE'VE LOST THIS BATTLE ALREADY?
AND WITHOUT THAT TALKING GAUNTLET, WE HAVE NO WAY OF GETTING BACK TO *VANISHING POINT.*
WE'VE BEEN HERE FOR HOURS AND WE DON'T EVEN KNOW WHO HAS US IN THIS BIRDCAGE...I THINK I'LL DIE OF BOREDOM!
YOU WERE THE FIRST OF US CHOSEN, *KAMANDI.* YOU MAY VERY WELL HOLD THE KEY TO ALL OF THIS. DO NOT LOSE HEART.
OKAY. HEART NOT LOST. SO NOW WHAT?
I WILL NOT SPEND ANOTHER DAY BEHIND BARS. NOT ON TAMARAN. NOR MALTUS. AND MOST CERTAINLY--
--NOT HERE!
STARFIRE, DON'T--

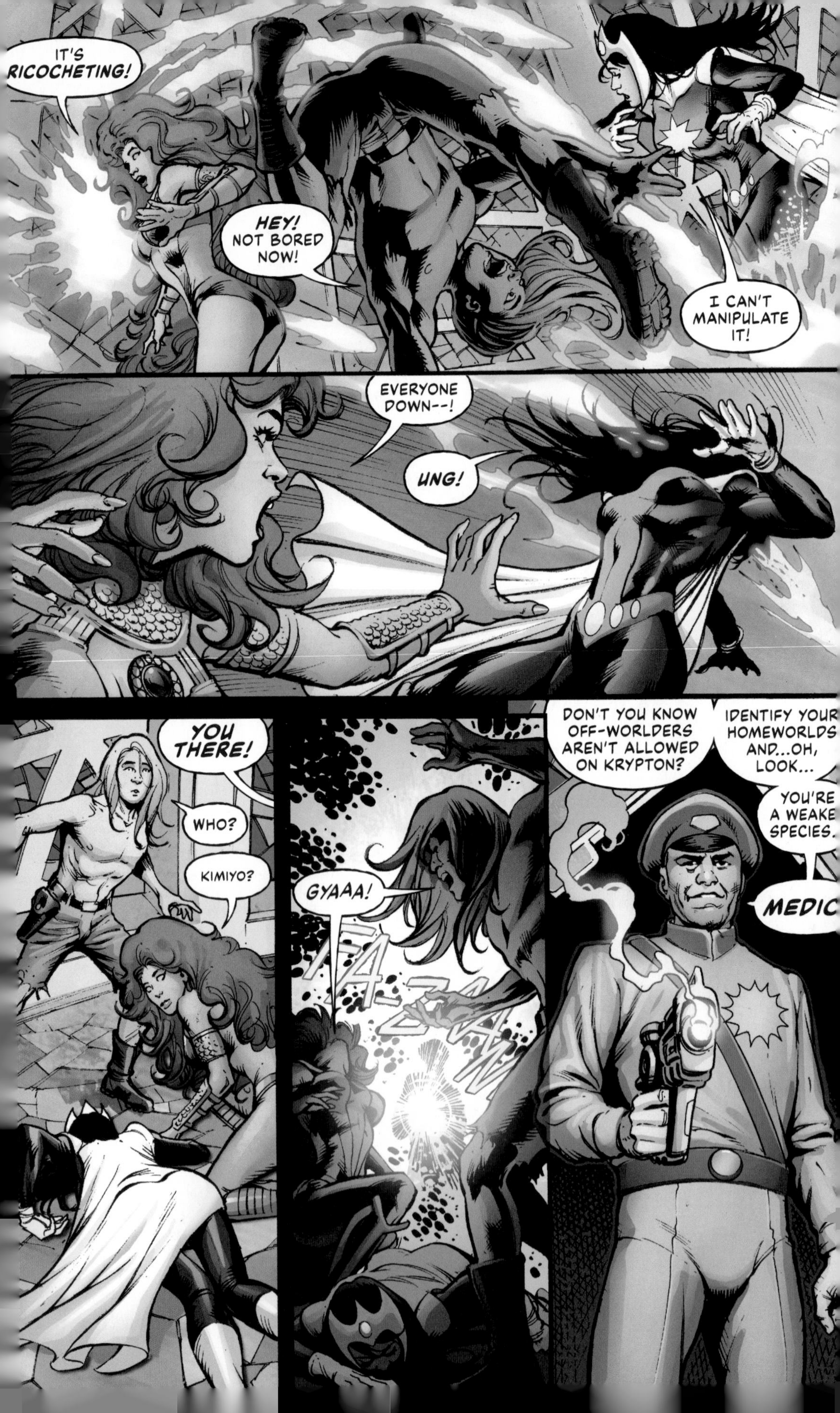

IT'S RICOCHETING!
HEY! NOT BORED NOW!
I CAN'T MANIPULATE IT!
EVERYONE DOWN--!
UNG!
YOU THERE!
WHO?
KIMIYO?
GYAAA!
DON'T YOU KNOW OFF-WORLDERS AREN'T ALLOWED ON KRYPTON?
IDENTIFY YOUR HOMEWORLDS AND...OH, LOOK...
YOU'RE A WEAKE SPECIES.
MEDIC

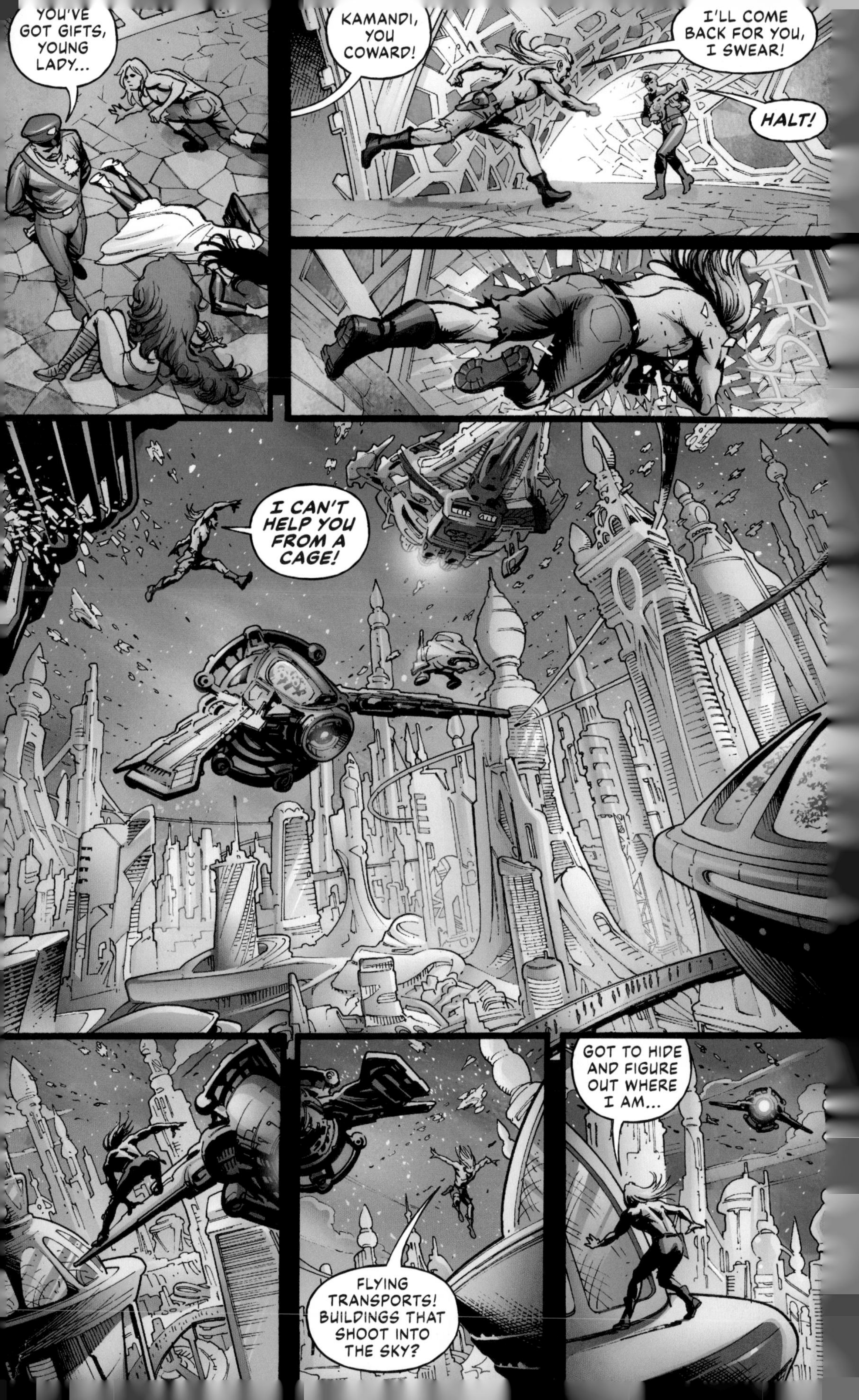
YOU'VE GOT GIFTS, YOUNG LADY...
KAMANDI, YOU COWARD!
I'LL COME BACK FOR YOU, I SWEAR!
HALT!
KRSSH
I CAN'T HELP YOU FROM A CAGE!
FLYING TRANSPORTS! BUILDINGS THAT SHOOT INTO THE SKY?
GOT TO HIDE AND FIGURE OUT WHERE I AM...

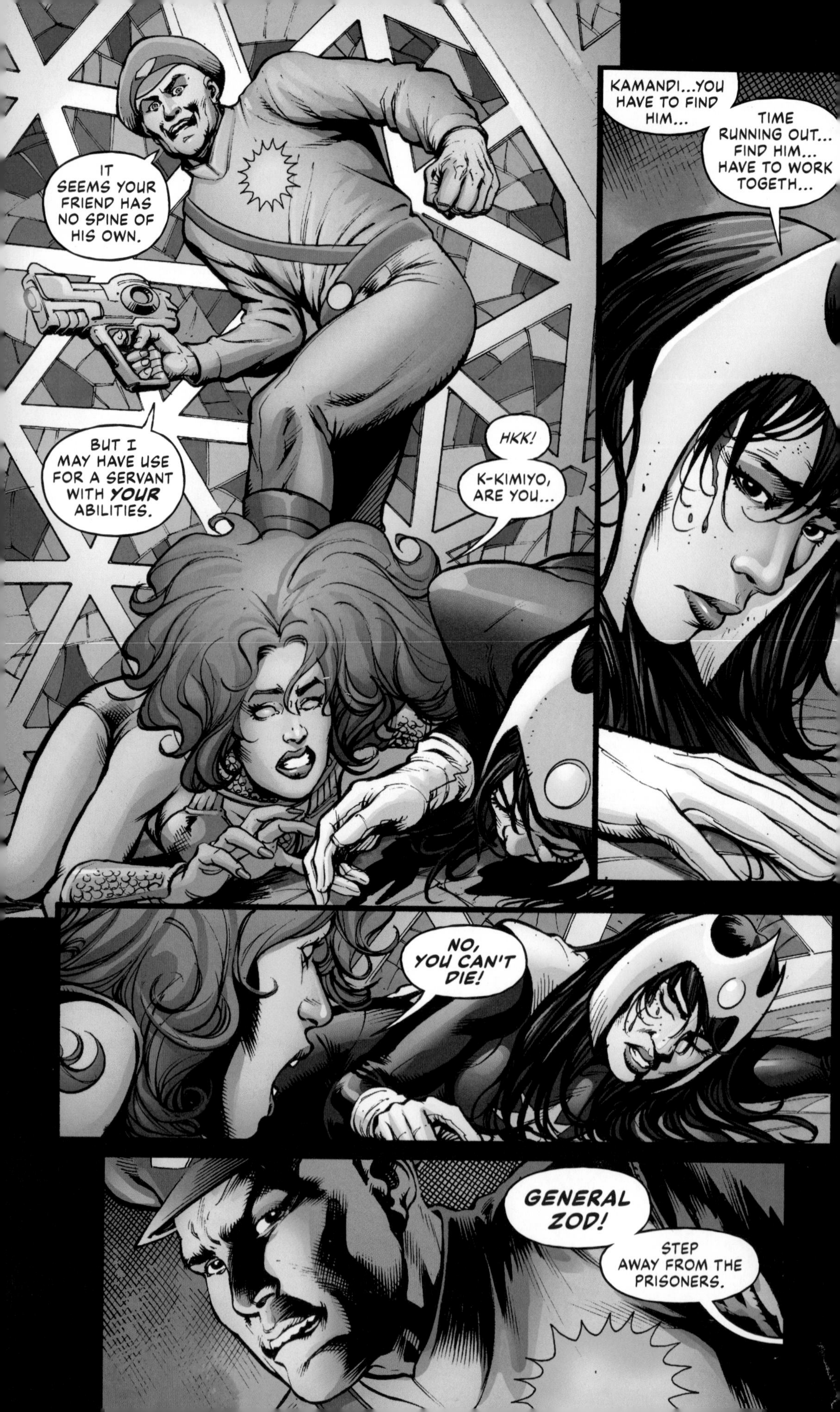
IT SEEMS YOUR FRIEND HAS NO SPINE OF HIS OWN.
BUT I MAY HAVE USE FOR A SERVANT WITH *YOUR* ABILITIES.
HKK!
K-KIMIYO, ARE YOU...
KAMANDI...YOU HAVE TO FIND HIM...
TIME RUNNING OUT... FIND HIM... HAVE TO WORK TOGETH...
NO, YOU CAN'T DIE!
GENERAL ZOD!
STEP AWAY FROM THE PRISONERS.

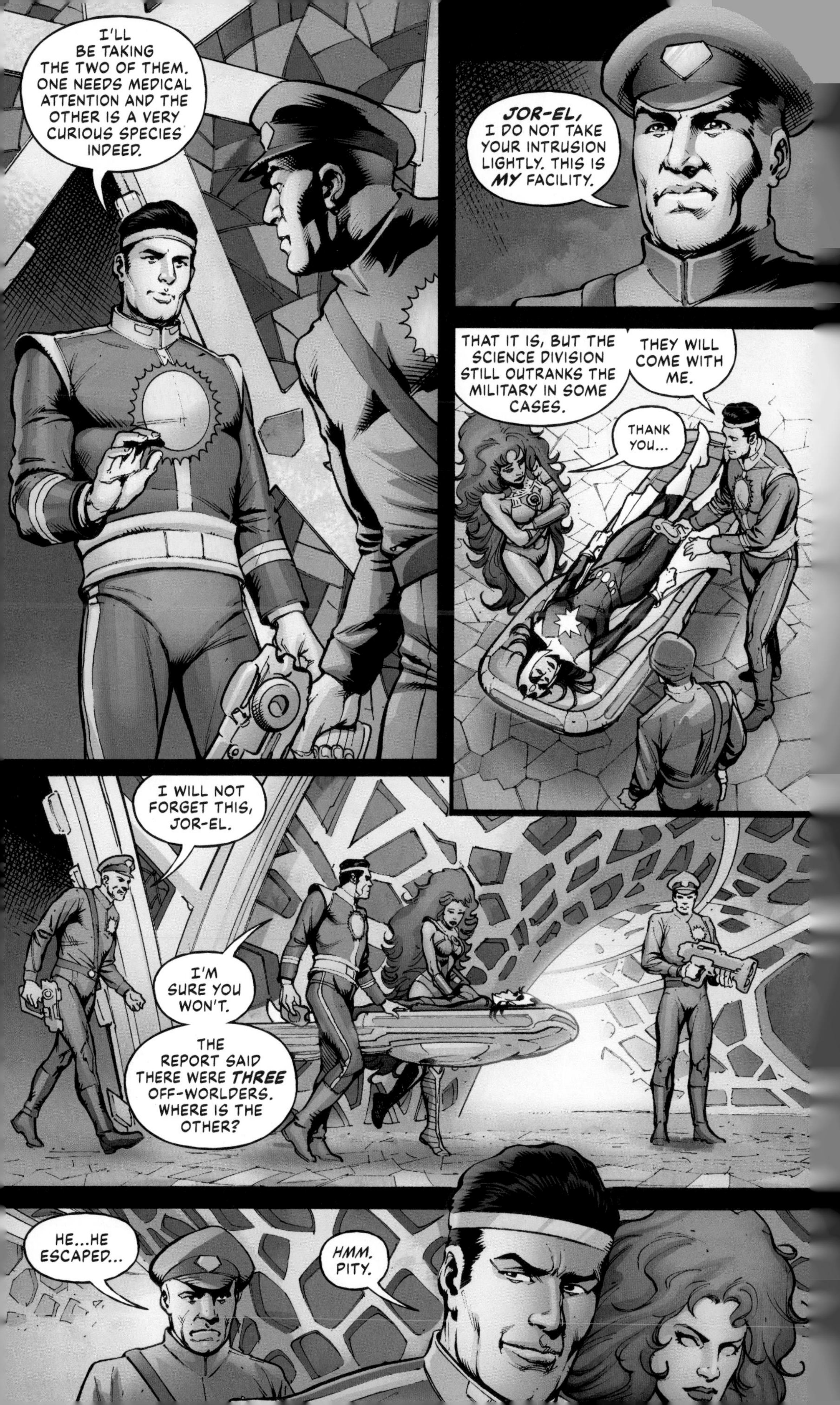
I'LL BE TAKING THE TWO OF THEM. ONE NEEDS MEDICAL ATTENTION AND THE OTHER IS A VERY CURIOUS SPECIES INDEED.
JOR-EL, I DO NOT TAKE YOUR INTRUSION LIGHTLY. THIS IS MY FACILITY.
THAT IT IS, BUT THE SCIENCE DIVISION STILL OUTRANKS THE MILITARY IN SOME CASES.
THEY WILL COME WITH ME.
THANK YOU...
I WILL NOT FORGET THIS, JOR-EL.
I'M SURE YOU WON'T.
THE REPORT SAID THERE WERE THREE OFF-WORLDERS. WHERE IS THE OTHER?
HE...HE ESCAPED...
HMM. PITY.

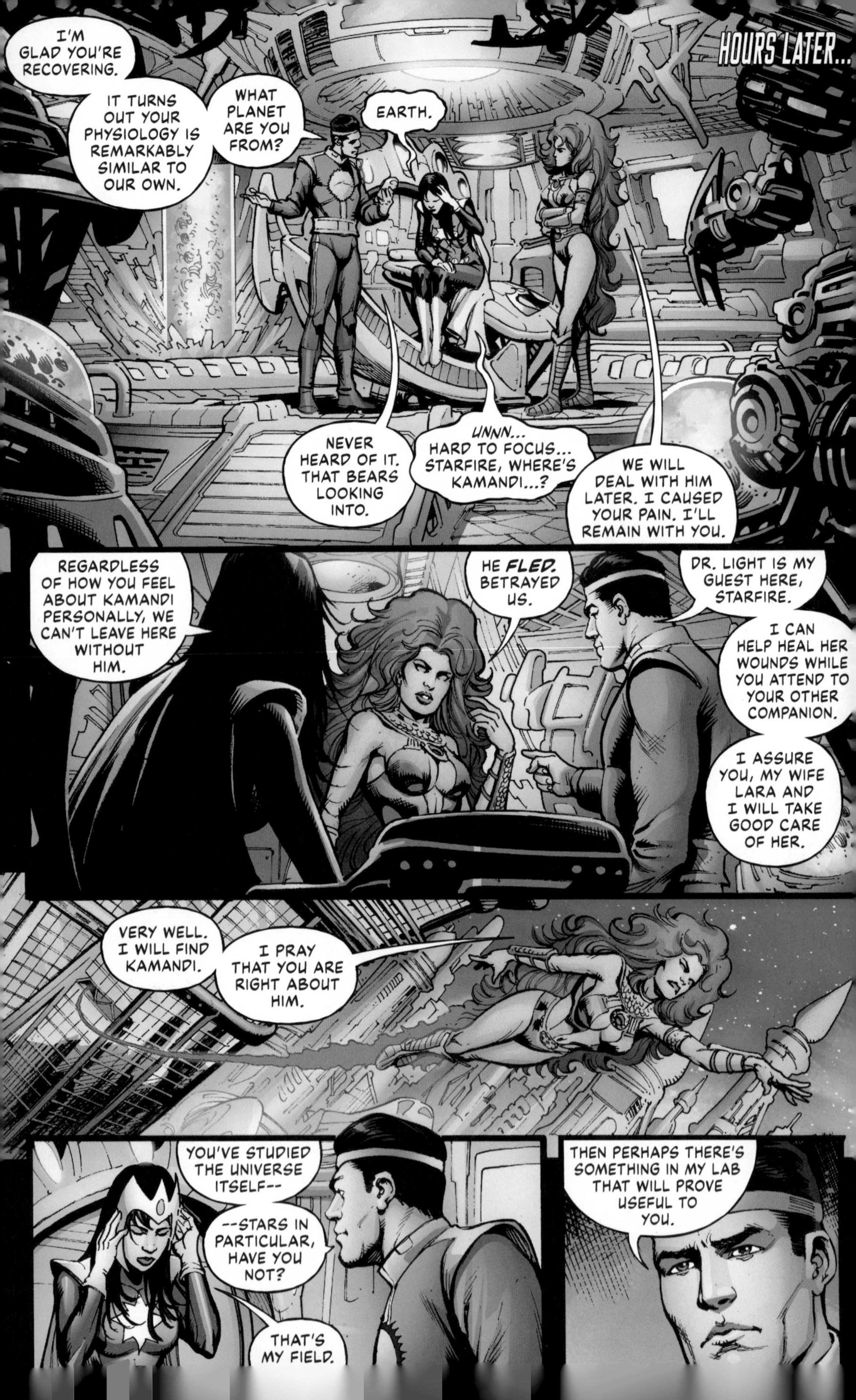
HOURS LATER...
I'M GLAD YOU'RE RECOVERING.
IT TURNS OUT YOUR PHYSIOLOGY IS REMARKABLY SIMILAR TO OUR OWN.
WHAT PLANET ARE YOU FROM?
EARTH.
NEVER HEARD OF IT. THAT BEARS LOOKING INTO.
UNNN... HARD TO FOCUS... STARFIRE, WHERE'S KAMANDI...?
WE WILL DEAL WITH HIM LATER. I CAUSED YOUR PAIN. I'LL REMAIN WITH YOU.
REGARDLESS OF HOW YOU FEEL ABOUT KAMANDI PERSONALLY, WE CAN'T LEAVE HERE WITHOUT HIM.
HE FLED. BETRAYED US.
DR. LIGHT IS MY GUEST HERE, STARFIRE.
I CAN HELP HEAL HER WOUNDS WHILE YOU ATTEND TO YOUR OTHER COMPANION.
I ASSURE YOU, MY WIFE LARA AND I WILL TAKE GOOD CARE OF HER.
VERY WELL. I WILL FIND KAMANDI.
I PRAY THAT YOU ARE RIGHT ABOUT HIM.
YOU'VE STUDIED THE UNIVERSE ITSELF--
--STARS IN PARTICULAR, HAVE YOU NOT?
THAT'S MY FIELD.
THEN PERHAPS THERE'S SOMETHING IN MY LAB THAT WILL PROVE USEFUL TO YOU.

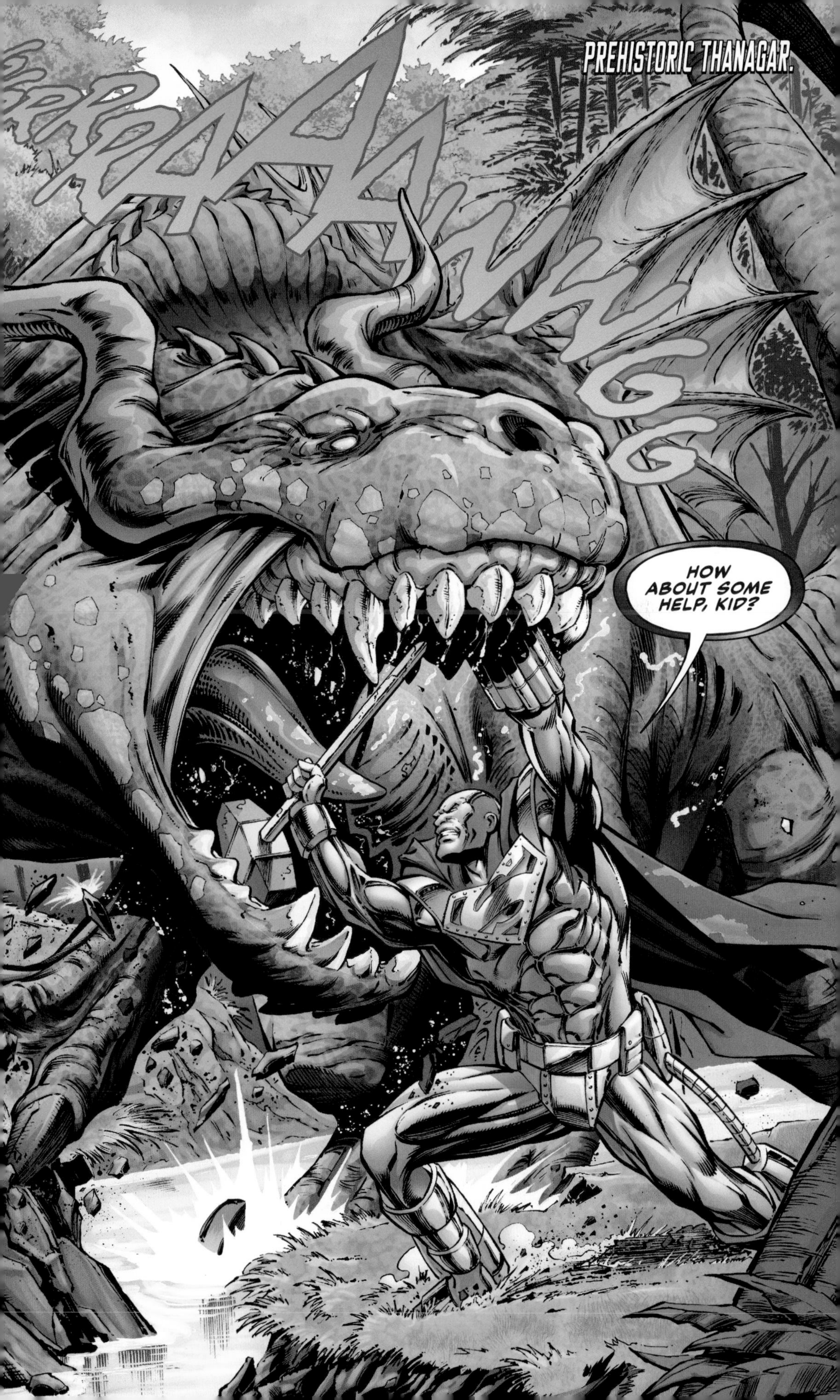
PREHISTORIC THANAGAR.
HOW ABOUT SOME HELP, KID?

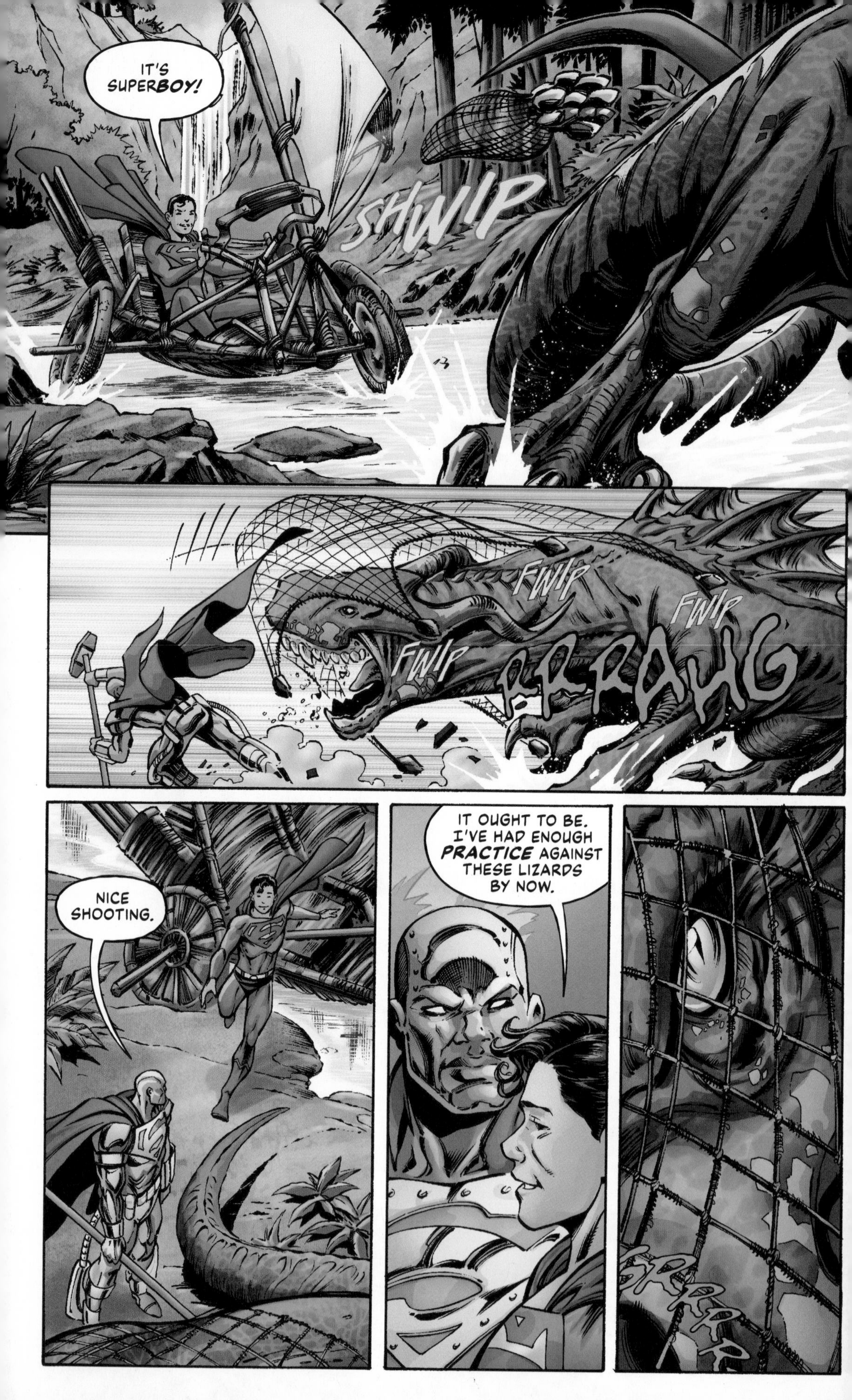
IT'S SUPERBOY!
SHWIP
FWIP
FWIP
FWIP
RRRAUG
NICE SHOOTING.
IT OUGHT TO BE. I'VE HAD ENOUGH PRACTICE AGAINST THESE LIZARDS BY NOW.
GRRRR

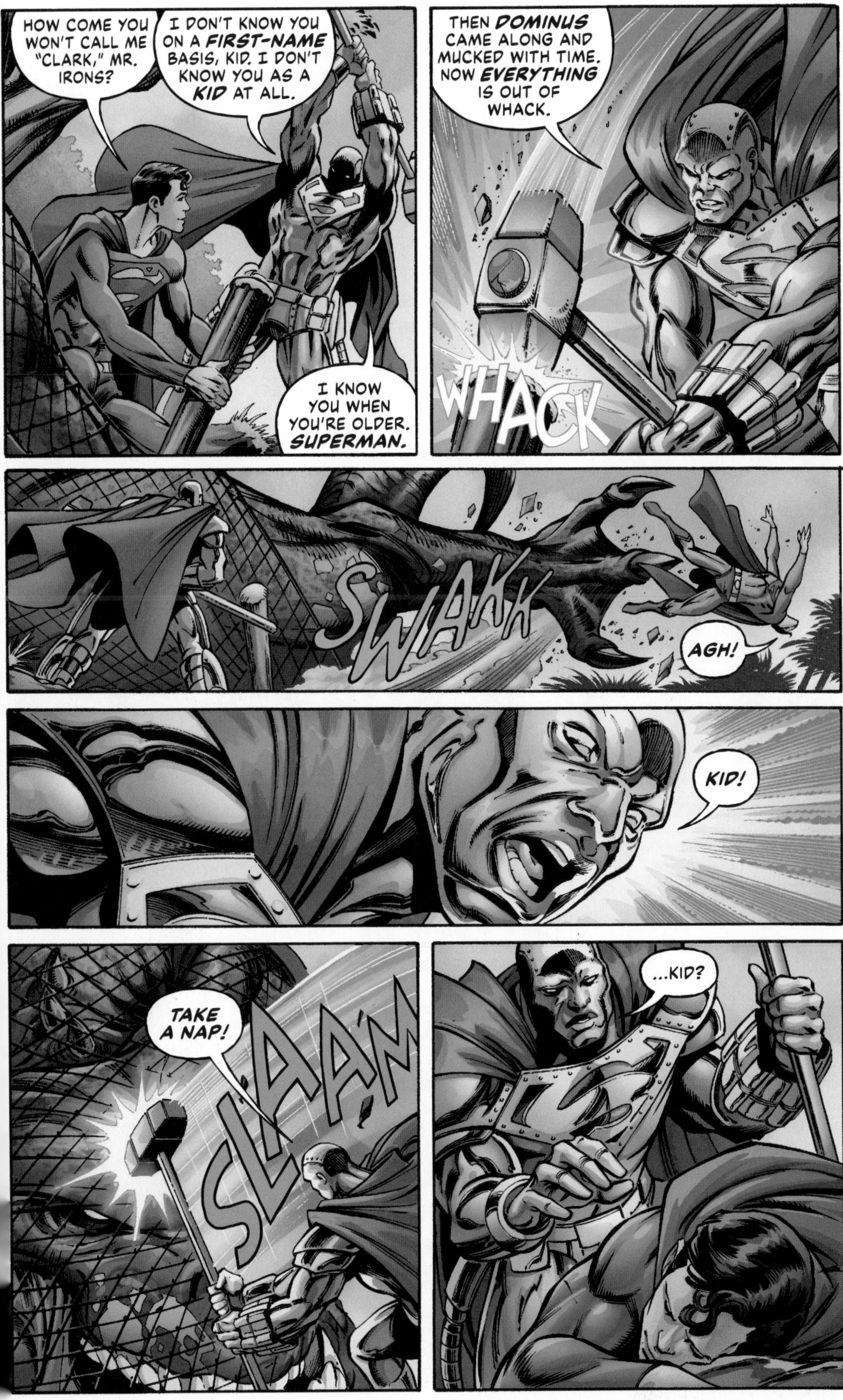
HOW COME YOU WON'T CALL ME "CLARK," MR. IRONS?
I DON'T KNOW YOU ON A FIRST-NAME BASIS, KID. I DON'T KNOW YOU AS A KID AT ALL.
I KNOW YOU WHEN YOU'RE OLDER. SUPERMAN.
THEN DOMINUS CAME ALONG AND MUCKED WITH TIME. NOW EVERYTHING IS OUT OF WHACK.
WHACK
SWAKK
AGH!
KID!
TAKE A NAP!
SLAAM
...KID?

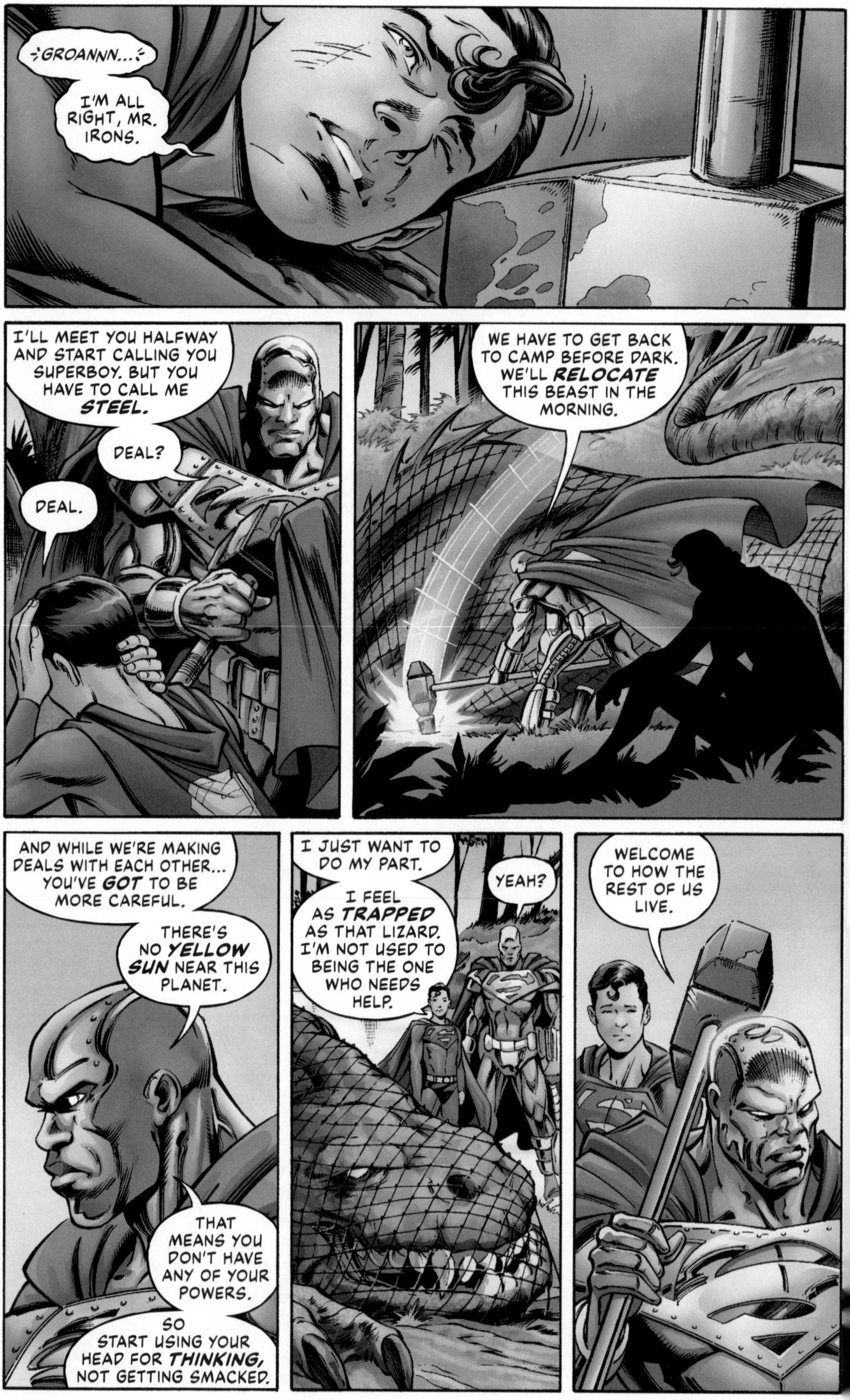
GROANNN...
I'M ALL RIGHT, MR. IRONS.
I'LL MEET YOU HALFWAY AND START CALLING YOU SUPERBOY. BUT YOU HAVE TO CALL ME STEEL.
DEAL?
DEAL.
WE HAVE TO GET BACK TO CAMP BEFORE DARK. WE'LL RELOCATE THIS BEAST IN THE MORNING.
AND WHILE WE'RE MAKING DEALS WITH EACH OTHER... YOU'VE GOT TO BE MORE CAREFUL.
THERE'S NO YELLOW SUN NEAR THIS PLANET.
THAT MEANS YOU DON'T HAVE ANY OF YOUR POWERS.
SO START USING YOUR HEAD FOR THINKING, NOT GETTING SMACKED.
I JUST WANT TO DO MY PART.
YEAH?
I FEEL AS TRAPPED AS THAT LIZARD. I'M NOT USED TO BEING THE ONE WHO NEEDS HELP.
WELCOME TO HOW THE REST OF US LIVE.

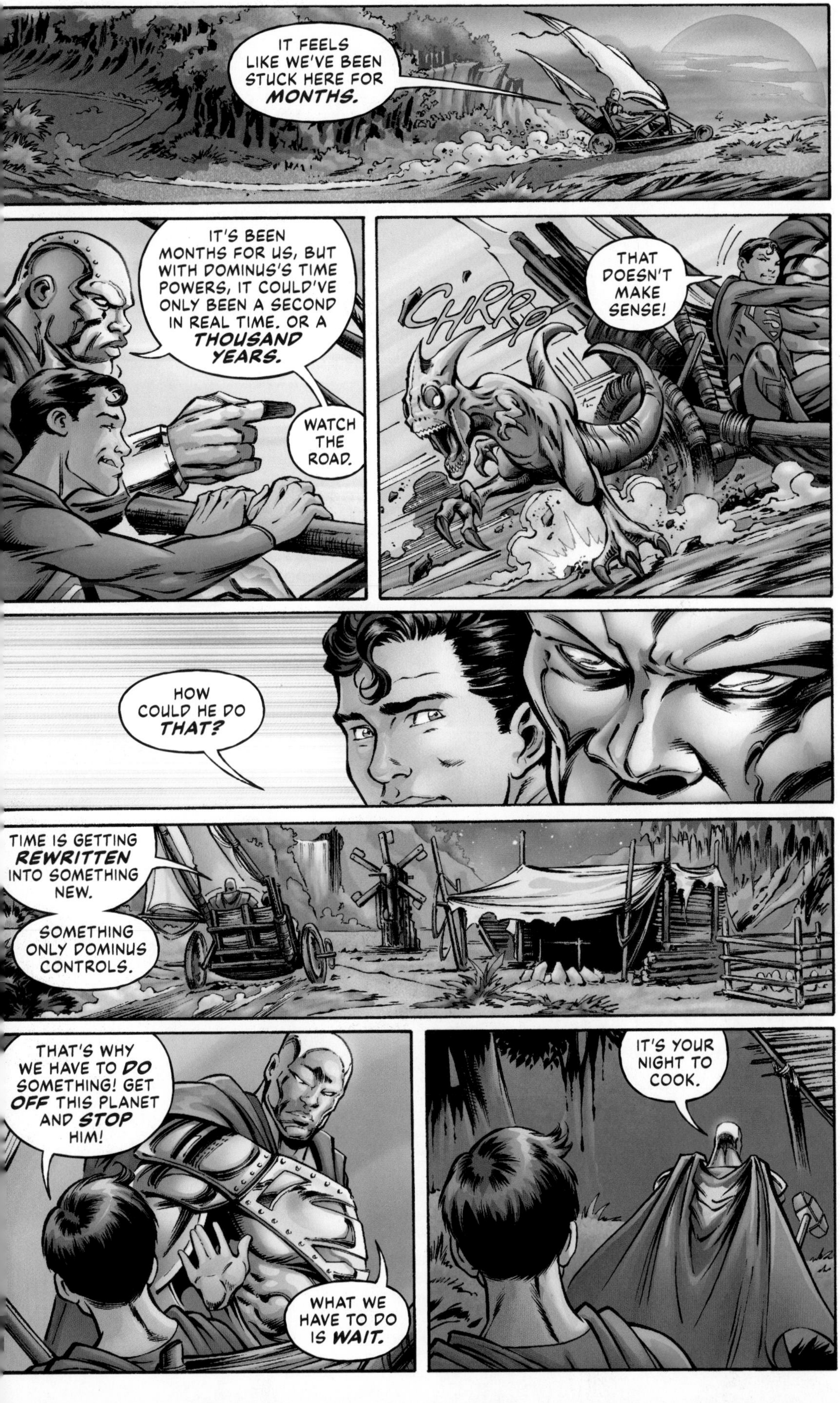
IT FEELS LIKE WE'VE BEEN STUCK HERE FOR MONTHS.
IT'S BEEN MONTHS FOR US, BUT WITH DOMINUS'S TIME POWERS, IT COULD'VE ONLY BEEN A SECOND IN REAL TIME. OR A THOUSAND YEARS.
WATCH THE ROAD.
CHRRP
THAT DOESN'T MAKE SENSE!
HOW COULD HE DO THAT?
TIME IS GETTING REWRITTEN INTO SOMETHING NEW.
SOMETHING ONLY DOMINUS CONTROLS.
THAT'S WHY WE HAVE TO DO SOMETHING! GET OFF THIS PLANET AND STOP HIM!
WHAT WE HAVE TO DO IS WAIT.
IT'S YOUR NIGHT TO COOK.

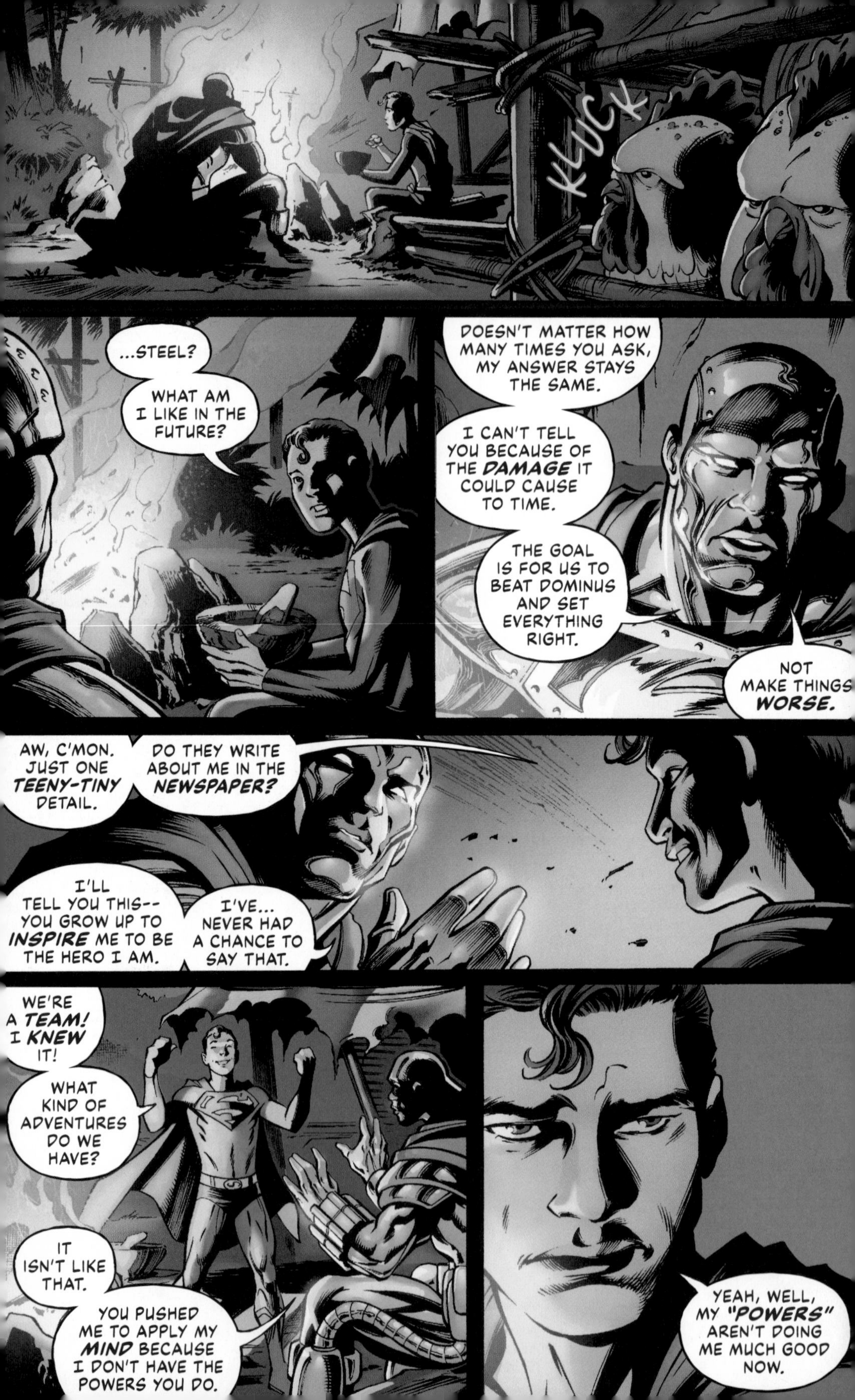
KLUCK
...STEEL?
WHAT AM I LIKE IN THE FUTURE?
DOESN'T MATTER HOW MANY TIMES YOU ASK, MY ANSWER STAYS THE SAME.
I CAN'T TELL YOU BECAUSE OF THE *DAMAGE* IT COULD CAUSE TO TIME.
THE GOAL IS FOR US TO BEAT DOMINUS AND SET EVERYTHING RIGHT.
NOT MAKE THINGS ***WORSE.***
AW, C'MON. JUST ONE ***TEENY-TINY*** DETAIL.
DO THEY WRITE ABOUT ME IN THE ***NEWSPAPER?***
I'LL TELL YOU THIS-- YOU GROW UP TO ***INSPIRE*** ME TO BE THE HERO I AM.
I'VE... NEVER HAD A CHANCE TO SAY THAT.
WE'RE A ***TEAM!*** I ***KNEW*** IT!
WHAT KIND OF ADVENTURES DO WE HAVE?
IT ISN'T LIKE THAT.
YOU PUSHED ME TO APPLY MY ***MIND*** BECAUSE I DON'T HAVE THE POWERS YOU DO.
YEAH, WELL, MY ***"POWERS"*** AREN'T DOING ME MUCH GOOD NOW.

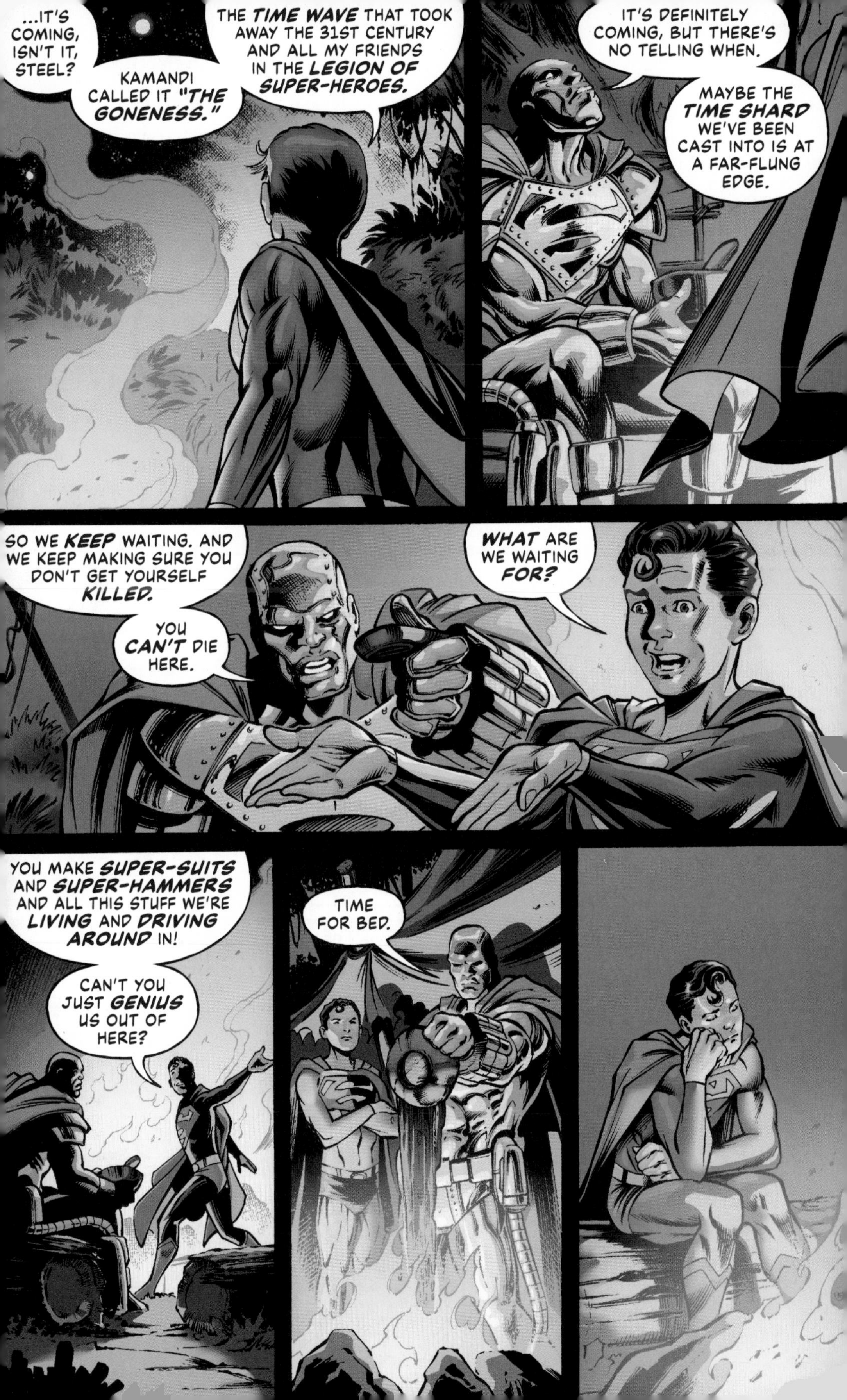
...IT'S COMING, ISN'T IT, STEEL?
KAMANDI CALLED IT "THE GONENESS."
THE TIME WAVE THAT TOOK AWAY THE 31ST CENTURY AND ALL MY FRIENDS IN THE LEGION OF SUPER-HEROES.
IT'S DEFINITELY COMING, BUT THERE'S NO TELLING WHEN.
MAYBE THE TIME SHARD WE'VE BEEN CAST INTO IS AT A FAR-FLUNG EDGE.
SO WE KEEP WAITING. AND WE KEEP MAKING SURE YOU DON'T GET YOURSELF KILLED.
YOU CAN'T DIE HERE.
WHAT ARE WE WAITING FOR?
YOU MAKE SUPER-SUITS AND SUPER-HAMMERS AND ALL THIS STUFF WE'RE LIVING AND DRIVING AROUND IN!
CAN'T YOU JUST GENIUS US OUT OF HERE?
TIME FOR BED.

SNORRRRE...

RISE AND SHINE.

HAIR AND TEETH. WE'RE GETTING AN EARLY START ON THE DAY.

YAWN

RIGHT. DON'T WANT TO BE LATE FOR ALL THE *WAITING AROUND* WE HAVE TO DO.

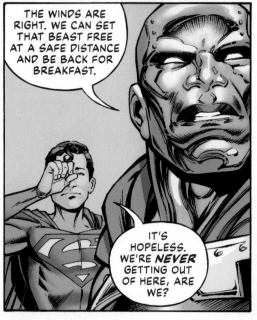

THE WINDS ARE RIGHT. WE CAN SET THAT BEAST FREE AT A SAFE DISTANCE AND BE BACK FOR BREAKFAST.

IT'S HOPELESS. WE'RE *NEVER* GETTING OUT OF HERE, ARE WE?

WE'RE THE *SWISS FAMILY SUPER-HEROES.*

WE'RE *BOTH* GOING TO GROW OLD AND DIE HERE.

KNOCK IT OFF.

GET IN. I'LL DRIVE.

THE BOY IS CORRECT.

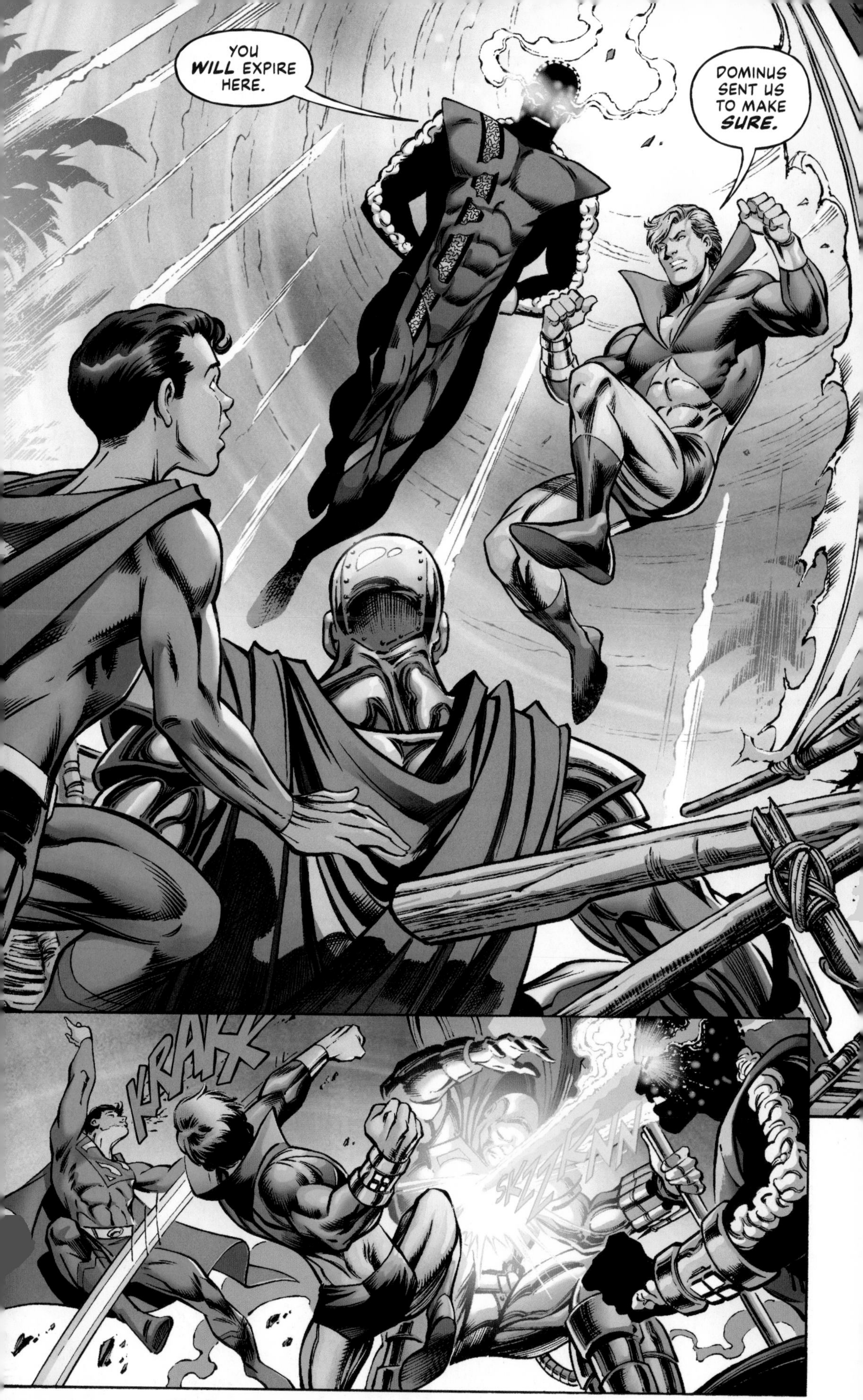
YOU WILL EXPIRE HERE.
DOMINUS SENT US TO MAKE SURE.
KRAKK
SKZZZRNN

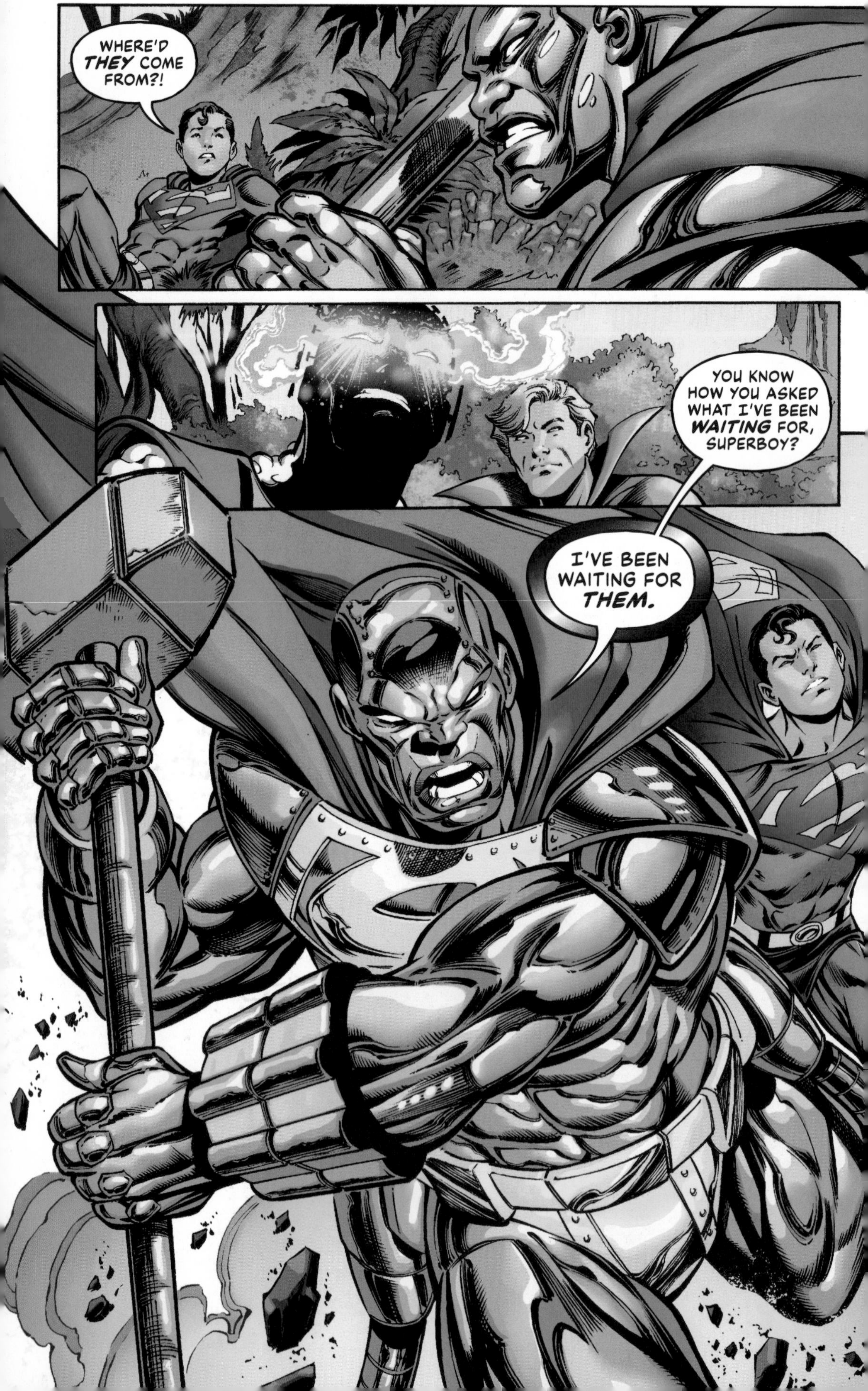

WHERE'D *THEY* COME FROM?!
YOU KNOW HOW YOU ASKED WHAT I'VE BEEN *WAITING* FOR, SUPERBOY?
I'VE BEEN WAITING FOR *THEM.*

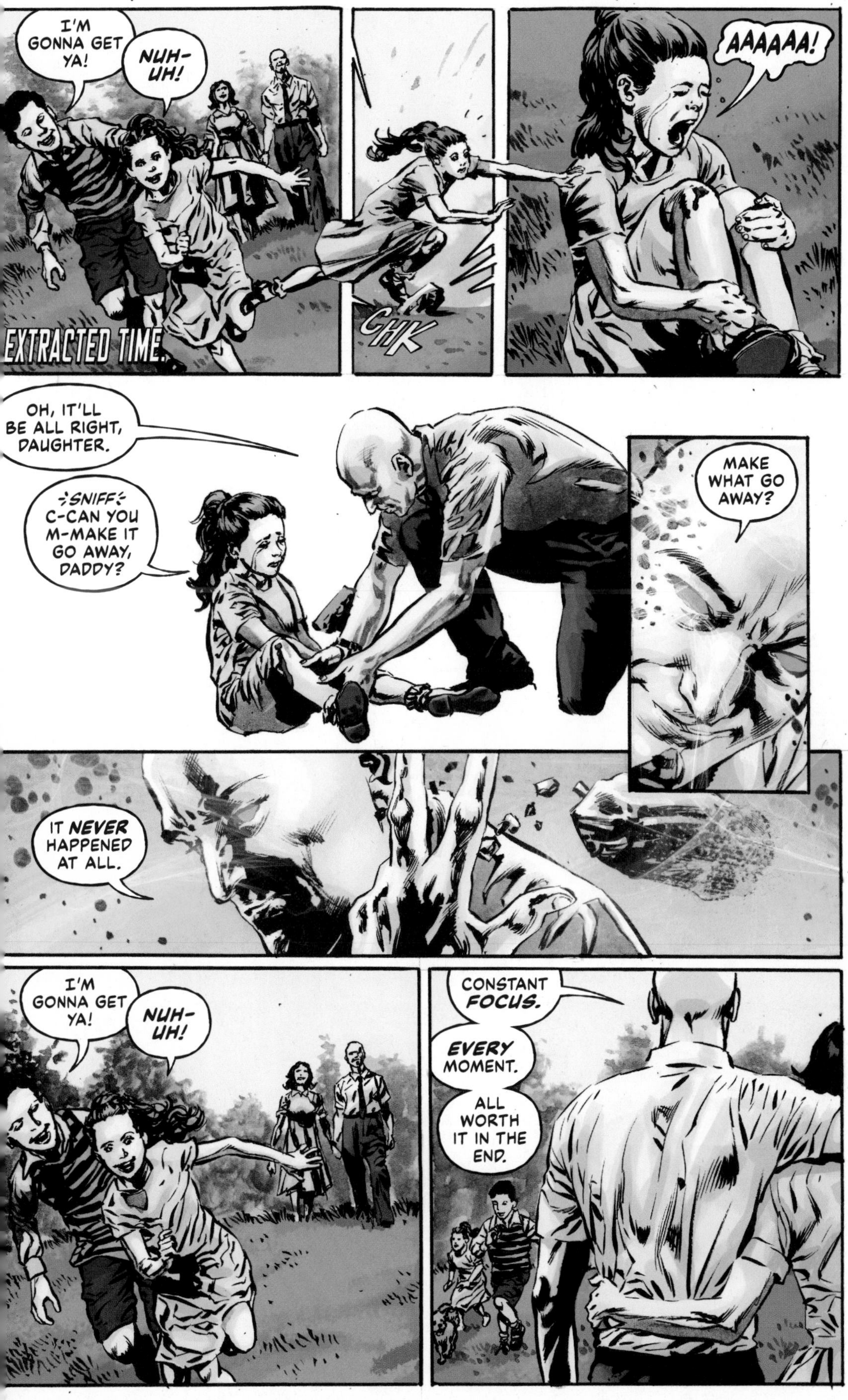

I'M GONNA GET YA!
NUH-UH!
EXTRACTED TIME.
CHK
AAAAAA!
OH, IT'LL BE ALL RIGHT, DAUGHTER.
SNIFF
C-CAN YOU M-MAKE IT GO AWAY, DADDY?
MAKE WHAT GO AWAY?
IT NEVER HAPPENED AT ALL.
I'M GONNA GET YA!
NUH-UH!
CONSTANT FOCUS.
EVERY MOMENT.
ALL WORTH IT IN THE END.

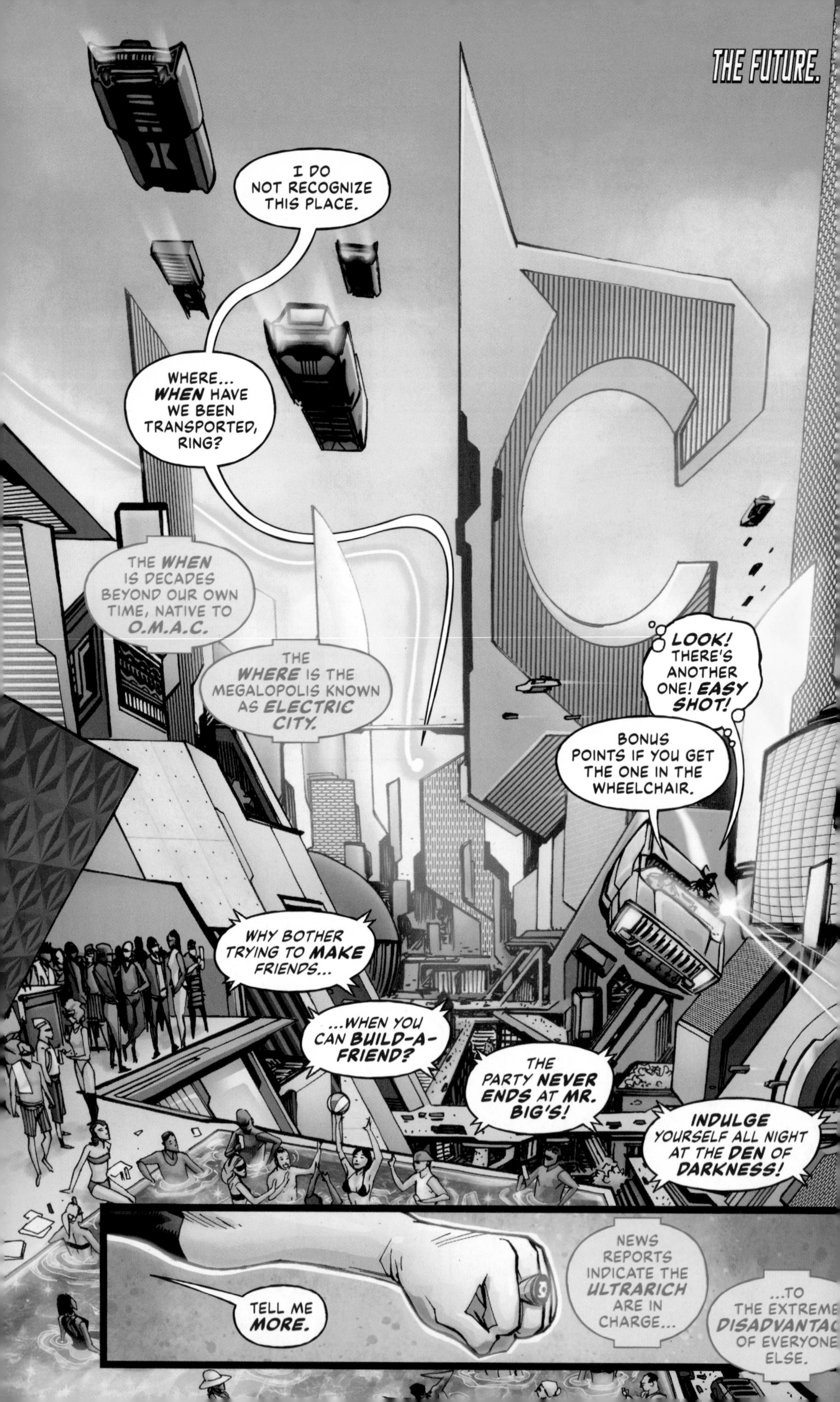

THE FUTURE.
I DO NOT RECOGNIZE THIS PLACE.
WHERE... WHEN HAVE WE BEEN TRANSPORTED, RING?
THE WHEN IS DECADES BEYOND OUR OWN TIME, NATIVE TO O.M.A.C.
THE WHERE IS THE MEGALOPOLIS KNOWN AS ELECTRIC CITY.
LOOK! THERE'S ANOTHER ONE! EASY SHOT!
BONUS POINTS IF YOU GET THE ONE IN THE WHEELCHAIR.
WHY BOTHER TRYING TO MAKE FRIENDS...
...WHEN YOU CAN BUILD-A-FRIEND?
THE PARTY NEVER ENDS AT MR. BIG'S!
INDULGE YOURSELF ALL NIGHT AT THE DEN OF DARKNESS!
TELL ME MORE.
NEWS REPORTS INDICATE THE ULTRARICH ARE IN CHARGE...
...TO THE EXTREME DISADVANTAG OF EVERYONE ELSE.

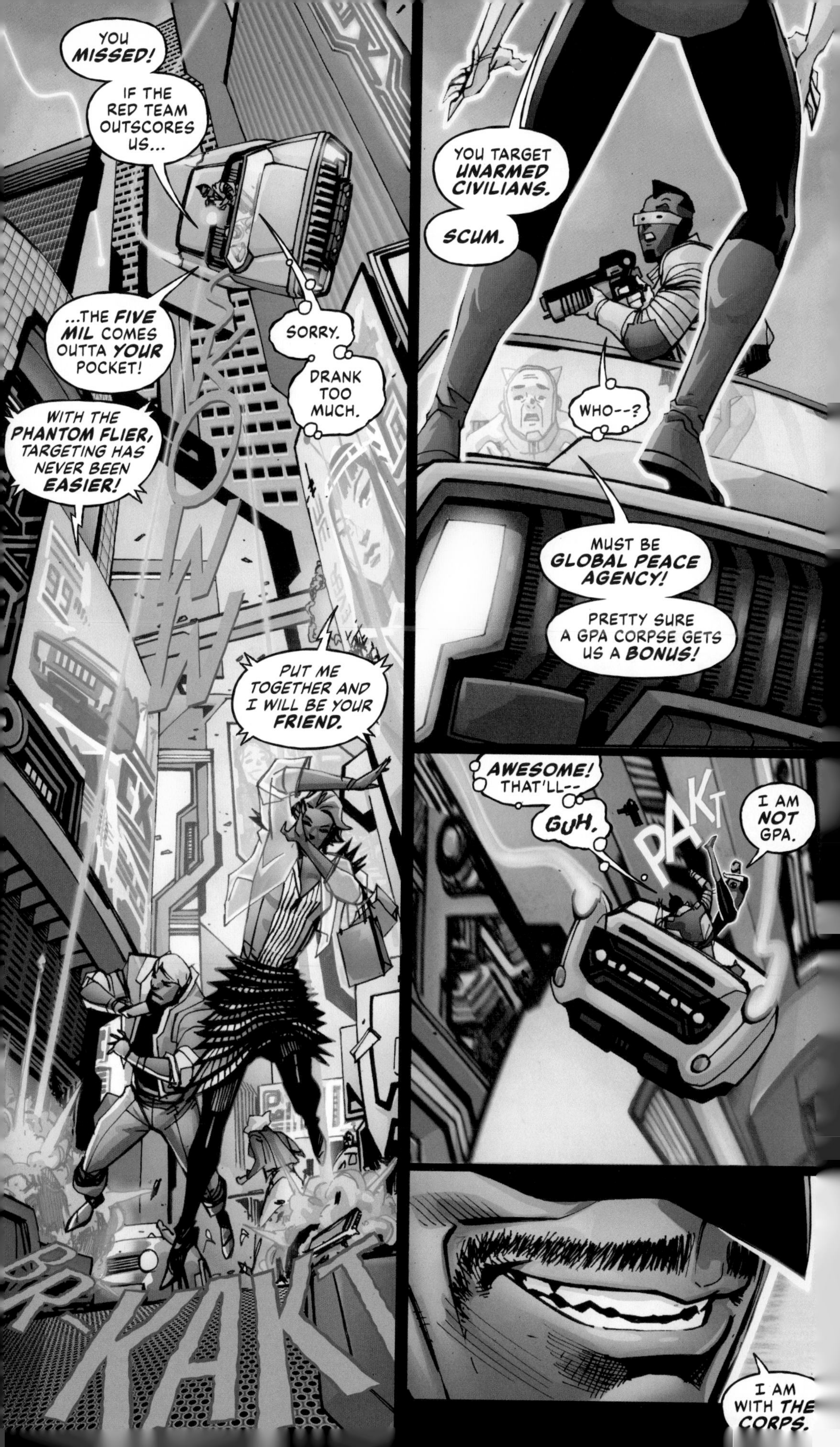

YOU MISSED!
IF THE RED TEAM OUTSCORES US...
...THE FIVE MIL COMES OUTTA YOUR POCKET!
SORRY.
DRANK TOO MUCH.
WITH THE PHANTOM FLIER, TARGETING HAS NEVER BEEN EASIER!
PUT ME TOGETHER AND I WILL BE YOUR FRIEND.
BRAKAK
YOU TARGET UNARMED CIVILIANS.
SCUM.
WHO--?
MUST BE GLOBAL PEACE AGENCY!
PRETTY SURE A GPA CORPSE GETS US A BONUS!
AWESOME! THAT'LL--
GUH.
PAKT
I AM NOT GPA.
I AM WITH THE CORPS.

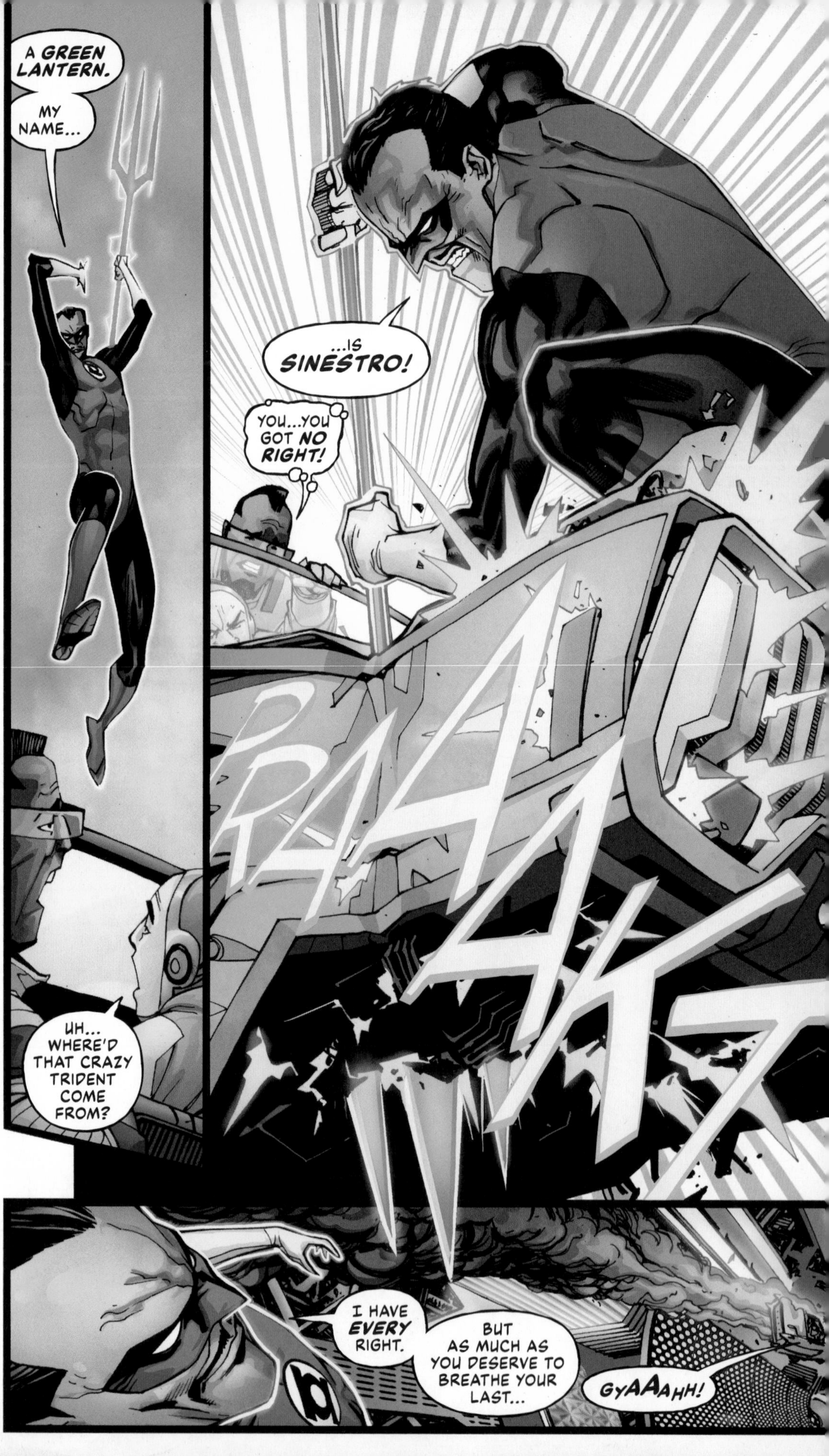
A GREEN LANTERN.
MY NAME...
...IS SINESTRO!
YOU...YOU GOT NO RIGHT!
UH... WHERE'D THAT CRAZY TRIDENT COME FROM?
I HAVE EVERY RIGHT.
BUT AS MUCH AS YOU DESERVE TO BREATHE YOUR LAST...
GYAAAHH!

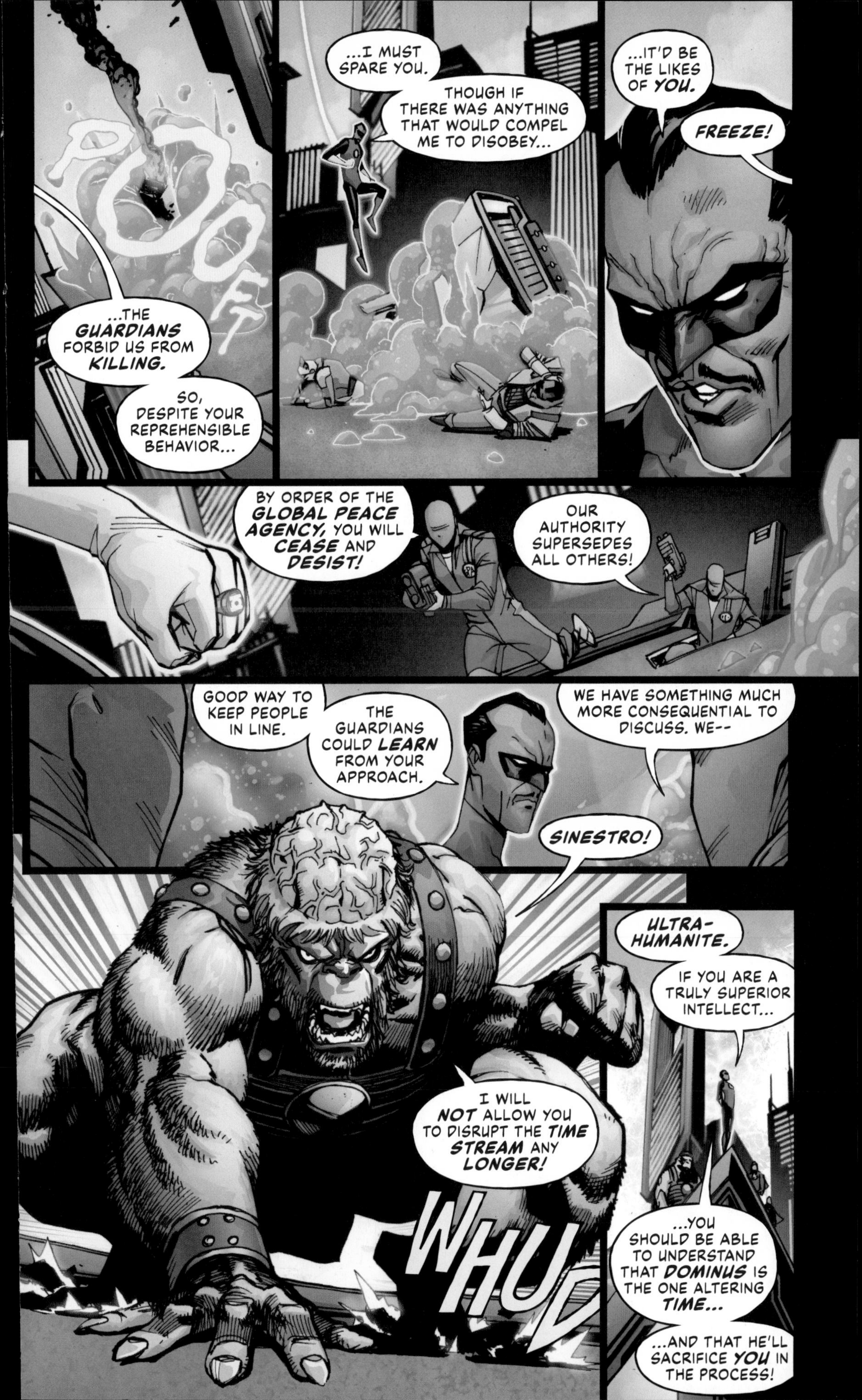
POOF
...THE GUARDIANS FORBID US FROM KILLING.
SO, DESPITE YOUR REPREHENSIBLE BEHAVIOR...
...I MUST SPARE YOU.
THOUGH IF THERE WAS ANYTHING THAT WOULD COMPEL ME TO DISOBEY...
...IT'D BE THE LIKES OF YOU.
FREEZE!
BY ORDER OF THE GLOBAL PEACE AGENCY, YOU WILL CEASE AND DESIST!
OUR AUTHORITY SUPERSEDES ALL OTHERS!
GOOD WAY TO KEEP PEOPLE IN LINE.
THE GUARDIANS COULD LEARN FROM YOUR APPROACH.
WE HAVE SOMETHING MUCH MORE CONSEQUENTIAL TO DISCUSS. WE--
SINESTRO!
I WILL NOT ALLOW YOU TO DISRUPT THE TIME STREAM ANY LONGER!
WHUD
ULTRA-HUMANITE.
IF YOU ARE A TRULY SUPERIOR INTELLECT...
...YOU SHOULD BE ABLE TO UNDERSTAND THAT DOMINUS IS THE ONE ALTERING TIME...
...AND THAT HE'LL SACRIFICE YOU IN THE PROCESS!

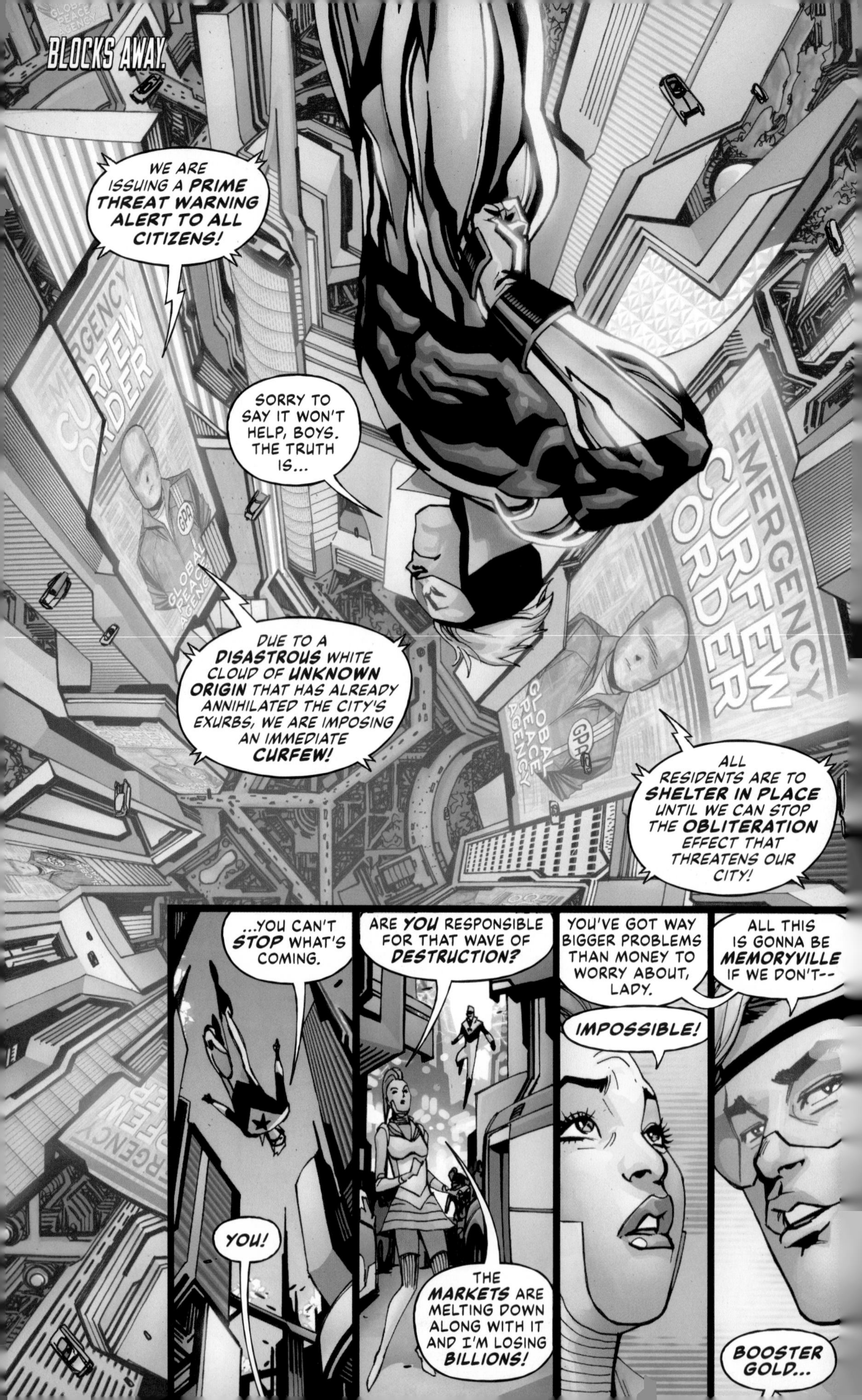
BLOCKS AWAY.
GLOBAL PEACE AGENCY
WE ARE ISSUING A PRIME THREAT WARNING ALERT TO ALL CITIZENS!
EMERGENCY CURFEW ORDER
SORRY TO SAY IT WON'T HELP, BOYS. THE TRUTH IS...
GLOBAL PEACE AGENCY
DUE TO A DISASTROUS WHITE CLOUD OF UNKNOWN ORIGIN THAT HAS ALREADY ANNIHILATED THE CITY'S EXURBS, WE ARE IMPOSING AN IMMEDIATE CURFEW!
EMERGENCY CURFEW ORDER
GLOBAL PEACE AGENCY
ALL RESIDENTS ARE TO SHELTER IN PLACE UNTIL WE CAN STOP THE OBLITERATION EFFECT THAT THREATENS OUR CITY!
...YOU CAN'T STOP WHAT'S COMING.
YOU!
ARE YOU RESPONSIBLE FOR THAT WAVE OF DESTRUCTION?
THE MARKETS ARE MELTING DOWN ALONG WITH IT AND I'M LOSING BILLIONS!
YOU'VE GOT WAY BIGGER PROBLEMS THAN MONEY TO WORRY ABOUT, LADY.
IMPOSSIBLE!
ALL THIS IS GONNA BE MEMORYVILLE IF WE DON'T--
BOOSTER GOLD...

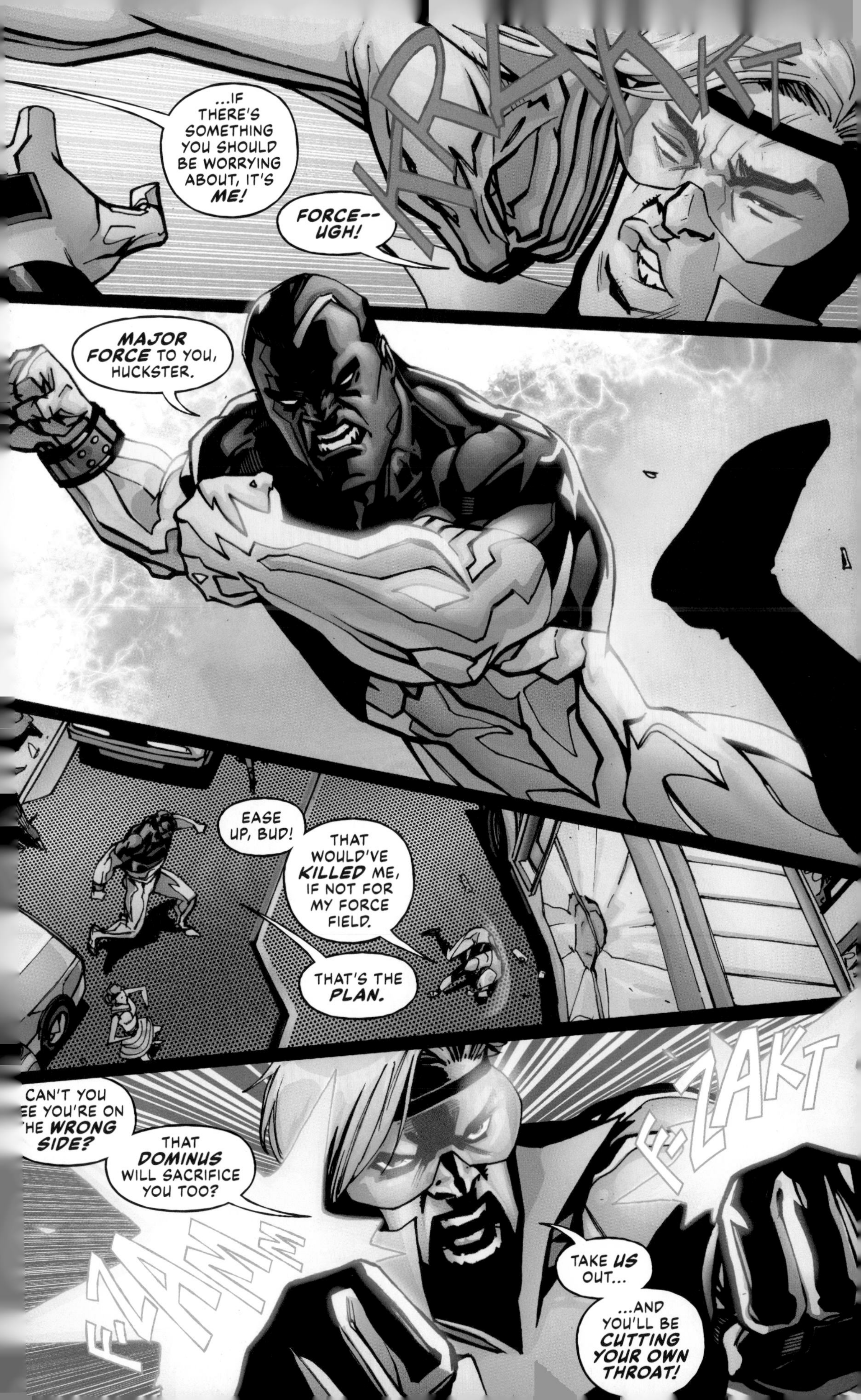

...IF THERE'S SOMETHING YOU SHOULD BE WORRYING ABOUT, IT'S **ME!**
FORCE-- UGH!
MAJOR FORCE TO YOU, HUCKSTER.
EASE UP, BUD!
THAT WOULD'VE **KILLED** ME, IF NOT FOR MY FORCE FIELD.
THAT'S THE **PLAN.**
CAN'T YOU EE YOU'RE ON HE **WRONG SIDE?**
THAT **DOMINUS** WILL SACRIFICE YOU TOO?
F-ZAKT
F-ZAMM
TAKE **US** OUT...
...AND YOU'LL BE **CUTTING YOUR OWN THROAT!**

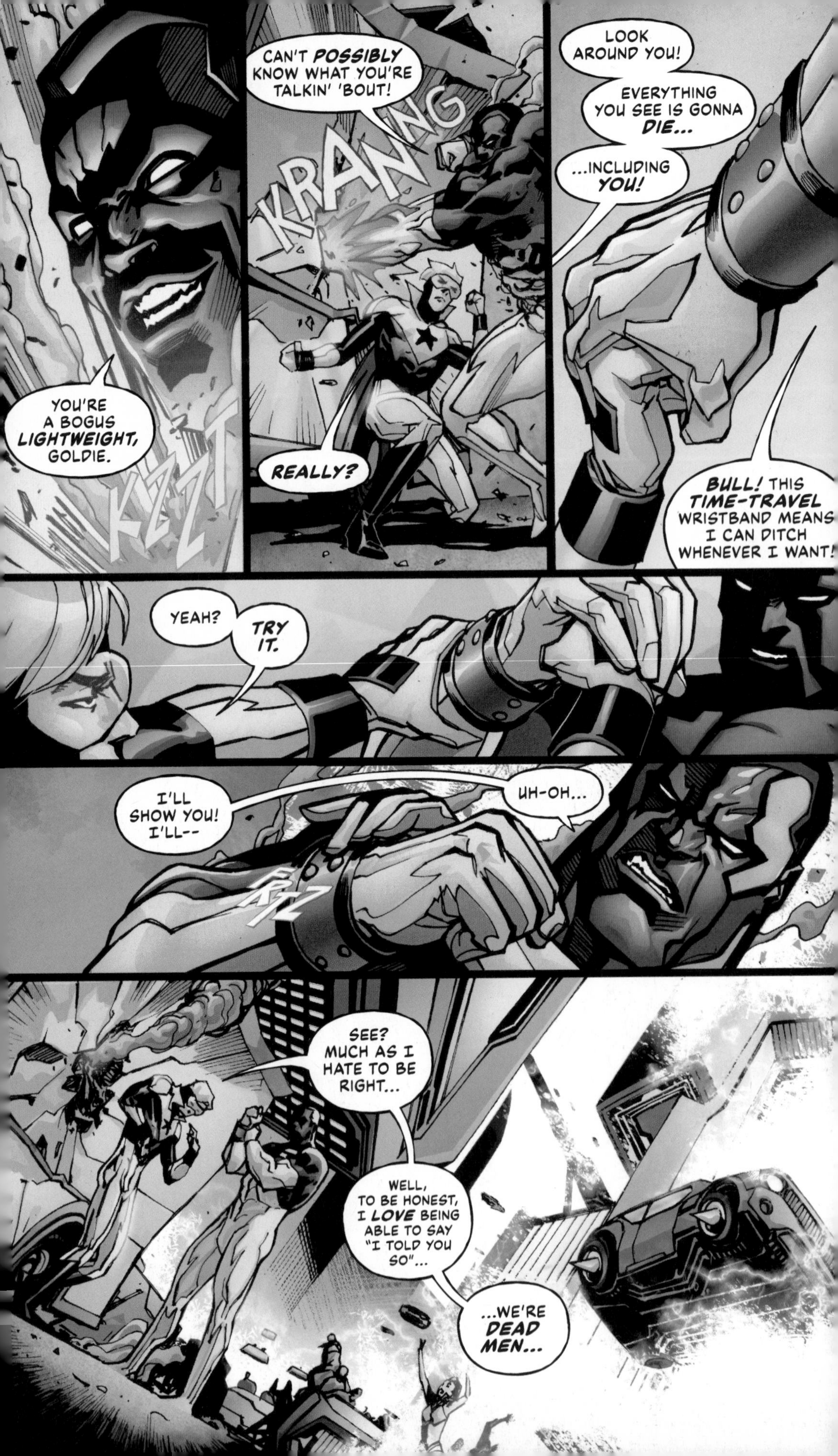

YOU'RE A BOGUS LIGHTWEIGHT, GOLDIE.
KZZT
CAN'T POSSIBLY KNOW WHAT YOU'RE TALKIN' 'BOUT!
KRANNG
REALLY?
LOOK AROUND YOU!
EVERYTHING YOU SEE IS GONNA DIE...
...INCLUDING YOU!
BULL! THIS TIME-TRAVEL WRISTBAND MEANS I CAN DITCH WHENEVER I WANT!
YEAH?
TRY IT.
I'LL SHOW YOU! I'LL--
UH-OH...
FRTZ
SEE? MUCH AS I HATE TO BE RIGHT...
WELL, TO BE HONEST, I LOVE BEING ABLE TO SAY "I TOLD YOU SO"...
...WE'RE DEAD MEN...

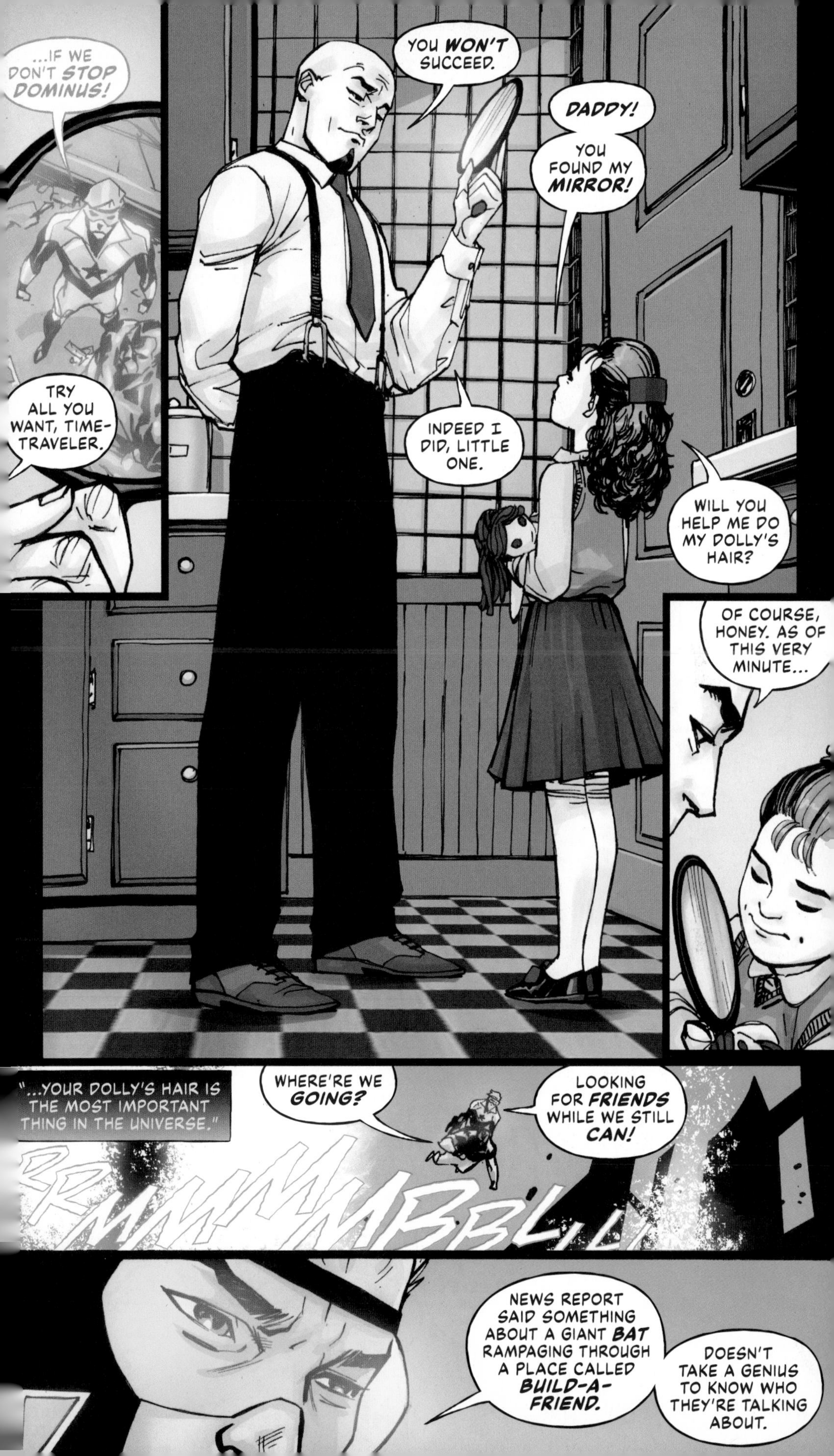

...IF WE DON'T STOP DOMINUS!
TRY ALL YOU WANT, TIME-TRAVELER.
YOU WON'T SUCCEED.
DADDY!
YOU FOUND MY MIRROR!
INDEED I DID, LITTLE ONE.
WILL YOU HELP ME DO MY DOLLY'S HAIR?
OF COURSE, HONEY. AS OF THIS VERY MINUTE...
"...YOUR DOLLY'S HAIR IS THE MOST IMPORTANT THING IN THE UNIVERSE."
WHERE'RE WE GOING?
LOOKING FOR FRIENDS WHILE WE STILL CAN!
RMMMMBBLLL
NEWS REPORT SAID SOMETHING ABOUT A GIANT BAT RAMPAGING THROUGH A PLACE CALLED BUILD-A-FRIEND.
DOESN'T TAKE A GENIUS TO KNOW WHO THEY'RE TALKING ABOUT.

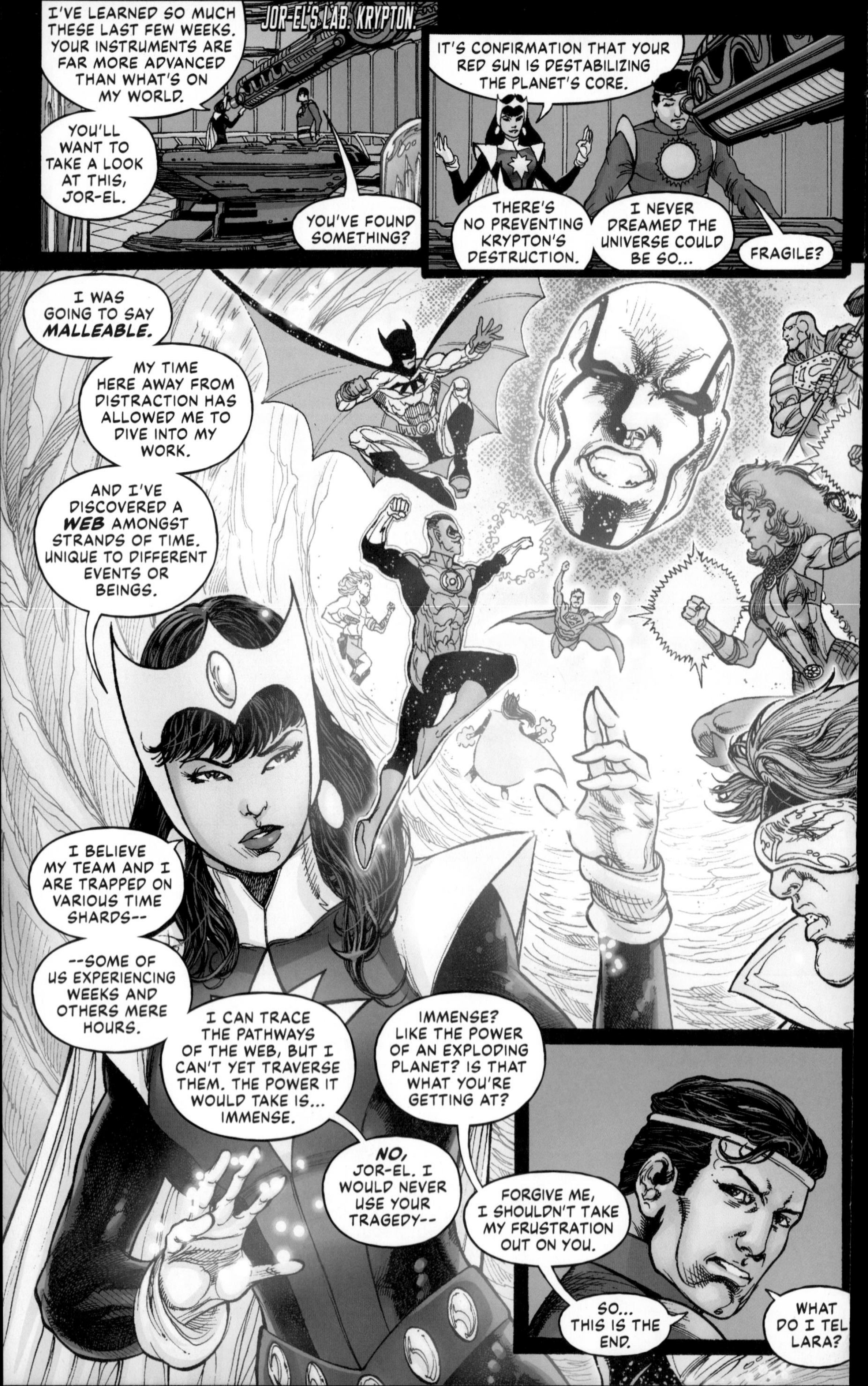
JOR-EL'S LAB. KRYPTON.
I'VE LEARNED SO MUCH THESE LAST FEW WEEKS. YOUR INSTRUMENTS ARE FAR MORE ADVANCED THAN WHAT'S ON MY WORLD.
YOU'LL WANT TO TAKE A LOOK AT THIS, JOR-EL.
YOU'VE FOUND SOMETHING?
IT'S CONFIRMATION THAT YOUR RED SUN IS DESTABILIZING THE PLANET'S CORE.
THERE'S NO PREVENTING KRYPTON'S DESTRUCTION.
I NEVER DREAMED THE UNIVERSE COULD BE SO...
FRAGILE?
I WAS GOING TO SAY MALLEABLE.
MY TIME HERE AWAY FROM DISTRACTION HAS ALLOWED ME TO DIVE INTO MY WORK.
AND I'VE DISCOVERED A WEB AMONGST STRANDS OF TIME. UNIQUE TO DIFFERENT EVENTS OR BEINGS.
I BELIEVE MY TEAM AND I ARE TRAPPED ON VARIOUS TIME SHARDS--
--SOME OF US EXPERIENCING WEEKS AND OTHERS MERE HOURS.
I CAN TRACE THE PATHWAYS OF THE WEB, BUT I CAN'T YET TRAVERSE THEM. THE POWER IT WOULD TAKE IS... IMMENSE.
IMMENSE? LIKE THE POWER OF AN EXPLODING PLANET? IS THAT WHAT YOU'RE GETTING AT?
NO, JOR-EL. I WOULD NEVER USE YOUR TRAGEDY--
FORGIVE ME, I SHOULDN'T TAKE MY FRUSTRATION OUT ON YOU.
SO... THIS IS THE END.
WHAT DO I TEL LARA?

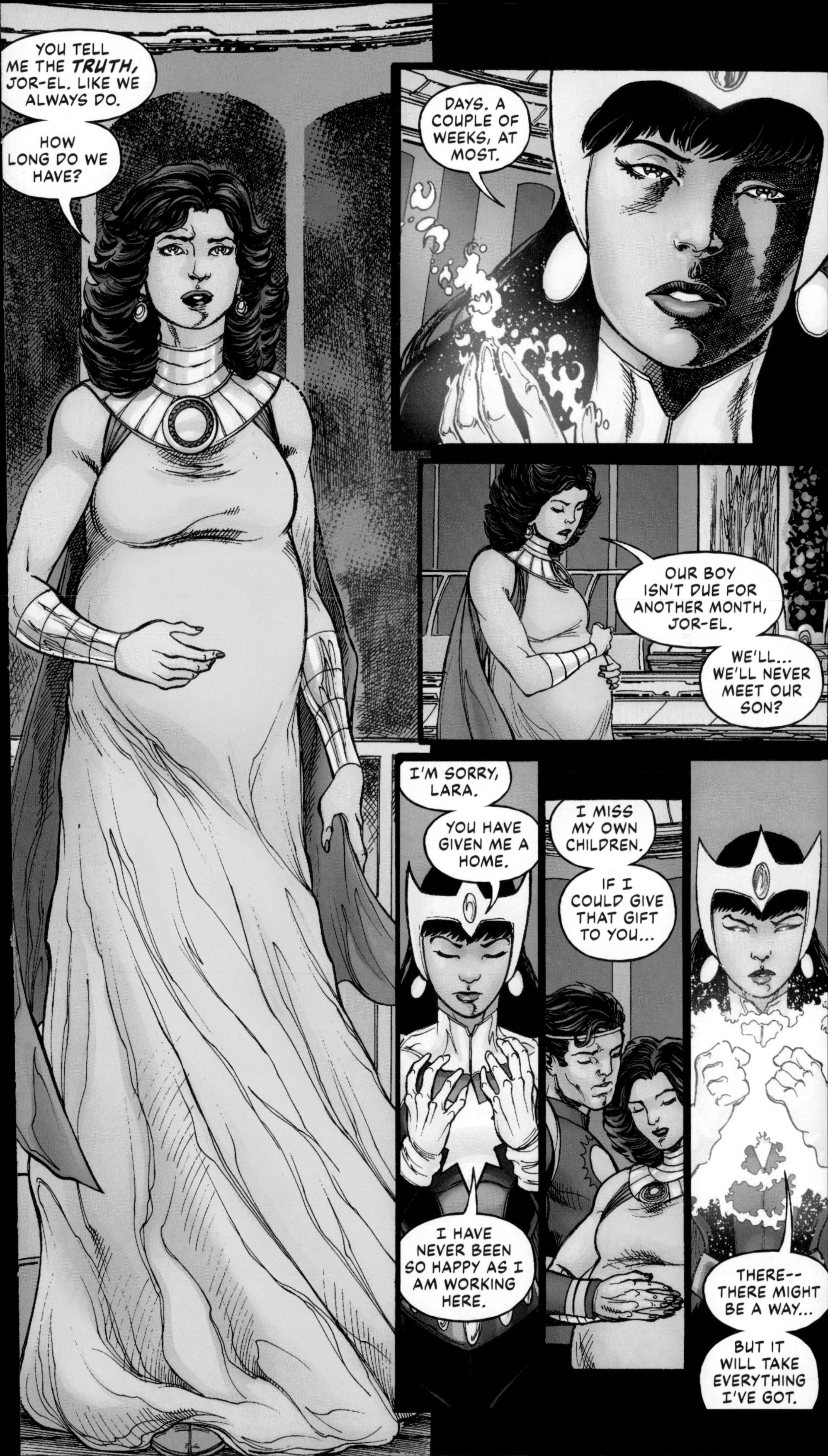
YOU TELL ME THE TRUTH, JOR-EL. LIKE WE ALWAYS DO.
HOW LONG DO WE HAVE?
DAYS. A COUPLE OF WEEKS, AT MOST.
OUR BOY ISN'T DUE FOR ANOTHER MONTH, JOR-EL.
WE'LL... WE'LL NEVER MEET OUR SON?
I'M SORRY, LARA.
YOU HAVE GIVEN ME A HOME.
I HAVE NEVER BEEN SO HAPPY AS I AM WORKING HERE.
I MISS MY OWN CHILDREN.
IF I COULD GIVE THAT GIFT TO YOU...
THERE-- THERE MIGHT BE A WAY...
BUT IT WILL TAKE EVERYTHING I'VE GOT.

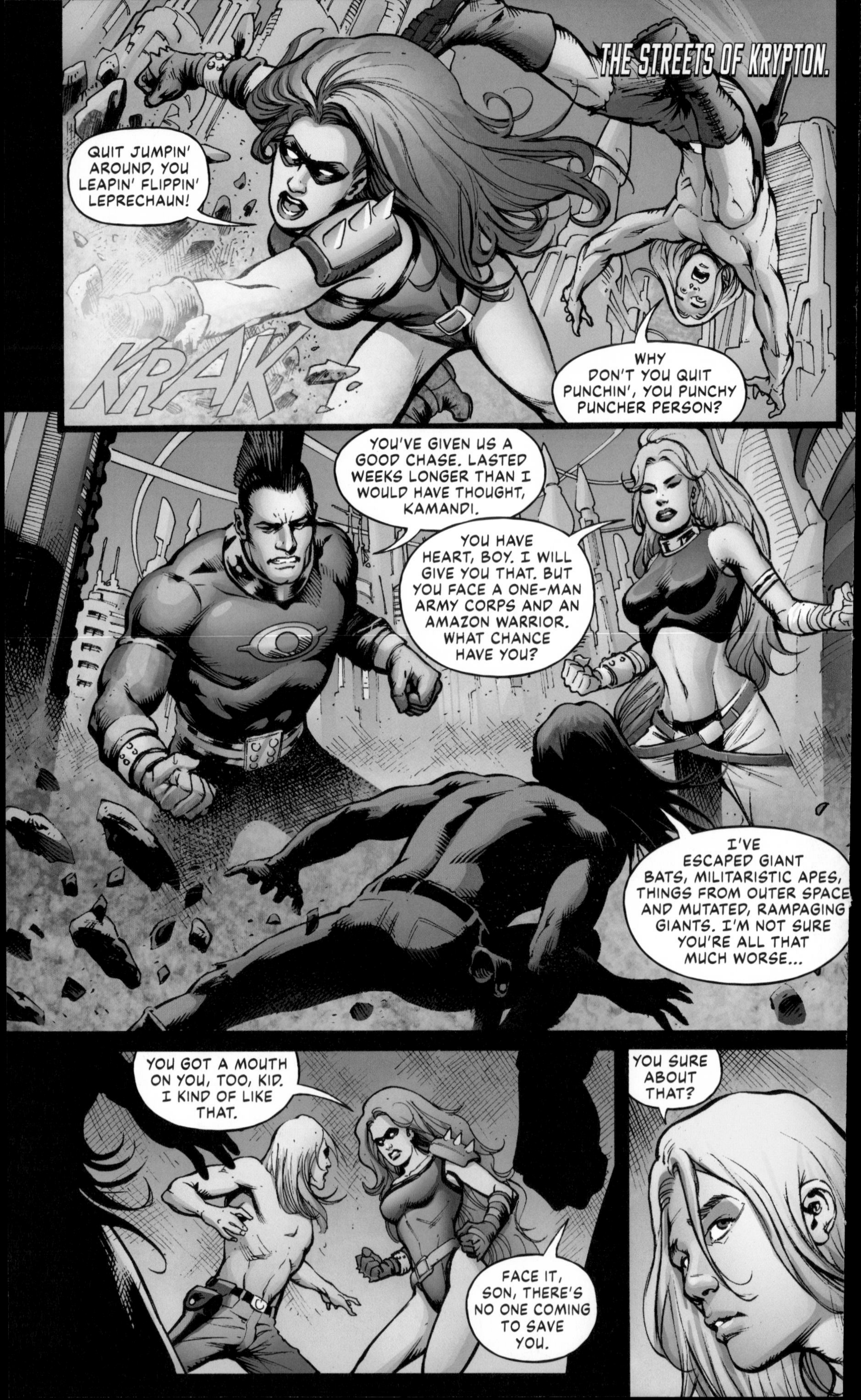
THE STREETS OF KRYPTON.
QUIT JUMPIN' AROUND, YOU LEAPIN' FLIPPIN' LEPRECHAUN!
KRAK
WHY DON'T YOU QUIT PUNCHIN', YOU PUNCHY PUNCHER PERSON?
YOU'VE GIVEN US A GOOD CHASE. LASTED WEEKS LONGER THAN I WOULD HAVE THOUGHT, KAMANDI.
YOU HAVE HEART, BOY. I WILL GIVE YOU THAT. BUT YOU FACE A ONE-MAN ARMY CORPS AND AN AMAZON WARRIOR. WHAT CHANCE HAVE YOU?
I'VE ESCAPED GIANT BATS, MILITARISTIC APES, THINGS FROM OUTER SPACE AND MUTATED, RAMPAGING GIANTS. I'M NOT SURE YOU'RE ALL THAT MUCH WORSE...
YOU GOT A MOUTH ON YOU, TOO, KID. I KIND OF LIKE THAT.
FACE IT, SON, THERE'S NO ONE COMING TO SAVE YOU.
YOU SURE ABOUT THAT?

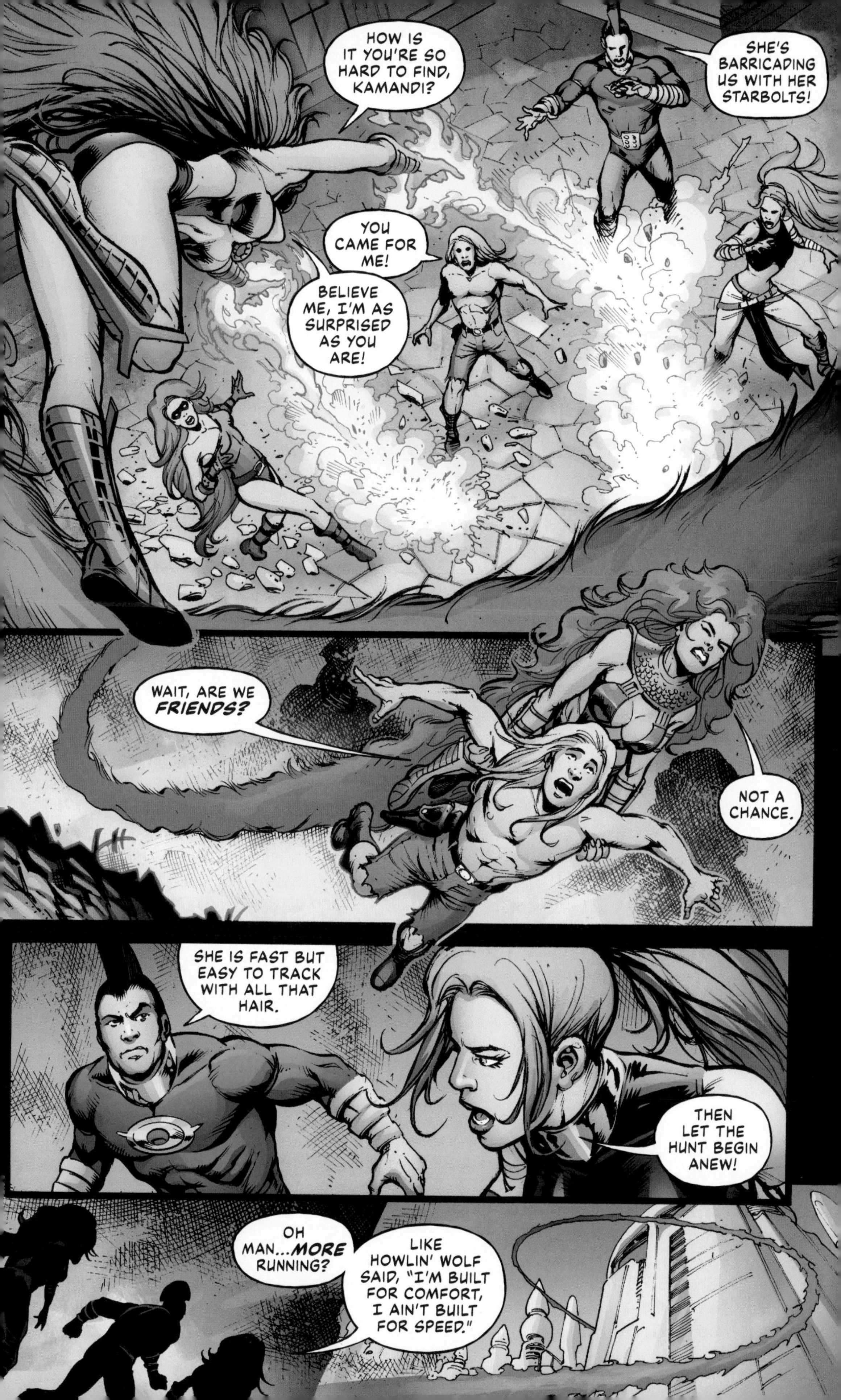
HOW IS IT YOU'RE SO HARD TO FIND, KAMANDI?
SHE'S BARRICADING US WITH HER STARBOLTS!
YOU CAME FOR ME!
BELIEVE ME, I'M AS SURPRISED AS YOU ARE!
WAIT, ARE WE *FRIENDS?*
NOT A CHANCE.
SHE IS FAST BUT EASY TO TRACK WITH ALL THAT HAIR.
THEN LET THE HUNT BEGIN ANEW!
OH MAN...*MORE* RUNNING?
LIKE HOWLIN' WOLF SAID, "I'M BUILT FOR COMFORT, I AIN'T BUILT FOR SPEED."

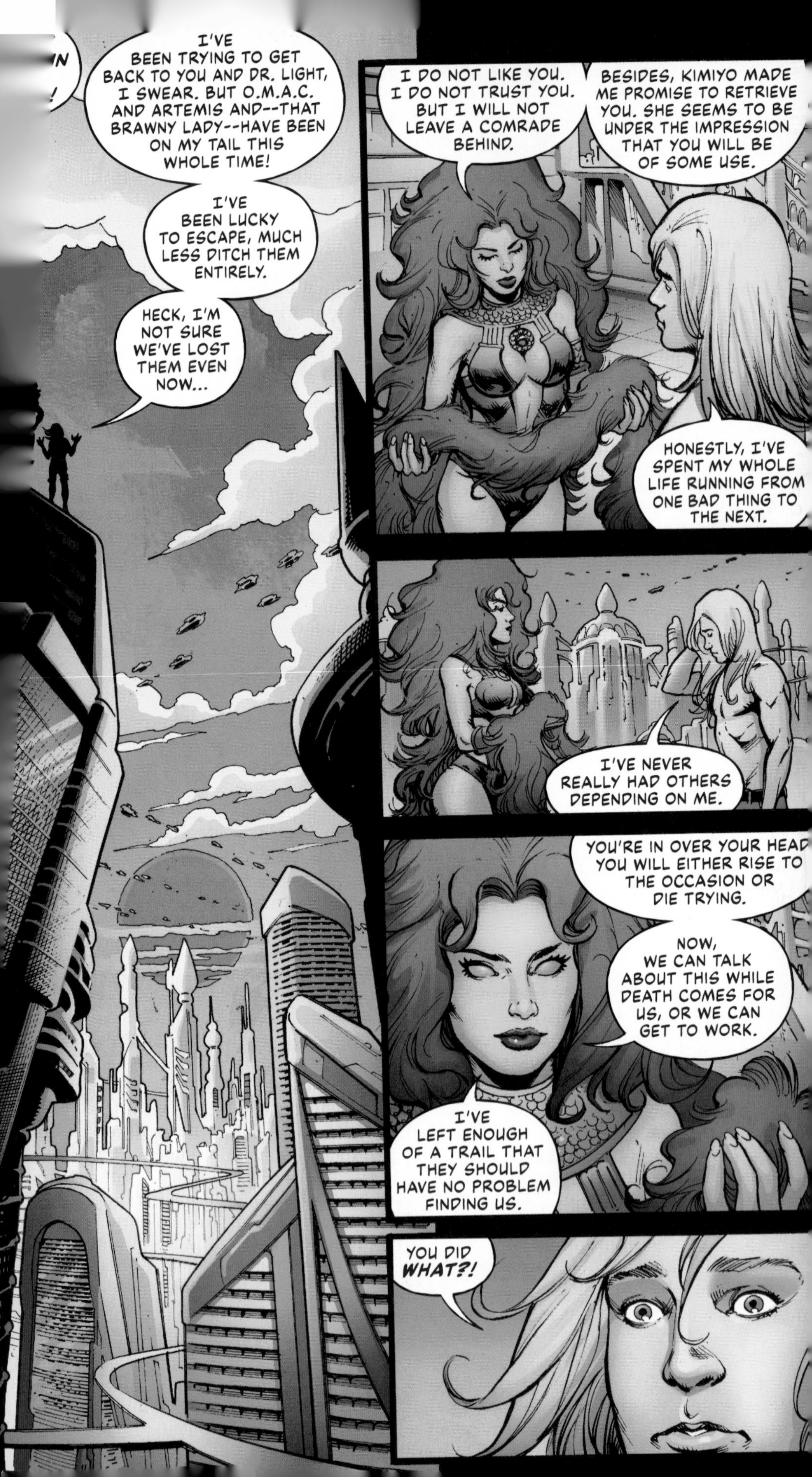
I'VE BEEN TRYING TO GET BACK TO YOU AND DR. LIGHT, I SWEAR. BUT O.M.A.C. AND ARTEMIS AND--THAT BRAWNY LADY--HAVE BEEN ON MY TAIL THIS WHOLE TIME!
I'VE BEEN LUCKY TO ESCAPE, MUCH LESS DITCH THEM ENTIRELY.
HECK, I'M NOT SURE WE'VE LOST THEM EVEN NOW...
I DO NOT LIKE YOU. I DO NOT TRUST YOU. BUT I WILL NOT LEAVE A COMRADE BEHIND.
BESIDES, KIMIYO MADE ME PROMISE TO RETRIEVE YOU. SHE SEEMS TO BE UNDER THE IMPRESSION THAT YOU WILL BE OF SOME USE.
HONESTLY, I'VE SPENT MY WHOLE LIFE RUNNING FROM ONE BAD THING TO THE NEXT.
I'VE NEVER REALLY HAD OTHERS DEPENDING ON ME.
YOU'RE IN OVER YOUR HEAD. YOU WILL EITHER RISE TO THE OCCASION OR DIE TRYING.
NOW, WE CAN TALK ABOUT THIS WHILE DEATH COMES FOR US, OR WE CAN GET TO WORK.
I'VE LEFT ENOUGH OF A TRAIL THAT THEY SHOULD HAVE NO PROBLEM FINDING US.
YOU DID WHAT?!

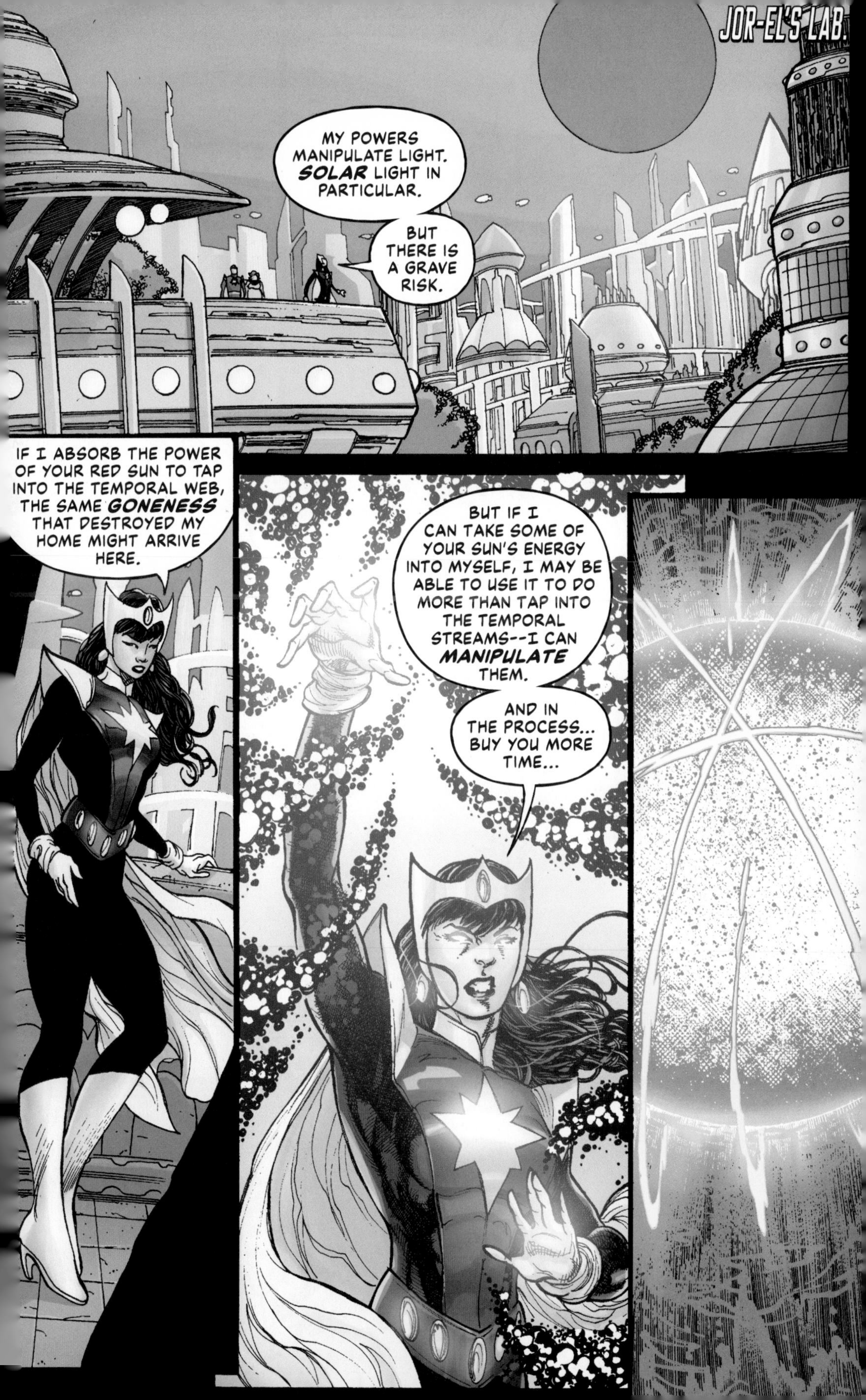
JOR-EL'S LAB.
MY POWERS MANIPULATE LIGHT. SOLAR LIGHT IN PARTICULAR.
BUT THERE IS A GRAVE RISK.
IF I ABSORB THE POWER OF YOUR RED SUN TO TAP INTO THE TEMPORAL WEB, THE SAME GONENESS THAT DESTROYED MY HOME MIGHT ARRIVE HERE.
BUT IF I CAN TAKE SOME OF YOUR SUN'S ENERGY INTO MYSELF, I MAY BE ABLE TO USE IT TO DO MORE THAN TAP INTO THE TEMPORAL STREAMS--I CAN MANIPULATE THEM.
AND IN THE PROCESS... BUY YOU MORE TIME...

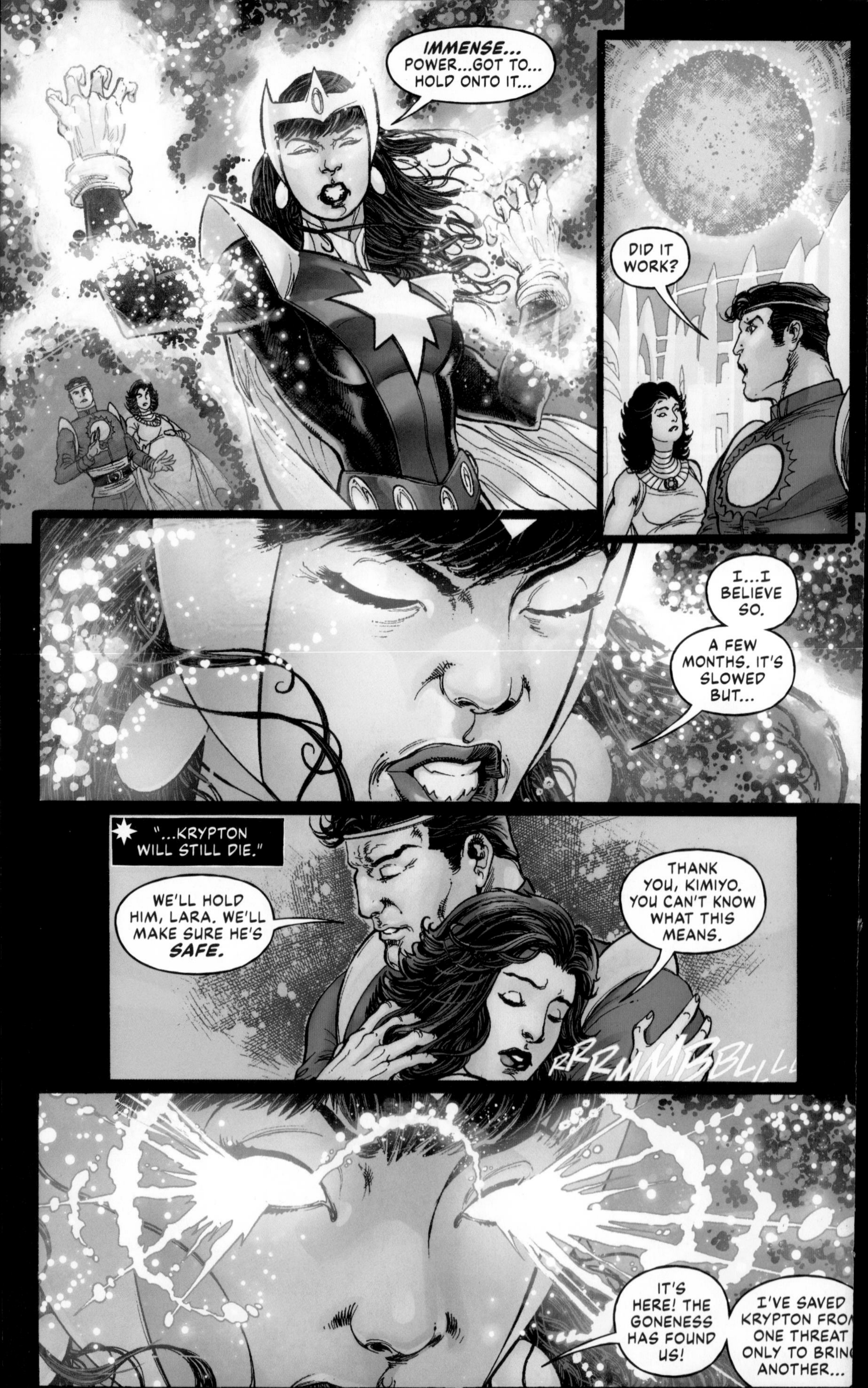
IMMENSE... POWER...GOT TO... HOLD ONTO IT...
DID IT WORK?
I...I BELIEVE SO.
A FEW MONTHS. IT'S SLOWED BUT...
"...KRYPTON WILL STILL DIE."
WE'LL HOLD HIM, LARA. WE'LL MAKE SURE HE'S SAFE.
THANK YOU, KIMIYO. YOU CAN'T KNOW WHAT THIS MEANS.
RRRMMBBLLL
IT'S HERE! THE GONENESS HAS FOUND US!
I'VE SAVED KRYPTON FROM ONE THREAT ONLY TO BRING ANOTHER...

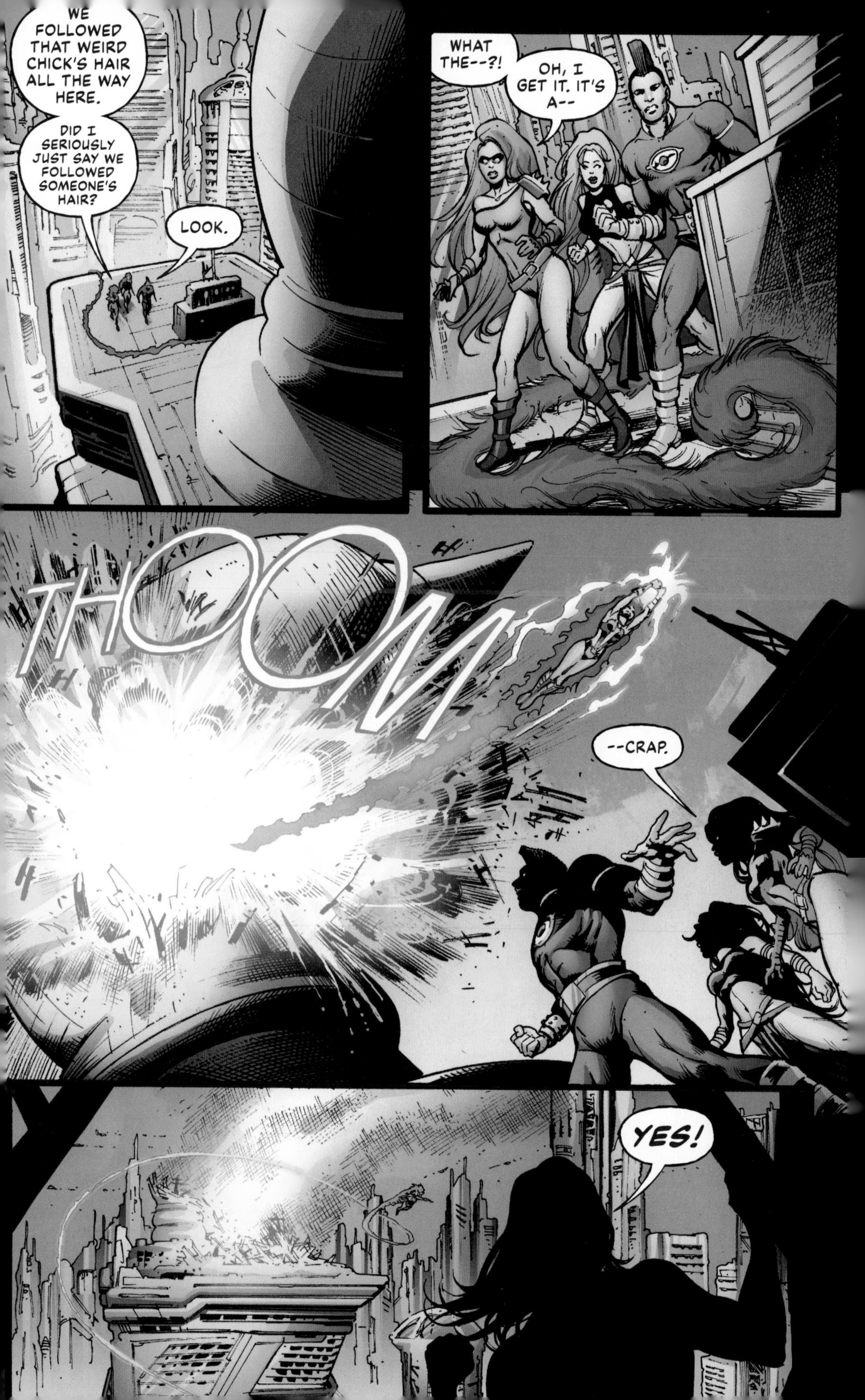
WE FOLLOWED THAT WEIRD CHICK'S HAIR ALL THE WAY HERE.
DID I SERIOUSLY JUST SAY WE FOLLOWED SOMEONE'S HAIR?
LOOK.
WHAT THE--?!
OH, I GET IT. IT'S A--
THOOM
--CRAP.
YES!

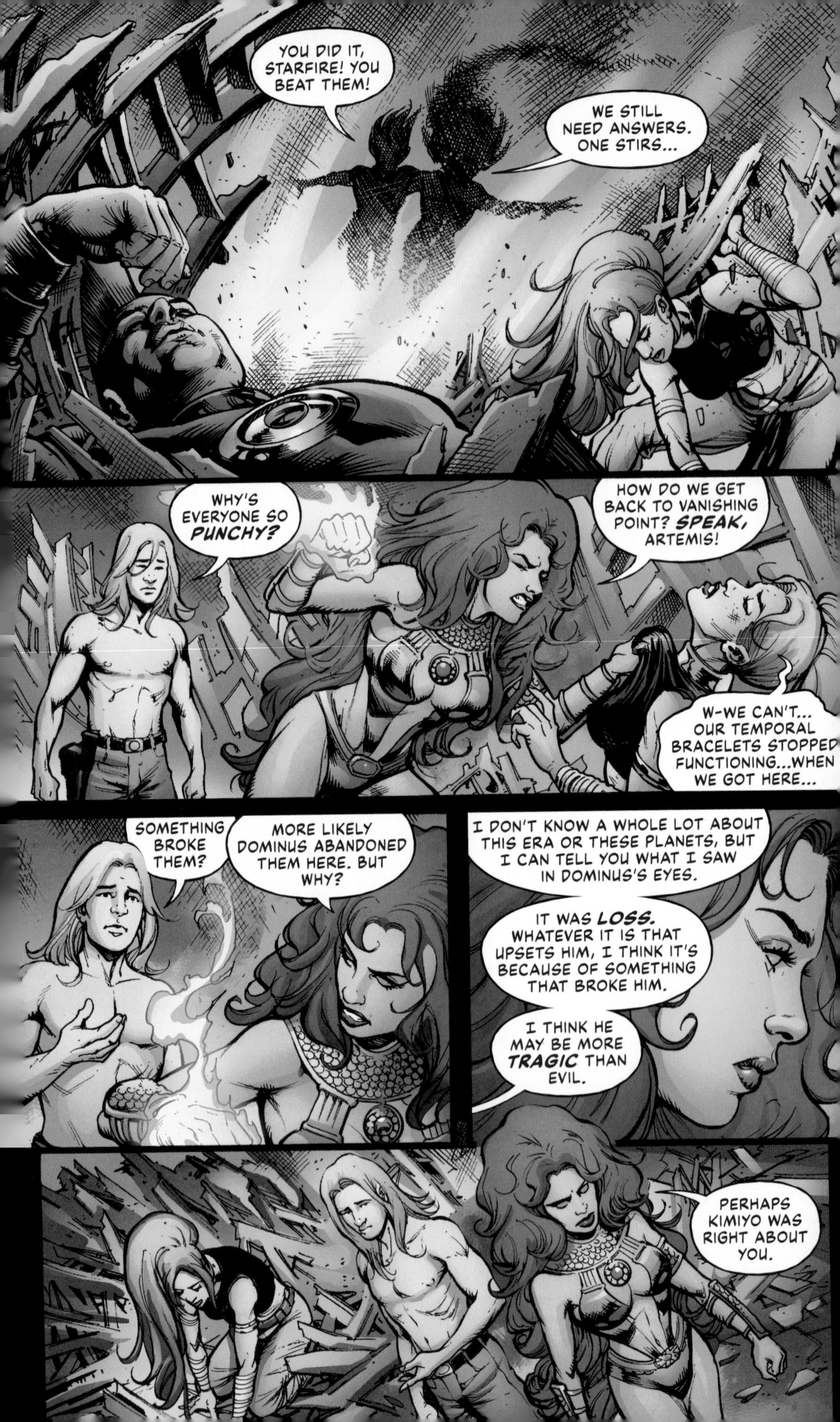
YOU DID IT, STARFIRE! YOU BEAT THEM!
WE STILL NEED ANSWERS. ONE STIRS...
WHY'S EVERYONE SO *PUNCHY?*
HOW DO WE GET BACK TO VANISHING POINT? ***SPEAK,*** ARTEMIS!
W-WE CAN'T... OUR TEMPORAL BRACELETS STOPPED FUNCTIONING...WHEN WE GOT HERE...
SOMETHING BROKE THEM?
MORE LIKELY DOMINUS ABANDONED THEM HERE. BUT WHY?
I DON'T KNOW A WHOLE LOT ABOUT THIS ERA OR THESE PLANETS, BUT I CAN TELL YOU WHAT I SAW IN DOMINUS'S EYES.
IT WAS ***LOSS.*** WHATEVER IT IS THAT UPSETS HIM, I THINK IT'S BECAUSE OF SOMETHING THAT BROKE HIM.
I THINK HE MAY BE MORE ***TRAGIC*** THAN EVIL.
PERHAPS KIMIYO WAS RIGHT ABOUT YOU.

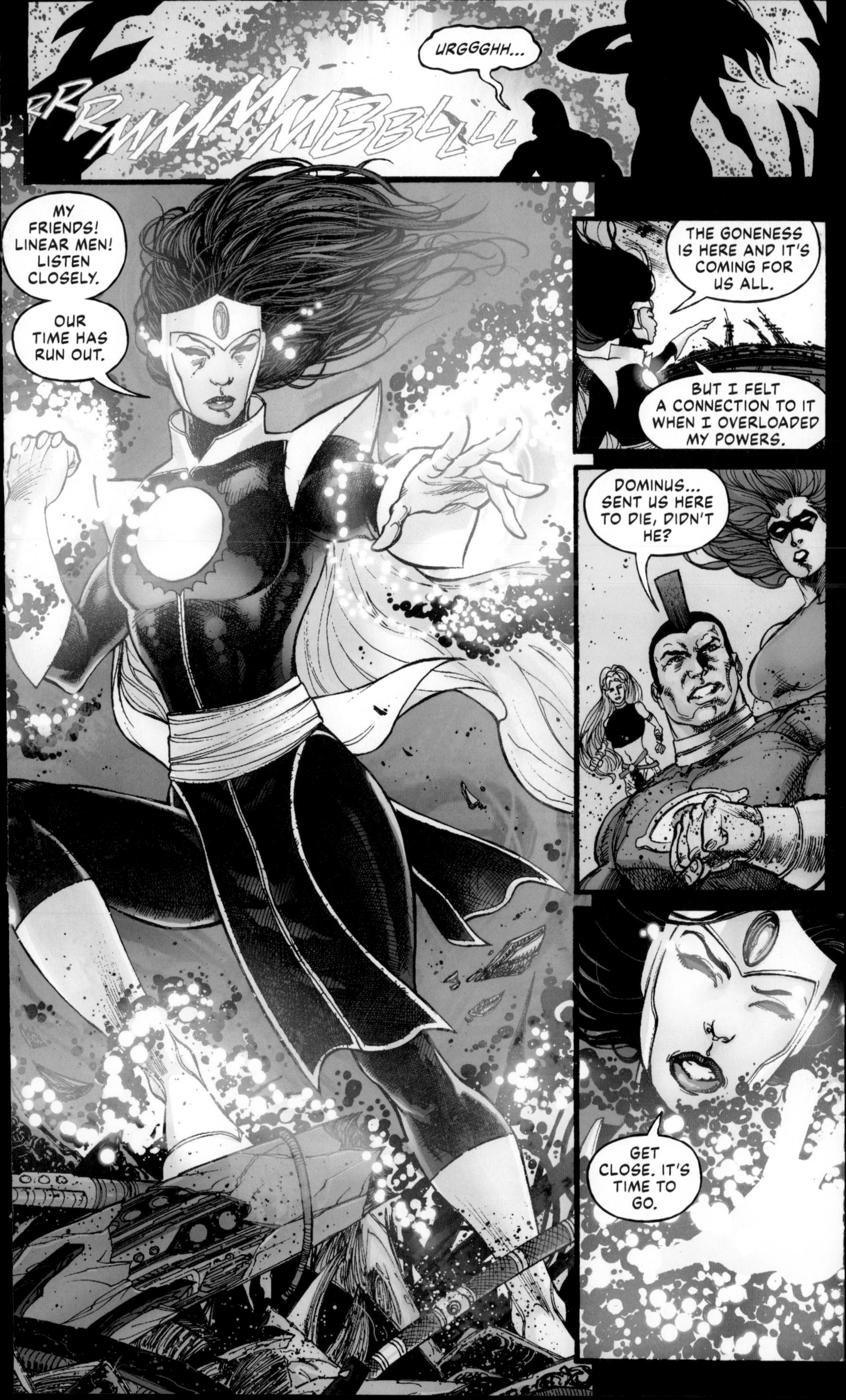
URGGGHH...
RRRMMMMMBBLLLL
MY FRIENDS! LINEAR MEN! LISTEN CLOSELY.
OUR TIME HAS RUN OUT.
THE GONENESS IS HERE AND IT'S COMING FOR US ALL.
BUT I FELT A CONNECTION TO IT WHEN I OVERLOADED MY POWERS.
DOMINUS... SENT US HERE TO DIE, DIDN'T HE?
GET CLOSE. IT'S TIME TO GO.

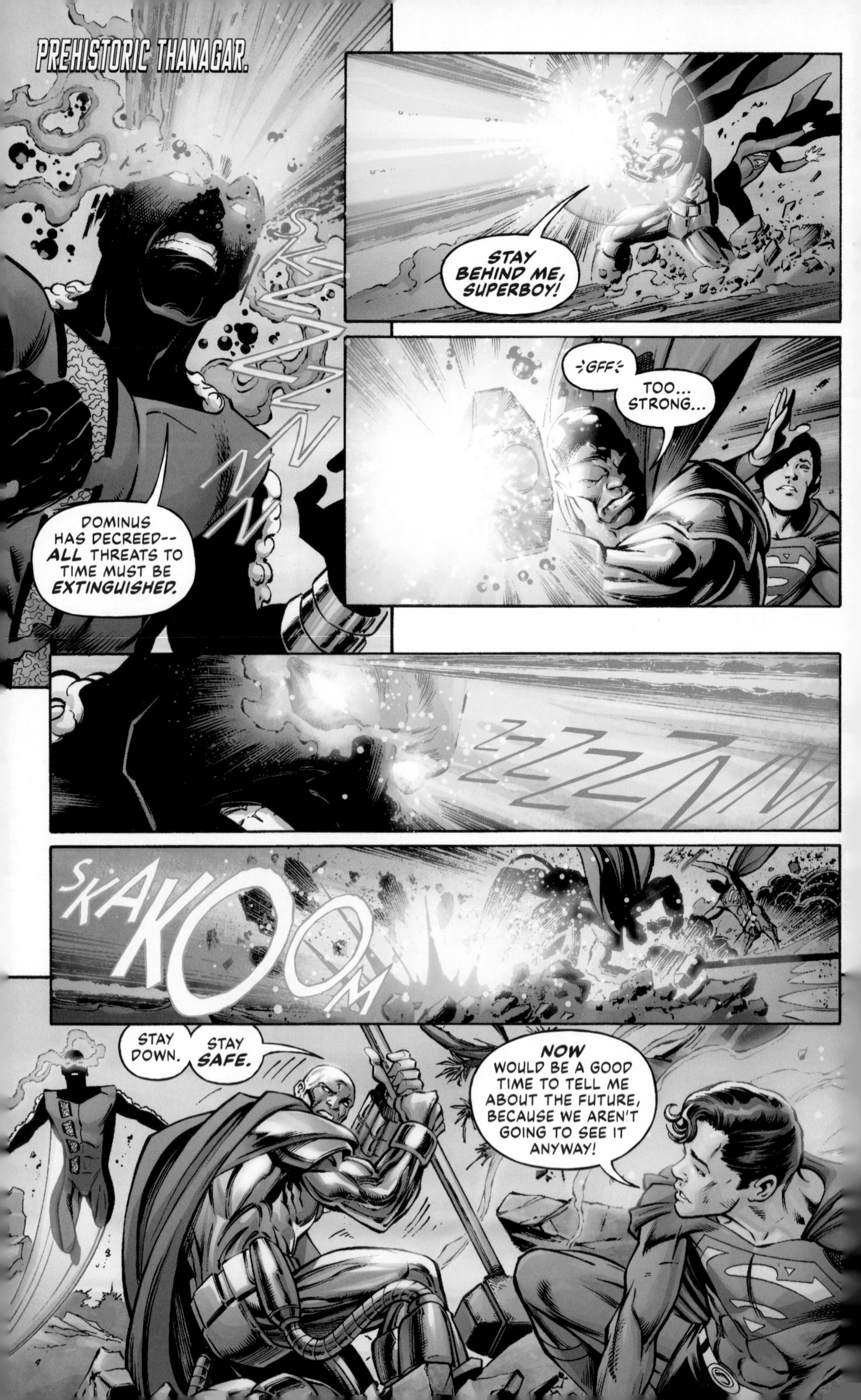
PREHISTORIC THANAGAR.
STAY BEHIND ME, SUPERBOY!
DOMINUS HAS DECREED-- ALL THREATS TO TIME MUST BE EXTINGUISHED.
SKWANNNNN
-GFF-
TOO... STRONG...
ZZZZZM
SKAKOOM
STAY DOWN.
STAY SAFE.
NOW WOULD BE A GOOD TIME TO TELL ME ABOUT THE FUTURE, BECAUSE WE AREN'T GOING TO SEE IT ANYWAY!

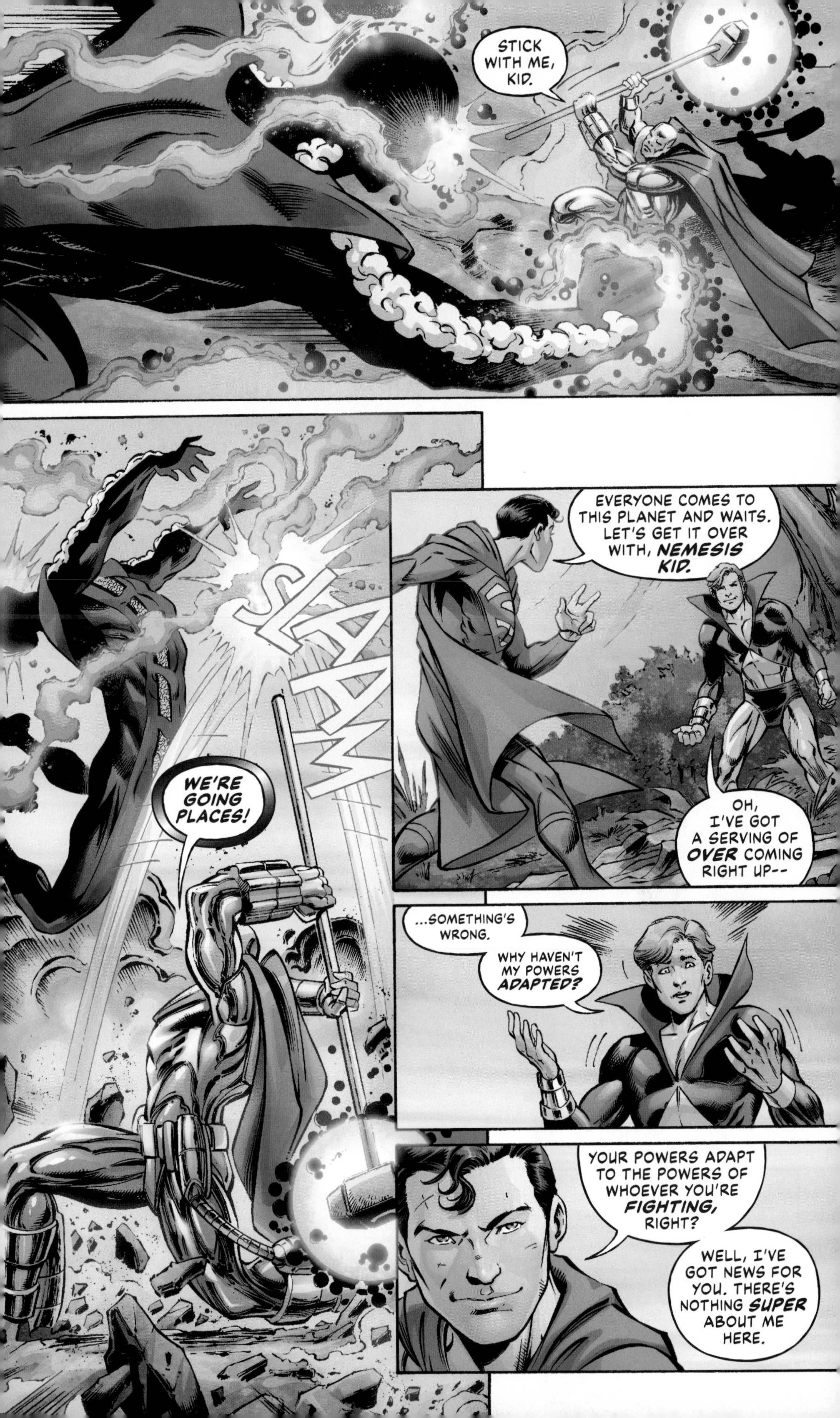

STICK WITH ME, KID.
SLAAAM
WE'RE GOING PLACES!
EVERYONE COMES TO THIS PLANET AND WAITS. LET'S GET IT OVER WITH, NEMESIS KID.
OH, I'VE GOT A SERVING OF OVER COMING RIGHT UP--
...SOMETHING'S WRONG.
WHY HAVEN'T MY POWERS ADAPTED?
YOUR POWERS ADAPT TO THE POWERS OF WHOEVER YOU'RE FIGHTING, RIGHT?
WELL, I'VE GOT NEWS FOR YOU. THERE'S NOTHING SUPER ABOUT ME HERE.

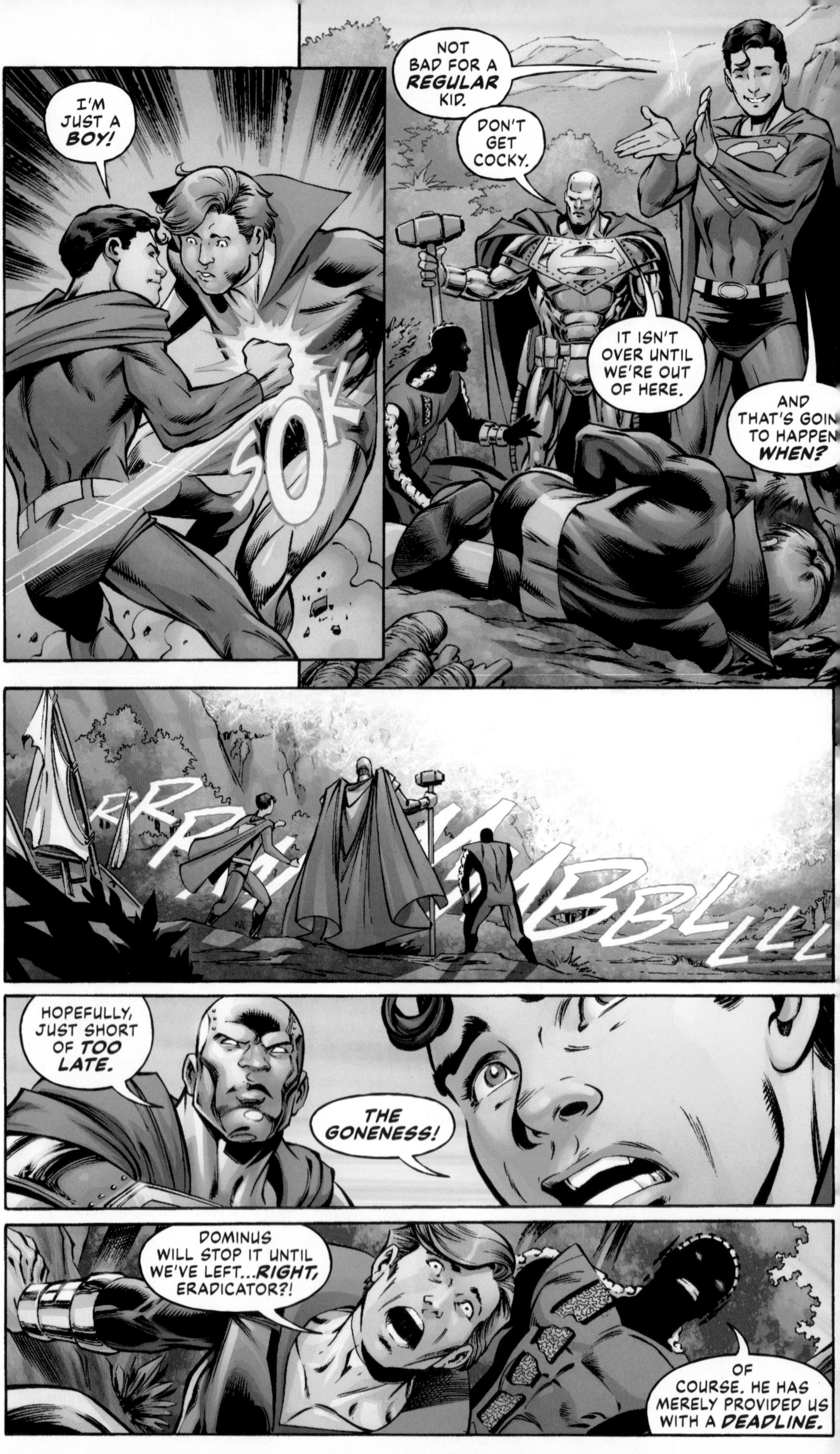
I'M JUST A BOY!
SOK
NOT BAD FOR A REGULAR KID.
DON'T GET COCKY.
IT ISN'T OVER UNTIL WE'RE OUT OF HERE.
AND THAT'S GOIN TO HAPPEN WHEN?
RRRMMMBBLLLL
HOPEFULLY, JUST SHORT OF TOO LATE.
THE GONENESS!
DOMINUS WILL STOP IT UNTIL WE'VE LEFT...RIGHT, ERADICATOR?!
OF COURSE. HE HAS MERELY PROVIDED US WITH A DEADLINE.

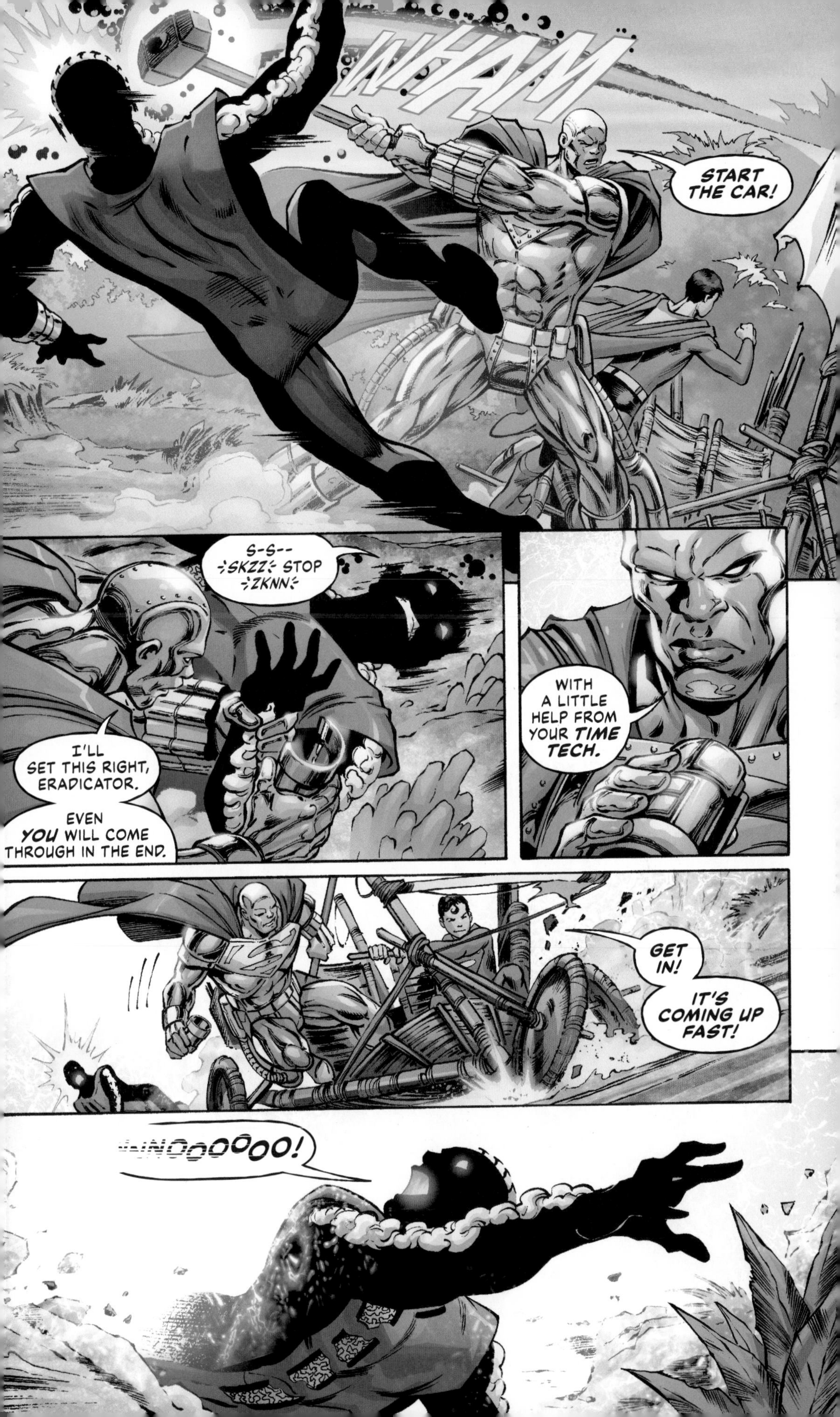
WHAM
START THE CAR!
S-S-- SKZZ STOP ZKNN
I'LL SET THIS RIGHT, ERADICATOR.
EVEN YOU WILL COME THROUGH IN THE END.
WITH A LITTLE HELP FROM YOUR TIME TECH.
GET IN!
IT'S COMING UP FAST!
NOOOOOOO!

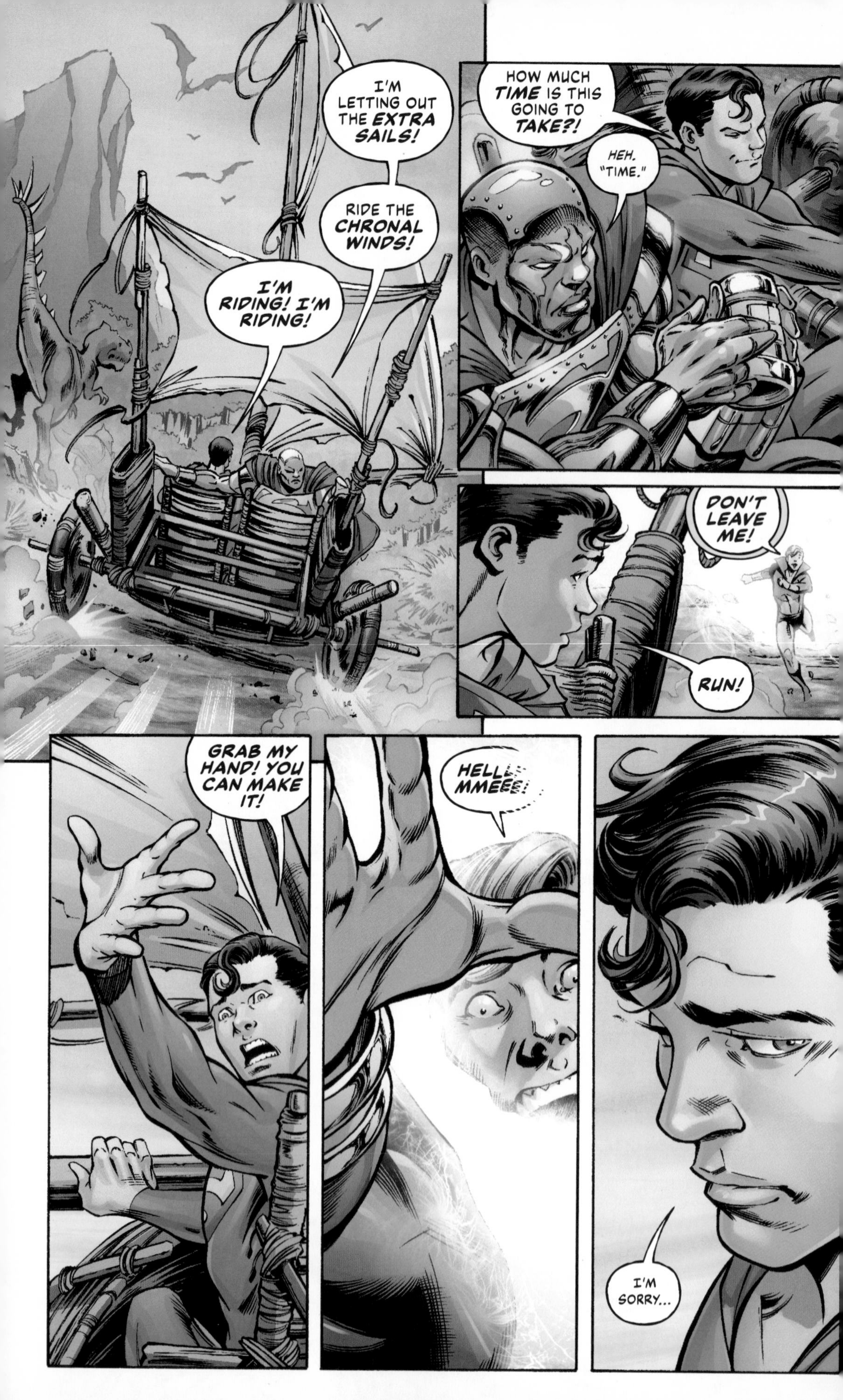
I'M LETTING OUT THE EXTRA SAILS!
RIDE THE CHRONAL WINDS!
I'M RIDING! I'M RIDING!
HOW MUCH TIME IS THIS GOING TO TAKE?!
HEH. "TIME."
DON'T LEAVE ME!
RUN!
GRAB MY HAND! YOU CAN MAKE IT!
I'M SORRY...

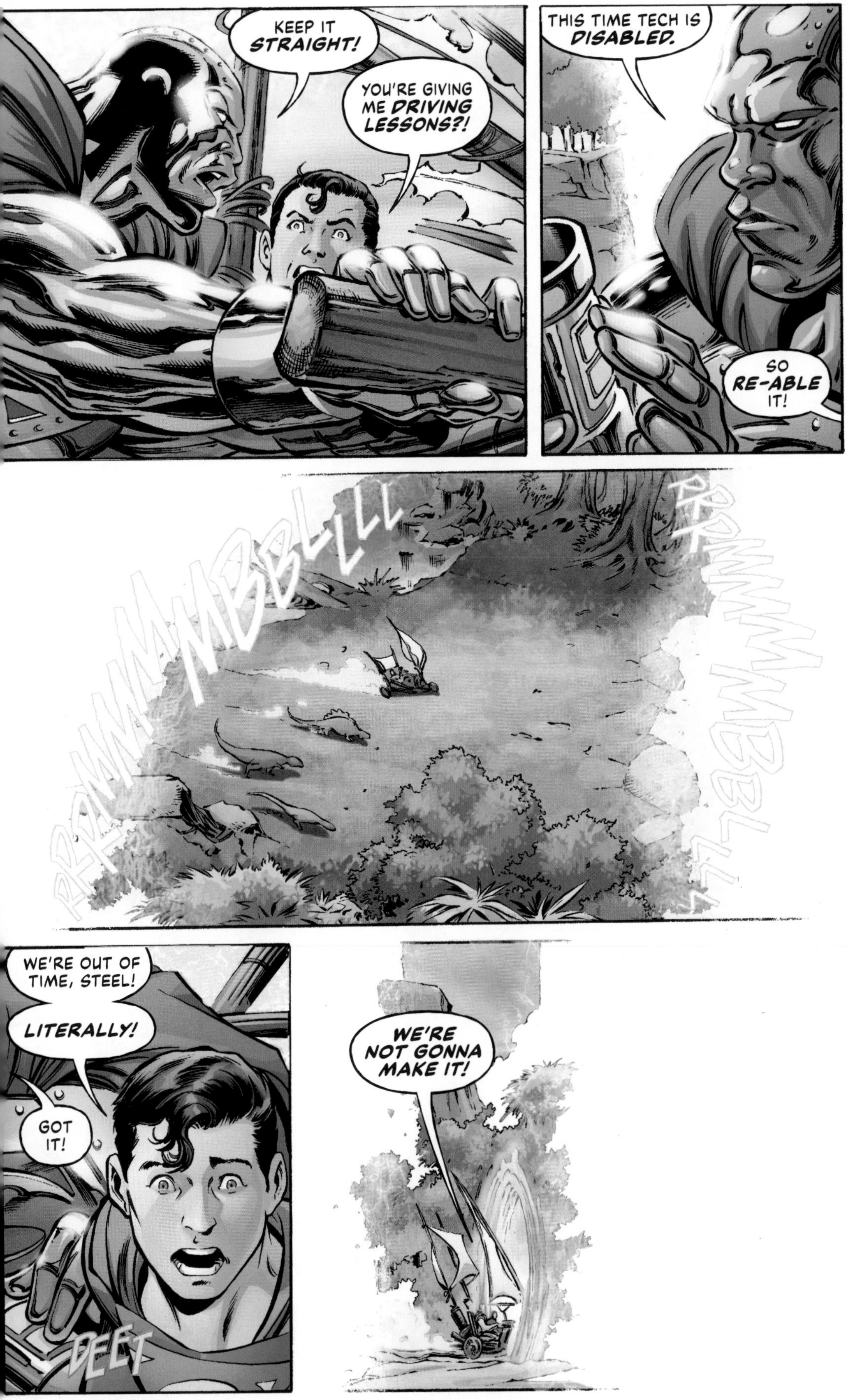
KEEP IT STRAIGHT!
YOU'RE GIVING ME DRIVING LESSONS?!
THIS TIME TECH IS DISABLED.
SO RE-ABLE IT!
BRRMMMMMBBLLLL
BRRMMMMMBBLLLL
WE'RE OUT OF TIME, STEEL!
LITERALLY!
GOT IT!
DEET
WE'RE NOT GONNA MAKE IT!

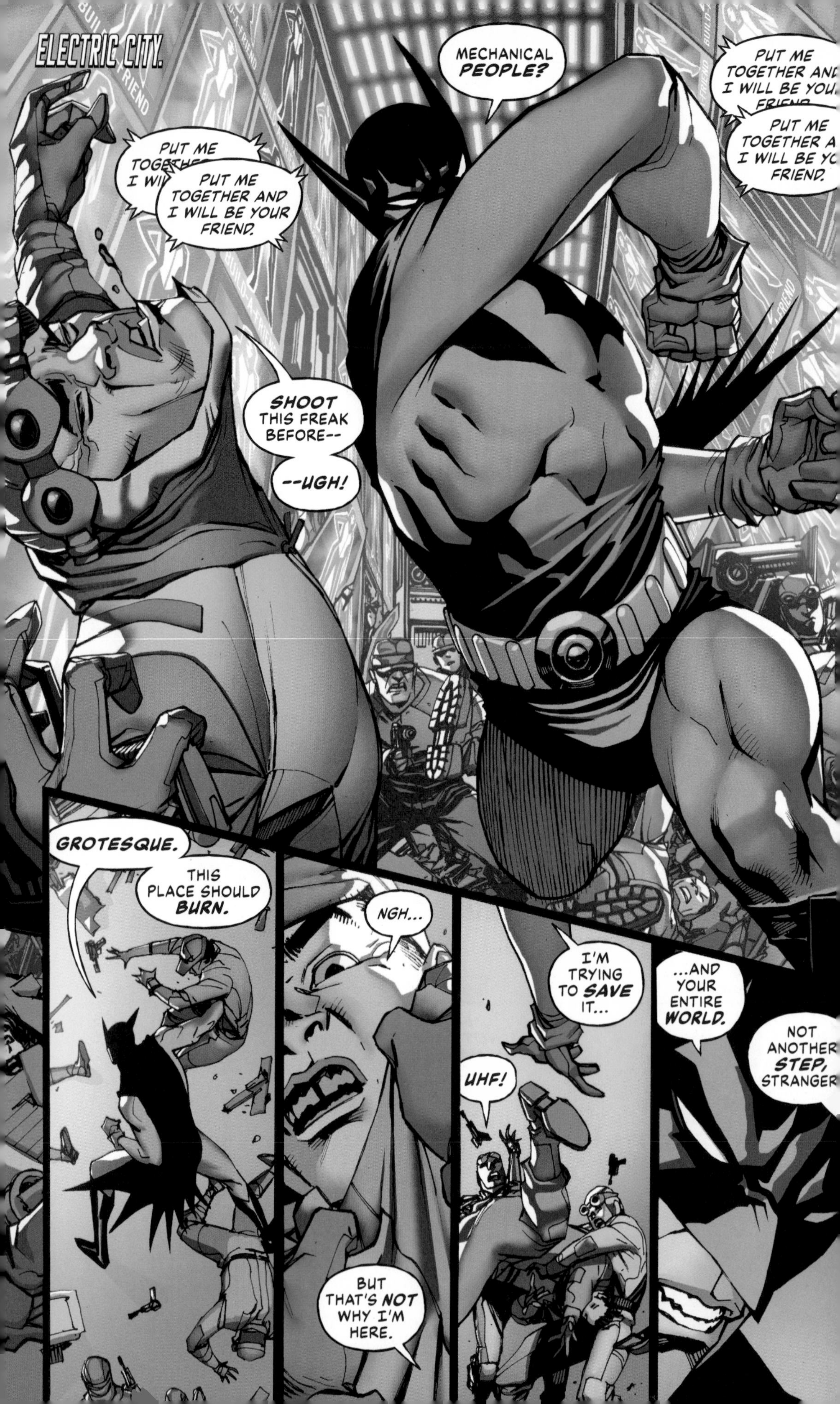
ELECTRIC CITY.
PUT ME TOGETHE I WI
PUT ME TOGETHER AND I WILL BE YOUR FRIEND.
MECHANICAL PEOPLE?
PUT ME TOGETHER AN I WILL BE YOU
PUT ME TOGETHER A I WILL BE YO FRIEND.
SHOOT THIS FREAK BEFORE--
--UGH!
GROTESQUE.
THIS PLACE SHOULD BURN.
NGH...
BUT THAT'S NOT WHY I'M HERE.
I'M TRYING TO SAVE IT...
UHF!
...AND YOUR ENTIRE WORLD.
NOT ANOTHER STEP, STRANGER

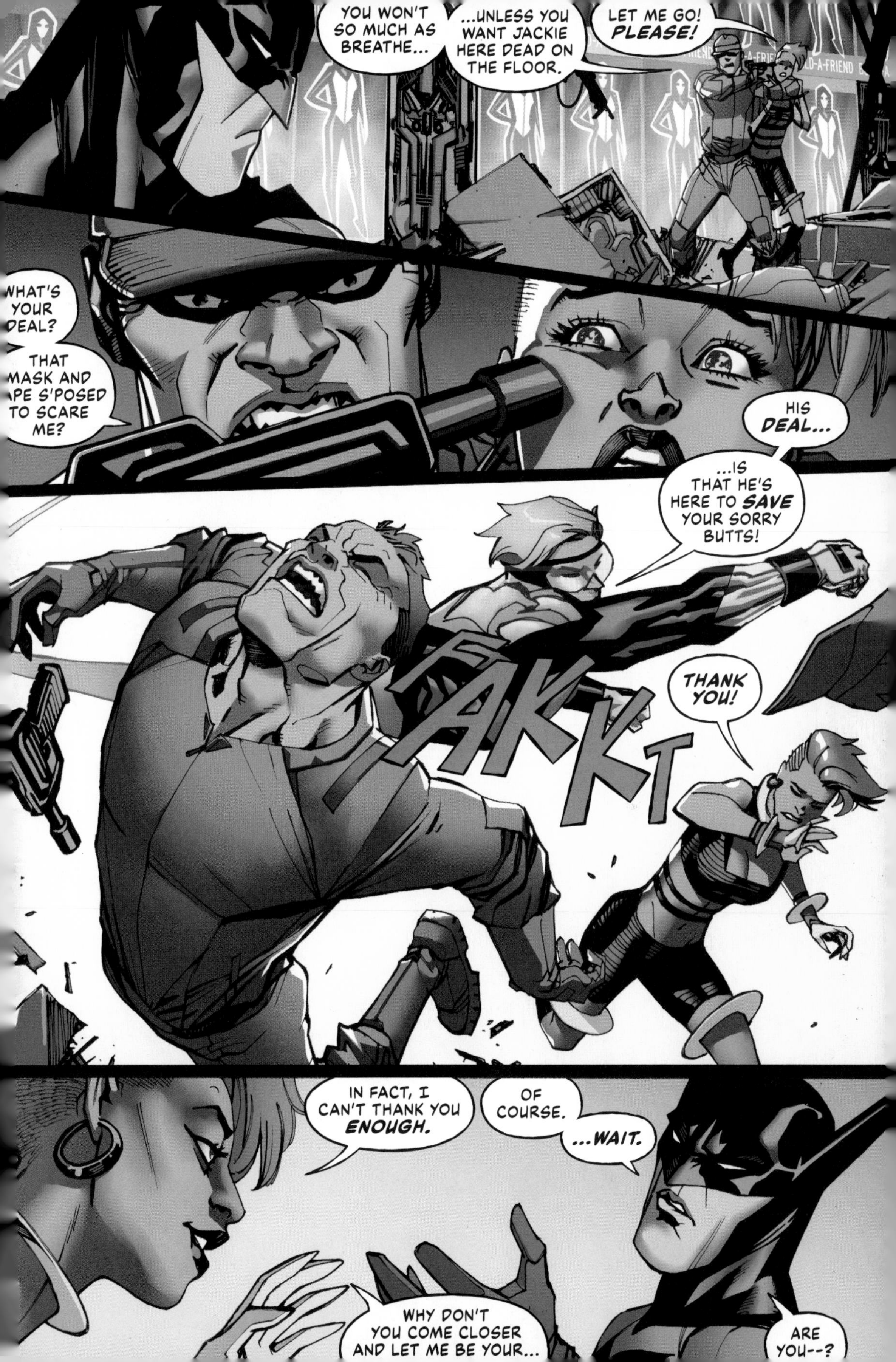
YOU WON'T SO MUCH AS BREATHE...
...UNLESS YOU WANT JACKIE HERE DEAD ON THE FLOOR.
LET ME GO! PLEASE!
WHAT'S YOUR DEAL?
THAT MASK AND CAPE S'POSED TO SCARE ME?
HIS DEAL...
...IS THAT HE'S HERE TO SAVE YOUR SORRY BUTTS!
FAKKT
THANK YOU!
IN FACT, I CAN'T THANK YOU ENOUGH.
OF COURSE.
...WAIT.
WHY DON'T YOU COME CLOSER AND LET ME BE YOUR...
ARE YOU--?

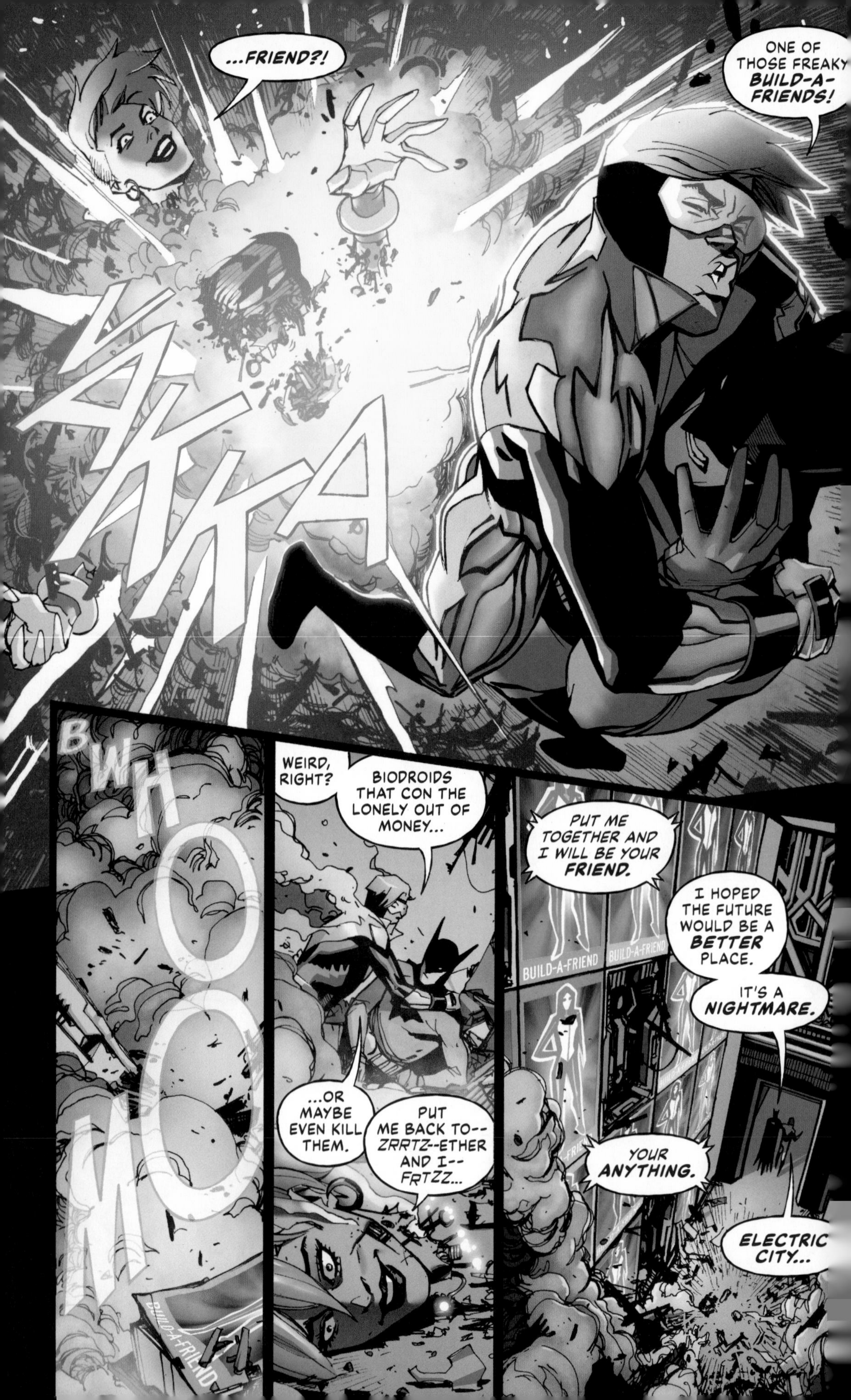
...FRIEND?!
ONE OF THOSE FREAKY BUILD-A-FRIENDS!
SKKA
BWHOOM
WEIRD, RIGHT?
BIODROIDS THAT CON THE LONELY OUT OF MONEY...
...OR MAYBE EVEN KILL THEM.
PUT ME BACK TO--ZRRTZ--ETHER AND I--FRTZZ...
BUILD-A-FRIEND
PUT ME TOGETHER AND I WILL BE YOUR FRIEND.
I HOPED THE FUTURE WOULD BE A BETTER PLACE.
IT'S A NIGHTMARE.
BUILD-A-FRIEND
BUILD-A-FRIEND
YOUR ANYTHING.
ELECTRIC CITY...

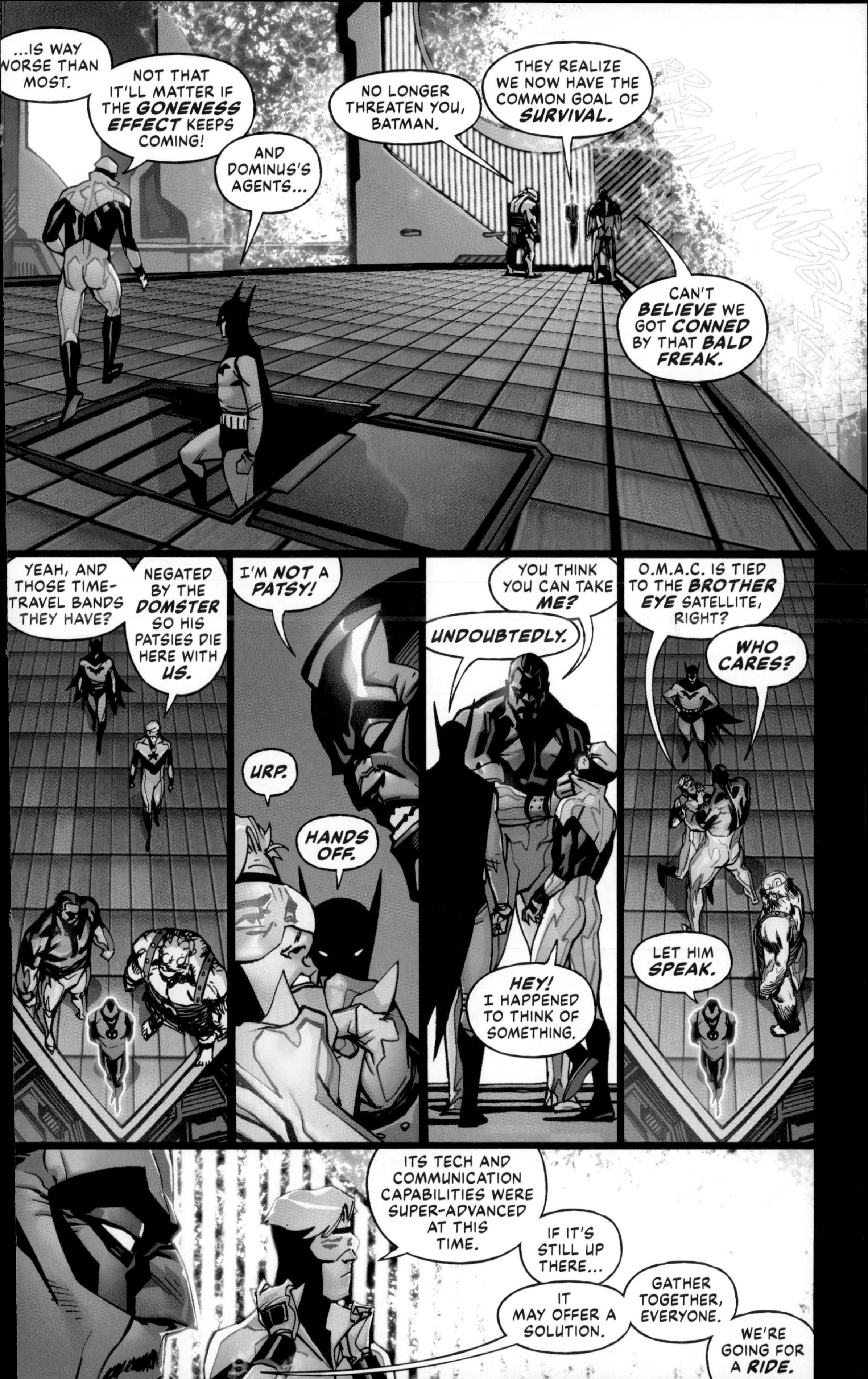
...IS WAY WORSE THAN MOST.
NOT THAT IT'LL MATTER IF THE GONENESS EFFECT KEEPS COMING!
AND DOMINUS'S AGENTS...
NO LONGER THREATEN YOU, BATMAN.
THEY REALIZE WE NOW HAVE THE COMMON GOAL OF SURVIVAL.
CAN'T BELIEVE WE GOT CONNED BY THAT BALD FREAK.
YEAH, AND THOSE TIME-TRAVEL BANDS THEY HAVE?
NEGATED BY THE DOMSTER SO HIS PATSIES DIE HERE WITH US.
I'M NOT A PATSY!
URP.
HANDS OFF.
YOU THINK YOU CAN TAKE ME?
UNDOUBTEDLY.
HEY! I HAPPENED TO THINK OF SOMETHING.
O.M.A.C. IS TIED TO THE BROTHER EYE SATELLITE, RIGHT?
WHO CARES?
LET HIM SPEAK.
ITS TECH AND COMMUNICATION CAPABILITIES WERE SUPER-ADVANCED AT THIS TIME.
IF IT'S STILL UP THERE...
IT MAY OFFER A SOLUTION.
GATHER TOGETHER, EVERYONE.
WE'RE GOING FOR A RIDE.

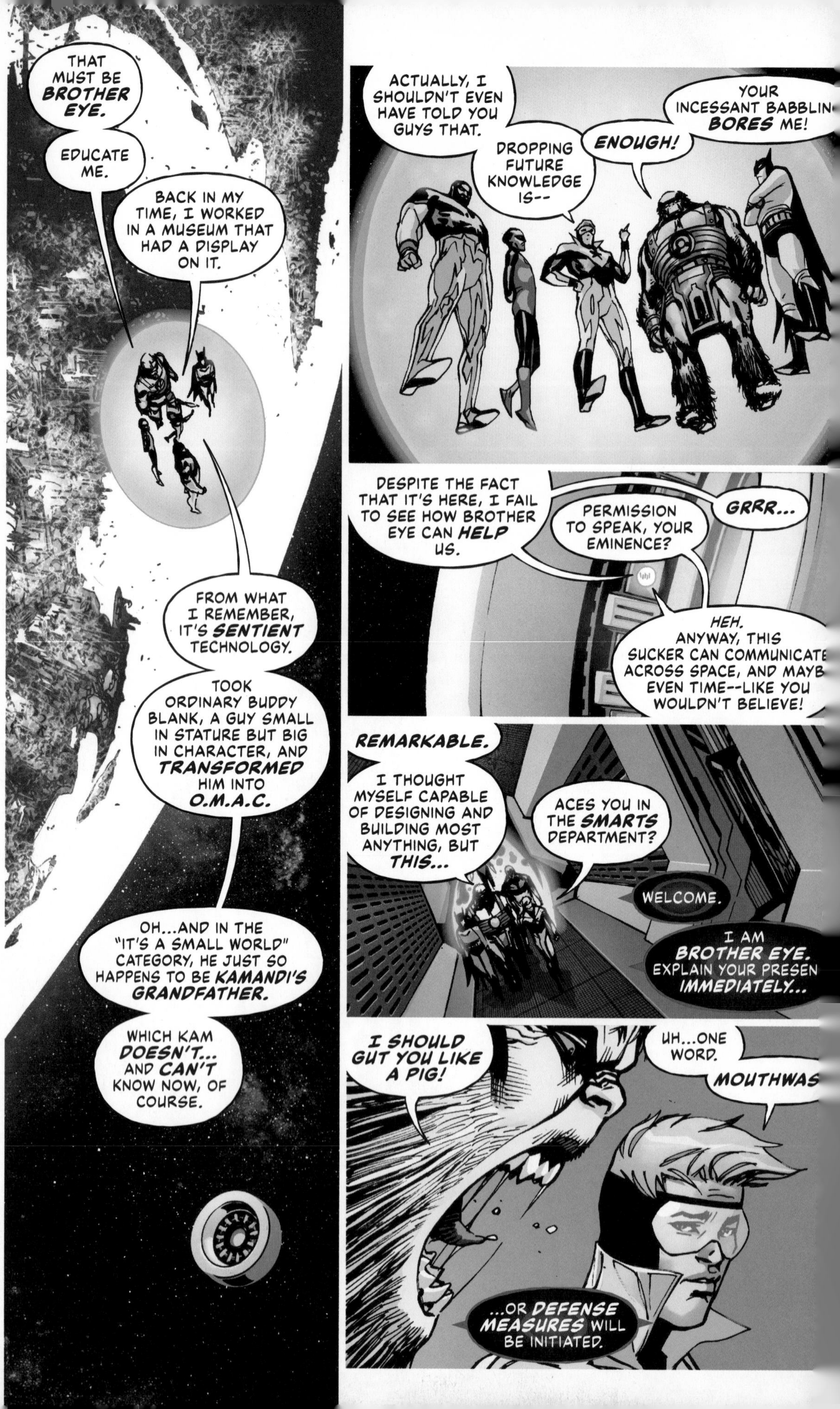

THAT MUST BE BROTHER EYE.
EDUCATE ME.
BACK IN MY TIME, I WORKED IN A MUSEUM THAT HAD A DISPLAY ON IT.
FROM WHAT I REMEMBER, IT'S SENTIENT TECHNOLOGY.
TOOK ORDINARY BUDDY BLANK, A GUY SMALL IN STATURE BUT BIG IN CHARACTER, AND TRANSFORMED HIM INTO O.M.A.C.
OH...AND IN THE "IT'S A SMALL WORLD" CATEGORY, HE JUST SO HAPPENS TO BE KAMANDI'S GRANDFATHER.
WHICH KAM DOESN'T... AND CAN'T KNOW NOW, OF COURSE.
ACTUALLY, I SHOULDN'T EVEN HAVE TOLD YOU GUYS THAT.
DROPPING FUTURE KNOWLEDGE IS--
ENOUGH!
YOUR INCESSANT BABBLIN BORES ME!
DESPITE THE FACT THAT IT'S HERE, I FAIL TO SEE HOW BROTHER EYE CAN HELP US.
GRRR...
PERMISSION TO SPEAK, YOUR EMINENCE?
HEH. ANYWAY, THIS SUCKER CAN COMMUNICATE ACROSS SPACE, AND MAYB EVEN TIME--LIKE YOU WOULDN'T BELIEVE!
REMARKABLE.
I THOUGHT MYSELF CAPABLE OF DESIGNING AND BUILDING MOST ANYTHING, BUT THIS...
ACES YOU IN THE SMARTS DEPARTMENT?
WELCOME.
I AM BROTHER EYE. EXPLAIN YOUR PRESEN IMMEDIATELY...
I SHOULD GUT YOU LIKE A PIG!
UH...ONE WORD.
MOUTHWAS
...OR DEFENSE MEASURES WILL BE INITIATED.

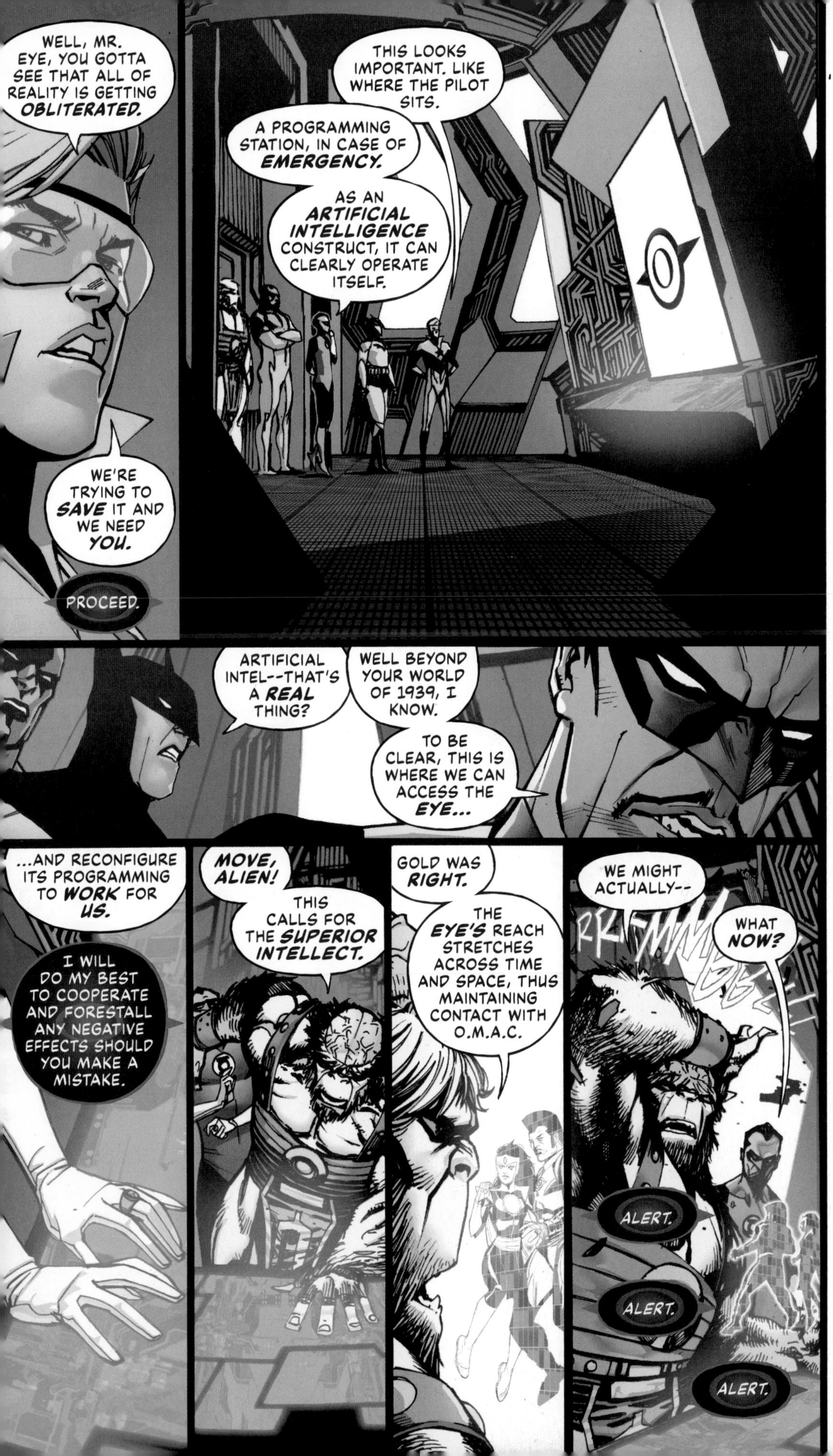
WELL, MR. EYE, YOU GOTTA SEE THAT ALL OF REALITY IS GETTING OBLITERATED.
WE'RE TRYING TO SAVE IT AND WE NEED YOU.
PROCEED.
THIS LOOKS IMPORTANT. LIKE WHERE THE PILOT SITS.
A PROGRAMMING STATION, IN CASE OF EMERGENCY.
AS AN ARTIFICIAL INTELLIGENCE CONSTRUCT, IT CAN CLEARLY OPERATE ITSELF.
ARTIFICIAL INTEL--THAT'S A REAL THING?
WELL BEYOND YOUR WORLD OF 1939, I KNOW.
TO BE CLEAR, THIS IS WHERE WE CAN ACCESS THE EYE...
...AND RECONFIGURE ITS PROGRAMMING TO WORK FOR US.
I WILL DO MY BEST TO COOPERATE AND FORESTALL ANY NEGATIVE EFFECTS SHOULD YOU MAKE A MISTAKE.
MOVE, ALIEN!
THIS CALLS FOR THE SUPERIOR INTELLECT.
GOLD WAS RIGHT.
THE EYE'S REACH STRETCHES ACROSS TIME AND SPACE, THUS MAINTAINING CONTACT WITH O.M.A.C.
WE MIGHT ACTUALLY--
WHAT NOW?
ALERT.
ALERT.
ALERT.

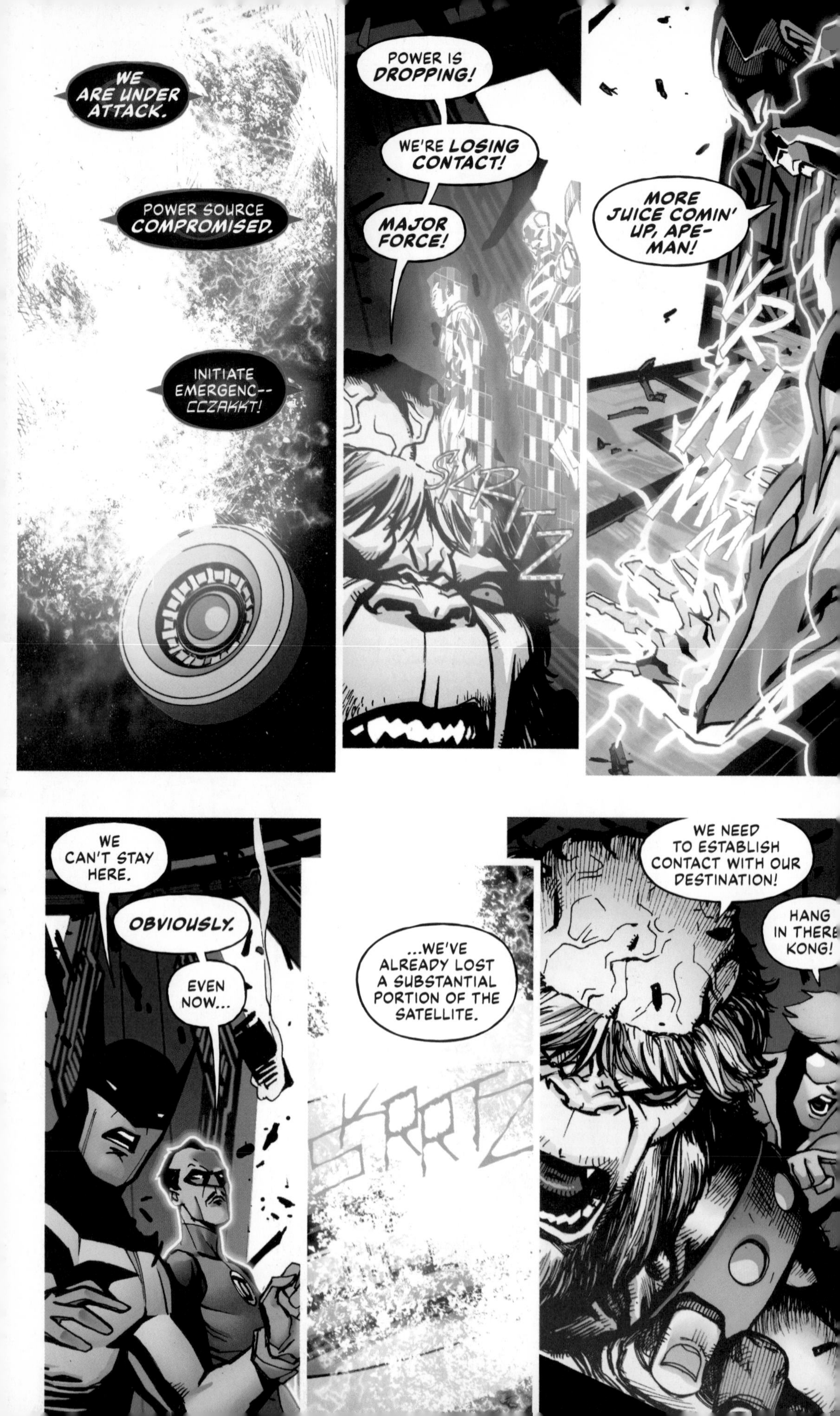

WE ARE UNDER ATTACK.
POWER SOURCE COMPROMISED.
INITIATE EMERGENC-- CCZAKKT!
POWER IS DROPPING!
WE'RE LOSING CONTACT!
MAJOR FORCE!
SKRITZ
MORE JUICE COMIN' UP, APE-MAN!
VRMMM
WE CAN'T STAY HERE.
OBVIOUSLY.
EVEN NOW...
...WE'VE ALREADY LOST A SUBSTANTIAL PORTION OF THE SATELLITE.
SKRRTZ
WE NEED TO ESTABLISH CONTACT WITH OUR DESTINATION!
HANG IN THERE KONG!

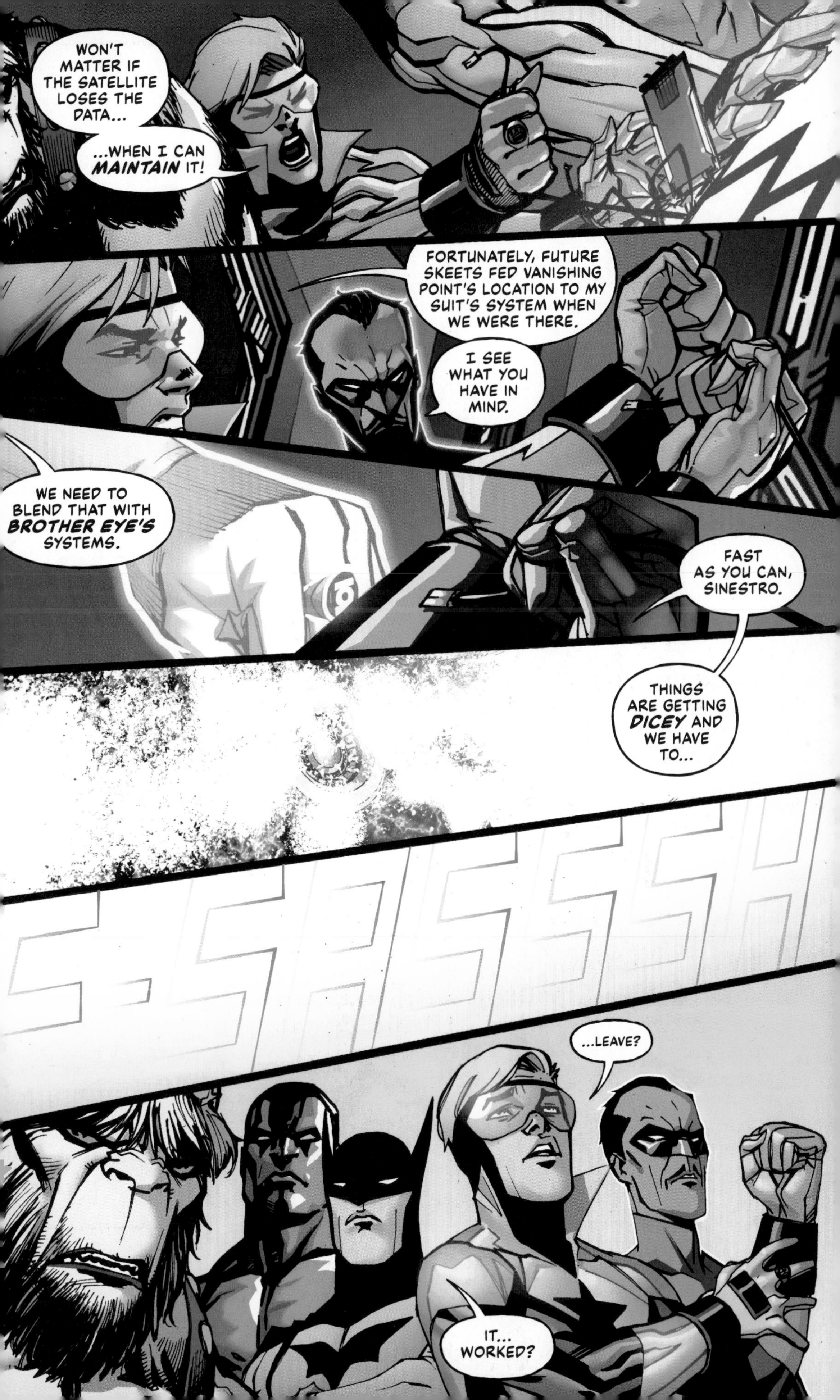
WON'T MATTER IF THE SATELLITE LOSES THE DATA...
...WHEN I CAN MAINTAIN IT!
FORTUNATELY, FUTURE SKEETS FED VANISHING POINT'S LOCATION TO MY SUIT'S SYSTEM WHEN WE WERE THERE.
I SEE WHAT YOU HAVE IN MIND.
WE NEED TO BLEND THAT WITH BROTHER EYE'S SYSTEMS.
FAST AS YOU CAN, SINESTRO.
THINGS ARE GETTING DICEY AND WE HAVE TO...
...LEAVE?
IT... WORKED?

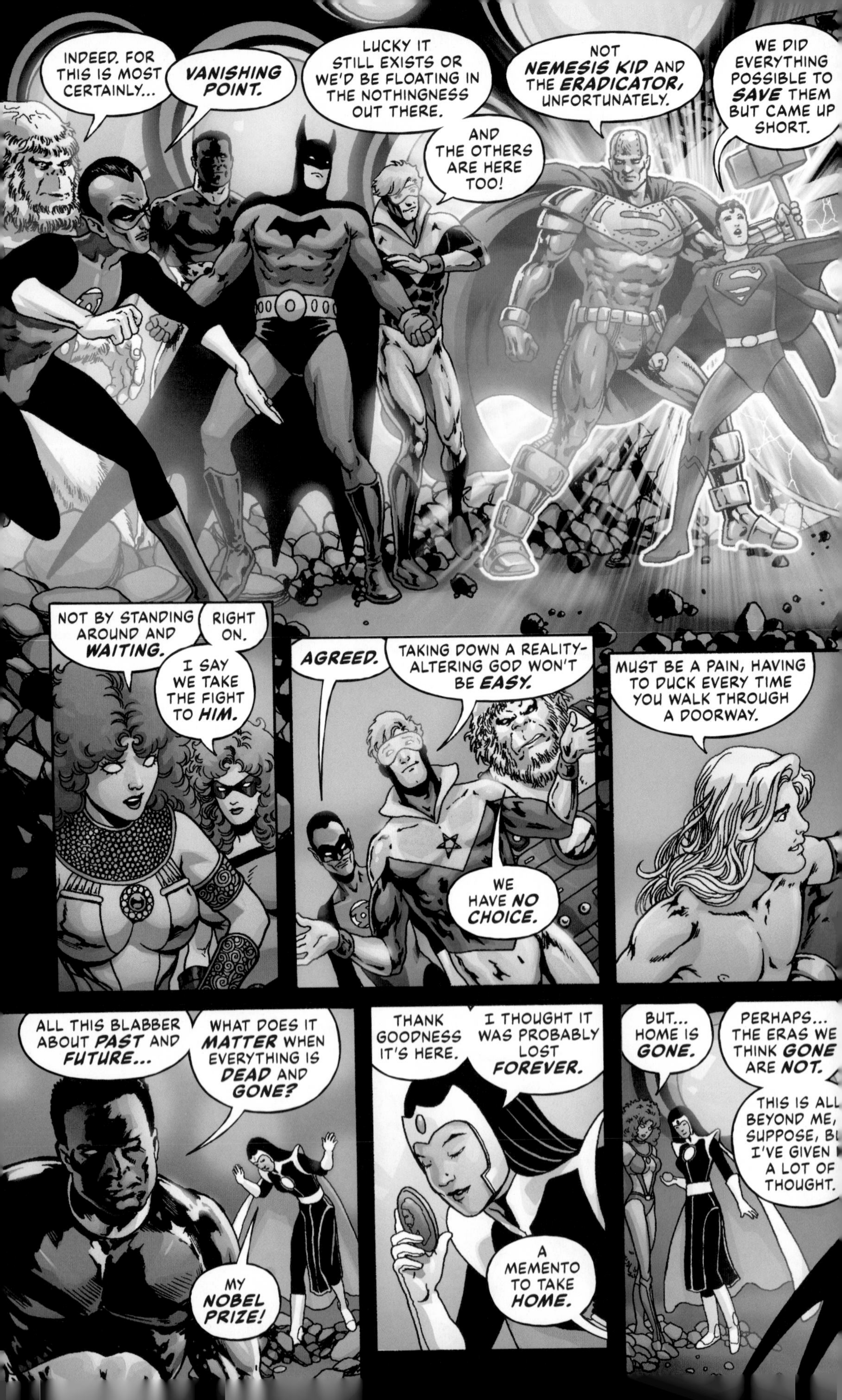
INDEED. FOR THIS IS MOST CERTAINLY...
VANISHING POINT.
LUCKY IT STILL EXISTS OR WE'D BE FLOATING IN THE NOTHINGNESS OUT THERE.
AND THE OTHERS ARE HERE TOO!
NOT NEMESIS KID AND THE ERADICATOR, UNFORTUNATELY.
WE DID EVERYTHING POSSIBLE TO SAVE THEM BUT CAME UP SHORT.
NOT BY STANDING AROUND AND WAITING.
RIGHT ON.
I SAY WE TAKE THE FIGHT TO HIM.
AGREED.
TAKING DOWN A REALITY-ALTERING GOD WON'T BE EASY.
WE HAVE NO CHOICE.
MUST BE A PAIN, HAVING TO DUCK EVERY TIME YOU WALK THROUGH A DOORWAY.
ALL THIS BLABBER ABOUT PAST AND FUTURE...
WHAT DOES IT MATTER WHEN EVERYTHING IS DEAD AND GONE?
MY NOBEL PRIZE!
THANK GOODNESS IT'S HERE.
I THOUGHT IT WAS PROBABLY LOST FOREVER.
A MEMENTO TO TAKE HOME.
BUT... HOME IS GONE.
PERHAPS... THE ERAS WE THINK GONE ARE NOT.

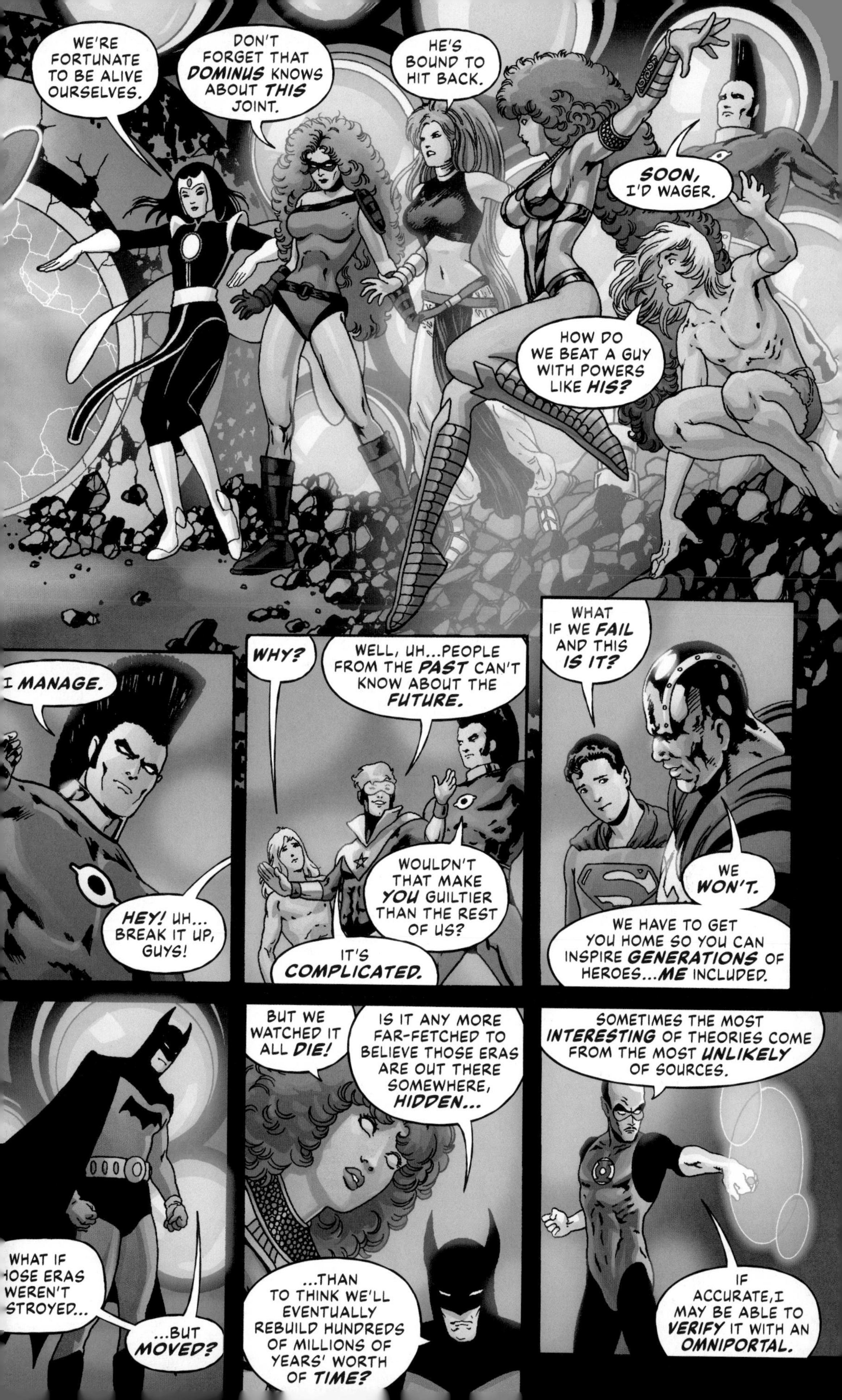

WE'RE FORTUNATE TO BE ALIVE OURSELVES.
DON'T FORGET THAT DOMINUS KNOWS ABOUT THIS JOINT.
HE'S BOUND TO HIT BACK.
SOON, I'D WAGER.
HOW DO WE BEAT A GUY WITH POWERS LIKE HIS?
I MANAGE.
HEY! UH... BREAK IT UP, GUYS!
WHY?
WELL, UH...PEOPLE FROM THE PAST CAN'T KNOW ABOUT THE FUTURE.
WOULDN'T THAT MAKE YOU GUILTIER THAN THE REST OF US?
IT'S COMPLICATED.
WHAT IF WE FAIL AND THIS IS IT?
WE WON'T.
WE HAVE TO GET YOU HOME SO YOU CAN INSPIRE GENERATIONS OF HEROES...ME INCLUDED.
WHAT IF
OSE ERAS WEREN'T
STROYED...
...BUT MOVED?
BUT WE WATCHED IT ALL DIE!
IS IT ANY MORE FAR-FETCHED TO BELIEVE THOSE ERAS ARE OUT THERE SOMEWHERE, HIDDEN...
...THAN TO THINK WE'LL EVENTUALLY REBUILD HUNDREDS OF MILLIONS OF YEARS' WORTH OF TIME?
SOMETIMES THE MOST INTERESTING OF THEORIES COME FROM THE MOST UNLIKELY OF SOURCES.
IF ACCURATE, I MAY BE ABLE TO VERIFY IT WITH AN OMNIPORTAL.

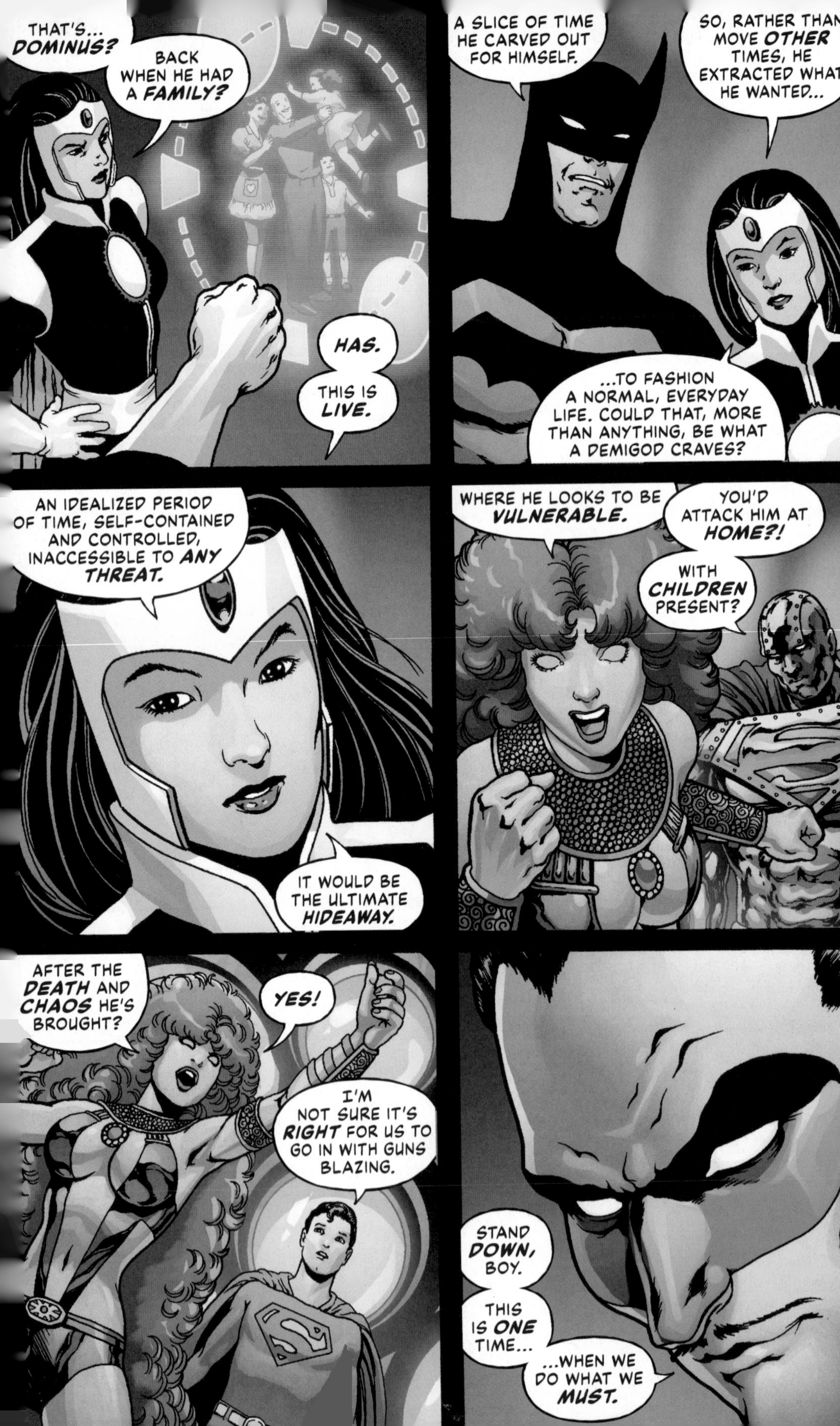
THAT'S... DOMINUS?
BACK WHEN HE HAD A FAMILY?
HAS.
THIS IS LIVE.
A SLICE OF TIME HE CARVED OUT FOR HIMSELF.
SO, RATHER THAN MOVE OTHER TIMES, HE EXTRACTED WHAT HE WANTED...
...TO FASHION A NORMAL, EVERYDAY LIFE. COULD THAT, MORE THAN ANYTHING, BE WHAT A DEMIGOD CRAVES?
AN IDEALIZED PERIOD OF TIME, SELF-CONTAINED AND CONTROLLED, INACCESSIBLE TO ANY THREAT.
IT WOULD BE THE ULTIMATE HIDEAWAY.
WHERE HE LOOKS TO BE VULNERABLE.
YOU'D ATTACK HIM AT HOME?!
WITH CHILDREN PRESENT?
AFTER THE DEATH AND CHAOS HE'S BROUGHT?
YES!
I'M NOT SURE IT'S RIGHT FOR US TO GO IN WITH GUNS BLAZING.
STAND DOWN, BOY.
THIS IS ONE TIME...
...WHEN WE DO WHAT WE MUST.

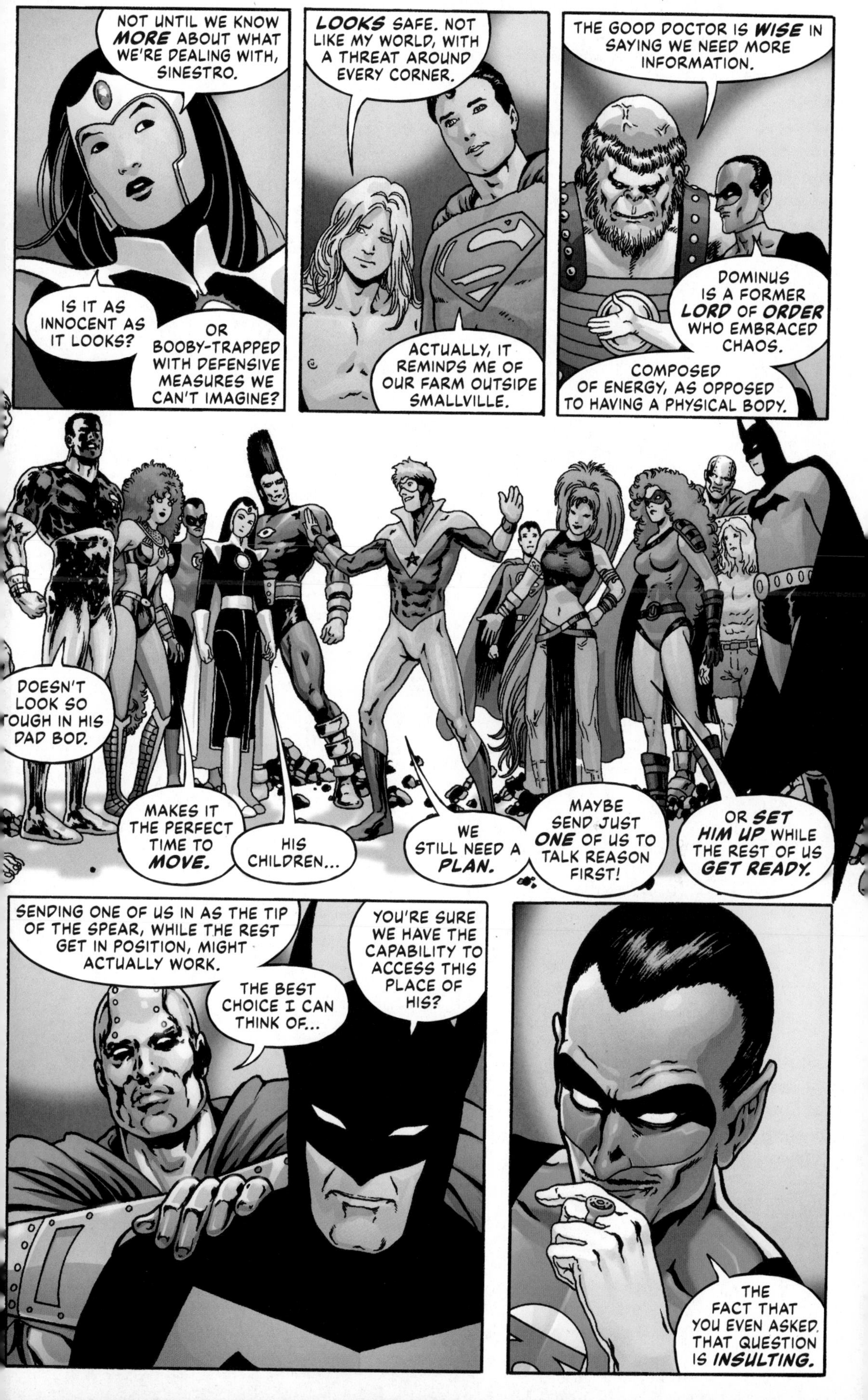

NOT UNTIL WE KNOW MORE ABOUT WHAT WE'RE DEALING WITH, SINESTRO.
IS IT AS INNOCENT AS IT LOOKS?
OR BOOBY-TRAPPED WITH DEFENSIVE MEASURES WE CAN'T IMAGINE?
LOOKS SAFE. NOT LIKE MY WORLD, WITH A THREAT AROUND EVERY CORNER.
ACTUALLY, IT REMINDS ME OF OUR FARM OUTSIDE SMALLVILLE.
THE GOOD DOCTOR IS WISE IN SAYING WE NEED MORE INFORMATION.
DOMINUS IS A FORMER LORD OF ORDER WHO EMBRACED CHAOS.
COMPOSED OF ENERGY, AS OPPOSED TO HAVING A PHYSICAL BODY.
DOESN'T LOOK SO TOUGH IN HIS DAD BOD.
MAKES IT THE PERFECT TIME TO MOVE.
HIS CHILDREN...
WE STILL NEED A PLAN.
MAYBE SEND JUST ONE OF US TO TALK REASON FIRST!
OR SET HIM UP WHILE THE REST OF US GET READY.
SENDING ONE OF US IN AS THE TIP OF THE SPEAR, WHILE THE REST GET IN POSITION, MIGHT ACTUALLY WORK.
THE BEST CHOICE I CAN THINK OF...
YOU'RE SURE WE HAVE THE CAPABILITY TO ACCESS THIS PLACE OF HIS?
THE FACT THAT YOU EVEN ASKED THAT QUESTION IS INSULTING.

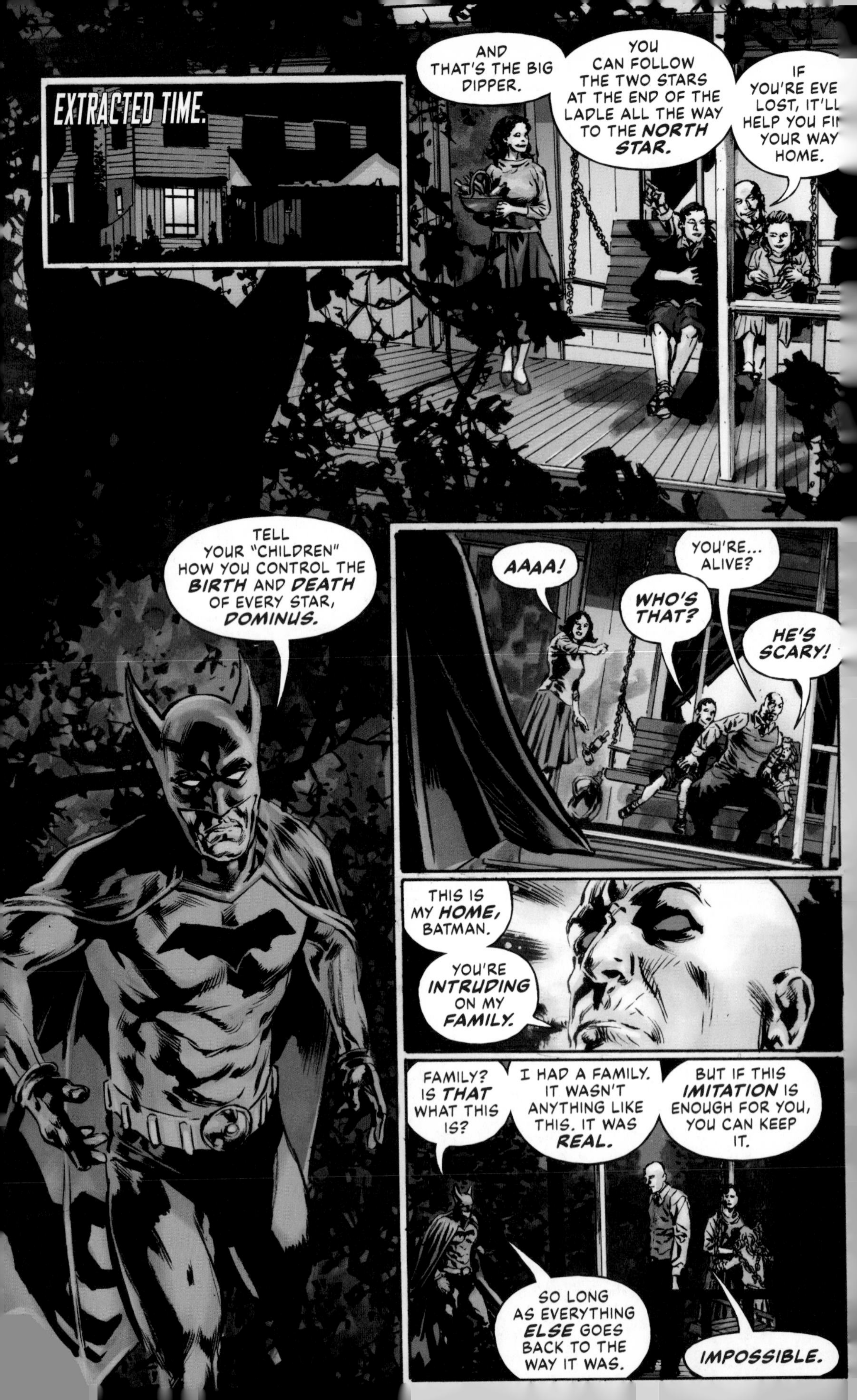

EXTRACTED TIME.
AND THAT'S THE BIG DIPPER.
YOU CAN FOLLOW THE TWO STARS AT THE END OF THE LADLE ALL THE WAY TO THE NORTH STAR.
IF YOU'RE EVE LOST, IT'LL HELP YOU FI YOUR WAY HOME.
TELL YOUR "CHILDREN" HOW YOU CONTROL THE BIRTH AND DEATH OF EVERY STAR, DOMINUS.
AAAA!
YOU'RE... ALIVE?
WHO'S THAT?
HE'S SCARY!
THIS IS MY HOME, BATMAN.
YOU'RE INTRUDING ON MY FAMILY.
FAMILY? IS THAT WHAT THIS IS?
I HAD A FAMILY. IT WASN'T ANYTHING LIKE THIS. IT WAS REAL.
BUT IF THIS IMITATION IS ENOUGH FOR YOU, YOU CAN KEEP IT.
SO LONG AS EVERYTHING ELSE GOES BACK TO THE WAY IT WAS.
IMPOSSIBLE.

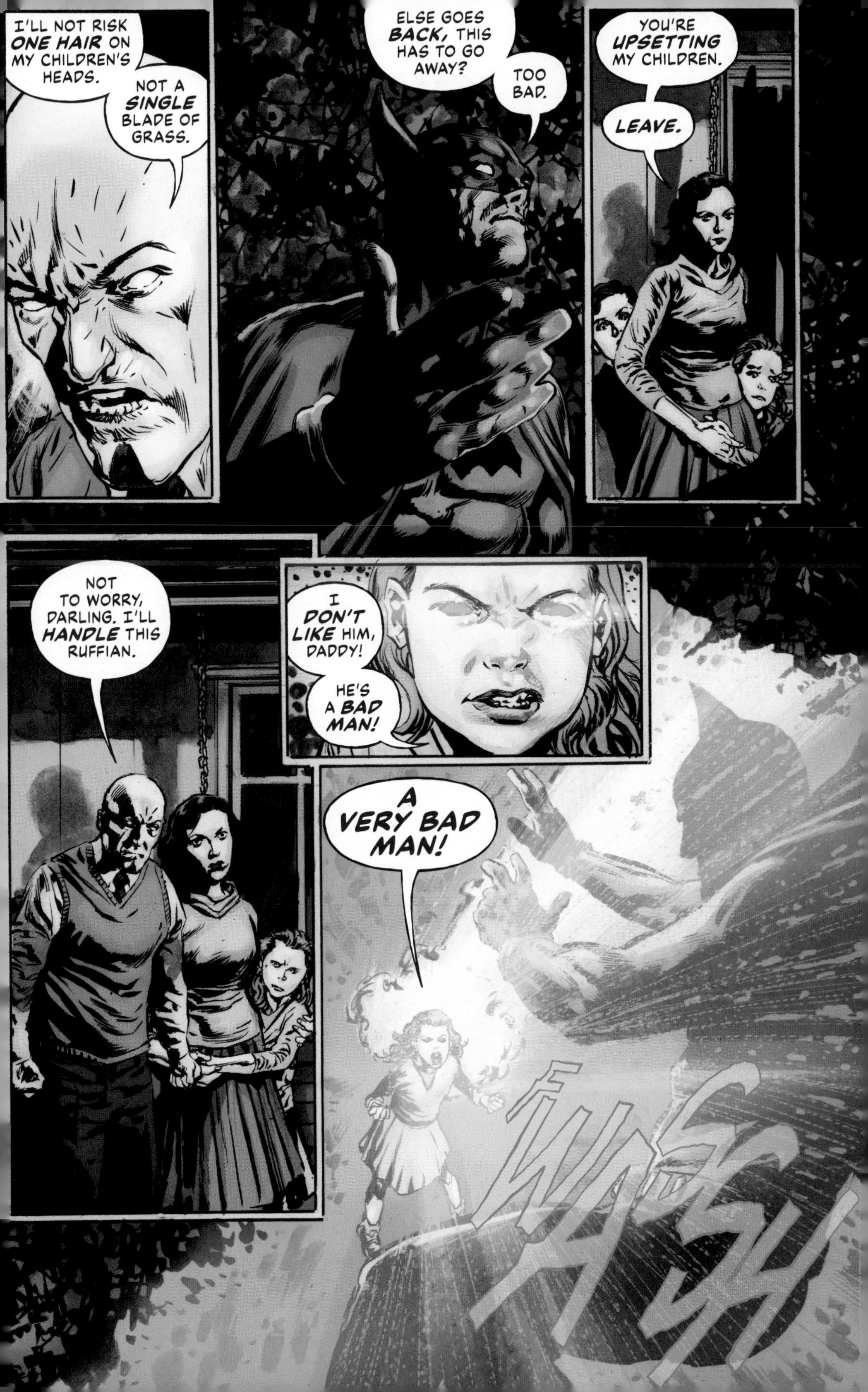
I'LL NOT RISK ONE HAIR ON MY CHILDREN'S HEADS.
NOT A SINGLE BLADE OF GRASS.
ELSE GOES BACK, THIS HAS TO GO AWAY?
TOO BAD.
YOU'RE UPSETTING MY CHILDREN.
LEAVE.
NOT TO WORRY, DARLING. I'LL HANDLE THIS RUFFIAN.
I DON'T LIKE HIM, DADDY!
HE'S A BAD MAN!
A VERY BAD MAN!

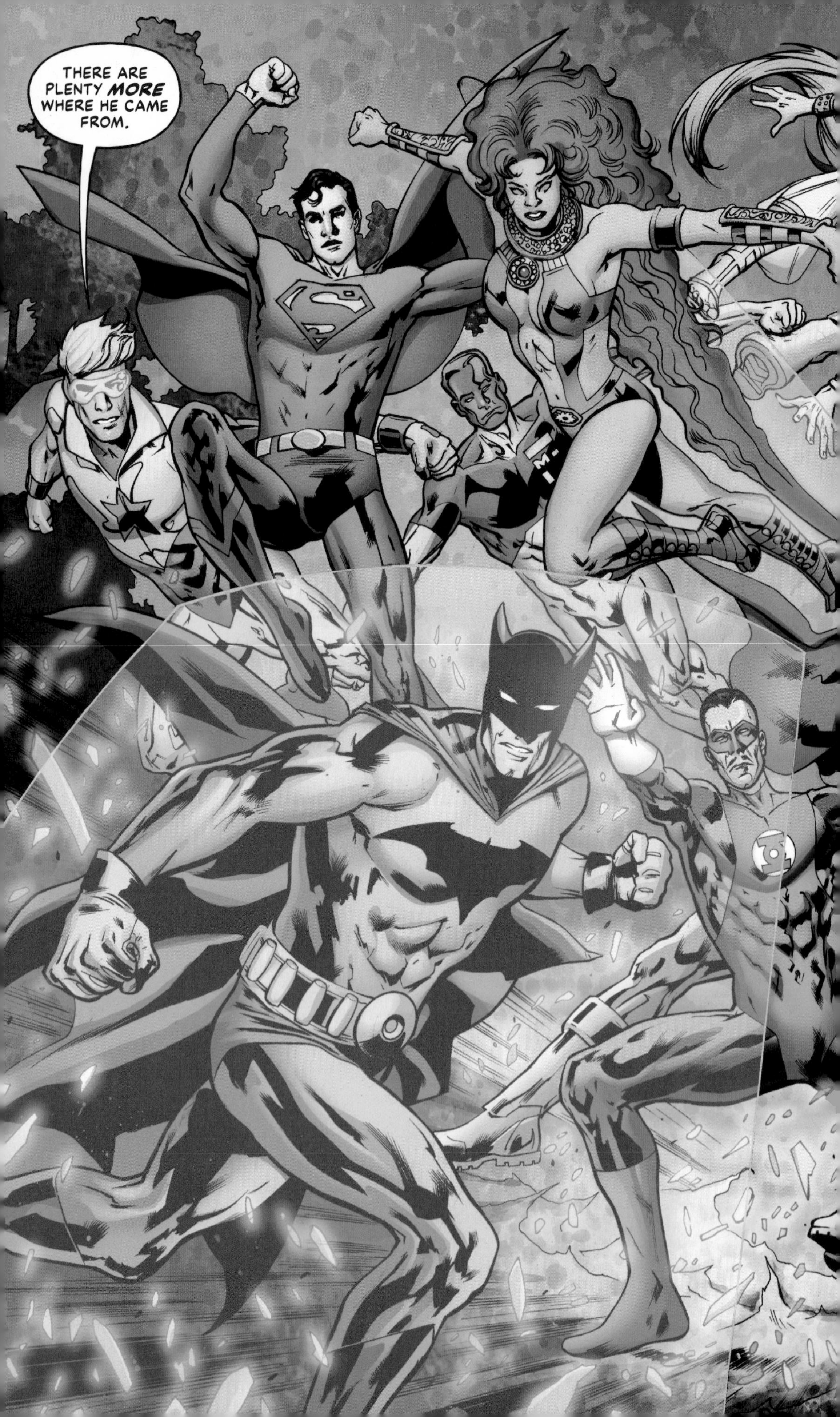
THERE ARE PLENTY MORE WHERE HE CAME FROM.

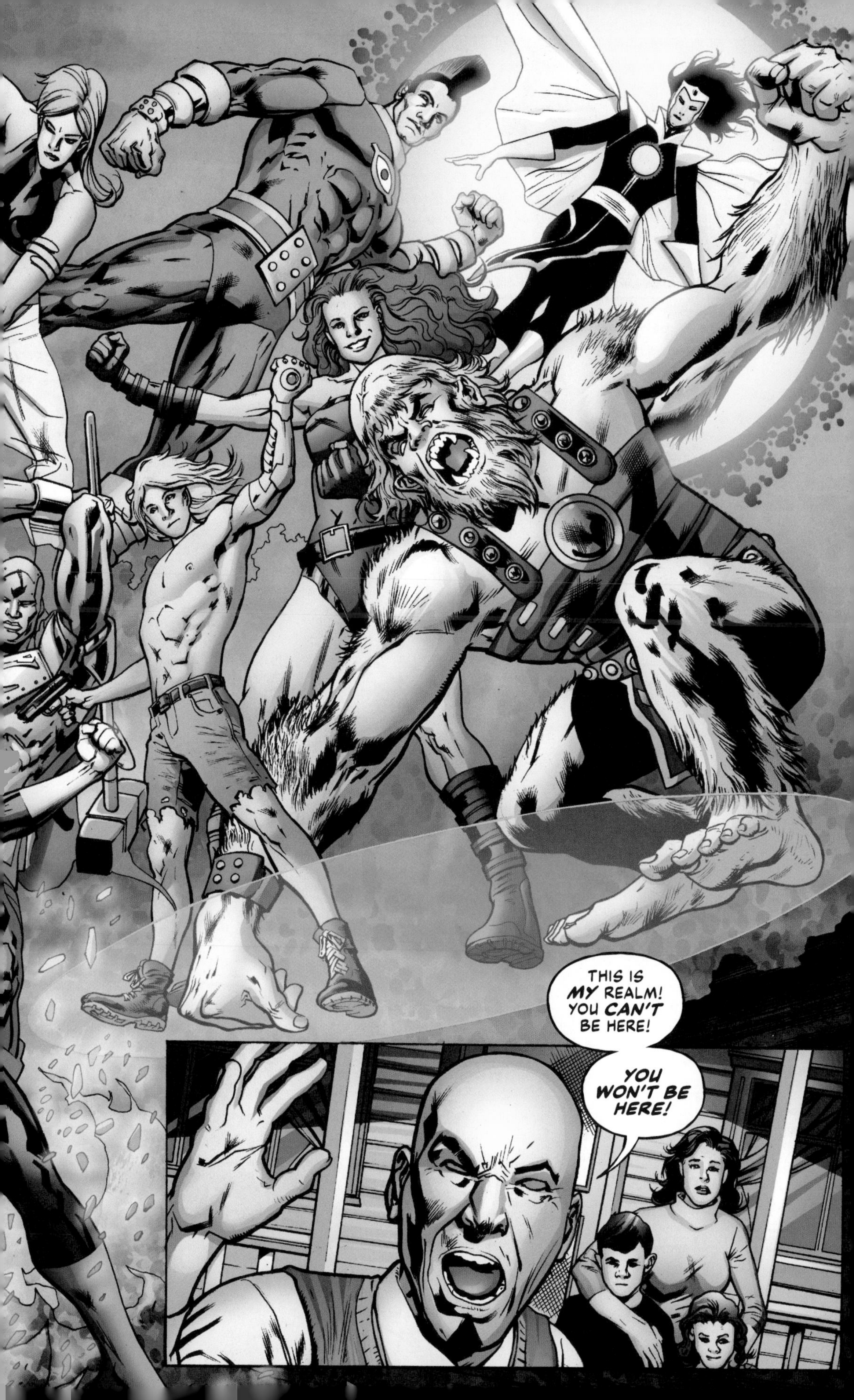
THIS IS *MY* REALM! YOU *CAN'T* BE HERE!
YOU WON'T BE HERE!

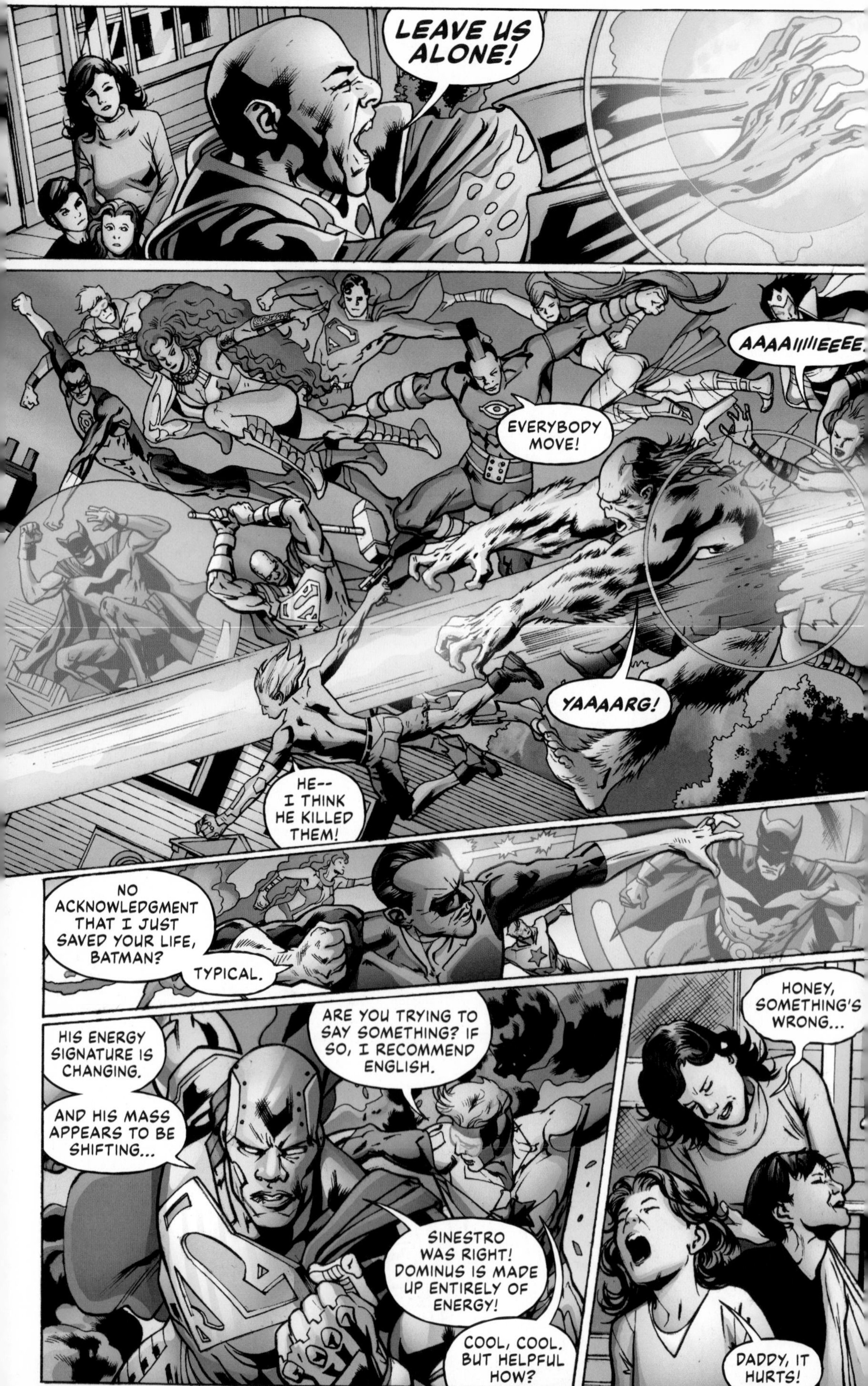
LEAVE US ALONE!
AAAAIIIIIEEEE.
EVERYBODY MOVE!
YAAAARG!
HE-- I THINK HE KILLED THEM!
NO ACKNOWLEDGMENT THAT I JUST SAVED YOUR LIFE, BATMAN?
TYPICAL.
HIS ENERGY SIGNATURE IS CHANGING.
AND HIS MASS APPEARS TO BE SHIFTING...
ARE YOU TRYING TO SAY SOMETHING? IF SO, I RECOMMEND ENGLISH.
SINESTRO WAS RIGHT! DOMINUS IS MADE UP ENTIRELY OF ENERGY!
COOL, COOL. BUT HELPFUL HOW?
HONEY, SOMETHING'S WRONG...
DADDY, IT HURTS!

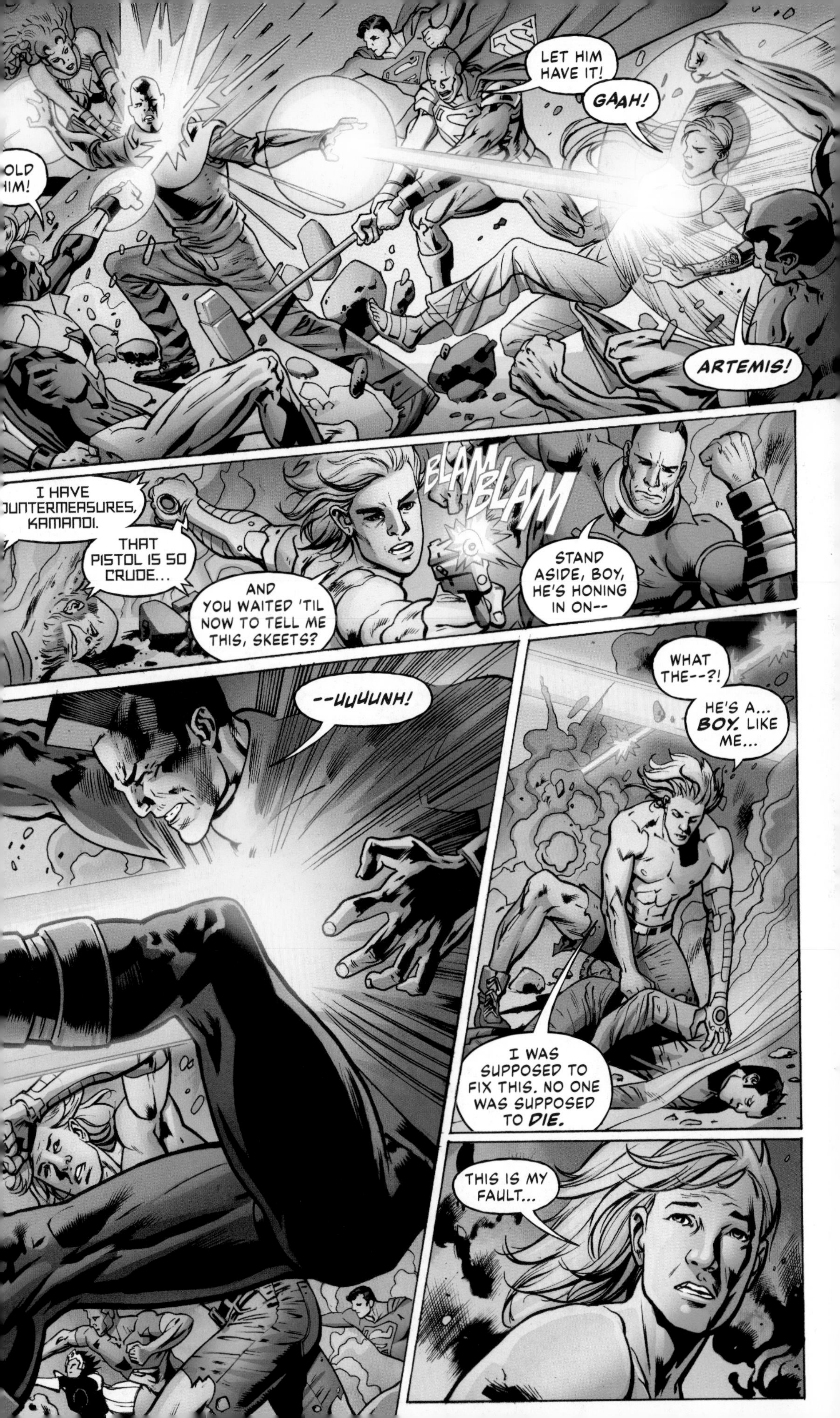

LET HIM HAVE IT!
GAAH!
OLD HIM!
ARTEMIS!
I HAVE OUNTERMEASURES, KAMANDI.
THAT PISTOL IS SO CRUDE...
AND YOU WAITED 'TIL NOW TO TELL ME THIS, SKEETS?
BLAM BLAM
STAND ASIDE, BOY, HE'S HONING IN ON--
--UUUUNH!
WHAT THE--?!
HE'S A... BOY. LIKE ME...
I WAS SUPPOSED TO FIX THIS. NO ONE WAS SUPPOSED TO DIE.
THIS IS MY FAULT...

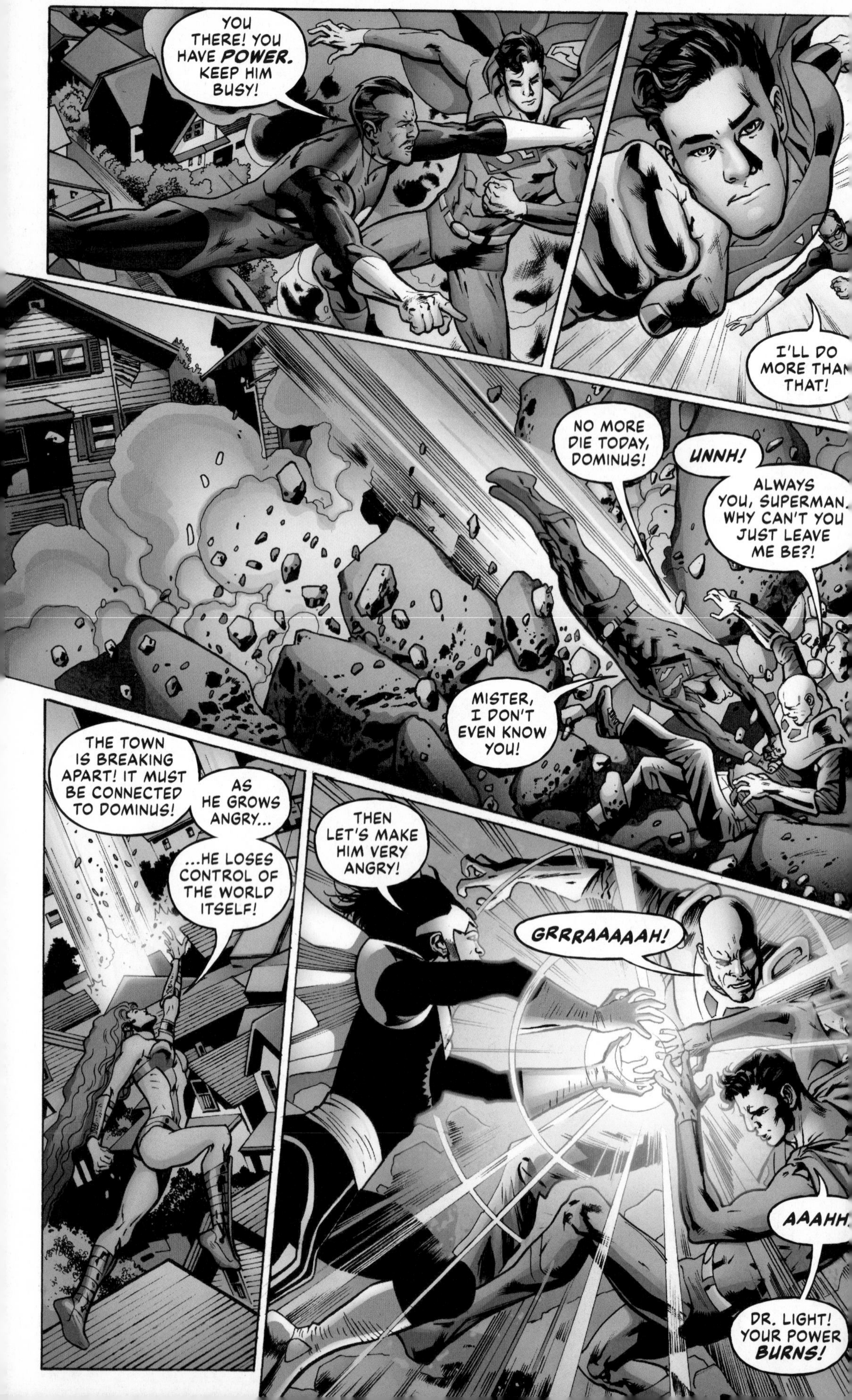
YOU THERE! YOU HAVE POWER. KEEP HIM BUSY!
I'LL DO MORE THAN THAT!
NO MORE DIE TODAY, DOMINUS!
UNNH!
ALWAYS YOU, SUPERMAN. WHY CAN'T YOU JUST LEAVE ME BE?!
MISTER, I DON'T EVEN KNOW YOU!
THE TOWN IS BREAKING APART! IT MUST BE CONNECTED TO DOMINUS!
AS HE GROWS ANGRY...
...HE LOSES CONTROL OF THE WORLD ITSELF!
THEN LET'S MAKE HIM VERY ANGRY!
GRRRAAAAAH!
AAAHH!
DR. LIGHT! YOUR POWER BURNS!

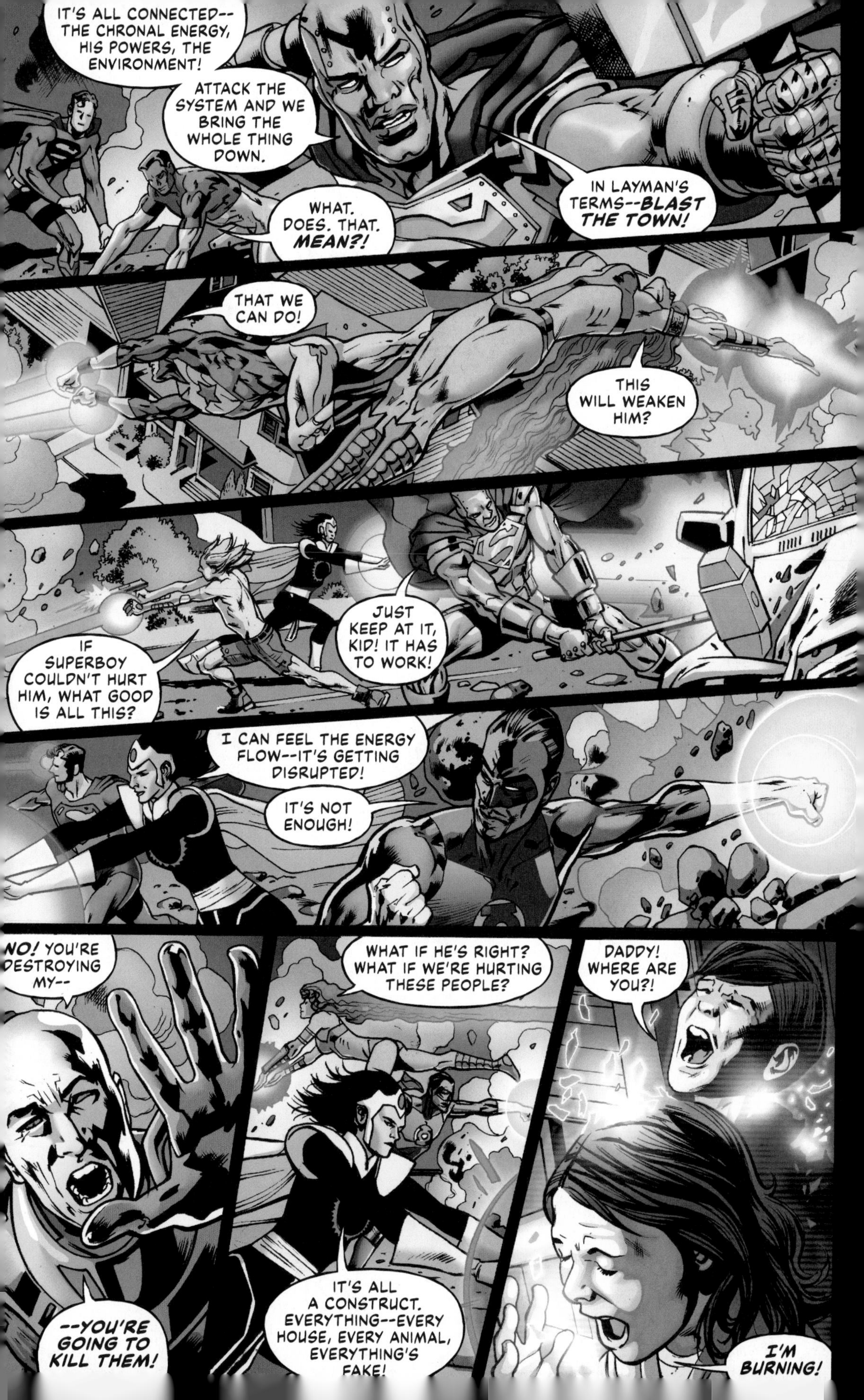
IT'S ALL CONNECTED-- THE CHRONAL ENERGY, HIS POWERS, THE ENVIRONMENT!
ATTACK THE SYSTEM AND WE BRING THE WHOLE THING DOWN.
WHAT. DOES. THAT. MEAN?!
IN LAYMAN'S TERMS--BLAST THE TOWN!
THAT WE CAN DO!
THIS WILL WEAKEN HIM?
JUST KEEP AT IT, KID! IT HAS TO WORK!
IF SUPERBOY COULDN'T HURT HIM, WHAT GOOD IS ALL THIS?
I CAN FEEL THE ENERGY FLOW--IT'S GETTING DISRUPTED!
IT'S NOT ENOUGH!
NO! YOU'RE DESTROYING MY--
--YOU'RE GOING TO KILL THEM!
WHAT IF HE'S RIGHT? WHAT IF WE'RE HURTING THESE PEOPLE?
IT'S ALL A CONSTRUCT. EVERYTHING--EVERY HOUSE, EVERY ANIMAL, EVERYTHING'S FAKE!
DADDY! WHERE ARE YOU?!
I'M BURNING!

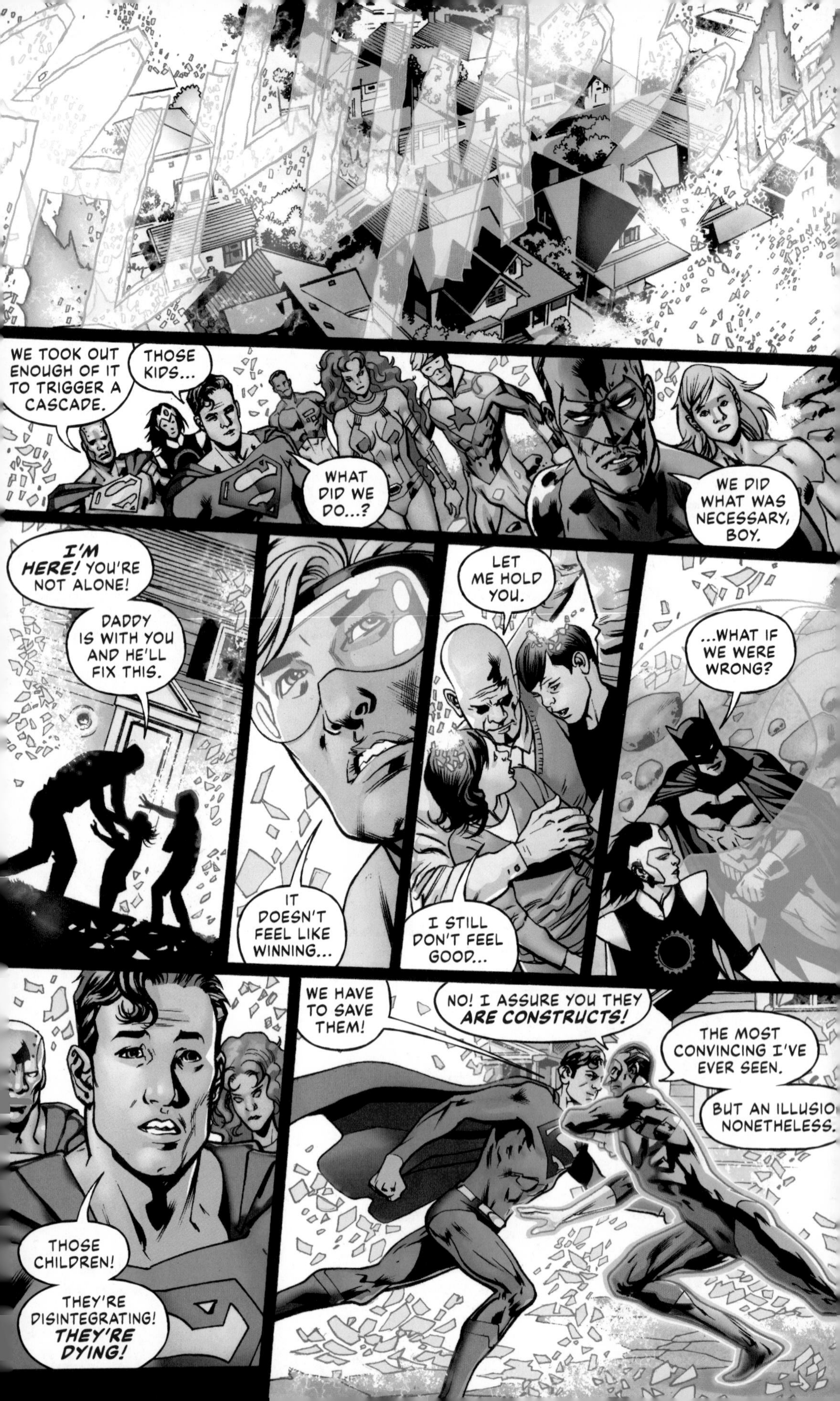
WE TOOK OUT ENOUGH OF IT TO TRIGGER A CASCADE.
THOSE KIDS...
WHAT DID WE DO...?
WE DID WHAT WAS NECESSARY, BOY.
I'M HERE! YOU'RE NOT ALONE!
DADDY IS WITH YOU AND HE'LL FIX THIS.
IT DOESN'T FEEL LIKE WINNING...
LET ME HOLD YOU.
I STILL DON'T FEEL GOOD...
...WHAT IF WE WERE WRONG?
THOSE CHILDREN!
THEY'RE DISINTEGRATING! THEY'RE DYING!
WE HAVE TO SAVE THEM!
NO! I ASSURE YOU THEY ARE CONSTRUCTS!
THE MOST CONVINCING I'VE EVER SEEN.
BUT AN ILLUSIO NONETHELESS.

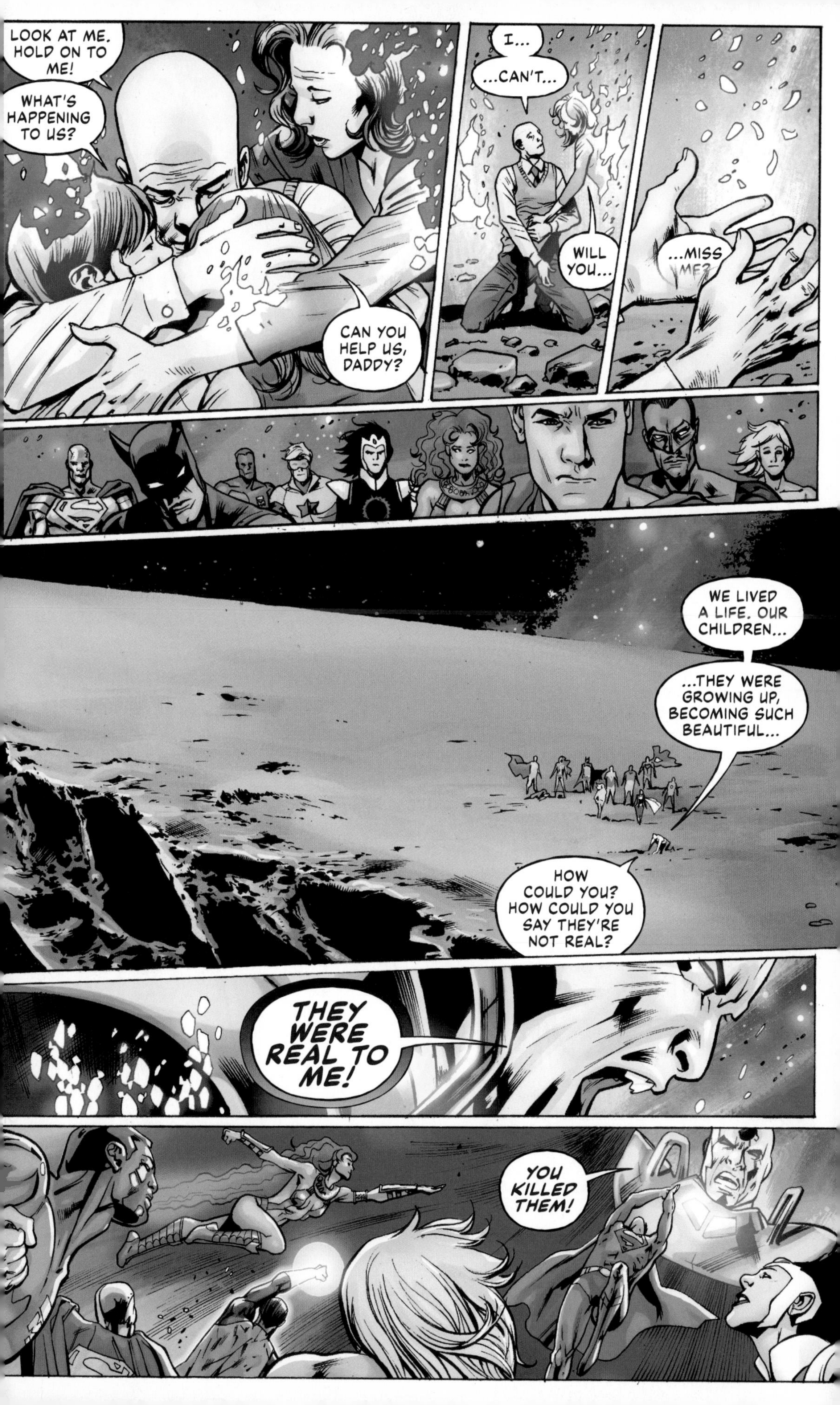

LOOK AT ME. HOLD ON TO ME!
WHAT'S HAPPENING TO US?
CAN YOU HELP US, DADDY?
I...
...CAN'T...
WILL YOU...
...MISS ME?
WE LIVED A LIFE. OUR CHILDREN...
...THEY WERE GROWING UP, BECOMING SUCH BEAUTIFUL...
HOW COULD YOU? HOW COULD YOU SAY THEY'RE NOT REAL?
THEY WERE REAL TO ME!
YOU KILLED THEM!

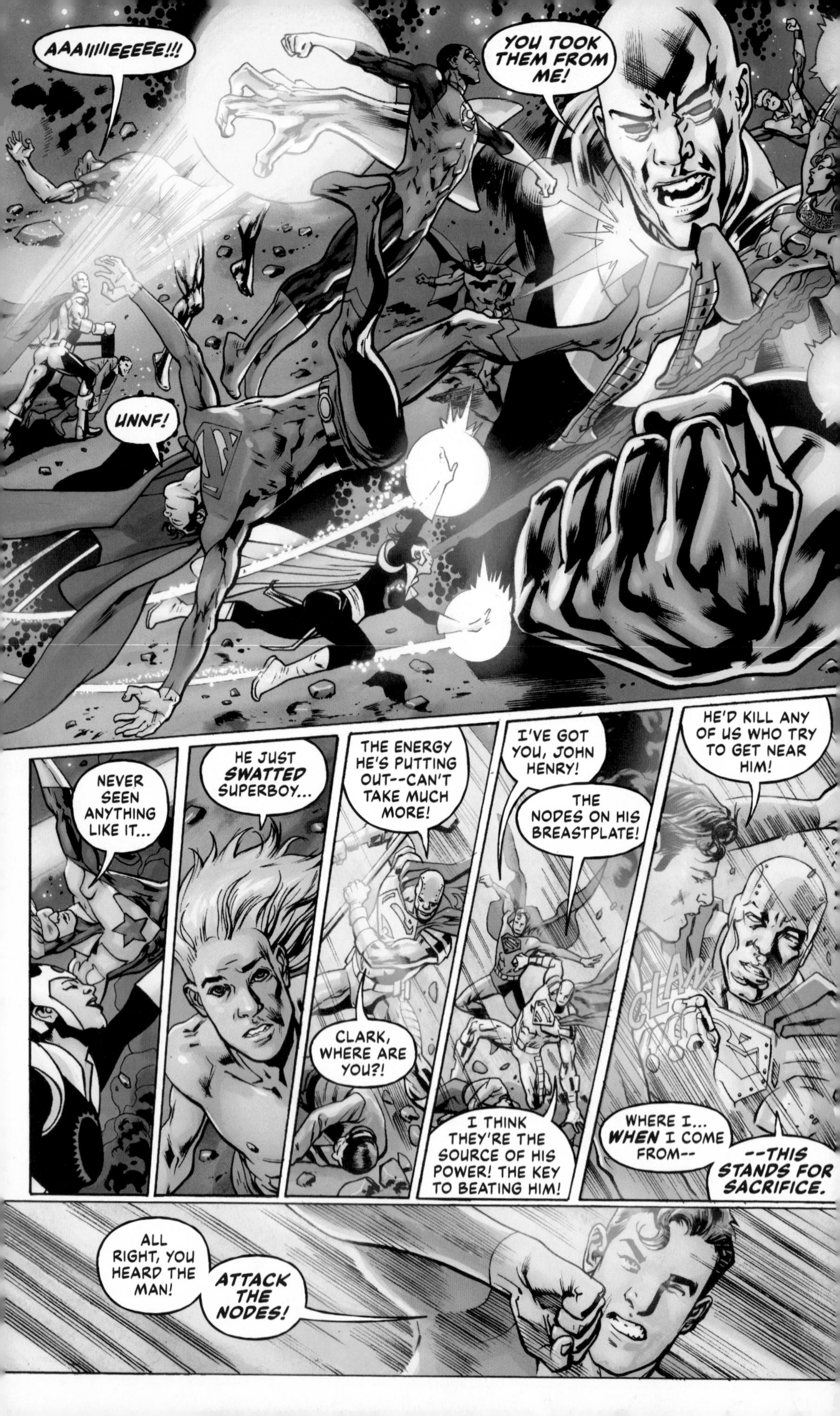

AAAIIIIIEEEEE!!!
YOU TOOK THEM FROM ME!
UNNF!
NEVER SEEN ANYTHING LIKE IT...
HE JUST **SWATTED** SUPERBOY...
THE ENERGY HE'S PUTTING OUT--CAN'T TAKE MUCH MORE!
CLARK, WHERE ARE YOU?!
I'VE GOT YOU, JOHN HENRY!
THE NODES ON HIS BREASTPLATE!
I THINK THEY'RE THE SOURCE OF HIS POWER! THE KEY TO BEATING HIM!
HE'D KILL ANY OF US WHO TRY TO GET NEAR HIM!
CLANK
WHERE I... **WHEN** I COME FROM--
--THIS STANDS FOR SACRIFICE.
ALL RIGHT, YOU HEARD THE MAN!
ATTACK THE NODES!

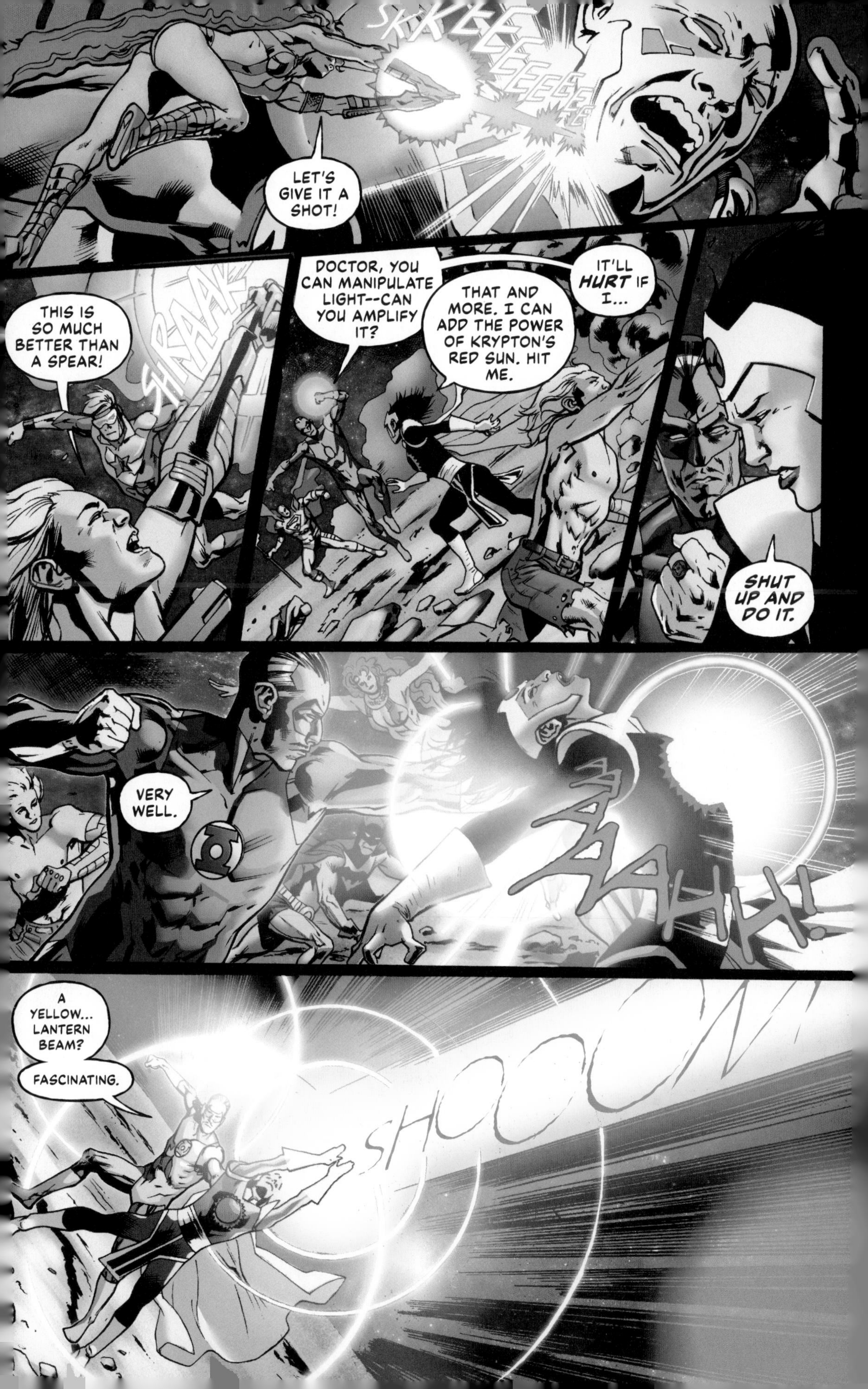
SKKEEEEEEEE
LET'S GIVE IT A SHOT!
SHRAAK
THIS IS SO MUCH BETTER THAN A SPEAR!
DOCTOR, YOU CAN MANIPULATE LIGHT--CAN YOU AMPLIFY IT?
THAT AND MORE. I CAN ADD THE POWER OF KRYPTON'S RED SUN. HIT ME.
IT'LL *HURT* IF I...
SHUT UP AND DO IT.
VERY WELL.
AAAAHH!
A YELLOW... LANTERN BEAM?
FASCINATING.
SHOOOOM

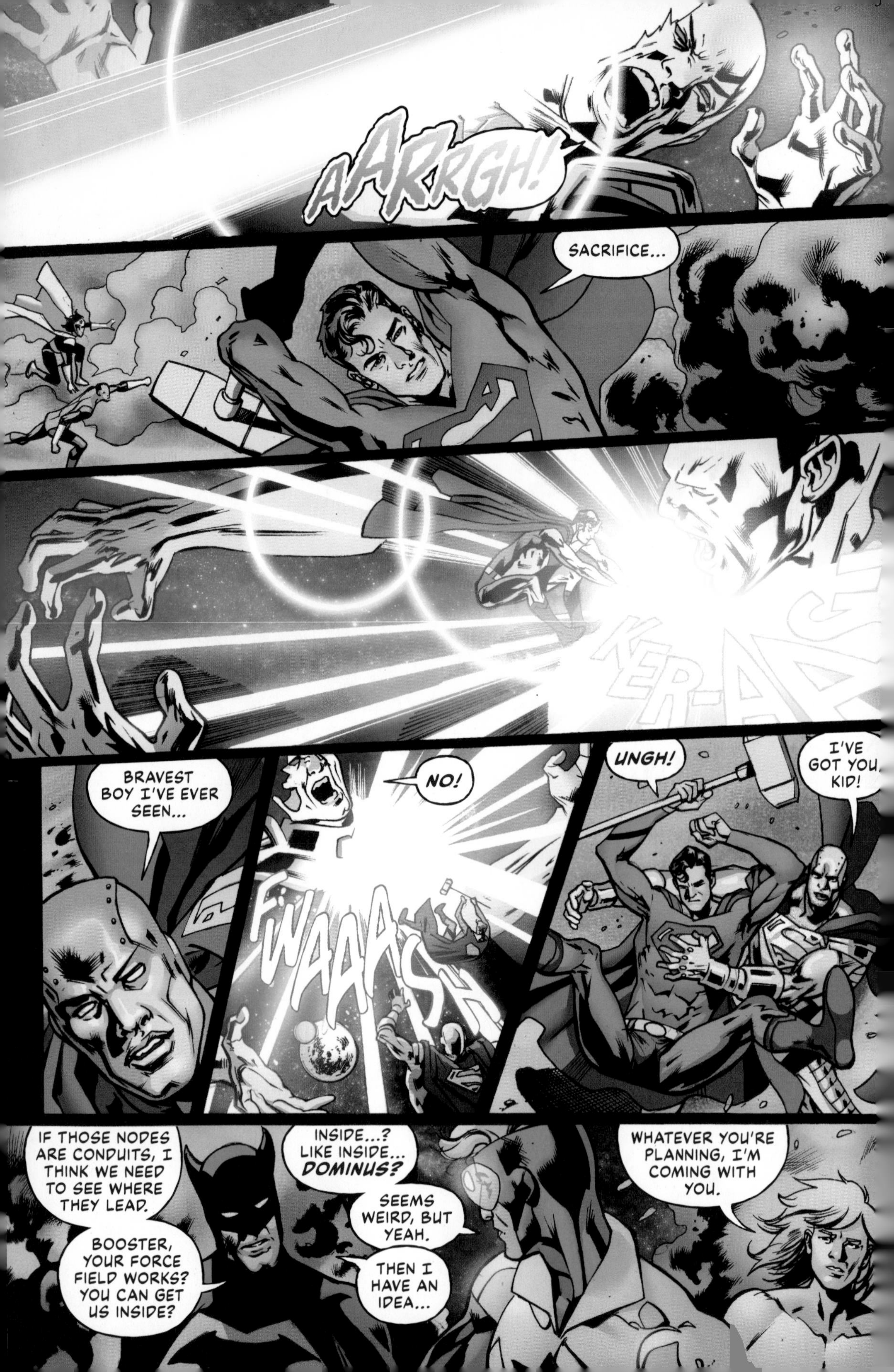
AARRGH!
SACRIFICE...
KER-AASH
BRAVEST BOY I'VE EVER SEEN...
NO!
FWAAASH
UNGH!
I'VE GOT YOU, KID!
IF THOSE NODES ARE CONDUITS, I THINK WE NEED TO SEE WHERE THEY LEAD.
BOOSTER, YOUR FORCE FIELD WORKS? YOU CAN GET US INSIDE?
INSIDE...? LIKE INSIDE... DOMINUS?
SEEMS WEIRD, BUT YEAH.
THEN I HAVE AN IDEA...
WHATEVER YOU'RE PLANNING, I'M COMING WITH YOU.

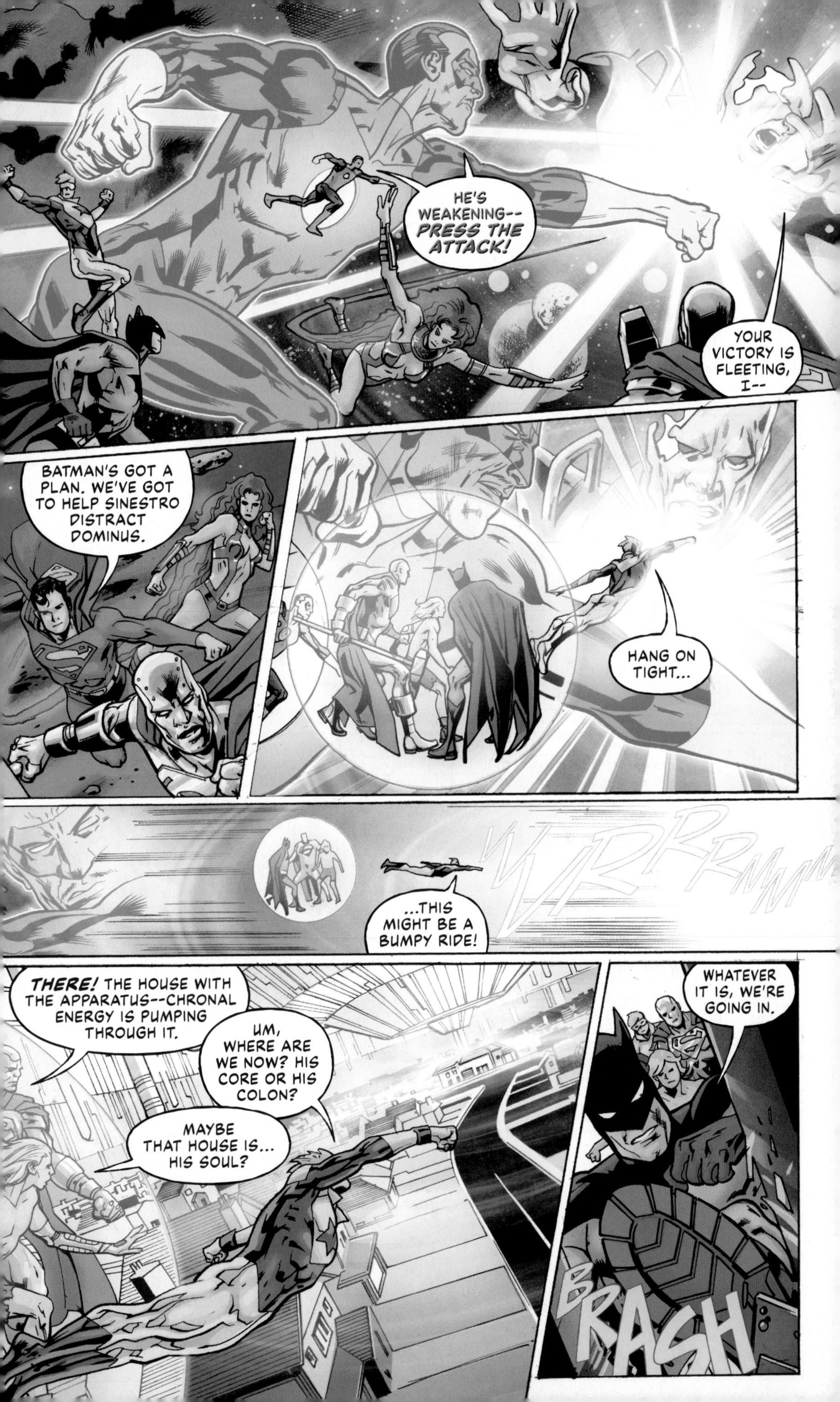
HE'S WEAKENING-- PRESS THE ATTACK!
YOUR VICTORY IS FLEETING, I--
BATMAN'S GOT A PLAN. WE'VE GOT TO HELP SINESTRO DISTRACT DOMINUS.
HANG ON TIGHT...
VRRRMMM
...THIS MIGHT BE A BUMPY RIDE!
THERE! THE HOUSE WITH THE APPARATUS--CHRONAL ENERGY IS PUMPING THROUGH IT.
UM, WHERE ARE WE NOW? HIS CORE OR HIS COLON?
MAYBE THAT HOUSE IS... HIS SOUL?
WHATEVER IT IS, WE'RE GOING IN.
BRASH

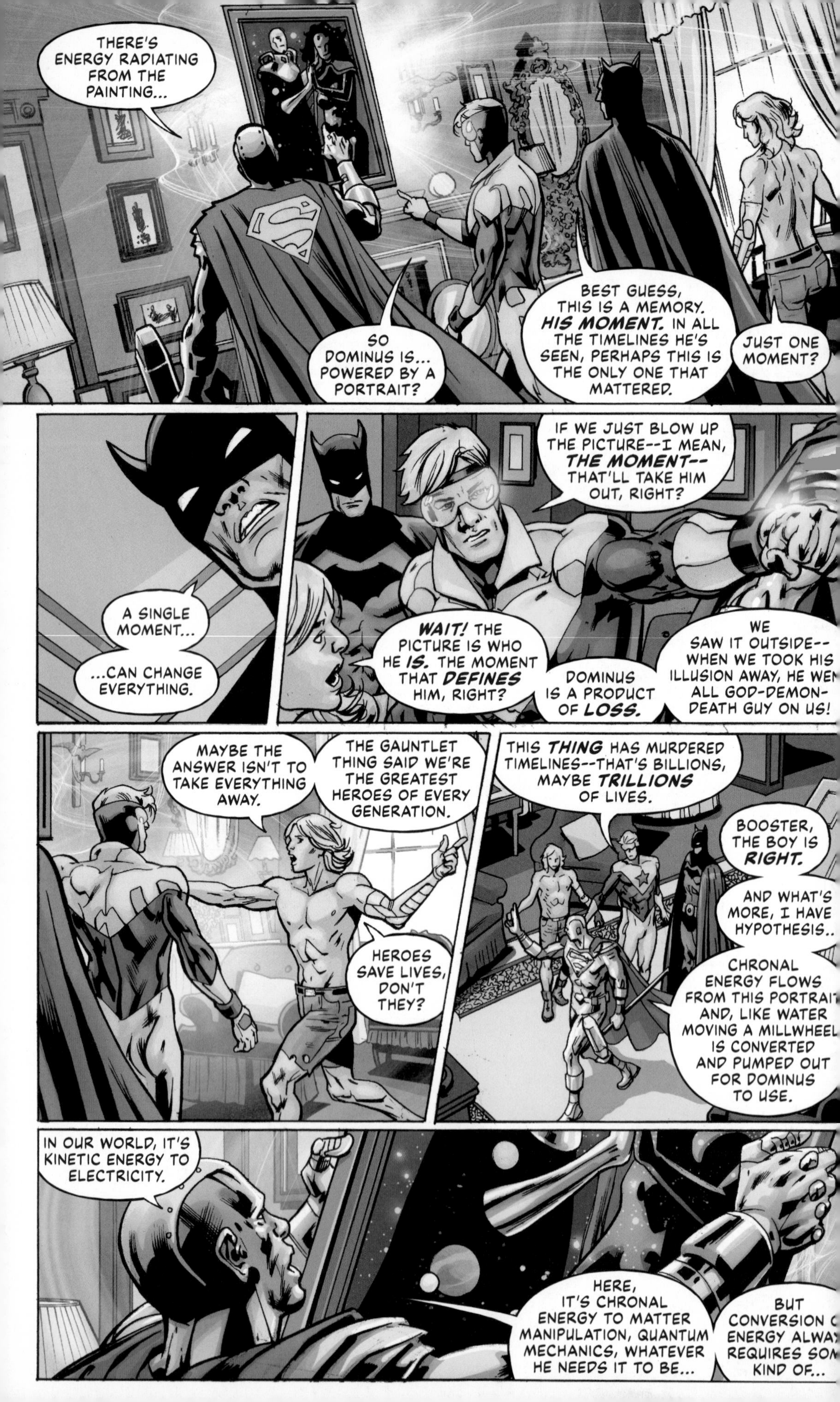
THERE'S ENERGY RADIATING FROM THE PAINTING...
SO DOMINUS IS... POWERED BY A PORTRAIT?
BEST GUESS, THIS IS A MEMORY. HIS MOMENT. IN ALL THE TIMELINES HE'S SEEN, PERHAPS THIS IS THE ONLY ONE THAT MATTERED.
JUST ONE MOMENT?
A SINGLE MOMENT...
...CAN CHANGE EVERYTHING.
IF WE JUST BLOW UP THE PICTURE--I MEAN, THE MOMENT--THAT'LL TAKE HIM OUT, RIGHT?
WAIT! THE PICTURE IS WHO HE IS. THE MOMENT THAT DEFINES HIM, RIGHT?
DOMINUS IS A PRODUCT OF LOSS.
WE SAW IT OUTSIDE--WHEN WE TOOK HIS ILLUSION AWAY, HE WEN ALL GOD-DEMON-DEATH GUY ON US!
MAYBE THE ANSWER ISN'T TO TAKE EVERYTHING AWAY.
THE GAUNTLET THING SAID WE'RE THE GREATEST HEROES OF EVERY GENERATION.
HEROES SAVE LIVES, DON'T THEY?
THIS THING HAS MURDERED TIMELINES--THAT'S BILLIONS, MAYBE TRILLIONS OF LIVES.
BOOSTER, THE BOY IS RIGHT.
AND WHAT'S MORE, I HAVE HYPOTHESIS..
CHRONAL ENERGY FLOWS FROM THIS PORTRAI AND, LIKE WATER MOVING A MILLWHEEL IS CONVERTED AND PUMPED OUT FOR DOMINUS TO USE.
IN OUR WORLD, IT'S KINETIC ENERGY TO ELECTRICITY.
HERE, IT'S CHRONAL ENERGY TO MATTER MANIPULATION, QUANTUM MECHANICS, WHATEVER HE NEEDS IT TO BE...
BUT CONVERSION ENERGY ALWA REQUIRES SOM KIND OF...

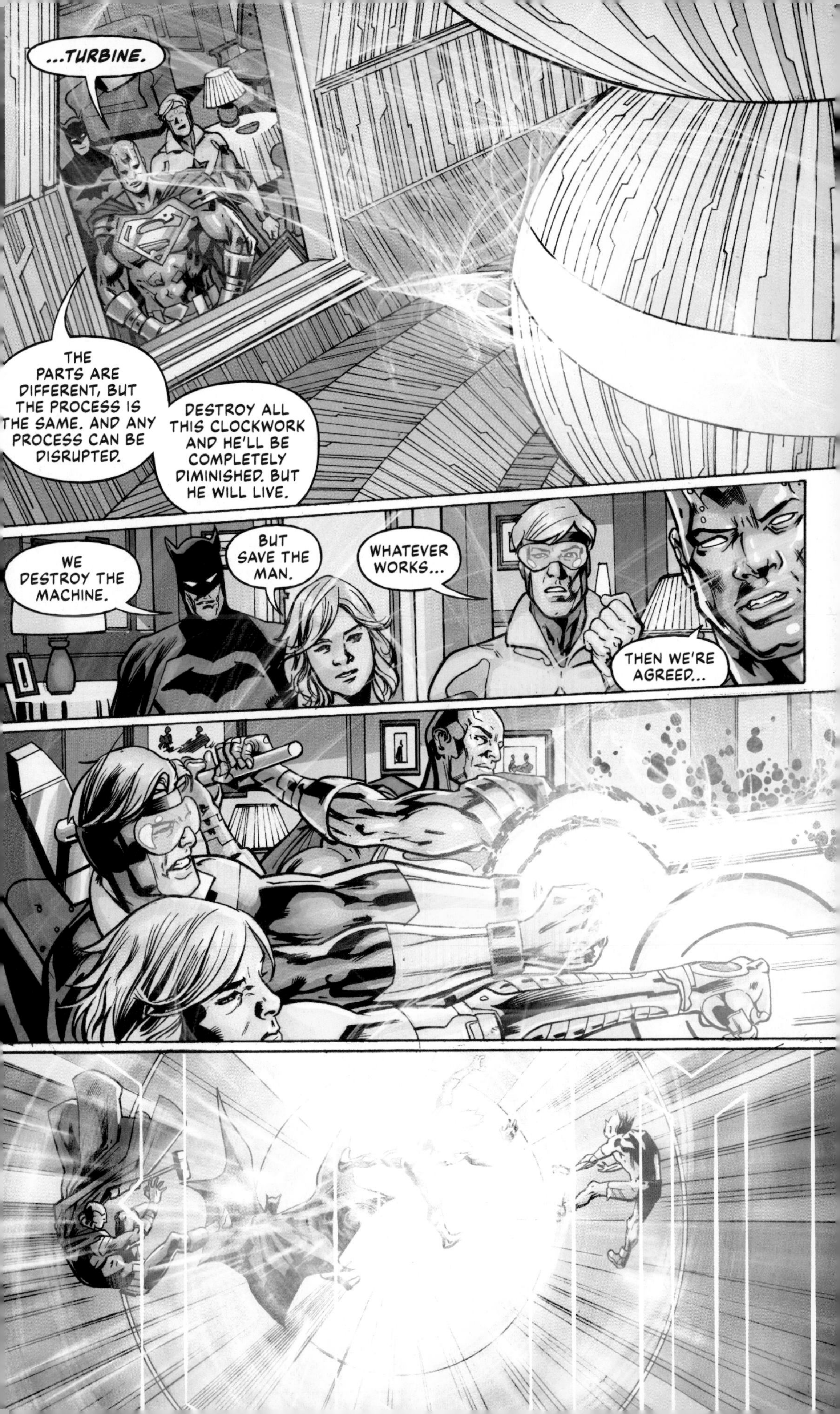

...TURBINE.
THE PARTS ARE DIFFERENT, BUT THE PROCESS IS THE SAME. AND ANY PROCESS CAN BE DISRUPTED.
DESTROY ALL THIS CLOCKWORK AND HE'LL BE COMPLETELY DIMINISHED. BUT HE WILL LIVE.
WE DESTROY THE MACHINE.
BUT SAVE THE MAN.
WHATEVER WORKS...
THEN WE'RE AGREED...

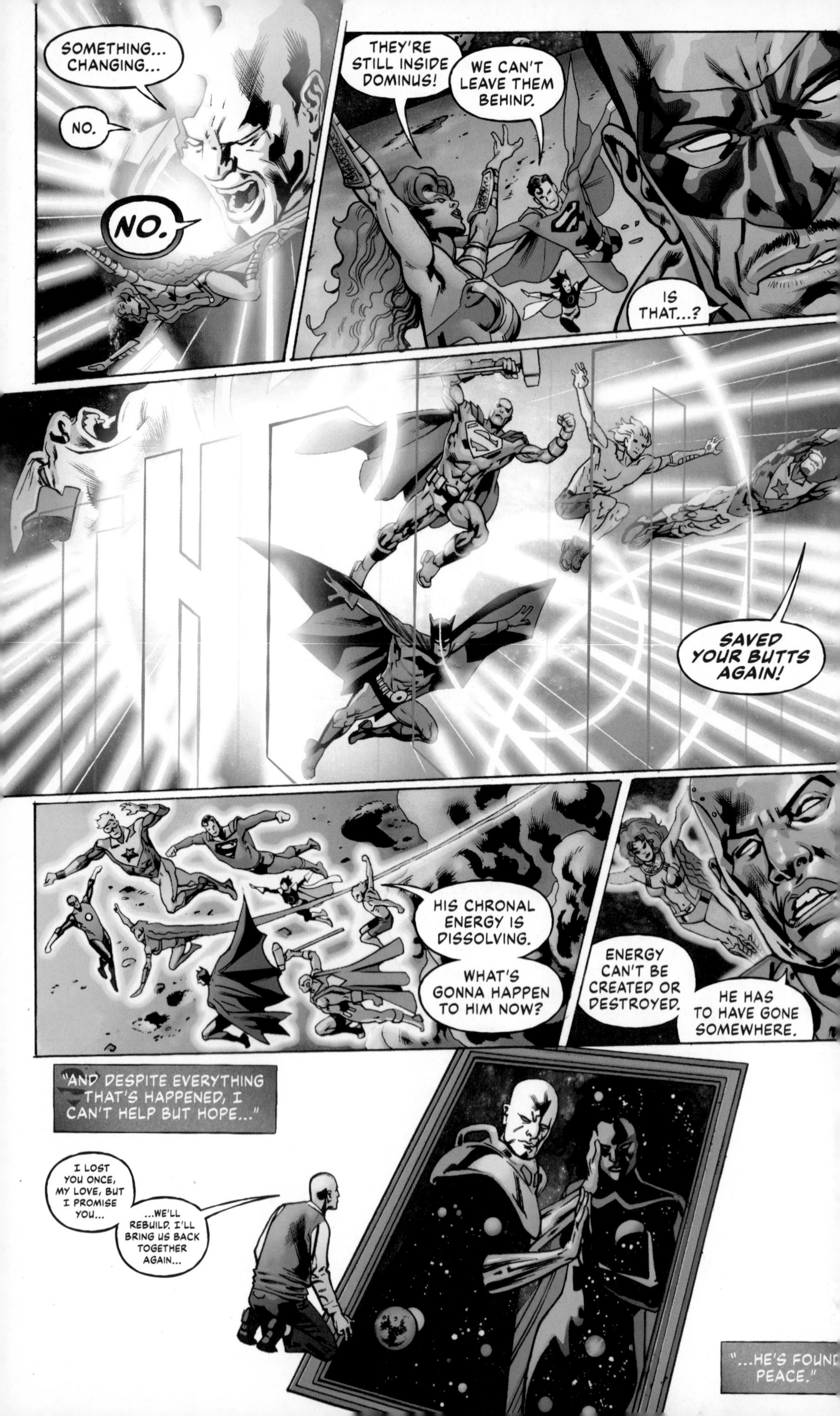
SOMETHING... CHANGING...
NO.
NO.
THEY'RE STILL INSIDE DOMINUS!
WE CAN'T LEAVE THEM BEHIND.
IS THAT...?
SAVED YOUR BUTTS AGAIN!
HIS CHRONAL ENERGY IS DISSOLVING.
WHAT'S GONNA HAPPEN TO HIM NOW?
ENERGY CAN'T BE CREATED OR DESTROYED.
HE HAS TO HAVE GONE SOMEWHERE.
"AND DESPITE EVERYTHING THAT'S HAPPENED, I CAN'T HELP BUT HOPE..."
I LOST YOU ONCE, MY LOVE, BUT I PROMISE YOU...
...WE'LL REBUILD. I'LL BRING US BACK TOGETHER AGAIN...
"...HE'S FOUND PEACE."

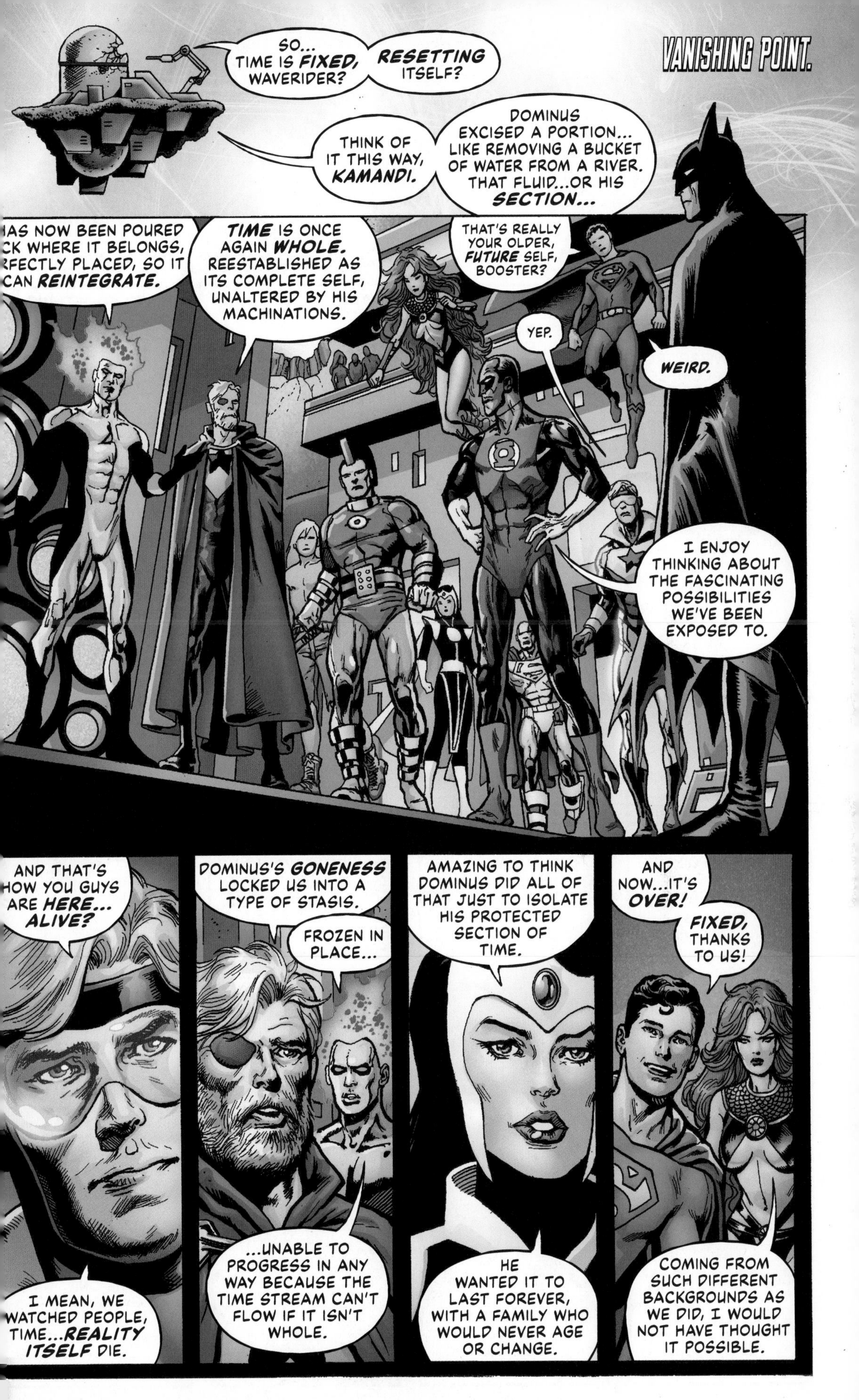

VANISHING POINT.
SO... TIME IS FIXED, WAVERIDER?
RESETTING ITSELF?
THINK OF IT THIS WAY, KAMANDI.
DOMINUS EXCISED A PORTION... LIKE REMOVING A BUCKET OF WATER FROM A RIVER. THAT FLUID...OR HIS SECTION...
HAS NOW BEEN POURED CK WHERE IT BELONGS, RFECTLY PLACED, SO IT CAN REINTEGRATE.
TIME IS ONCE AGAIN WHOLE. REESTABLISHED AS ITS COMPLETE SELF, UNALTERED BY HIS MACHINATIONS.
THAT'S REALLY YOUR OLDER, FUTURE SELF, BOOSTER?
YEP.
WEIRD.
I ENJOY THINKING ABOUT THE FASCINATING POSSIBILITIES WE'VE BEEN EXPOSED TO.
AND THAT'S HOW YOU GUYS ARE HERE... ALIVE?
I MEAN, WE WATCHED PEOPLE, TIME...REALITY ITSELF DIE.
DOMINUS'S GONENESS LOCKED US INTO A TYPE OF STASIS.
FROZEN IN PLACE...
...UNABLE TO PROGRESS IN ANY WAY BECAUSE THE TIME STREAM CAN'T FLOW IF IT ISN'T WHOLE.
AMAZING TO THINK DOMINUS DID ALL OF THAT JUST TO ISOLATE HIS PROTECTED SECTION OF TIME.
HE WANTED IT TO LAST FOREVER, WITH A FAMILY WHO WOULD NEVER AGE OR CHANGE.
AND NOW...IT'S OVER!
FIXED, THANKS TO US!
COMING FROM SUCH DIFFERENT BACKGROUNDS AS WE DID, I WOULD NOT HAVE THOUGHT IT POSSIBLE.

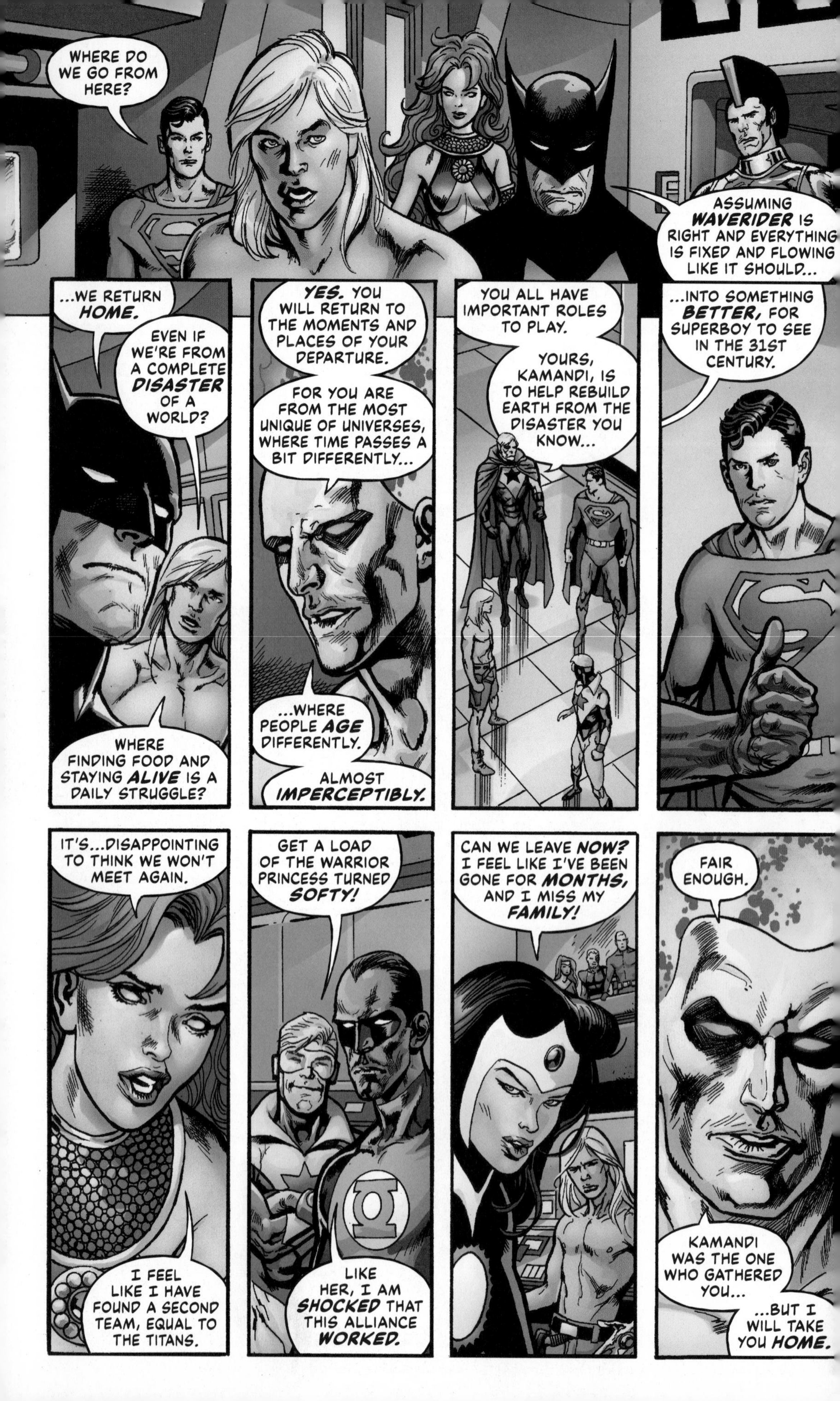
WHERE DO WE GO FROM HERE?
ASSUMING WAVERIDER IS RIGHT AND EVERYTHING IS FIXED AND FLOWING LIKE IT SHOULD...
...WE RETURN HOME.
EVEN IF WE'RE FROM A COMPLETE DISASTER OF A WORLD?
WHERE FINDING FOOD AND STAYING ALIVE IS A DAILY STRUGGLE?
YES. YOU WILL RETURN TO THE MOMENTS AND PLACES OF YOUR DEPARTURE.
FOR YOU ARE FROM THE MOST UNIQUE OF UNIVERSES, WHERE TIME PASSES A BIT DIFFERENTLY...
...WHERE PEOPLE AGE DIFFERENTLY.
ALMOST IMPERCEPTIBLY.
YOU ALL HAVE IMPORTANT ROLES TO PLAY.
YOURS, KAMANDI, IS TO HELP REBUILD EARTH FROM THE DISASTER YOU KNOW...
...INTO SOMETHING BETTER, FOR SUPERBOY TO SEE IN THE 31ST CENTURY.
IT'S...DISAPPOINTING TO THINK WE WON'T MEET AGAIN.
I FEEL LIKE I HAVE FOUND A SECOND TEAM, EQUAL TO THE TITANS.
GET A LOAD OF THE WARRIOR PRINCESS TURNED SOFTY!
LIKE HER, I AM SHOCKED THAT THIS ALLIANCE WORKED.
CAN WE LEAVE NOW? I FEEL LIKE I'VE BEEN GONE FOR MONTHS, AND I MISS MY FAMILY!
FAIR ENOUGH.
KAMANDI WAS THE ONE WHO GATHERED YOU...
...BUT I WILL TAKE YOU HOME.

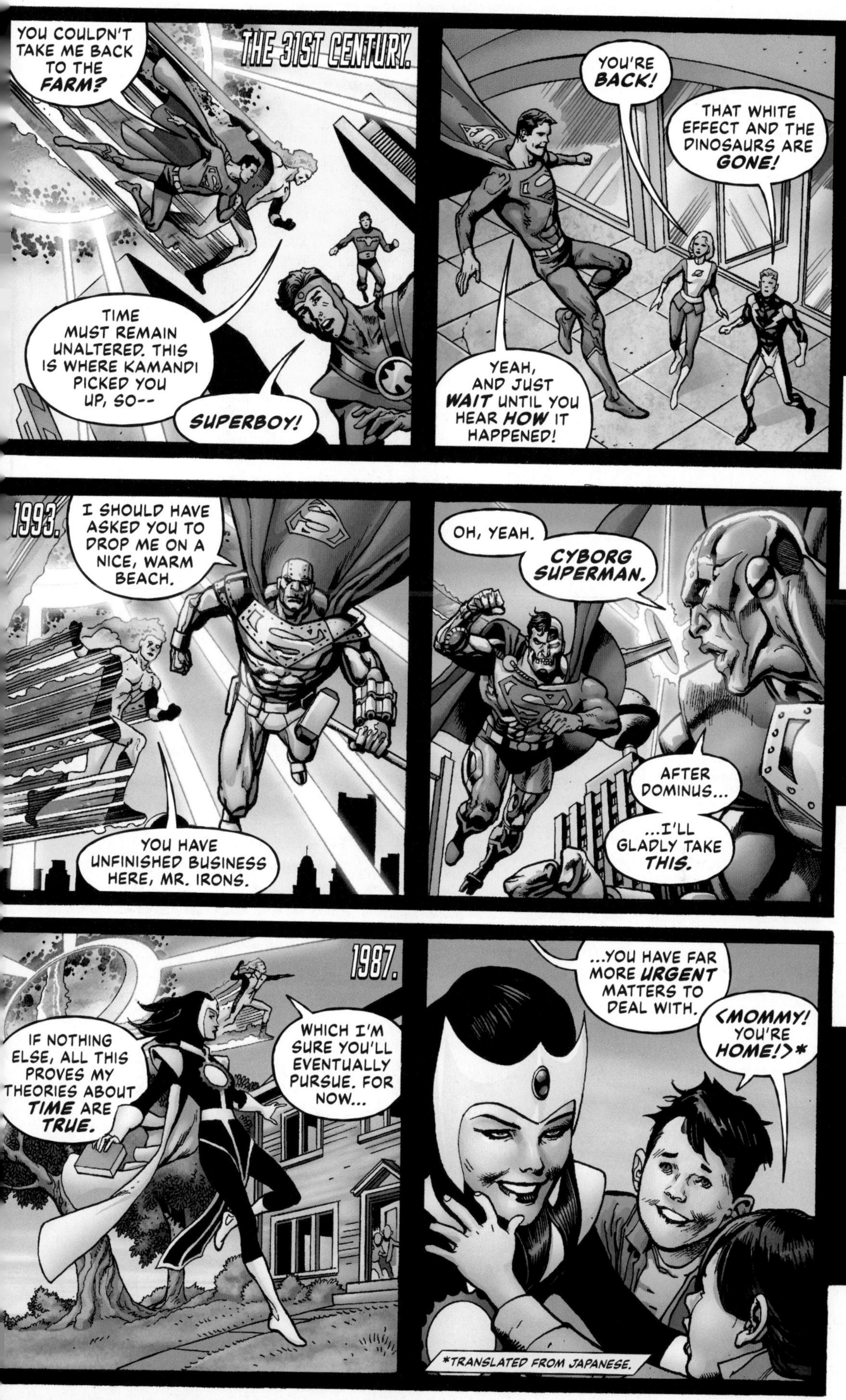
THE 31ST CENTURY.
YOU COULDN'T TAKE ME BACK TO THE FARM?
TIME MUST REMAIN UNALTERED. THIS IS WHERE KAMANDI PICKED YOU UP, SO--
SUPERBOY!
YOU'RE BACK!
THAT WHITE EFFECT AND THE DINOSAURS ARE GONE!
YEAH, AND JUST WAIT UNTIL YOU HEAR HOW IT HAPPENED!
1993.
I SHOULD HAVE ASKED YOU TO DROP ME ON A NICE, WARM BEACH.
YOU HAVE UNFINISHED BUSINESS HERE, MR. IRONS.
OH, YEAH.
CYBORG SUPERMAN.
AFTER DOMINUS...
...I'LL GLADLY TAKE THIS.
1987.
IF NOTHING ELSE, ALL THIS PROVES MY THEORIES ABOUT TIME ARE TRUE.
WHICH I'M SURE YOU'LL EVENTUALLY PURSUE. FOR NOW...
...YOU HAVE FAR MORE URGENT MATTERS TO DEAL WITH.
<MOMMY! YOU'RE HOME!>*
*TRANSLATED FROM JAPANESE.

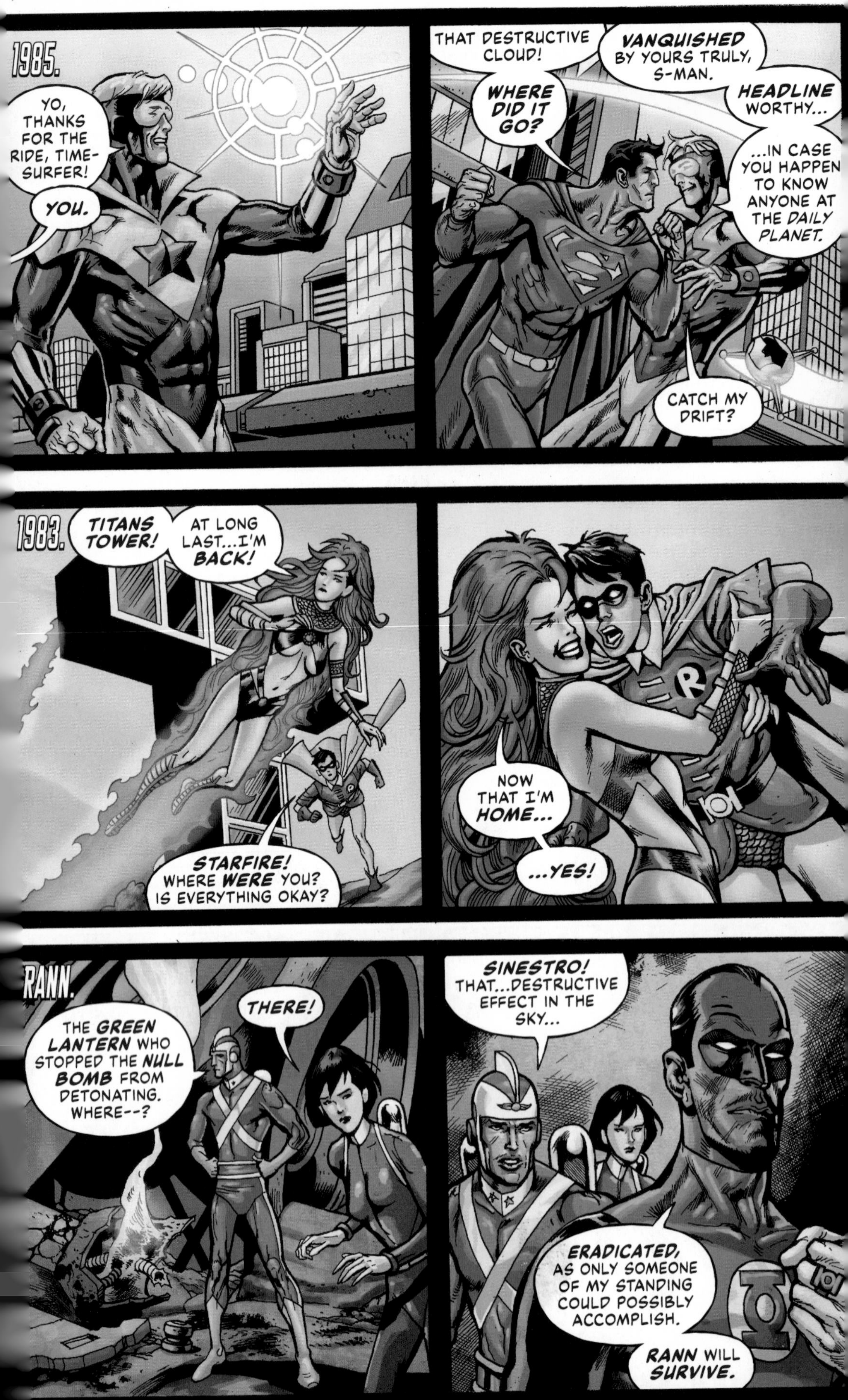
1985.
YO, THANKS FOR THE RIDE, TIME-SURFER!
YOU.
THAT DESTRUCTIVE CLOUD!
WHERE DID IT GO?
VANQUISHED BY YOURS TRULY, S-MAN.
HEADLINE WORTHY...
...IN CASE YOU HAPPEN TO KNOW ANYONE AT THE DAILY PLANET.
CATCH MY DRIFT?
1983.
TITANS TOWER!
AT LONG LAST...I'M BACK!
STARFIRE! WHERE WERE YOU? IS EVERYTHING OKAY?
NOW THAT I'M HOME...
...YES!
RANN.
THE GREEN LANTERN WHO STOPPED THE NULL BOMB FROM DETONATING. WHERE--?
THERE!
SINESTRO! THAT...DESTRUCTIVE EFFECT IN THE SKY...
ERADICATED, AS ONLY SOMEONE OF MY STANDING COULD POSSIBLY ACCOMPLISH.
RANN WILL SURVIVE.

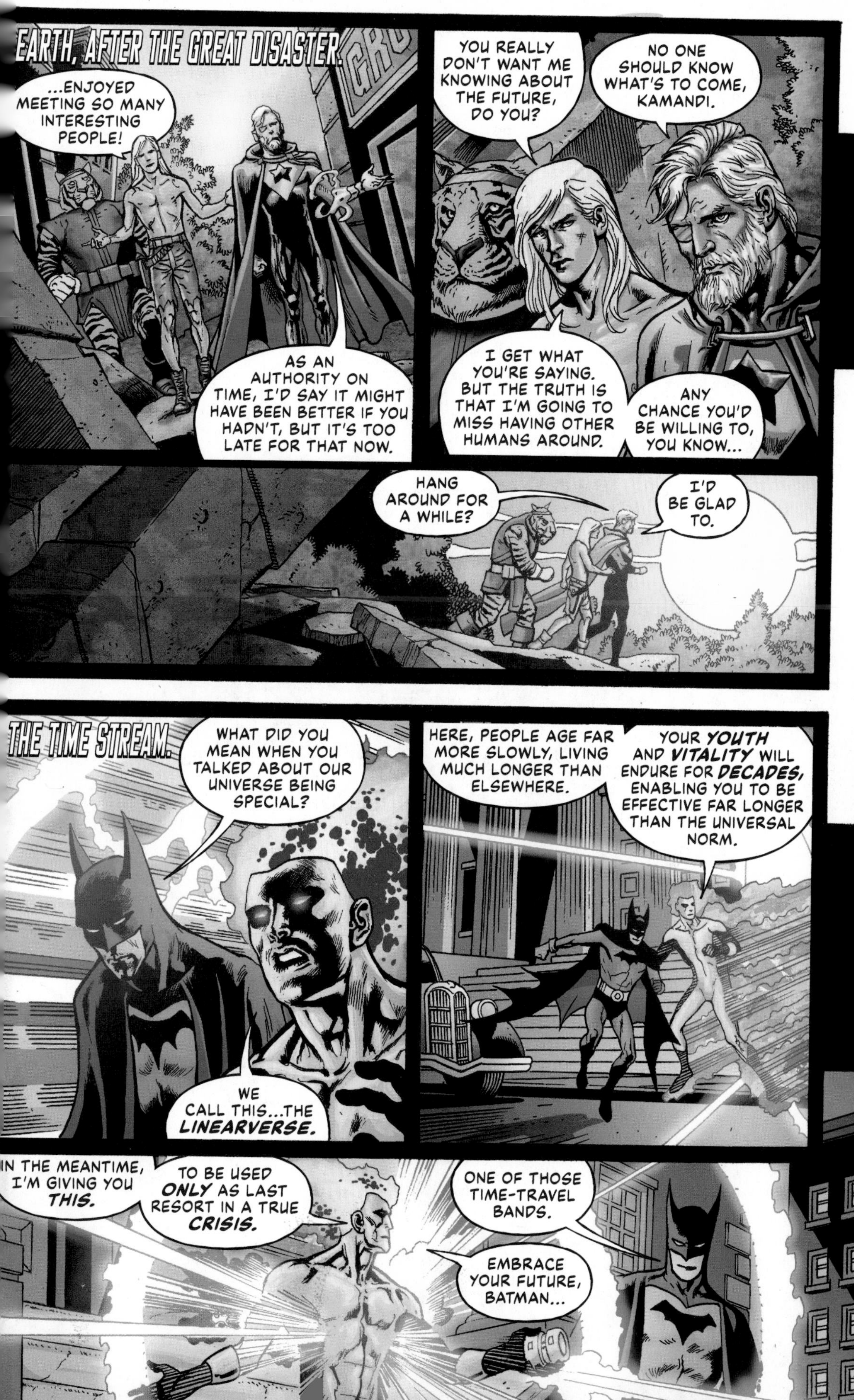
EARTH, AFTER THE GREAT DISASTER.
...ENJOYED MEETING SO MANY INTERESTING PEOPLE!
AS AN AUTHORITY ON TIME, I'D SAY IT MIGHT HAVE BEEN BETTER IF YOU HADN'T, BUT IT'S TOO LATE FOR THAT NOW.
YOU REALLY DON'T WANT ME KNOWING ABOUT THE FUTURE, DO YOU?
NO ONE SHOULD KNOW WHAT'S TO COME, KAMANDI.
I GET WHAT YOU'RE SAYING. BUT THE TRUTH IS THAT I'M GOING TO MISS HAVING OTHER HUMANS AROUND.
ANY CHANCE YOU'D BE WILLING TO, YOU KNOW...
HANG AROUND FOR A WHILE?
I'D BE GLAD TO.
THE TIME STREAM.
WHAT DID YOU MEAN WHEN YOU TALKED ABOUT OUR UNIVERSE BEING SPECIAL?
WE CALL THIS...THE ***LINEARVERSE.***
HERE, PEOPLE AGE FAR MORE SLOWLY, LIVING MUCH LONGER THAN ELSEWHERE.
YOUR ***YOUTH*** AND ***VITALITY*** WILL ENDURE FOR ***DECADES,*** ENABLING YOU TO BE EFFECTIVE FAR LONGER THAN THE UNIVERSAL NORM.
IN THE MEANTIME, I'M GIVING YOU ***THIS.***
TO BE USED ***ONLY*** AS LAST RESORT IN A TRUE ***CRISIS.***
ONE OF THOSE TIME-TRAVEL BANDS.
EMBRACE YOUR FUTURE, BATMAN...

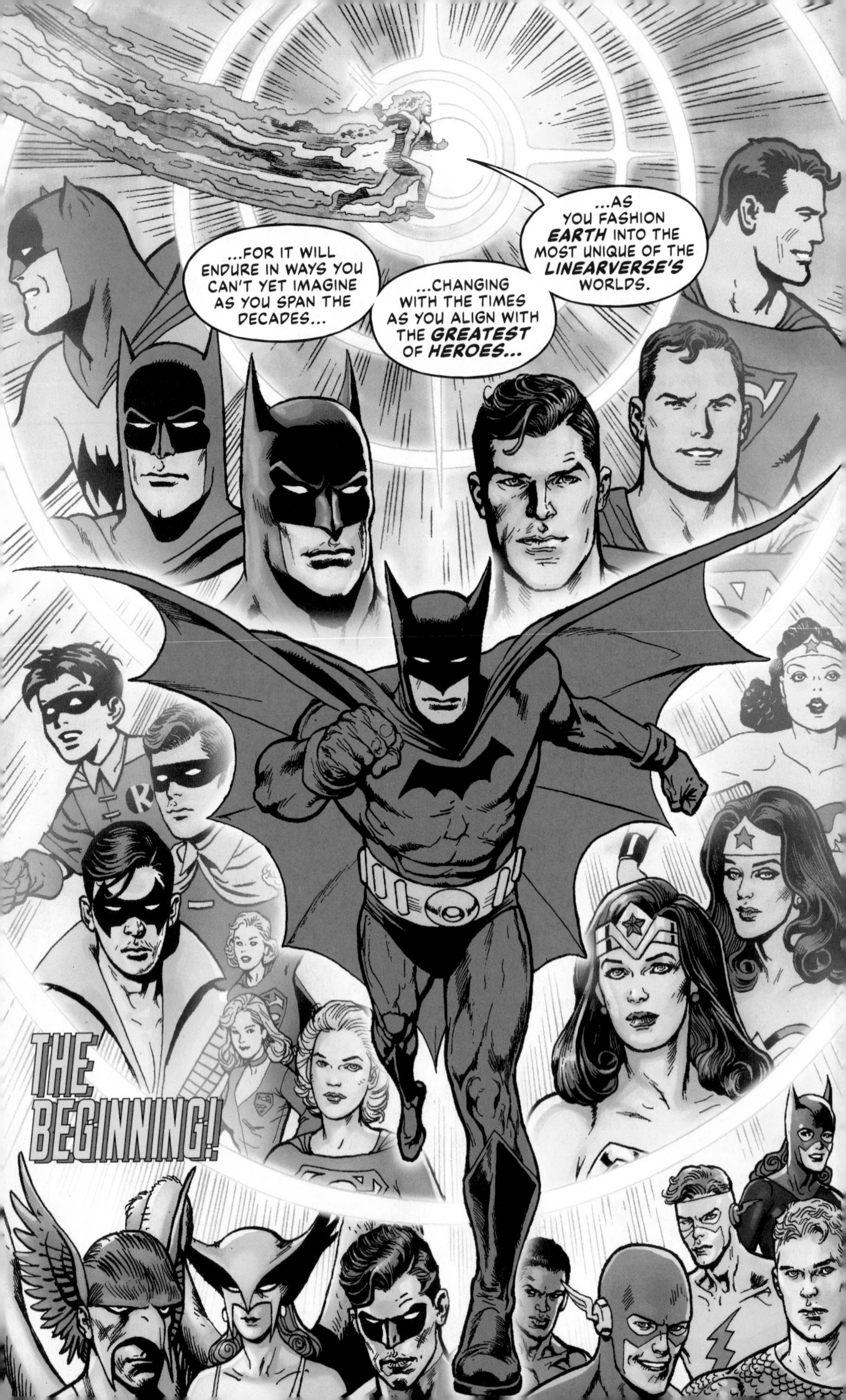
...FOR IT WILL ENDURE IN WAYS YOU CAN'T YET IMAGINE AS YOU SPAN THE DECADES...
...CHANGING WITH THE TIMES AS YOU ALIGN WITH THE GREATEST OF HEROES...
...AS YOU FASHION EARTH INTO THE MOST UNIQUE OF THE LINEARVERSE'S WORLDS.
THE BEGINNING!

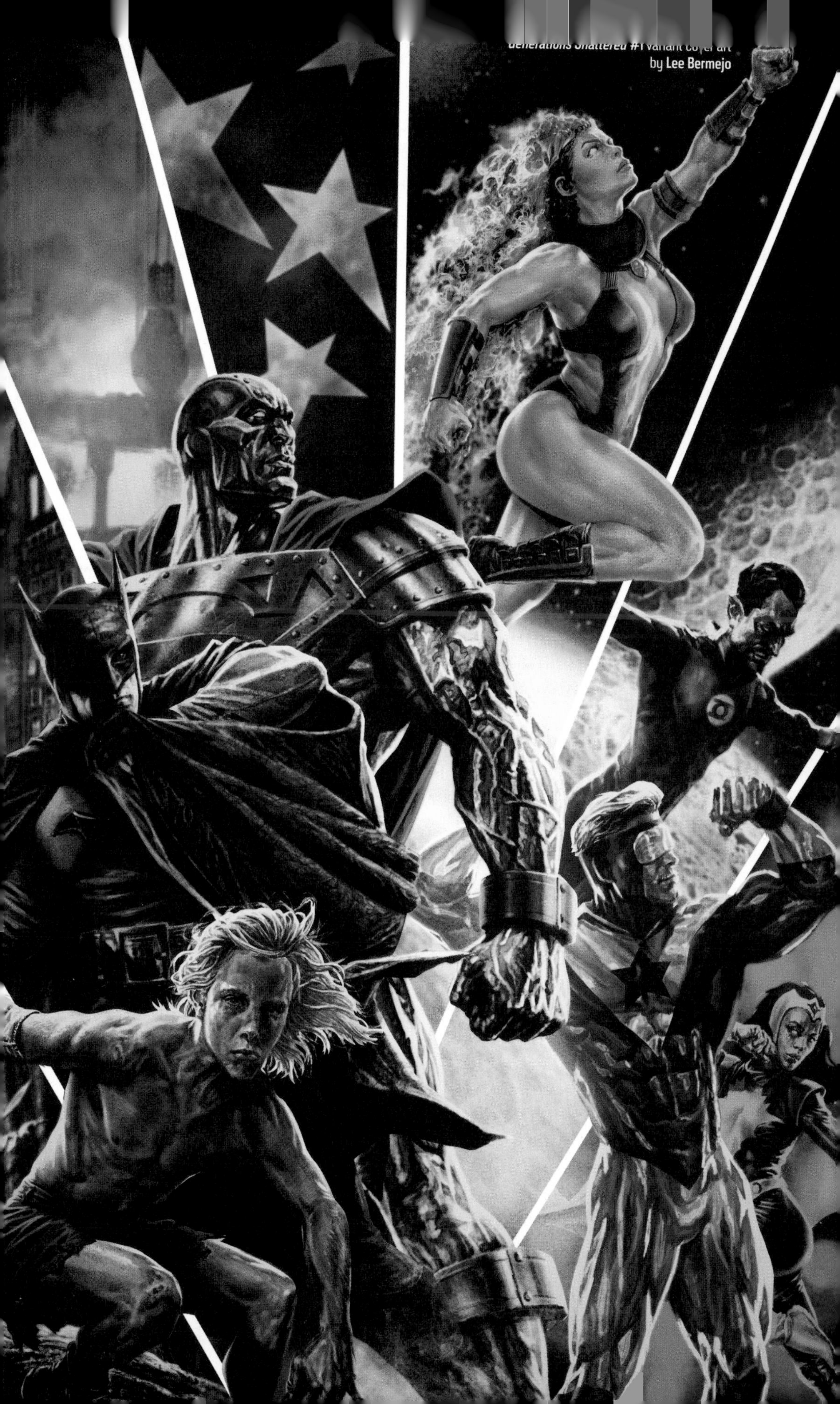

Generations Shattered #1 variant cover art
by Lee Bermejo

Generations Forged **#1** variant cover art
by **Rafael Albuquerque** & **Brad Anderson**

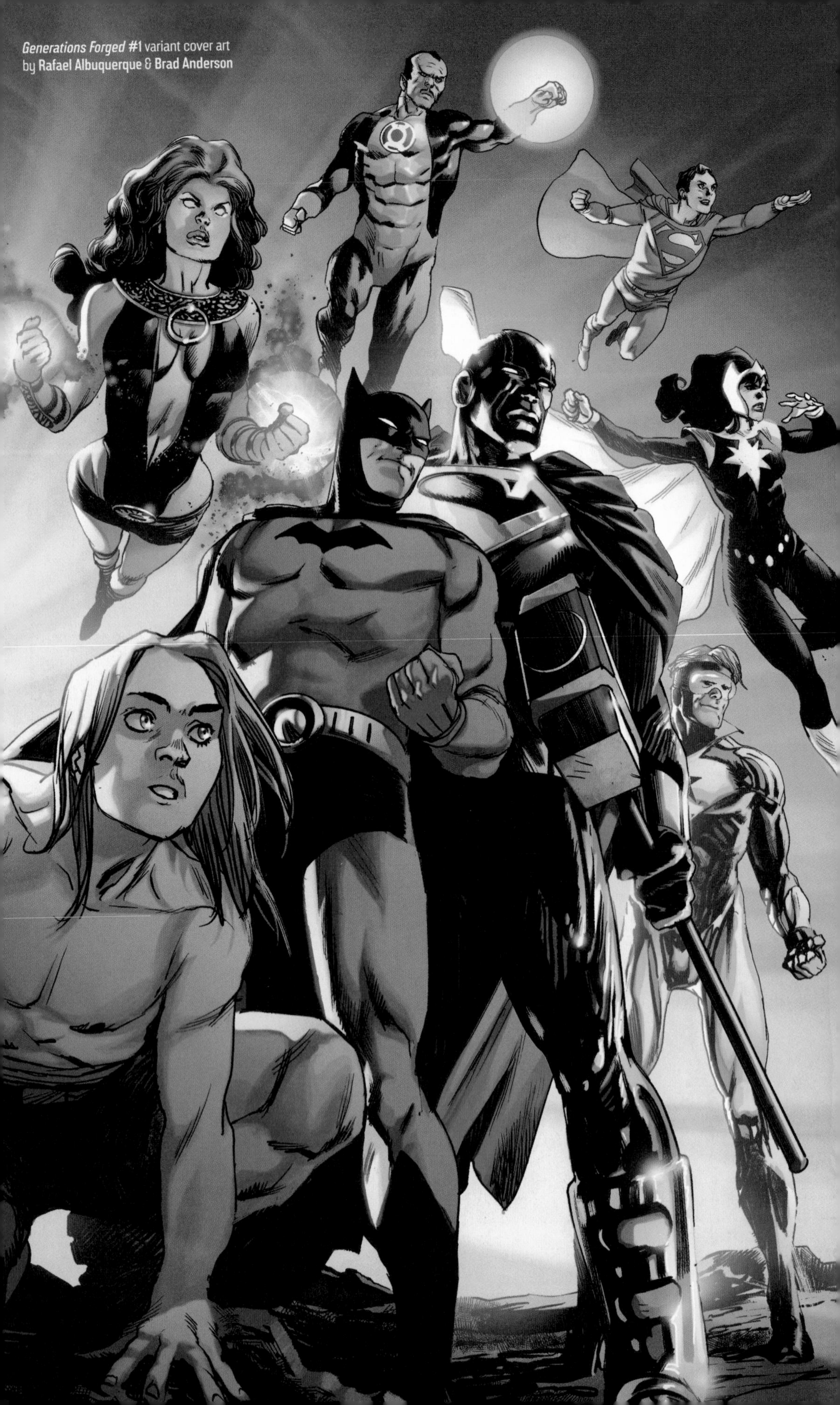

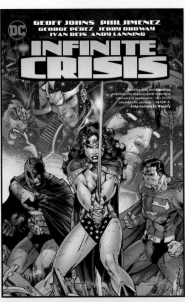

"Dynamite."
–IGN

"Intriguing."
–AIN'T IT COOL NEWS

"Comic-book art at its finest."
–ENTERTAINMENT WEEKLY SHELF LIFE

"Ambitious."
–USA TODAY

"Heroic comic-book art at its finest" – ENTERTAINMENT WEEKLY / SHELF LIFE
GEOFF JOHNS · ANDY KUBERT · SANDRA HOPE
FLASHPOINT
"A soaring, if radical, tale that uses superheroes in ways that may surprise both first-time readers and long-time fans."
– THE ASSOCIATED PRESS

FLASHPOINT
GEOFF JOHNS with ANDY KUBERT

THE WORLD OF
FLASHPOINT
FEATURING
BATMAN
$100
Wayne Casino
"BRIAN AZZARELLO and EDUARDO RISSO continue their track record of excellent collaborations here."
– CBR, on BATMAN: KNIGHT OF VENGEANCE
"One of the best BATMAN stories ever"
– Newsarama, on BATMAN: KNIGHT OF VENGEANCE

FLASHPOINT: THE WORLD OF FLASHPOINT FEATURING BATMAN

THE WORLD OF
FLASHPOINT
FEATURING
GREEN LANTERN
"One of the triumphs of DC's latest event."
– IGN, on FRANKENSTEIN AND THE CREATURES OF THE UNKNOWN

FLASHPOINT: THE WORLD OF FLASHPOINT FEATURING GREEN LANTERN

READ THE ENTIRE EP

FLASHP

FLASHPOINT: THE WORL
FLASHPOINT FEATURING BAT

FLASHPOINT: THE WORL
FLASHPOINT FEATURING THE FL

FLASHPOINT: THE WORL
FLASHPOINT FEATURING GREEN LAN

FLASHPOINT: THE WORL
FLASHPOINT FEATURING SUPER

FLASHPOINT: THE WORL
FLASHPOINT FEATURING WONDER WO